"America's leading source of self-help legal information." ★★★★
— YAHOO!

LEGAL INFORMATION ONLINE ANYTIME
24 hours a day

www.nolo.com

AT THE NOLO.COM SELF-HELP LAW CENTER, YOU'LL FIND

- Nolo's comprehensive Legal Encyclopedia filled with plain-English information on a variety of legal topics
- Nolo's Law Dictionary—legal terms <u>without</u> the legalese
- Auntie Nolo—if you've got questions, Auntie's got answers
- The Law Store—over 200 self-help legal products including Downloadable Software, Books, Form Kits and eGuides
- Legal and product updates
- Frequently Asked Questions
- NoloBriefs, our free monthly email newsletter
- Legal Research Center, for access to state and federal statutes
- Our ever-popular lawyer jokes

Quality LAW BOOKS & SOFTWARE FOR EVERYONE

Nolo's user-friendly products are consistently first-rate. Here's why:

- A dozen in-house legal editors, working with highly skilled authors, ensure that our products are accurate, up-to-date and easy to use
- We continually update every book and software program to keep up with changes in the law
- Our commitment to a more democratic legal system informs all of our work
- We appreciate & listen to your feedback. Please fill out and return the card at the back of this book.

OUR "NO-HASSLE" GUARANTEE

Return anything you buy directly from Nolo for any reason and we'll cheerfully refund your purchase price. No ifs, ands or buts.

Read This First

The information in this book is as up to date and accurate as we can make it. But it's important to realize that the law changes frequently, as do fees, forms, and other important legal details. If you handle your own legal matters, it's up to you to be sure that all information you use—including the information in this book—is accurate. Here are some suggestions to help you do this:

First, check the edition number on the book's spine to make sure you've got the most recent edition of this book. To learn whether a later edition is available, go to Nolo's online Law Store at www.nolo.com or call Nolo's Customer Service Department at 800-728-3555.

Next, because the law can change overnight, users of even a current edition need to be sure it's fully up to date. At www.nolo.com, we post notices of major legal and practical changes that affect a book's current edition only. To check for updates, go to the Law Store portion of Nolo's website and find the page devoted to the book (use the "A to Z Product List" and click on the book's title). If you see an "Updates" link on the left side of the page, click on it. If you don't see a link, there are no posted changes—but check back regularly.

Finally, while Nolo believes that accurate and current legal information in its books can help you solve many of your legal problems on a cost-effective basis, this book is not intended to be a substitute for personalized advice from a knowledgeable lawyer. If you want the help of a trained professional, consult an attorney licensed to practice in your state.

Sixth Edition

Make Your Own
Living Trust

by Attorney Denis Clifford

Illustrated by Mari Stein

SIXTH EDITION	JANUARY 2004
Production	SARAH HINMAN
Illustrations	MARI STEIN
Book Design	JACKIE MANCUSO
Cover Design	TONI IHARA
Proofreading	MU'AFRIDA BELL
Index	JULIE SHAWVAN
Printing	DELTA PRINTING SOLUTIONS, INC.

Clifford, Denis.
    Make your own living trust / by Denis Clifford.-- 6th ed.
        p. cm.
    Includes index.
    ISBN 0-87337-985-3
        1. Living trusts--United States--Popular works.   I. Title: Living Trust II. Title.

KF734.Z9C57 2004
346.7305'2--dc22

2003059361

Quantity sales: For information on bulk purchases or corporate premium sales, please contact the Special Sales department. For academic sales or textbook adoptions, ask for Academic Sales, 800-955-4775. Nolo, 950 Parker St., Berkeley, CA, 94710.

Dedication

Once again, to Naomi.

Acknowledgments

My thanks to all those friends who helped me with this book, both putting it together and over the years:

First, to four friends at Nolo, without whose aid this book would never have come into existence: Mary Randolph, my once and now again superb editor and writer, and organizer extraordinaire; Shae Irving, equally superb editor and writer, and kindred spirit; and Stephanie Harolde, who prepared so many drafts of the book so well and did much fine editing, too; and Ella Hirst, for her fine research.

Second, to Mark Peery, of Greenbrae, California, a superb estate planning lawyer (and great friend).

Third, to Jake Warner, for his brilliant editing and assistance on this book and all his help through the years.

Fourth, to Toni Ihara, a spirit forever joyous—thanks again for getting me into all this.

Fifth, to all my other friends and colleagues at Nolo. In the past, I listed everyone, but now we have 80 or more employees, plus more outside writers and an employee manual. Still, Nolo retains the relaxed, friendly atmosphere that makes it such a pleasant (as well as productive) place to work.

Sixth, to Attorney Magdalen Gaynor, of White Plains and New York City, New York, an excellent estate planning lawyer who gave me information generously and cheerfully.

Seventh, to other friends who helped me with this book: Linda Moody, of Mill Valley, California, a law school friend who's become another superb estate planning lawyer; Ken Fisher, of Pleasant Hill, California, a fine insurance agent, and the many, many other people who helped with this book and over the years, with earlier materials I've written about living trusts.

And finally, my heartfelt thanks to my clients from past years, from whom I learned so much reality I could never have learned in books or school (sure never did in law school), and also to the many readers of earlier books of mine that discussed living trusts, who wrote me with suggestions, comments, corrections, and other thoughts that contributed greatly to this book.

About the Author

DENIS CLIFFORD is a lawyer who specializes in estate planning. He is the author of several Nolo books, including *Plan Your Estate* and *Nolo's Simple Will Book*. A graduate of Columbia Law School, where he was an editor of the *The Law Review*, he has practiced law in various ways, and became convinced that people can do much of their own legal work.

Contents

4

WHAT TYPE OF TRUST DO YOU NEED?

5

NOLO'S TAX-SAVING AB TRUST

6

CHOOSING WHAT PROPERTY TO PUT IN YOUR LIVING TRUST

7

TRUSTEES

8

CHOOSING YOUR BENEFICIARIES

9

PROPERTY LEFT TO MINOR CHILDREN OR YOUNG ADULTS

10

PREPARING YOUR LIVING TRUST DOCUMENT

11

TRANSFERRING PROPERTY TO YOUR TRUST

12

COPYING, STORING, AND REGISTERING YOUR TRUST DOCUMENT

13

LIVING WITH YOUR LIVING TRUST

14

AFTER A GRANTOR DIES

15

A LIVING TRUST AS PART OF YOUR ESTATE PLAN

16

WILLS

17

IF YOU NEED EXPERT HELP

Glossary

Appendix A

HOW TO USE THE FORMS CD-ROM

Appendix B

FORMS

Form 1: Basic Living Trust for One Person

Form 2: Basic Shared Living Trust

Form 3: AB Living Trust

Form 4: Witness Statement for a Florida Living Trust

Form 5: Assignment of Property to a Trust for One Person

Form 6: Assignment of Shared Property to a Trust for a Couple

Form 7: Amendment to Living Trust for One Person

Form 8: Amendment to Basic Shared Living Trust or AB Trust

Form 9: Revocation of Living Trust

Form 10: Basic Will for One Person

Form 11: Basic Will for a Member of a Couple

Form 12: Affidavit of Successor Trustee

Index

Introduction

HOW TO USE THIS BOOK

Whether you are single or a member of a couple, this book lets you prepare your own basic living trust. A basic living trust enables people with small or moderate estates—in estate tax terms, those with a net worth of less than $1.5 million, depending on the year of death—to transfer their property after their death to whomever they want to have it, without any attorneys or court involvement. The people who inherit your property can avoid probate—that expensive, lawyer-ridden process required of most wills.

This book also enables more prosperous couples with a combined estate worth over $1.5 million to create a living trust that both avoids probate and saves on estate taxes. I call this type of trust an AB trust or a "living trust with marital life estate." As you read through the book, you'll learn whether or not it's wise for you to create this type of trust with the forms in this book.

Any intelligent person can create a valid, effective living trust. You don't have to be a nuclear physicist—or an attorney. Indeed, with the aid of this book, most people can safely create their living trusts themselves, without any need for a lawyer.

⚠️ **Louisiana residents.** This book is designed for residents of all states except Louisiana, which has a legal system based on the Napoleonic Code, different from all other states.

Many books or so-called authorities on living trusts assert that it is foolish to try to do your own living trust. They maintain that you must hire a lawyer or even a

"team of experts" (lawyer, accountant, financial planner)—and they'll see to it that you don't have much of an estate left. Some even argue that doing your own living trust is like trying to do your own brain surgery. This is ridiculous. For most people, there is nothing difficult about preparing a living trust. After all, most people simply want to transfer their own property after their death to those they want to have it, without involving lawyers and courts. There is nothing inherently complex about that. For most people, there's no reason to hire a lawyer to accomplish this goal.

As you read the book, you'll learn exactly how living trusts work and what form is right for you. Some readers, particularly those with net estates worth more than $1.5 million, may decide they want a lawyer's assistance to prepare their final living trust. This book doesn't claim to present definitive advice on all aspects of living trusts. There are volumes of books on the topic in any good-sized law library. As you'll see, in some situations I urge you to consult a lawyer or other expert. When I do so, I also use an identifying symbol (see "Icons Used in This Book," below), so you can readily see that an expert is recommended.

Even if you decide to get an expert's help with preparing your living trust, you'll benefit greatly by comprehending the basic issues and objectives involved. The information you gain by reading this book will help you deal with a professional and get the help you really need, for a reasonable fee.

Before you actually start to prepare a living trust, read through the book once. You need to know how a living trust really works and how it fits in with your overall estate plan. Also, obviously, you need to resolve basic personal issues, such as what property to transfer to your trust and who your beneficiaries are (who gets what).

Keep in mind that creating a living trust has important, long-term consequences for your family and their finances. You can do it yourself, in most cases, but you must do it right, which means educating yourself about your options so you can make well-informed decisions.

The trust forms in this book have been carefully prepared to be both clear and fully acceptable in the real world. There is no "standard" living trust. Anyone (or any book) who asserts that trusts must be written in "legalese" (language that is peculiar to the legal profession) is flat-out wrong. A living trust functions just fine if it covers the basics, such as what property is in the trust, who gets it, and who manages the trust after you die. And although no legalese is mandated, it is prudent to have a trust form that, like the ones in this book, is sufficiently traditional that it looks familiar to institutions that may be presented with it—such as banks, title companies, or stock brokerage companies. ∎

ICONS USED IN THIS BOOK

Throughout this book, the following icons will help you along.

Warns you to slow down and consider potential problems.

Advises you to consult a lawyer or other legal expert. Although quite a few of these symbols appear throughout the book, most readers won't be affected by them.

Alerts you to instructions that apply only to marital living trusts.

Refers you to other helpful resources.

Make Your Own Living Trust is a workbook, not a treasure to cherish unmarked. Its purpose, after all, is to help you understand and prepare your own living trust. While reading this book, take notes, record information about your own situation, use the worksheets to the extent you find them helpful, and then decide how you want your trust to work. Finally, use one of the trust forms provided in Appendix B to draft your own living trust, or use one of these forms provided on the CD-ROM at the back of the book.

AN OVERVIEW OF LIVING TRUSTS

*L*iving trusts are an efficient and effective way to transfer property, at your death, to the relatives, friends, or charities you've chosen. Essentially, a living trust performs the same function as a will, with the important difference that property left by a will must go through the probate court process. In probate, a deceased person's will is proved valid in court, the person's debts are paid and, usually after about a year, the remaining property is finally distributed to the beneficiaries. In the vast majority of instances, these probate court proceedings are an utter waste of time and money.

By contrast, property left by a living trust can go promptly and directly to your inheritors. They don't have to bother with a probate court proceeding. That means they won't have to spend any of your hard-earned money (at least, I presume it was hard-earned) to pay for court and lawyer fees.

You don't need to maintain separate tax records for your living trust. While you live, all transactions that are technically made by your living trust are simply reported on your personal income tax return. Indeed, while some paperwork is necessary to establish a probate-avoidance living trust and transfer property to it, there are no serious drawbacks or risks involved in creating or maintaining the trust.

These trusts are called "living" or sometimes "inter vivos" (Latin for "among the living") because they're created while you're alive. They're called "revocable" because you can revoke or change them at any time, for any reason, before you die.

While you live, you effectively keep ownership of all property that you've technically transferred to your living trust. You can do whatever you want to with any trust property, including selling it, spending it, or giving it away. Basically, a revocable living trust is merely a piece of paper that becomes operational at your death. At that point, it allows your trust property to be transferred, privately and outside of probate, to the people or organizations you name as beneficiaries of the trust.

A. Living Trusts Explained

A trust can seem like a mysterious creature, dreamed up by lawyers and wrapped in legal jargon. Trusts were an invention of medieval England, used as a method to evade restrictions on ownership and inheritance of land. Don't let the word "trust" scare you. True, the word can have an impressive, slightly ominous sound. Historically, monopolists used trusts to dominate entire industries—for example, the Standard Oil Trust in the era of Teddy Roosevelt's "trust-busting." And trusts have traditionally been used by the very wealthy to preserve their riches from generation to generation. (Indeed, isn't one version of the American dream to be the beneficiary of your very own trust fund?) But happily, the types of living trusts this book covers aren't complicated or beyond the reach of ordinary folks. Here are the basics.

1. The Concept of a Trust

A trust, like a corporation, is an intangible legal entity ("legal fiction" might be a more accurate term). You can't see a trust, or touch it, but it does exist. The first step in creating a working trust is to prepare and sign a document called a *Declaration of Trust*.

Once you create and sign the Declaration of Trust, the trust exists, and you can transfer property to it. There must, however, be a flesh-and-blood person actually in charge of this property; that person is called the *trustee*. With traditional trusts, the trustee manages the property on the behalf of someone else, called the *beneficiary*. However, with a living trust, until you die, you can be the trustee of the trust you create and also, in effect, the beneficiary. Only after your death do the trust beneficiaries you've named in the Declaration of Trust have any rights to your trust property.

2. Creating a Living Trust

When you create a living trust document with this book, you must identify:

- Yourself, as the *grantor*—or for a couple, the grantors. The grantor is the person who creates a trust.
- The *trustee*, who manages the trust property. You are also the trustee, as long as you (or your spouse, if you make a trust together) are alive.
- The *successor trustee*, who takes over after you (or you and your spouse) die. This successor trustee turns the trust property over to the trust beneficiaries and performs any other task required by the trust.
- The *trust beneficiary* or beneficiaries, those who are entitled to receive the trust property at your death.
- The *property* that is subject to the trust.

A Declaration of Trust also includes other basic terms, such as the authority of the grantor to amend or revoke the document at any time, and the authority of the trustee.

3. How a Living Trust Works

The key to establishing a living trust to avoid probate is that the grantor—remember, that's you, the person who sets up the trust—isn't locked into anything during the grantor's life. You can revise, amend, or revoke the trust for any (or no) reason, any time before your death, as long as you're legally competent. And because you appoint yourself as the initial trustee, you can control and use the property as you see fit while you live.

WHAT IS COMPETENCE?

"Competent" means having the mental capacity to make and understand decisions regarding your property. A person can become legally "incompetent" if declared so in a court proceeding, such as a custodianship or guardianship proceeding. If a person tries to make or revoke or amend a living trust and someone challenges her mental capacity, or competence, to do so, the matter can end up in a nasty court battle. Fortunately, such court disputes are quite rare.

And now for the legal magic of the living trust device. Although a living trust is really only a legal fiction during your life, it assumes a very real presence for a brief period after your death. When you die, the living trust can no longer be revoked or altered. It is now irrevocable.

With a trust for a single person, after you die, the person you named in your trust document to be successor trustee takes over. He or she is in charge of transferring the trust property to the family, friends, or charities you named as your trust beneficiaries.

With a trust for a married couple, the surviving spouse manages the trust. A successor trustee takes over after both spouses die.

There is no court or governmental supervision to ensure that your successor trustee complies with the terms of your living trust. That means that a vital element of an effective living trust is naming someone you fully trust as your successor trustee. If there is no person you trust sufficiently to name as successor trustee, a living trust probably isn't for you. You can name a bank, trust company, or other financial institution as successor trustee, but that has serious drawbacks. (See Chapter 7, Section C.)

After the trust grantor dies, some paperwork is necessary to transfer the trust property to the beneficiaries, such as preparing new ownership documents. (See Chapter 14.) But because no probate is necessary for property that was transferred to the living trust, the whole thing can generally be handled within a few weeks, in most cases without a lawyer. No court proceedings or papers are required to terminate the trust. Once the job of getting the property to the beneficiaries is accomplished, the trust just evaporates, by its own terms. No formal documents need be filed to end the trust.

Some types of living trusts, however, are designed to last much longer. First, the living trust forms in this book include provisions for creating what's called a "child's trust" (discussed in Chapter 9, Section D). You can use this type of trust for property you leave to a minor or young adult beneficiary. These trusts are managed by your successor trustee and can last for years, until the young beneficiary reaches the age you specified in your Declaration of Trust. Then the beneficiary receives the trust property, and the trust ends.

If you and your spouse create an AB living trust (discussed in Chapters 4 and 5) designed both to avoid probate and save on estate taxes after one spouse dies, that spouse's trust keeps going until the second spouse dies.

A MINI-GLOSSARY OF LIVING TRUST TERMS

Although I've already used and defined some of these terms, I want to give you a summary of all basic trust terms that are essential when preparing or understanding a living trust. Unfortunately, you can't escape legal jargon entirely when you deal with living trusts.

- The person who sets up the living trust (that's you, or you and your spouse) is called a **grantor, trustor,** or **settlor.** These terms mean the same thing and are used interchangeably. I use the term **grantor** in this book.

- All the property you own at death, whether in your living trust or owned in some other form, is your **estate.**

- The market value of your property at your death, less all debts and liabilities on that property, is your net or **taxable estate.** The IRS allows your successor trustee to choose market value at your death or six months later.

- The property you transfer to the trust is called, collectively, the **trust property, trust principal,** or **trust estate.** (And, of course, there's a Latin version: the trust corpus.)

- The person who has power over the trust property is called the **trustee.**

- The person the grantor names to take over as trustee after the grantor's death (or, with a trust made jointly by a couple, after the death of both spouses) is called the **successor trustee.**

- The people or organizations who get the trust property when the grantor dies are called the **beneficiaries** of the trust. (While the grantors are alive, technically they themselves are the beneficiaries of the trust.)

B. Probate and Why You Want to Avoid It

Given that you're reading this book, you probably already know that you want to avoid probate. If you still need any persuasion that avoiding probate is desirable, here's a brief look at how the process actually works.

Probate is the legal process that includes:

- filing the deceased person's will with the local probate court (called "surrogate" or "chancery" court in some places)

- taking inventory of the deceased person's property

- having that property appraised

- paying legal debts, including death taxes

- proving the will valid in court, and

- eventually distributing what's left as the will directs.

If the deceased person didn't leave a will, or a will isn't valid, the estate must still undergo probate. The process is called an "intestacy" proceeding, and the property is distributed to the closest relatives as state law dictates.

People who defend the probate system (mostly lawyers, which is surely no surprise) assert that probate prevents fraud in transferring a deceased person's property. In addition, they claim it protects inheritors by promptly resolving claims creditors have against a deceased person's property. In truth, however, most property is transferred within a close circle of family and friends, and very few estates have problems with creditors' claims. In short, most people have no need of these so-called benefits, so probate usually amounts to a lot of time-wasting, expensive mumbo-jumbo of aid to no one but the lawyers involved.

The actual probate functions are essentially clerical and administrative. In the vast majority of probate cases, there's no conflict, no contesting parties—none of the normal reasons for court proceedings or lawyers' adversarial skills. Likewise, probate doesn't usually call for legal research or lawyers' drafting abilities. Instead, in the normal, uneventful probate proceeding, the family or other heirs of the deceased person provide a copy of the will and other financial information. The attorney's secretary then fills in a small mound of forms and keeps track of filing deadlines and other procedural technicalities. Some lawyers hire probate form preparation companies to do all the real work. In most instances, the existence of these freelance paralegal companies is not disclosed to clients, who assume that lawyers' offices at least do the routine paperwork they are paid so well for. In some states, the attorney makes a couple of routine court appearances; in others, normally the whole procedure is handled by mail.

Because of the complicated paperwork and waiting periods imposed by law, a typical probate takes up to a year or more, often much more. (I once worked in a law office that was profitably entering its seventh year of handling a probate estate—and a very wealthy estate it was.) During probate, the beneficiaries generally get nothing unless the judge allows the decedent's immediate family a "family allowance." In some states, this allowance is a pittance—only a few hundred dollars. In others, it can amount to thousands.

Some states now allow simplified probate for certain types of estates. (See Chapter 15, Section B.) While simplified probate can speed up the process, and may even result in lower attorney fees, the truth is that probate—simplified or not—is simply a waste for most people.

Probate usually requires both an "executor" (called a "personal representative" in some states) and someone familiar with probate procedures, normally a probate attorney. The executor is a person appointed in the will who is responsible for supervising the estate, which means making sure that the will is followed. If the person died without a will, the court appoints an "administrator" (whose main qualification may sometimes be that he's a crony of the judge) to serve the same function. The executor, who is usually the spouse or a friend of the deceased, hires a probate lawyer to do the paperwork. The executor often hires the decedent's lawyer (who may even have possession of the will), but this is not required. Then the executor does little more than sign where the lawyer directs, wondering why the whole business is taking so long. For these services, the lawyer and the executor are each entitled to a hefty fee from the probate estate. Some lawyers even persuade (or dupe) clients into naming them as executors, enabling the lawyers to hire themselves as probate attorneys and collect two fees—one as executor, one as probate attorney. By contrast, most relatives and friends who serve as executors do not take the fee, especially if the person who serves is a substantial inheritor.

Probate can evoke exaggerated images of greedy lawyers consuming most of an estate in fees, while churning out reams of gobbledygook-filled paper as slowly as possible. While there is truth in these images (far more than lawyers care to admit), lawyer fees rarely actually devour the entire estate. In many states, the fees are what a court approves as "reasonable." In a few states, the fees are based on a percentage of the estate subject to probate. Either way, probate attorney fees for a routine estate with a gross value of $400,000 (these days, in many urban areas, this may be little more than a modest home, some savings and a car) can amount to $10,000 or more. Fees based on the "gross" probate estate means that debts on property are not deducted to determine value. Thus, if a house has a market value of $200,000 with a mortgage balance of $160,000 (net equity of $40,000), the gross value of the house is $200,000.

In addition, there are court costs, appraiser's fees, and other possible expenses. Moreover, if the basic fee is set by statute and there are any "extraordinary" services performed for the estate, the attorney or executor can ask the court for additional fees.

EXTREME PROBATE FEES

Marilyn Monroe's estate offers an extreme example of how outrageous probate fees can be. She died in debt in 1962, but over the next 18 years, her estate received income, mostly from movie royalties, in excess of $1.6 million. When her estate was settled in 1980, her executor announced that debts of $372,136 had been paid, and $101,229 was left for inheritors. Well over $1 million of Monroe's estate was consumed by probate fees.

Then there's the 1997 U.S. Tax Court case upholding an attorney's probate fee of $1,600 an hour, totaling $368,100. The court declared the fee was "reasonable under New York law."

Even England—the source of our antiquated probate laws—abolished its elaborate probate system years ago. It survives in this country because it is so lucrative for lawyers.

C. Avoiding Probate

The most popular probate-avoidance method is, undoubtedly, the living trust. However, there are a number of other methods.

1. Informal Probate Avoidance

You may wonder why surviving relatives and friends can't just divide up your property as your will directs (or as you said you wanted, if you never got around to writing a will), and ignore the laws requiring probate. Some small estates are undoubtedly disposed of this way, directly and informally by family members.

For example, say an older man lives his last few years in a nursing home. After his death, his children meet and divide the personal items their father had kept over the years. What little savings he has have long since been put into a joint account with the children anyway, so there's no need for formalities there.

For this type of informal procedure to work, the family must be able to gain possession of all of the deceased's property, agree on how to distribute it, and pay all the creditors. Gaining possession of property isn't difficult when the only property left is personal effects and household items. However, if real estate, securities, bank accounts, cars, boats, or other property bearing legal title papers are involved, informal family property distribution can't work. Title to a house, for example, can't be changed on the say-so of the next of kin. Someone with legal authority must prepare, sign, and record a deed transferring title to the house to the new owners, the inheritors.

One good rule is that whenever outsiders are involved with a deceased's property, do-it-yourself division by inheritors is not feasible. For instance, creditors can be an obstacle; a creditor concerned about being paid can usually file a court action to compel a probate proceeding.

Another stumbling block for an informal family property disposition is disagreement among family members on how to divide the deceased's possessions. All inheritors must agree to the property distribution if probate is bypassed. Any inheritor who is unhappy with the result can, like creditors, file for a formal probate. If there's a will, the family will probably follow its provisions. If there is no will, the family may look up and agree to abide by the inheritance rules established by the law of the state where the deceased person lived. Or, in either case, the family may simply agree on their own settlement. For example, if, despite a will provision to the contrary, one sibling wants the furniture and the other wants the tools, they can simply trade.

In sum, informal probate avoidance, even for a small estate, isn't something you can count on. Realistically, you must plan ahead to avoid probate.

2. Other Probate-Avoidance Methods

Besides the living trust, these are the most popular probate-avoidance methods:

- joint tenancy or tenancy by the entirety
- pay-on-death financial accounts
- transfer-on-death registration for stocks and bonds
- retirement accounts
- life insurance
- state laws that exempt certain (small) amounts of property left by will from probate, and
- gifts made while you are alive.

These methods are discussed briefly in Chapter 15, Section B.

These and other probate-avoidance techniques are discussed in detail in *Plan Your Estate* (Nolo).

While I'm a fan of living trusts, I don't believe they are always the best probate-avoidance device for all property of all people in all situations. It's up to you to determine whether a living trust is the best way for you to avoid probate for all your property, or whether you want to use other methods. In rare cases, you may even want to use other methods exclusively. (See Chapter 3, Section A, and Chapter 15.)

D. Reducing Estate Taxes

A basic probate-avoidance living trust, either for a single person or a couple, does not, by itself, reduce federal or state estate taxes. The taxing authorities don't care whether or not your property goes through probate; all they care about is how much you owned at your death. Property you leave in a revocable living trust is definitely considered part of your estate for federal estate tax purposes.

Under federal law, the personal estate tax exemption allows a set dollar amount of property to pass tax-free, no matter who it is left to. This amount varies, depending on the year of death, as shown below.

THE PERSONAL ESTATE TAX EXEMPTION

Year of Death	Estate Tax Exemption
2004	$1.5 million
2005	$1.5 million
2006	$2 million
2007	$2 million
2008	$2 million
2009	$3.5 million
2010	Estate tax repealed
2011	$1 million unless Congress extends repeal

DEFINITION: AMOUNT OF PROPERTY SUBJECT TO ESTATE TAX

Since the amount of the personal exemption depends on the year of death, no one dollar figure can define the amount of an estate that can be transferred tax-free under this exemption. Rather than repeat this table each time I refer to the personal exemption, I use the term "estate tax threshold" to mean the amount of the personal exemption in any and all years. It refers to the range of exempt amounts, from $1.5 million to $3.5 million.

In addition to the personal exemption, all property left to a spouse (if that spouse is a U.S. citizen) or to a tax-exempt charity is exempt from estate tax.

Some specialized kinds of living trusts can save on estate taxes. This book contains one such tax-saving trust, called Nolo's "AB" trust or, sometimes, a "marital life estate" trust.

If you are a member of a couple with combined property worth over the estate tax threshold, you can save your inheritors substantial estate taxes by using Nolo's AB trust. Couples can use this trust to shield a combined estate worth between $3 million to $7 million

from estate taxes, depending on the years of death. Basically, Nolo's AB trust allows each member of a couple to use a separate personal estate tax exemption (that is, use two exemptions in total) while leaving one spouse's property for the use of the surviving spouse. How Nolo's AB trust works is explained in depth in Chapters 4 and 5.

 If the combined value of your and your spouse's estates exceeds the estate tax threshold, you'll need estate tax planning help that's beyond the scope of this book, although an AB trust will likely be a key component of your final plan.

E. Other Advantages of a Living Trust

As you know, the main reason for setting up a revocable living trust is to save your family time and money by avoiding probate and perhaps estate taxes as well. But there are other advantages as well. Here is a brief rundown of the other major positive features of a living trust.

1. Out-of-State Real Estate Doesn't Have to Be Probated in That State

The only thing worse than regular probate is out-of-state probate. Usually, an estate is probated in the probate court of the county where the decedent was living before he or she died. But if the decedent owned real estate in more than one state, it's usually necessary to have a whole separate probate proceeding in each one. That means the surviving relatives must find and hire a lawyer in each state, and pay for multiple probate proceedings.

With a living trust, out-of-state property can normally be transferred to the beneficiaries without probate in that state.

2. You Can Avoid the Need for a Conservatorship

A living trust can be useful if the person who created it (the grantor) becomes incapable, because of physical or mental illness, of taking care of his or her financial affairs. The person named in the living trust document to take over as trustee at the grantor's death (the successor trustee) can also take over management of the trust if the grantor becomes incapacitated. (If you use this book's trust forms, the grantor's incapacity must be certified in writing by a physician.) When a couple sets up a trust, if one person becomes incapacitated, the other takes sole responsibility. If both members of the couple are incapacitated, their successor trustee takes over. The person who takes over has authority to manage all property in the trust, and to use it for the grantor or grantors' benefit.

Example

Wei creates a revocable living trust, appointing herself as trustee. The trust document states that if she becomes incapacitated and a physician signs a statement saying she can no longer manage her own affairs, her daughter Li-Shan will replace her as trustee and manage the trust property for Wei's benefit.

If there is no living trust and no other arrangements have been made for someone to take over property management if you become incapacitated, someone must get legal authority, from a court, to take over. Typically, the spouse or adult child of the person seeks this authority and is called a "conservator" or "guardian." Conservatorship proceedings are intrusive and often expensive, and they get a court involved in your personal finances on a continuing basis.

DURABLE POWER OF ATTORNEY

You should also give your successor trustee (or spouse) the authority to manage property that has not been transferred to the trust if you become incapacitated. The best way to do that is to prepare and sign a document called a "Durable Power of Attorney for Finances." (See Chapter 15, Section E.)

Your successor trustee has no power to make health care decisions for you if you become incapacitated. If your preference is to die a natural death without the unauthorized use of life support systems, you'll want to prepare and sign health care directives. (This is discussed in Chapter 15, Section E.)

3. Your Estate Plan Remains Confidential

When your will is filed with the probate court after you die, it becomes a matter of public record. A living trust, on the other hand, is a private document. Because the

living trust document is never filed with a court or other government entity, what you leave, and to whom, generally remains private. There are just a couple of exceptions. First, records of real estate transfers are always public, so if your successor trustee transfers real estate to a beneficiary after your death, there will be a public record of it. Second, a few states require the successor trustee to disclose information about your living trust. These requirements are explained in Chapter 14, Section B.

A handful of states do require that you register your living trust with the local court, but there are no legal consequences or penalties if you don't. (Registration is explained in Chapter 12.) Also, registration of a living trust normally requires that you just file a paper stating the existence of the trust and the main players—you don't file the document itself, so the terms aren't part of the public record.

In most cases, the only way the terms of a living trust might become public is if—and this is very unlikely—after your death someone files a lawsuit to challenge the trust or collect a court judgment you owe them.

4. You Can Change Your Mind at Any Time

You have complete control over your revocable living trust and all the property you transfer to it. You can:

- sell, mortgage, or give away property in the trust
- put ownership of trust property back in your own name
- add property to the trust
- change the beneficiaries
- name a different successor trustee (the person who distributes trust property after your death), or
- revoke the trust completely.

If you and your spouse create the trust together, both spouses must consent to changes, although either of you can revoke the trust entirely. (See Chapter 13.)

5. No Trust Record Keeping Is Required While You Are Alive

Even after you create a valid trust that will avoid probate after your death, you do not have to maintain separate trust records. This means you do not have to keep a separate trust bank account, maintain trust financial records, or spend any time on trust paperwork.

As long as you remain the trustee of your trust, the IRS does not require that a separate trust income tax return be filed. (IRS Reg. § 1.671-4.) You do not have to obtain a trust taxpayer ID number. You report all trust transactions on your regular income tax returns. In sum, for tax purposes, living trusts don't exist while you live.

6. You Can Name Someone to Manage Trust Property for Young Beneficiaries

If there's a possibility that any of your beneficiaries will inherit trust property while still young (not yet 35), you may want to arrange to have someone manage that property for them until they're older. If they might inherit before they're legally adults (age 18), you should definitely arrange for management. Minors are not allowed to legally control significant amounts of property, and if you haven't provided someone to do it, a court will have to appoint a property guardian.

When you create a living trust with this book, you can arrange for someone to manage property for a young beneficiary. In most states, you have two options:

- Have your successor trustee (or your spouse, if you created a living trust together) manage the property in a "child's trust" until the child reaches an age you designate.

- In most states, you can appoint someone as a "custodian" to manage the property until the child reaches an age specified by your state's Uniform Transfers to Minors Act (18 in a few states, 21 in most, but up to 25 in California, Alaska, Nevada, Oregon, Pennsylvania, and Tennessee).

Both methods are explained in Chapter 9.

7. No Lawyer Is Necessary to Distribute Your Property

With a living trust, the person you named as your successor trustee has total control over how the property is transferred to the beneficiaries you named in the trust document. With a will, technically the person in charge of the property that passes under the terms of the will is the executor you named in the will, but the probate lawyer usually runs the show. This can be the personal show as well as the silly court show. I've heard of a lawyer calling a family in for a "reading" of the deceased's will immediately after the funeral service, which some family members found highly insensitive. There's much less

chance of this type of crassness if only close personal relations are involved in the transfer of the property.

F.   Possible Drawbacks of a Living Trust

A basic living trust, which serves just to avoid probate, can have some drawbacks. They aren't significant to most people, but you should be aware of them before you create a living trust. Aside from the problems discussed below, an AB living trust, which is designed to save on estate taxes as well as avoid probate, has a whole set of its own potential problems and drawbacks, which are covered in Chapter 4.

1.   Initial Paperwork

Setting up a living trust obviously requires some paperwork. The first step is to use this book to create a trust document, which you must sign in front of a notary public. So far, the amount of work required is no more than writing a will.

There is, however, one more essential step to make your living trust effective. You must make sure that ownership of all the property you listed in the trust document is legally transferred to the living trust. (Chapter 11 explains this process in detail.) Transferring property into your trust is simply a matter of doing the paperwork correctly. What you have to do depends on the kind of property you're putting in the trust.

- If an item of property doesn't have a title (ownership) document, then in most states, listing it in the trust document is enough to transfer it. So, for example, no additional paperwork is legally required for most books, furniture, electronics, jewelry, appliances, musical instruments, paintings, and many other kinds of property.

- If an item has a title document—real estate, stocks, mutual funds, bonds, money market accounts, or vehicles, for example—you must change the title document to show that the property is owned by the trustee of the trust. For example, if you want to put your house into your living trust, you must prepare and sign a new deed, transferring ownership from you to your living trust.

After the trust is created, you must keep written records sufficient to identify what's in and out of the trust, whenever you transfer property to or from the trust.

This isn't burdensome unless you're frequently transferring property in and out, which is rare.

Example

Misha and David Feldman put their house in a living trust to avoid probate, but later decide to sell it. In the real estate contract and deed transferring ownership to the new owners, Misha and David sign their names "as trustees of the Misha and David Feldman Revocable Living Trust, dated March 18, 1998."

2. Transfer Taxes

In virtually all states, including California, New York, Florida, and Texas, transfers of real estate to revocable living trusts are exempt from transfer taxes usually imposed on real estate transfers. Washington, DC, used to tax transfers of real estate to living trusts, but repealed those laws.

If you're the cautious type, you can check with your county tax assessor to learn if there will be any transfer tax imposed on transfer of your real estate to your trust. Your county land records office (County Recorder's office or Registry of Deeds) may also be able to provide this information. As I've said, you're very likely to learn that no tax is imposed. If there is a tax, but it is minor, it may impose no serious burden on creating your trust. If the tax is substantial, you may decide it's too costly to place your real estate in a trust.

3. Difficulty Refinancing Trust Real Estate

Because legal title to trust real estate is held in the name of the trustee of the living trust—not your name—some banks, and especially title companies, may balk if you want to refinance it. They should be sufficiently reassured if you show them a copy of your trust document, which specifically gives you, as trustee, the power to borrow against trust property.

In the unlikely event you can't convince an uncooperative lender to deal with you in your capacity as trustee, you'll have to find another lender (which shouldn't be hard) or simply transfer the property out of the trust and back into your name. Later, after you refinance, you can transfer it back into the living trust. It's a silly process, but one that does work.

4. No Cutoff of Creditors' Claims

Most people don't have to worry that after their death creditors will try to collect large debts from property in their estate. In most situations, there are no massive debts. Those that exist, such as outstanding bills, taxes, and last illness and funeral expenses, can be readily paid from the deceased's property. But if you are concerned about the possibility of large claims, you may want to let your property go through probate instead of a living trust.

If your property goes through probate, creditors have only a set amount of time to file claims against your estate. A creditor who was properly notified of the probate court proceeding cannot file a claim after the period—about six months, in most states—expires.

Example

Elaine is a real estate investor with a good-sized portfolio of property. She has many creditors and is involved in a couple of lawsuits. It's sensible for her to have her estate transferred by a probate court procedure, which allows creditors to present claims, resolves conflicts, and cuts off the claims of creditors who are notified of the probate proceeding but don't present timely claims.

On the other hand, when property isn't probated, creditors still have the right to be paid (if the debt is valid) from that property. In most states, there is no formal claim procedure. (California has enacted a statutory scheme for creditors to get at property transferred by living trust.) The creditor may not know who inherited the deceased debtor's property, and once the property is found, the creditor may have to file a lawsuit, which may not be worth the time and expense.

If you want to take advantage of probate's creditor cutoff, you must let all your property pass through probate. If not, there's a good chance the creditor could still sue (even after the probate claim cutoff) and try to collect from the property that didn't go through probate and passed instead through your living trust. ■

chapter 2

HUMAN EMOTIONS AND LIVING TRUSTS

*B*efore plunging deeper into the mechanics of creating your own living trust, I want to switch gears and acknowledge the underlying reality we're talking about here: death, and the transfer of your property after death. Although property concerns can be minor indeed in the face of the overwhelming force and mystery of death, these deep imponderables are beyond the scope of this book and are appropriately left to poets, philosophers, clergy, and—ultimately—to you.

Even when the focus shifts to property, this is basically a technical how-to-do-it book. Yet clearly, planning for the transfer of property on your death can raise deep emotional concerns, problems, or potential conflicts. No matter how well you deal with the legal technicalities, your living trust won't achieve what you want unless you take human concerns into account.

For many people—probably most—no serious personal problems arise when preparing a living trust. They know to whom they want to give their property. They have no difficulty deciding who to name as successor trustee. They do not foresee conflict among their beneficiaries or threat of a lawsuit by someone angry at not being named a beneficiary. On the human level, these people can, happily, focus on the satisfactions they expect their gifts to bring.

Other people's situations are not so clear and straightforward. They must deal with more difficult human dynamics, such as possible family conflicts, dividing property unequally between children, providing care for minor children, or handling complexities arising from second or subsequent marriages.

Before beginning the work of preparing your living trust, it's vital that you assess your personal circumstances and resolve any potential human problems regarding distribution of your property. If you're sure you don't face any such problems, wonderful. If, however, you think you might face complications—or if you're not sure what kinds of problems can come up—try to identify and resolve those problems now, or as you go along. After all, you surely don't want the distribution of your property to result in bitterness, family feuds, or fights between former friends.

A self-evident truth about a living trust is that it transfers property—money or things that can be converted into money. Money, as most of us have learned, is strange stuff indeed. It has power to do good in a number of material ways, and can alleviate anxiety and provide security. Unfortunately, however, human flaws and fears are sometimes unleashed when substantial sums of money are involved; meanness, greed, and dishonesty have certainly been known to surface. Naturally, in making your gifts, you don't want to unnecessarily stir up negative feelings or emotions. What about your beneficiaries? Are they clearheaded enough to accept your gifts in the spirit in which you give them, or are some of them likely to create their own brand of trouble? Sadly, bitterness, strife, and lawsuits are far from unheard of upon distribution of property after one's death. This chapter discusses a number of personal concerns, based on examples drawn from my living trust legal practice.

A. Leaving Unequal Amounts of Property to Children

Most parents feel it's very important to treat their children equally regarding the distribution of property, to avoid giving the impression that they value one child more than another. However, in some family situations, parents sensibly conclude that the abstract goal of equal division of property isn't the fairest or wisest solution for their children. The most important issue here, I suggest, is to explain your reasoning to your children.

Example

A widower with three grown children feels that one, a struggling pianist, needs far more financial support than his other two, who have more conventional and well-paying jobs. He wants to give the pianist the bulk of his money, but worries this might cause problems among his children. So he writes a letter explaining that he loves all three children equally and that his decision to give the pianist more is a reflection of need, not preference. He attaches the letter to his living trust. He also leaves most family heirlooms, which are emotionally but not monetarily valuable, to the other two children to emphasize how much he cares for them.

Example

An elderly couple owns a much-loved summer home in the Poconos. Only one of their four children, Skip, cares about the home as much as they do, and they plan to give it to him. But they question whether they should reduce his portion of the rest of their estate by the value of the home, or divide the rest of their estate equally among their four children, and on top of this, give the summer home to Skip.

As the family is a close one, they discuss the problem with the kids. One of them doesn't think their last alternative is fair. Skip doesn't think so either. The parents decide to give Skip less than one-fourth of the rest of their estate, but not to reduce his share by the full value of the summer home. They explain their decision to the others on the basis that Skip helped maintain the summer home for many years, and that his work should be recognized. It is, and the plan is accepted in good grace by all.

B. Second or Subsequent Marriages

People who marry more than once may face problems reconciling their desires for their present spouse (and family) with their wishes for children from prior marriages. Individual situations vary greatly here, and you must work carefully through your needs and desires. How much of one spouse's property might a surviving spouse need? How much property does each spouse want to leave to his or her own children? Sometimes, spouses can readily resolve such concerns and use a Nolo living trust to leave their property.

Example

Ben and Estelle met in the 1970s, as teachers in an alternative school. They fell in love, ran away to Oregon to live in a commune, and had two daughters. What a long, strange trip it was; they wound up, to their considerable surprise, owning a prosperous business in San Francisco. Now that it is time to draw up their living trust, Ben and Estelle are in complete accord about how to distribute their property, with one exception—Ben's daughter Susan (now age 47) from his first marriage. Ben wants to leave her a substantial part of his estate; he suggests 20%. Estelle thinks that is outrageous, since his daughter has long treated him terribly, and is a wastrel with money besides. Estelle says it's too late to try to buy her love. Ben insists he feels a duty to his child no matter how she treats him.

Fortunately, both Ben and Estelle recognize signs of trouble and understand they're talking about a lot more than property here. What, if anything, does Ben owe his child? Will his ex-wife get involved if his daughter inherits money? If so, so what? Ben and Estelle discuss these problems themselves and with a therapist they see from time to time.

Eventually, they reach a compromise. Ben will leave some property to Susan, but not a percentage of his total estate. He and Estelle agree on a figure of $40,000.

Other couples find they want more control than a Nolo living trust offers. Many couples with substantial assets create a trust leaving property to the surviving spouse for his or her life, with specific, limiting controls over how that property can be spent for that spouse. Then, when that spouse dies, the trust property goes to children from the other spouse's prior marriage(s). These types of "life estate" trusts are briefly discussed in Chapter 15, Section F. (They are discussed in more depth in Nolo's *Plan Your Estate*.) You need a lawyer to draft this kind of trust.

Example

Ellen and Alex, a married couple, each have children from prior marriages. Both spouses want to eventually leave their property to their own children, but both also want to protect the interest of the survivor. They own a house in equal shares. If the first spouse to die leaves half directly to his or her children, they may want to sell it or use it before the other spouse dies. At best, the surviving spouse will be insecure and, at worst, may be thrown out of the house. Neither spouse wants to risk that.

They decide to each leave the other what's called a "life estate" in their one-half of the house, specifying that the other spouse cannot sell the house. For instance, if Alex dies first, Ellen can live in the house during her lifetime, but when she dies, Alex's share automatically goes to his children. Because Ellen's share will go to her kids, the house will probably be sold, and the proceeds divided, when she dies.

C. Disinheriting a Child

Sometimes, people are troubled by deciding how much, if any, property to leave to a child. Legally, you can completely disinherit a child if you want to. But deciding to disinherit a child is often not emotionally easy to do. Many people decide that something less harsh than disinheritance is desirable. Rather than completely cutting off a child by direct words, they decide that it's wiser to leave some small, lesser amount to this out-of-favor child.

Example

Toshiro and Miya have three daughters and a substantial estate. They are very close to two of the daughters, but are bitterly on the outs with the third, Kimiko. Toshiro and Miya had originally intended to leave most of their property to the surviving spouse, with some to the two daughters they're close to. Then, when the surviving spouse dies, the remaining property is to be divided between these two daughters.

But they have second thoughts. Do they really want to cut Kimiko out entirely? If they do, aren't they creating an incentive for her to sue and try to invalidate their estate plan? They decide that good hearts and prudence both dictate the same decision. Each will leave Kimiko $25,000 in their living trust and include a "no-contest" clause in both their wills and trusts. This clause states that if any beneficiary challenges a will or trust, she gets nothing if her challenge is unsuccessful. The parents expect Kimiko to take the certain $50,000 rather than risk an expensive lawsuit she's very likely to lose. Also, Toshiro and Miya are relieved that they haven't had to formally disinherit one of their own children.

If you decide to disinherit a child, you must make that explicitly clear in your will. (See Chapter 8, Section H.)

No-contest clauses. The trust and will forms in this book do not contain "no contest" clauses. These clauses are not, technically, hard to draft. But the reason to include a no-contest clause in a living trust or will isn't a simple, technical matter. It indicates a serious problem and conflict with a family member. If you think you need a no-contest clause, you should see a lawyer to be sure you've done all you can to discourage a lawsuit against your trust or will.

D. Special Concerns of Unmarried Couples

Unlike married couples, unmarried couples have no automatic legal right to inherit any of each other's property. (Except in California, Hawaii, and Vermont, where domestic partner laws allow unmarried lesbian and gay couples to register with the state and obtain the same legal rights as married spouses to inherit each other's property.) A major concern of most unmarried couples—

whether lesbian, gay, or heterosexual—is to ensure that each will inherit property from the other. Happily, people have the right to leave their property by living trust to whomever they want, as long as they're mentally competent. As a general rule, a person must be very far gone, mentally, before a court will declare him incompetent. In case of serious threat by hostile family members, a couple may take action to establish by clear proof that they were competent when they prepared their trusts.

Example

Ernesto and Teresa have lived together for several years. Aside from a few small gifts to friends or family, each wants to leave all their property to the other after death. They're concerned with efficiency and economy, but above all they want to be sure that their estate plan can't be successfully attacked by several close relatives who have long been hostile to their lifestyle. Ernesto and Teresa discuss their situation with a sympathetic lawyer. Each then prepares a living trust leaving their property as they desire. They videotape their signing and the notarization of this document to provide additional proof they were both mentally competent and not under duress.

E. Communicating Your Decisions to Family and Friends

Most of the examples in this chapter demonstrate my belief that talking can help resolve many potential difficulties with family and friends. But talking is not a panacea. Certainly, there are times when someone doesn't want to listen or talk, or times when communication reveals only a deep and unbridgeable gulf. Still, most of the people I've worked with have been aided by talking openly about what they want to accomplish with their living trusts. If you have a personal problem or two, something to work out on an emotional level, it can require a good deal of thought, understanding, and consideration. For these problems, two or more heads do seem better than one. ■

chapter 3

COMMON QUESTIONS ABOUT LIVING TRUSTS

*C*omplexities and doubts sometimes arise between considering a living trust and deciding to prepare one, so before you move into the heart of this book, read through this chapter. It answers a number of questions about living trusts I've been asked over the years, both by clients and by readers of my estate planning books.

A. Does Everyone Need a Living Trust?

For those who want to arrange now to avoid probate— the elderly, the seriously ill, as well as anyone who is cautious and doesn't want any risk of subjecting property to probate—living trusts are usually the best probate-avoidance device. Indeed, most people who plan their estates ultimately choose a living trust to transfer their property, at least their big-ticket assets—house, stocks and bonds, and other valuable items.

Given the advantages of avoiding probate that a living trust confers, shouldn't every prudent person use one for all his or her property? Norman Dacey, in his pioneering work *How to Avoid Probate* (Macmillan), essentially asserted that living trusts should be used by all people in all situations. A number of lawyers now make the same claim in advertisements and seminars. These sweeping claims are too extreme. First, some people don't really need to plan now to avoid probate. Second, other probate-avoidance methods may fit an individual's needs better, at least for certain types of property.

Generally, you may conclude that you don't need a living trust, at least not right now, if:

- **You are young and healthy**. Your primary goals probably are to be sure your property will be distributed as you want, and to provide financial resources and arrange for someone to care for your minor children, if you have any. A will (perhaps coupled with life insurance) often achieves these goals more easily than a living trust.

  Here's why: A will is simpler to prepare than a living trust. While using a will usually means property goes through probate, probate occurs only after death. As long as you are alive, the fact that probate will be avoided is obviously of no benefit. Because very few healthy younger people die without any warning (and because they often don't yet own enough property that probate fees would amount to much), it can make good sense to use a will for a number of years. Later in life, when the prospect of death is more imminent and

you have accumulated more property, you can create a revocable living trust to avoid probate.

- **You can more sensibly transfer your assets, or at least some of them, by other probate-avoidance devices.** Other easy ways to avoid probate include joint tenancy, pay-on-death bank accounts, transfer-on-death securities accounts, life insurance, and gifts. In addition, the laws in some states allow certain amounts or types of property (and occasionally all property left to certain classes of beneficiaries, such as a surviving spouse) to be transferred without probate even if a will is used. None of these devices has the breadth of a living trust, which can be used to transfer virtually all types of assets. However, each can be easier to use, and equally efficient, in particular circumstances. It's best to understand all probate-avoidance methods and then to decide which ones will work best for you. (See Chapter 15, Section B.)

- **You have complex debt problems.** As I've discussed, if you have a serious debt problem, such as a business that has many creditors, probate provides an absolute cut-off time for notified creditors to file claims. If they don't do so in the time permitted (a few months, in most states), your inheritors can take your property free of concern that these creditors will surface later and claim a share. A living trust normally doesn't create any such cut-off period, which means your property could be subject to creditors' claims for a much longer time.

- **Your primary goal is to name a personal guardian to care for your minor children.** A living trust shouldn't be used for this purpose. You do this in your will.

NAMING A GUARDIAN FOR MINOR CHILDREN IN A LIVING TRUST

A few states' laws, such as California's, can be read to allow the appointment of your minor children's personal or property guardian in your living trust. However, this is most definitely not common practice. A judge must confirm the appointment of any acting personal or property guardian. It's unwise to present judges with novel legal documents when important matters are at stake.

A will can always be used to name a personal guardian for your minor children. (See Chapter 16.) Of course, if you have a great deal of valuable property, you will probably create a living trust (or other probate-avoidance device) to transfer it and name a personal guardian for your minor children in a "back-up" will.

- **Your state has streamlined probate procedures.** Wisconsin lets married couples avoid probate altogether for their marital property by using a written agreement. For Wisconsin couples who don't want a tax-saving AB trust, this procedure could work fine. By contrast, in most other states with simplified probate, you still have to pay a lawyer. For example, in Texas, probate is usually not very complicated, but property still must go through court, and a lawyer will take fees. The process will probably be more costly than using one of Nolo's do-it-yourself living trusts.

- **You are separated but not yet divorced.** To protect the rights of divorcing spouses, your state may have very specific rules about what you can and cannot do with property after separation but before your divorce is final. See a lawyer before trying to create a living trust or transferring property in or out of one.

- **You own little property.** If you don't have a lot of assets, there isn't much point in bothering with a living trust and probate avoidance, because probate won't cost that much. Often parents in this situation provide money for their young children, in case of a parent's death, by purchasing life insurance. (Insurance proceeds do not go through probate.) However, insurance proceeds (above a minimal amount) cannot be turned over to children under 18. So you may need to leave the proceeds under your state's Uniform Transfers to Minors Act (available in all states except South Carolina and Vermont). Using this Act, you name an adult custodian to manage the money for the benefit of the child until the child becomes an adult. (See Chapter 9, Sections B and E.)

How large should your estate be before you need to concern yourself with avoiding probate? There's no mathematical rule here. Even a relatively small estate—say $50,000—might cost $1,000 or more to transfer by probate. One sensible approach for smaller estates is to check out the dollar amount of property your state allows to be transferred by a will without formal probate. This varies widely from state to state. California, one of the more generous states, allows you to transfer up to $100,000 by will free of probate. Most states allow much less. (You can find a state-by-state list of each state's rules regarding exemption from normal probate in Nolo's *Plan Your Estate*.) Basically, if you own any significant amount of property, it's desirable to avoid probate.

B. If I Prepare a Living Trust, Do I Need a Will?

Yes. Even if you arrange to transfer almost all your property by a living trust, you should always prepare a "back-up" will. A back-up will can serve several purposes. First, you use it to name beneficiaries for property that it is generally not desirable to transfer to a living trust, such as your personal checking account or car. (See Chapter 6, Section B.) Also, a back-up will ensures that any of your property that didn't make it into your trust—for example, a last-minute inheritance or lottery winnings—goes to who you want to have it. Also, just in case you haven't properly transferred some item of property to your trust, you want to control who receives that property, by use of your will.

Finally, a living trust won't work for property you don't presently own, but expect to receive, like an inheritance from someone else, or property in a trust that you haven't actually yet obtained. A living trust works to transfer only property you currently own. If you've been left property by someone's will that is still in probate, or you expect to get money from a lawsuit settlement, only a will can transfer that property.

(Back-up wills are covered in Chapter 16. Tear-out will forms are included in Appendix B and on the CD-ROM.)

C. How Can I Leave Trust Property to Children and Young Adults?

How you can use your living trust to leave property to minor children or young adults is covered in depth in Chapter 9. Here I cover some basic, preliminary questions.

1. Providing for Minor Children

You can leave property to minor children (those under 18) in your living trust and name an adult to manage that trust property.

If any of your living trust property is left to a beneficiary who's a minor when you die, an adult must manage that property for the minor. Minors cannot own any substantial amount of property outright.

WHAT YOUR LIVING TRUST CAN'T DO FOR CHILDREN

Do not name a personal guardian (someone responsible for raising your children if you die) for your own minor child or children in your living trust. Similarly, do not name a general property guardian, responsible for managing all property owned by your minor children, in a living trust document. You must use your will for those purposes.

Various legal devices can be used to leave property to minors:

- **Small gifts for children's benefit.** If your estate is relatively modest and there is a trusted person to care for the child (usually the other parent), it's often easiest simply to leave property directly to the adult who will care for the child.

- **Larger gifts.** If the gift is larger—as a rough rule, say up to $50,000—it can be desirable to leave the property by using the Uniform Transfers to Minors Act in your living trust. You name an adult "custodian" to manage the property you leave to the child.

- **Very large gifts.** The best way to leave even larger gifts—more than $50,000—to minor children is by using a "child's trust" as part of your living trust. A child's trust allows you to designate the age at which the child will receive the property. Your successor trustee manages the trust property for the child's benefit until the child receives it outright.

The trust forms in this book have specific provisions allowing you to use the Uniform Transfers to Minors Act if your state has it. All but South Carolina and Vermont have it. The forms also allow you to create a child's trust as a part of your living trust. If you die before a minor beneficiary has reached the age you've chosen, that child's trust property is held in a child's trust. If you don't specify an age, the trust form provides that the property remains in the child's trust until that child becomes age 35. This trust is irrevocable after your death. If the child has already reached that age when you die, she receives her property outright, and no child's trust is created for her.

Example

One of the beneficiaries of Edward's living trust is Abigail, age 17. Edward establishes a child's trust for her, as part of his living trust. She is to receive her trust property when she becomes 35. Edward dies when Abigail is 26. Her property is maintained in the trust until she becomes 35.

While a child's trust is operational, the trustee (the successor trustee of your living trust) has broad powers to spend any of that trust's income or principal for the child's health, support, maintenance, or education. When the child reaches the age you specified for her to receive her property outright (or age 35, if you didn't specify an age), the successor trustee turns the trust property over to her.

2. Young Adult Beneficiaries Who Can't Handle Money Responsibly Now

A child's trust does not have to be used solely for minors. You can leave a gift in a child's trust for any beneficiary who is under 35 when you create your trust.

Example

Julio's son Enrique is 22. Julio wants to leave Enrique a large amount of property, worth over $100,000. Julio worries (sadly, with good reason) that Enrique isn't mature enough to handle this money responsibly if he happens to inherit it soon. So Julio creates a child's trust for this gift to Enrique, and provides that Enrique will receive the gift outright at age 35.

D. Will My Living Trust Reduce Estate Taxes?

When some people hear the word "trust," they feel it must mean "tax savings." Not necessarily. Indeed, most living trusts are designed solely to avoid probate. A basic trust for a single person (Form 1 in this book), or a basic shared living trust for a couple (Form 2), will not reduce federal estate taxes.

By contrast, an AB living trust (the other kind of trust in this book; Form 3) can achieve substantial federal estate tax savings for a couple with a combined estate that may be liable for estate taxes. (See Chapter 4, Section E, and Chapter 5.)

E. Will I Have to Pay Gift Taxes?

Some people worry that by creating a living trust, they'll become enmeshed in gift taxes. Not to worry.

No gift tax is assessed when you transfer property to your living trust. Legally, to make a taxable gift you must relinquish all control over the property. Since you keep complete control over property in your living trust (and you can revoke the trust at any time before you die), you don't make a gift simply by transferring property to the trust. (See Chapter 15, Section C, for a discussion of gifts and gift taxes.)

F. Will a Living Trust Shield My Property From Creditors?

Some people think that a living trust can protect their assets from creditors. No such luck.

1. While You're Alive

Property in a revocable living trust is not immune from attack by your creditors while you're alive. Some "authorities" have inaccurately stated that property in a revocable living trust can't be grabbed by the grantor's creditors, because for collection purposes a revocable living trust is legally distinct from its creator. I know of no law or court ruling that supports this position. It's most unlikely that any judge would accept it, because during your life you have complete and exclusive power over the trust property.

On the other hand, if property is put in an irrevocable trust—and you no longer have any control over it—it's a different legal matter. Property transferred to a bona fide irrevocable trust is immune from your creditors. The key words here are "bona fide." If an irrevocable trust is set up to defraud creditors, it's not bona fide. This book does not include irrevocable trusts.

 Keeping creditors away from your property. If you're concerned about protecting your assets from creditors, see a lawyer.

2. After Your Death

A living trust won't shield your assets from your creditors after your death either, even after the property has been turned over to your beneficiaries.

One advantage claimed for probate is that it ensures that one's debts and taxes are paid before property is distributed to inheritors. If duly notified creditors don't make their claims within an allotted time, they're simply cut off. Does that mean you should worry about how your debts, including death taxes, get paid if there's no probate and no probate court supervision? In most cases—no.

Many people leave no significant debts, and even if they do, they normally leave sufficient assets to pay them. The most common kinds of large debts—mortgages on real estate or loans on cars—don't have to be paid off when the owner dies. Normally, these kinds of debts are transferred with the asset to an inheritor, who then becomes liable for the mortgage or loan. In other words, mortgages or car loans pass with the property and don't need to be paid off separately.

Your successor trustee (who should also be named as executor of your will—see Chapter 7, Section C, and Chapter 16, Section C) has the legal responsibility of paying your debts. If no probate occurs to cut off creditors' claims, all your property, including all property that was in the living trust, remains liable for your debts. This is true even after the property is transferred to inheritors. If only one person inherits from you, that person will wind up paying your debts and any death taxes from the inherited property.

If there are several inheritors, who will pay your last debts and taxes might cause more confusion. You can eliminate this problem by designating a specific trust asset—often a bank account or stock market account—to be used to pay your debts. If you don't have a suitable asset available to do this, consider purchasing insurance to provide quick cash to pay debts. (Providing in your trust for payment of your debts is covered in Chapter 10, Section D, Step 9.)

G. Do I Need a "Catastrophic Illness Clause" in My Trust?

The term "catastrophic illness clause" commonly refers to a clause that, hopefully, prevents assets from being used for the costs of a major illness that strikes you or your spouse, when you want government aid to help pay the bills. Many people are concerned with becoming eligible for Medicaid or Medicare without having to use up all (or even any) of their assets. Indeed, they don't want their assets counted at all when eligibility for government aid is determined. Married couples want to protect at least the assets owned by the healthier spouse.

A catastrophic illness clause certainly sounds like a good idea. But unfortunately, no simple clause can protect your assets. Bluntly put, the law doesn't allow people to easily retain their assets and still become eligible for federal aid. There are various, more complex, ways of protecting some of your assets if you're faced with huge medical bills, including making gifts, paying children for services, or using certain complex types of trusts.

Methods of hanging onto your assets are discussed in *Choose the Right Long-Term Care: Home Care, Assisted Living & Nursing Homes*, by Joseph Matthews (Nolo).

If you want to take concrete actions to protect your assets from possible medical costs, see a lawyer knowledgeable in this distinct legal area. To help you, a lawyer must be up to date on relevant federal and state statutes and regulations, which can change fast.

H. How Does Where I Live Affect My Living Trust?

Living trusts are valid under the laws of every state. Still, a number of questions can arise about living trusts and where you live.

1. Determining Your Legal Residence

In your trust document, you'll name the state where you live; that state's laws govern the document. If you live in one state but work in another, it's the state where you live whose laws apply. You must also sign appropriate documents to transfer property to your trust in that state. (See Chapter 11.)

For most people, determining what state they reside in (in legalese, their "domicile") is self-evident. But for others, it can be more complex.

If during the course of a year you live in more than one state, your residence is the state with which you have the most significant contacts—where you vote, register vehicles, own valuable property, have bank accounts, or run a business.

If you might be justified in claiming more than one state as your legal residence, you may want to arrange your affairs so that your legal residence is in the state with the most advantageous state death tax laws. Some states (such as New Jersey and Iowa) impose inheritance or estate taxes; others (California and Florida, for example) essentially have no estate or inheritance tax. (See Chapter 15, Section D.)

Example

Carlo and Sophia, a couple in their 60s, spend about half the year in Florida and the other half in Michigan. They have bank accounts and real estate in both states. To take advantage of Florida's lack of a state inheritance tax, they register their car in Florida, vote there, and move their bank accounts there. This leaves them owning nothing in Michigan but a condominium near where their son lives. They decide to sell him the condo and lease it back six months of every year, severing their last important property ownership contact with Michigan.

If you have significant contacts with more than one state and a substantial estate, it may be worthwhile to have a lawyer with tax and estate planning experience advise you.

2. If You Live Out of the Country

If you are living outside the United States, your residence is the state you still have contacts with and expect to return to.

If you don't maintain ties with any particular state and have a large estate, see a lawyer to discuss what state you should declare as your residence.

If you are in the Armed Forces and living out of the country temporarily, your legal residence is the state you declared as your Home of Record—the state you lived in before going overseas, or where your spouse or parents live.

If you acquire property in a foreign country, such as real estate, you must check out that country's laws regarding transfer of real estate on death.

3. If You Move to Another State or Country

Revocable living trusts are valid and used in every state, and your trust remains valid if you move to a different state. However, if you're married and you move from a community property state to a common law state, or vice versa, you may want to check the marital property ownership laws of your new state. (See Chapter 6, Section D.) Also, if you moved from a state that allows gifts to be made under the Uniform Transfers to Minors Act (see Chapter 9, Section D) to a state that has not adopted the Act, and you made a gift using that Act, you'll have to amend this portion of your trust. (See Chapter 13, Sections D, E, and F.)

If you move to another country after creating a living trust, the trust remains valid. Under the 1961 Hague Convention (effective for U.S. citizens since 1981), a document notarized as a valid document in one country is recognized as valid by other countries which agreed to the treaty.

4. Out-of-State Beneficiaries or Successor Trustee

Your trust beneficiaries can live in any state, or indeed, any country. Similarly, your successor trustee does not have to live in your state.

5. Registration

A few states require "registration" of living trusts. These requirements are not a serious burden, or reason not to use a trust. (See Chapter 12, Section C.)

I. Can I Place Real Estate in a Living Trust?

Generally, it's easy—and quite common—to place valuable real estate, usually your home, in a living trust. You simply prepare and record a deed, transferring the real estate from you, personally, to you as trustee of your trust. (See Chapter 11, Section E.)

1. Property Tax Reassessment

In some states, certain real estate transfers, such as sales to new owners who aren't family members, result in property being immediately reappraised for property tax purposes. By contrast, if the property is not transferred to new owners, it usually won't be reappraised for a set period of years, or is reappraised at a reduced rate.

In states that reappraise property when it's transferred to a new owner, placing title to property in a living trust very rarely, if ever, triggers a property tax reappraisal. For instance, California law (Cal. Rev. & Tax. Code § 62) expressly prohibits reappraisals for transfers to a living trust where the grantor is a trustee. To be absolutely sure that this is true in your state if you're transferring real estate into a living trust, you can check with your local property tax collector to learn exactly what reappraisal rules apply.

2. Transfer Taxes

Very rarely, if ever, are transfer taxes imposed when you transfer your real estate to your living trust. But to be absolutely safe here, check this out with your County Assessor or Recorder's Office.

3. Deducting Mortgage Interest

For income tax purposes, the trust doesn't exist. You retain the right to deduct all mortgage interest from your income taxes, even though your home is technically owned by the trustee of your trust.

4. Insurance Policies

Insurance policies on your home—fire, liability, theft, and other particular policies—do not have to be re-registered in the trust's name. Like the IRS, insurance companies are concerned with the real form of ownership, not legal technicalities to avoid probate or reduce estate taxes. So there's no reason at all to contact your insurance company when you transfer your home or other real estate to your living trust.

5. Tax Breaks for Sellers

You have the right to sell your principal home once every two years and exclude $250,000 of profit from income taxation. A couple can exclude all profits up to $500,000.

During your life, you retain that right even if you have transferred that home to a living trust (IRC § 121).

6. Homestead Rights

Generally, transferring your home to a living trust does not affect the protection offered by state homestead laws. These laws typically protect a homeowner's equity interest in a home, up to a designated amount, from creditors. The living trust forms in this book each contain a specific statement that the grantor(s) intend to remain eligible for the state homestead exemption they would be entitled to if they still owned the real estate outside the trust.

"HOMESTEAD" DEFINED

A homestead is a legal device, available under the laws of most states, to protect your equity in your home, up to a certain amount, from creditors. In some states that allow homesteads, you record a Declaration of Homestead with the county land records office; in others, the protection is automatic. In either case, if you qualify for a homestead, your home is protected against forced sale by creditors (other than mortgage holders) if your equity is below the dollar limit set out in the statute.

However, if you're in debt and concerned that a creditor may try to force a sale of your house, check your state's homestead rules carefully. If you are not seriously in debt, there is no need to worry about this one.

7. Selling or Refinancing Your House

If you try to sell or refinance a house that is in a living trust, you might encounter some paperwork hassles, but nothing more serious. Some banks balk at refinancing a home that technically is owned by the trustee of a living trust, even if you show them the original trust document. Similarly, some title companies are reluctant to insure sales of a home by a trustee while the grantor is alive. By contrast, once an owner dies and a house is transferred to the beneficiaries, title companies routinely approve the sale of that real estate, even though it is transferred by a successor trustee.

If you encounter a problem trying to sell or refinance a house owned by your trust, you have two options:

- seek a bank or title company that is reasonable and will allow the transaction in the trustee's name, which is fully legal, or

- transfer the property out of the trustee's name, back into your individual name. Then go ahead with the sale or refinancing. Once the refinancing is completed, you can prepare yet another deed, again transferring the property back to the trustee. Convoluted, yes, but not really onerous.

8. Due-on-Sale Clauses

Federal law expressly prohibits enforcing a "due-on-sale" clause in a mortgage because of a transfer of one's home ("principal residence") to one's own revocable living trust. (The Garn-St. Germain Depository Institutions Act, 12 U.S.C. §§ 1464, 1701.)

CITATIONS TO FEDERAL STATUTES

Federal laws are codified in the United States Code, cited as U.S.C. A citation to a law lists the appropriate volume and sections of the U.S.C. For example, in the citation above, you can find the Garn-St. Germain Depository Institutions Act in Volume 12 of the United States Code, Sections 1464 and 1701.

The Internal Revenue Code is contained in Volume 26 of the U.S.C. This volume is often cited simply as I.R.C.

No statute expressly prohibits a bank from enforcing a due-on-sale clause when other real estate is transferred to a trust. However, I've never heard of it happening, probably because banks know it wouldn't make sense. After all, the transfer is flatly not a sale. No money changes hands. The IRS doesn't consider the transaction a sale. If a bank did try to claim that a due-on-sale clause was activated by a transfer of, say, investment or commercial real estate to a trust, you could always rescind the transaction and transfer the property back to your individual name.

Some cautious lawyers do obtain a bank (mortgage holder's) prior consent to transfers of commercial real estate to a living trust. Sometimes banks charge a fee of $100 or $200 for consenting to the transfer.

9. Transferring Part Interests in Real Estate

Any portion of real estate you own, such as a timeshare or percentage of ownership, can be transferred to a living trust. (See Chapter 11, Section E.)

10. Owning Real Estate in More Than One State

You must record a transfer deed in the land records office of the county where the real estate is located. So if you own one piece of real estate in Arizona, one in New York, and another in Vermont, you must record transfer deeds in all three states.

11. Rental (Income) Property

Under federal tax law, net profits received from rental property are "passive income." Losses in passive income cannot be used to offset profits or gains from "active income." However, there is a limited $25,000 exception to this rule for owners who "actively participate" in operation of the rental property. This $25,000 exception remains applicable if the rental property is placed in a living trust (I.R.C. § 469).

12. Contaminated Property

Under federal law "responsible parties" are liable for the costs of cleaning up contaminated land. Responsible parties include past and current owners of the real estate—whether or not the present owners contributed to the contamination. Contamination includes pollution from various toxic or dangerous substances, such as petroleum products, dry cleaning solvents, and many other chemicals.

If you own land that may be contaminated. If you own real estate that you know, or suspect, is contaminated, do not simply leave that property under your living trust, or by other means. You may be leaving someone a massive, very costly problem. See a lawyer experienced with problems of contaminated property.

J. Can I Sell or Give Away Trust Property While I'm Alive?

You can readily sell, transfer, or give away property in your trust.

1. Making Gifts

While you are alive, you can give away property held in your living trust. There are no restrictions on your power to make gifts from your trust. However, federal gift tax rules apply to gifts you make from trust property, as well as to gifts you make from your own nontrust property. (See Chapter 15, Section C.)

2. Selling Trust Property

You can readily sell any property in your trust. There are two ways to go about it:

- Sell the property directly from the trust, acting in your capacities as grantor and trustee to sign the title document, bill of sale, sales contract, or other document. The trust documents in this book specifically state that the trustee has the power to sell trust property, including stocks or bonds.

- In your capacity as trustee of the living trust, first transfer title of the particular item of trust property back to yourself as an individual, and then sell the property in your own name.

The only reason for using the second option, which requires more paperwork, is if some institution involved in the sale insists you sell it in your own name. This rarely happens. For instance, stock brokerage companies are familiar with sales by a trustee from a living trust. At most you might have to point out to some overcautious bureaucrat that the specific trustee powers clause of your trust document specifically gives you authority to make the sale.

AMENDING YOUR TRUST AFTER SALE OR GIFT OF TRUST PROPERTY

You should amend your revocable living trust if you sell or give away property that the trust leaves to a particular trust beneficiary. Obviously, the trust document cannot give away what the trust no longer owns. (Amending living trusts is discussed in Chapter 13, Section D.)

K. Is My Bank Account in the Trust's Name Insured by the FDIC?

Yes. If the bank is covered by the FDIC, any bank account in the trust's or trustee's name is insured up to the $100,000 maximum per institution.

Banks also offer "pay-on-death" accounts, which function as de facto living trusts for the funds in the accounts, and which also are protected by the FDIC. (See Chapter 15, Section B.)

L. Will Property in My Living Trust Get a "Stepped-Up" Tax Basis When I Die?

Yes. Property left through a revocable living trust does get a stepped-up tax basis. This is an important concern for many people, who rightly understand that, for inheritors of their property, a stepped-up basis is highly desirable for income tax reasons. Here's how it works.

To understand the concept of stepped-up basis, you must first understand what "basis" means. Put simply, the basis of property is the figure used to determine taxable profit when the property is sold. Usually, the basis of real estate is its purchase price, plus the cost of any capital improvements, less any depreciation. Once you know the basis, you subtract that figure from what you sell the property for. The result is your taxable profit.

Example

Phyllis bought a home for $140,000. She puts $25,000 into capital improvements (new roof and foundation). So her basis in the property is $165,000. If she sells the property for $375,000, her profit is $210,000.

Under federal law, the basis of inherited property is increased, or "stepped-up," to its market value as of the date the deceased owner died. (This is only fair, as the same property is valued, for estate tax purposes, at its market value as of the date the owner died.) At your death, the inheritors' basis of living trust property becomes the market value of that property at your death, not your original acquisition cost. Of course, if the property has declined in value since you bought it, the change in basis is a negative. However, given the long-term inflationary economy, property owned for a while usually increases in value. Thus, for most estates, the basis is "stepped-up."

Example

Continuing the above example, Phyllis dies and, through her living trust, leaves the house (with a market value of $275,000) to her niece, Nancy. Nancy's basis in the house is $275,000. If she promptly sells it for that amount, she has no taxable profit.

In community property states (see the list in Chapter 8, Section H), both halves of property owned jointly by both spouses receive a stepped-up basis when one spouse dies. In all other states (called "common law" states), the property of a married person who dies receives a stepped-up basis. However, property already owned by the surviving spouse does not get a stepped-up basis; it retains the basis it had.

Example

Alexander and Harriet, residents of New York, share ownership of a house with a basis of $200,000. When Alexander dies, the house is worth $800,000. The basis of Alexander's share is "stepped up" to its value at the time of death, or $400,000. However, Harriet's share retains its original basis, which is one-half of $200,000, or $100,000.

If Alexander and Harriet lived in Texas, a community property state, and had the same property situation, both spouses' shares of the house would receive a stepped-up basis to $400,000 when Alexander died.

⚠ **Stepped-up basis rules repealed for 2010.** Under the 2001 estate tax "repeal," in 2010 inheritors will receive a stepped-up basis only for inherited property worth a total of $1.3 million when the deceased person dies (plus an additional $3 million for a surviving spouse). During 2010, all property above this $1.3 million limit received by inheritors will carry the same basis as it had before the deceased person died. As of now, in 2011 the estate tax will return. Whether the stepped-up basis rules will also return is not certain. Indeed, the entire estate tax "repeal" is so confusing that it seems certain that Congress will have to reexamine that question sometime before 2010. (See Chapter 4, Section E.)

M. Who Must Know About My Living Trust?

Normally, the only person who must know about your living trust is your successor trustee. And even he or she need only know where the trust document is, not what's in it. However, most people do show the trust document to their successor trustee. After all, you should fully trust this person. And it should make his or her job easier to know in advance what property the trust owns, and who gets it after your death.

A few states require registration of a living trust. (See Chapter 12, Section C.) If you register your trust in one of these states, it is possible for others to have access to certain information about the trust. But only minimal information need be made public through registration—the name of the grantor, the date of the trust—not the key terms of the trust, such as the property in it, and who are the beneficiaries.

Whether or not to tell your beneficiaries what's in your trust and who gets what is entirely your personal decision. Personally, I believe it's wisest to inform at least your major beneficiaries of your trust gifts, unless you have a compelling reason not to do so.

N. Could Someone Challenge My Living Trust?

Of course a trust can be challenged in court. In our judicial system, any legal document, including a living trust, can be challenged this way. But theory doesn't matter here, reality does. The important questions to ask are:

- Is there any likelihood someone will challenge my living trust?

- If there is, what can I do to protect myself?

Legal challenges to a living trust are quite rare. (Indeed, I've never encountered one, either in my own practice or that of colleagues in estate planning.) You don't need to concern yourself unless you think a close relative might have an axe to grind after your death.

Some people ask about including a "no-contest" clause as a protection against a lawsuit attacking their trust. A no-contest clause doesn't prevent anyone from contesting the validity of your trust. It simply says that if a beneficiary contests your living trust and loses, he or she gets nothing. Thus, a no-contest clause will not discourage a nonbeneficiary from suing. Nor will a no-contest clause necessarily deter a disgruntled beneficiary who wants more, and is willing to risk losing what you've given them by suing.

Adding a no-contest clause. If you think you need a no-contest clause, it's an indication you have a potentially serious problem—someone who might challenge your trust. See a lawyer.

Following are the kinds of legal challenges that can theoretically be made against a living trust.

1. Challenges to the Validity of the Trust

Someone who wanted to challenge the validity of your living trust would have to bring a lawsuit and prove that:

- when you made the trust, you were mentally incompetent or unduly influenced by someone, or

- the trust document itself is flawed—for example, because the signature was forged.

Proving any of this is not easy. It's generally considered more difficult to successfully challenge a living trust than a will. That's because your continuing involvement with a living trust after its creation (transferring property in and out of the trust, or making amendments) is evidence that you were competent to manage your affairs.

2. Lawsuits by Spouses

Most married people leave much, if not all, of their property to their spouses. But if you don't leave your spouse at least half of your property, your spouse may have the right to go to court and claim some of your property after your death. Such a challenge wouldn't wipe out your whole living trust, but might take some of the property you had earmarked for other beneficiaries and give it to your spouse.

The rights of spouses vary from state to state. (See Chapter 6, Section D, and Chapter 8, Section H.)

3. Lawsuits by a Child

Children usually have no right to inherit anything from their parents. There are two exceptions: laws that give minor children certain rights and laws that are designed to protect children who are unintentionally overlooked in a will.

a. Minor Children

State law may give your minor children (those under age 18) the right to inherit the family residence. The Florida constitution, for example, prohibits the head of a family from leaving his residence in his will (except to his spouse) if he is survived by a spouse or minor child. (Fla. Const. Art. 10, § 4.)

b. Overlooked Children

Some state laws protect offspring who appear to have been unintentionally overlooked in a parent's will. The legal term for such an overlooked offspring is a "pretermitted heir." In most states, this term means a child born after the will was signed. In a few states, the term includes any child not mentioned in the will. Though the law is unclear, it could be argued that a child omitted from a living trust was also a pretermitted heir. Fortunately, it's easy to avoid these problems. See Chapter 8, Section H, and Chapter 16, Section B.

O. Will Congress or My State Legislature Abolish or Restrict Living Trusts?

Probate-avoidance living trusts seem clearly safe from government restrictions and limits. There would be howls of protest if Congress or a state legislature tried to abolish or restrict living trusts from being used as a probate-avoidance device. Certainly there's no legitimate reason for Congress or a legislature to do so. Probate-avoidance living trusts have been successfully used for decades, without any reports of serious problems. Literally millions of people have prepared them. Also, probate-avoidance living trusts don't cost the federal government or states serious money. (Some lost revenue from court filing fees, but that's about it.)

Really, the only people who have an interest in curtailing probate-avoidance living trusts are some conservative probate lawyers. But their self-interest is so blatant that it's inconceivable they could persuade a legislature to seriously restrict living trusts. Indeed, more savvy lawyers have long since moved into selling living trusts themselves. It's also extremely unlikely that Congress would change the tax laws to restrict or abolish tax-saving AB trusts (discussed in Chapters 4 and 5). Many thousands, perhaps hundreds of thousands, of Americans have already created these trusts. Their estate plans rely on the continuing validity of AB trusts. Congress won't want to pick a fight with so many prosperous voters. ■

chapter 4

WHAT TYPE OF TRUST DO YOU NEED?

*N*o law specifies the form a living trust must take. As a result, there is no such thing as a "standard" living trust. Indeed, there are a bewildering variety of living trust forms. Some attorney-created forms contain vast piles of verbiage, which serve little real-world purpose except to generate attorney fees.

This book offers three types of legal living trusts, as clear and understandable as I can make them:

- a probate-avoidance trust for an individual

- a probate-avoidance trust for a couple that owns property together, called a "basic shared living trust," and

- a probate-avoidance and estate tax-saving AB trust for a prosperous couple.

Nolo's AB estate tax-saving trust in this book is beneficial for couples with a net combined estate worth at least $1.5 million. The maximum estate a couple can have and still safely use Nolo's AB trust is $7 million, depending on the year of death of the first spouse. The reason for this range, from $1.5 million to $7 million, is the way that the estate tax exemption increases between 2004 and 2009. This is explained in Sections E and F below, and in Chapter 5.

A. If You Are Single

If you are single and making a living trust by yourself, you must use Nolo's living trust for one person (Form 1). So if you are a single parent, you'll need to use Trust Form 1 to create a living trust to leave property for your minor children. You can use it to leave all of your property, or any part of it, including your share of co-owned property. For instance, if you own a house together with your sister, you simply transfer your share of that house into your trust. Similarly, you can transfer your share of a partnership or shares in a small corporation to your trust, assuming the partnership agreement or corporate charter and by-laws permit it.

With Nolo's individual trust, you can also:

- name your successor trustee or trustees, and

- leave property to minors or young adults—including your own children, of course—through a child's trust, or a gift under the Uniform Transfers to Minors Act. (See Chapter 9.)

If you decide to make an individual trust, go to Chapter 6, "Choosing What Property to Put in Your Living Trust."

USING MORE THAN ONE LIVING TRUST

Legally, you can have more than one living trust for different types of property. Although it isn't necessary for most people, in complex property ownership situations using more than one trust can make sense. For example, you might set up one trust for your business and another for the rest of your property, if you want one of your business associates to act as successor trustee to handle and transfer your business property, but a spouse, friend, or close relative to distribute your other property.

A MORE COMPLEX TRUST

Some single people want to create a trust that does more than avoid probate. For example, a sibling might want to create a "life estate" trust that first avoids probate, then leaves property for the benefit of a brother for his life, and then at the brother's death leaves the property outright to other beneficiaries.

Preparing a complex trust. If you are single and want to create a living trust that accomplishes goals other than avoiding probate and, if you need them, establishing children's trusts, see a lawyer. Drafting a complex trust requires careful attention to the specifics of your situation. You cannot use Nolo's individual living trust or AB trust to accomplish these goals.

B. If You Are Part of a Couple

Couples—married or unmarried—often own property together. They can legally set up a living trust that doesn't change that shared ownership. In their trust, they can also include property that is separately owned by either spouse.

This book provides three ways for members of a couple to create a living trust:

- Each spouse prepares an individual trust.
- Both spouses prepare one basic shared living trust.
- Both spouses prepare one AB living trust.

The next sections examine each option in detail.

TERMINOLOGY FOR UNMARRIED COUPLES

Because most couples who use shared living trusts are married, my discussion of these trusts is cast in terms of "spouses" and "marital property." However, the discussion applies equally to unmarried couples. Since it's too awkward to restate this point in each sentence or sprinkle the text with terms such as "partners," "significant others," or "lovers," please, if you are a member of an unmarried couple, make the necessary semantic substitutions for yourself.

C. Individual Trusts for Members of a Couple

A member of a couple can legally use a separate, individual trust for all of his or her property, or can use two living trusts, one trust for separately owned property and another trust for property shared with the other spouse. But this is rarely necessary or advisable. As you'll see in Sections D and E, below, both separately owned and shared property can be conveniently handled in a shared living trust.

Most couples prefer not to create two individual trusts because it requires dividing property they own together, which is normally the bulk of their property. Splitting ownership of co-owned assets can be a clumsy process. For example, to transfer a co-owned house into two separate trusts would require the spouses to sign and record two deeds transferring a half-interest in the house to two separate trusts. And to transfer household furnishings to separate trusts, spouses would have to allocate each item to a trust or do something as silly as each transferring a half-interest in a couch to his or her trust.

In some common law states (see the list in Chapter 6, Section D), some attorneys advise couples to go this route. The claimed advantage for this is that it's then easier, upon the death of a spouse, to tell what property each spouse owns. I think this type of caution is unnecessary, and not worth the drawbacks of dividing shared property while both members of the couple are living. With a properly drafted trust—either a basic shared living trust or an AB trust—there should be no difficulty identifying what property belonged to which spouse.

If, however, you and your spouse own most or all of your property separately, you may each want to make an individual trust. Most couples in this situation fit one of these profiles:

- You live in a community property state, and you and your spouse signed an agreement stating that each spouse's property, including earnings and other income, is separate, not community property. (See Chapter 6, Section D, for a discussion of community property.)
- You don't want to give your spouse legal authority as your successor trustee over your property when you die. (See Chapter 7.)
- You are recently married, have little or no shared or community property, and want to keep future property acquisitions separate. (To accomplish this,

you'll both need to sign a written statement of your intentions.)

- You each own mostly separate property acquired before your marriage (or by gift or inheritance), which you conscientiously keep from being mixed with any shared property you own. Couples who marry later in life and no longer work often fit into this category. Not only is the property they owned before the marriage separate, but Social Security benefits and certain retirement plan benefits are also separate, not shared or community, property.

Example

Howard and Luisa live in Indiana, a noncommunity property state. Both have adult children from prior marriages. When they married, they moved into Howard's house. They both have their own bank accounts and investments, and one joint checking account that they own as joint tenants with right of survivorship.

Each makes an individual living trust. Howard, who dies first, leaves his house to Luisa, but most of his other property is left to his children. The funds in the joint checking account are not included in his living trust, but pass to Luisa, also without probate, because the account was held in joint tenancy. Howard's other accounts go to his children, under the pay-on-death arrangement he has with the bank. (Joint tenancy, pay-on-death accounts, and other probate-avoidance methods are discussed in Chapter 15.)

If you and your spouse decide on separate living trusts, each of you will transfer your separately owned property to your individual trust. If you own some property together—a house, for example—you each transfer your portion of it to your individual trust.

Preparing separate trusts. If you and your spouse decide to prepare two separate trusts and do not name each other as successor trustees, you may want to see a lawyer to be as certain as you can that there won't be any conflict between your spouse and your successor trustee.

D. A Basic Shared Living Trust

Most married couples (and many unmarried ones) own most or all of their property equally together and don't want to divide it up and transfer it into two separate trusts. They choose to make one living trust to avoid probate, and transfer all of their property—both shared and separately owned—to it. They are willing to do this because, while they live, each retains full ownership of all his or her separate property, as well as her or his share of jointly owned property.

Example

Lorenzo and Marsha are married and own a house together. Marsha also owns, as her own property, some valuable jewels left to her by her mother. Lorenzo owns, as his separate property, some stock his uncle gave him.

Lorenzo and Marsha create one shared living trust and transfer all of their jointly owned property to it. Marsha's jewelry is also placed in this trust, identified as her separate property. Similarly, Lorenzo's stock is placed in this trust, identified as his separate property. Neither loses any ownership rights to her or his separate property by placing it in the shared living trust.

If probate avoidance is your only goal, you can use a basic living trust no matter how much all of your property is worth. But if your and your spouse's combined estates exceed $1 million or more, you should at least consider an estate tax-saving trust, such as Nolo's AB living trust, explained in Sections E and F, below.

1. How a Basic Shared Trust Works

With the basic shared marital trust in this book, designed to avoid probate, you and your spouse will be cotrustees of your living trust. You'll both have control over your shared ownership property in the trust. In theory, this means either spouse can act alone on behalf of the trust, including selling or giving away shared trust property. However, because banks, title companies, and others often have their own rules requiring both signatures, as a practical matter, the consent of both spouses to sell or transfer shared property is commonly necessary.

If one spouse will not be a trustee. If for any reason—health, mistrust, whatever—you don't want your spouse to serve with you as a trustee of your basic shared trust, see a lawyer.

As I've said, each spouse retains sole control over his or her separate property, because in the trust document it's identified and listed as property owned by only that spouse. With his or her separate trust property, each spouse may:

- sell it, give it away, or leave it in the trust

- in the trust document, name a beneficiary, or beneficiaries, to inherit that property

- amend the trust document to name a new beneficiary or beneficiaries for that property. Technically, trust amendments require consent of both spouses, but this is a mere formality in most cases where a spouse wants to amend the trust to name new beneficiaries for her property. If the other spouse is recalcitrant—say the couple is getting divorced—either spouse can revoke the entire trust and prepare a new one for his or her property.

Each spouse is also free to add separately owned property to the trust later.

In the trust document, each spouse names beneficiaries for his or her share of co-owned property, as well as all of his or her separate property. Commonly, spouses leave all, if not the bulk, of their property to each other. But leaving all or most of your property to your spouse isn't legally required. Each spouse has complete freedom in choosing beneficiaries, subject to legal restrictions in many states that entitle a surviving spouse to claim a certain share of a deceased spouse's estate. (See Chapter 6, Section D.)

A spouse's separate property is kept separate in a shared trust by means of trust "schedules," which are just lists of trust property attached to the trust document. Schedule A lists co-owned property. Property listed on Schedule B is the separate property of the wife, and all property listed on Schedule C is the separate property of the husband.

If spouses want to leave significant amounts of property to each other, a basic shared living trust provides another big advantage over individual trusts. With a basic shared trust, property left by one spouse to the survivor automatically stays in the living trust when the first spouse dies. It becomes part of the property the surviving spouse has in what is now her individual living trust. No formal transfer documents are needed. If separate, individual trusts were used, property left to the surviving spouse would need to be transferred first from the deceased spouse's trust to the name of the surviving spouse and then, to avoid probate, the second spouse would have to transfer it into his or her own living trust.

Either spouse can revoke the trust at any time. If either spouse revokes the trust, the couple's property ownership situation returns to exactly what it was before the trust was formed. Shared property is returned to the

ownership of both spouses, and separately owned property goes to the spouse who owned it. By contrast, amendments to the trust document require the consent of both spouses. For example, both must agree to change the successor trustee or name new beneficiaries.

2. What Happens When One Spouse Dies

When one spouse dies, the shared living trust is split into two trusts, Trust 1 and Trust 2; this is automatic under the terms of the basic living trust document. The surviving spouse is sole trustee of both trusts. (The surviving spouse's duties are discussed in Chapter 14.)

Trust 1 contains the deceased spouse's share of trust property, except any trust property left to the surviving spouse. Trust 1 is irrevocable; that is, the surviving spouse can't change its terms, which dictate what happens to the property in it.

Trust 2, the survivor's trust, contains the surviving spouse's share of the trust property, plus any trust property left to him or her by the deceased spouse.

In many situations, since all property is left to the survivor, nothing need be done at this point. However, if the deceased left property in Trust 1 to others, the surviving spouse, as sole trustee of Trust 1, distributes that property to the named beneficiaries.

The trustee simply hands over the property to the beneficiaries, except for gifts left to minors or young adults in a child's trust or through the Uniform Transfers to Minors Act (UTMA). (See Chapter 9.) If the property is left in a child's trust, the surviving spouse manages that trust for the child until the child reaches the age specified by the deceased spouse in the trust document to receive the property outright. If the property is left to a custodian under the UTMA, the custodian manages the property until the child is old enough to be legally entitled to the property.

When all the property in Trust 1 has been distributed to the beneficiaries, including any property placed in a child's trust, Trust 1 ceases to exist. No formal documents need be prepared or filed to officially end the trust. Once its mission is accomplished, it just evaporates.

Trust 2 (the survivor's trust) is basically a continuation of the original revocable living trust. It contains any trust property the survivor inherited from the deceased spouse, as well as the surviving spouse's share of shared trust property and any separately owned trust property that belongs to the survivor. The surviving spouse is free to change or amend Trust 2 if he or she wishes to. For example, the surviving spouse might name a new successor trustee or name a new beneficiary for property that was to have gone to the deceased spouse.

Example

Harry and Maude, a married couple, set up a basic shared revocable living trust to avoid probate. In their trust document, they name themselves cotrustees and appoint Maude's brother Al as successor trustee, to take over as trustee after they have both died. They transfer much of their co-owned property—their house, money market accounts, and stocks—to the living trust. Maude also puts some of her family heirlooms, which are her separate property, in the trust.

The trust document states that Maude's brother Al is to receive the heirlooms when she dies; everything else goes to Harry. Harry leaves all his trust property to Maude. Both name their son, Edward, as alternate and residuary beneficiary. (The residuary beneficiary is the person who receives all property not left to other named beneficiaries. See Chapter 8.)

Maude dies first. The basic shared living trust splits into Trust 1, which contains Maude's heirlooms, and Trust 2, which contains everything else—Harry's half of the co-owned trust property and the trust property he inherits from Maude. Harry becomes the sole trustee of both trusts.

Following the terms of the trust document, Harry distributes Maude's heirlooms (from Trust 1) to Al, without probate. Trust 1 then ceases to exist. Harry doesn't have to do anything with the trust property Maude left him; it's already in Trust 2, his revocable living trust.

When the second spouse dies, the person named in the original trust document as successor trustee takes over as trustee of Trust 2. This successor trustee is responsible for distributing the surviving spouse's trust property to the surviving spouse's beneficiaries, named in the trust document. If any trust property is left to a young beneficiary in a child's trust, the trustee will also manage it. Again, no formal documents are required to terminate Trust 2.

Example

Continuing the example of Harry and Maude, after Maude dies, Harry needs to change his beneficiaries. (This is normally done when one spouse dies, if that spouse was the major beneficiary of the other spouse's trust.) Harry names his son Edward as the new primary beneficiary of his trust. He names Edward's three minor children as alternate beneficiaries, and creates a child's trust for each one. Harry also leaves some property outright to his niece, Cecelia. Finally, he names Edward as successor trustee, denoting Al as alternate successor trustee.

When Harry dies, Edward becomes trustee and distributes the trust property following Harry's instructions in the trust document. He transfers the property Harry left to Cecelia to her. The rest of the property he transfers to himself, and the trust ends.

If your combined estate isn't large enough to trigger estate taxes, and you just want to create a basic shared living trust, you can proceed to Chapter 6.

EXAMPLE 1: TRUST CONTAINS ALL SHARED PROPERTY

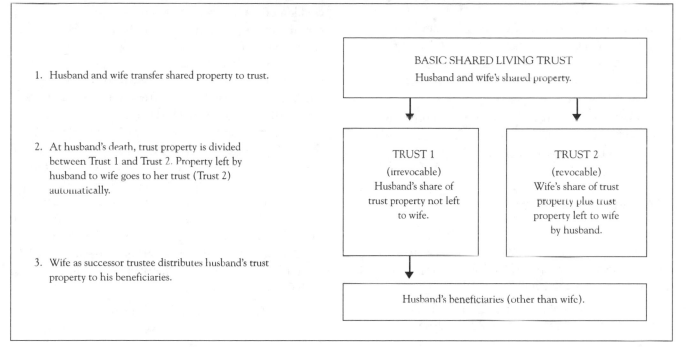

1. Husband and wife transfer shared property to trust.

2. At husband's death, trust property is divided between Trust 1 and Trust 2. Property left by husband to wife goes to her trust (Trust 2) automatically.

3. Wife as successor trustee distributes husband's trust property to his beneficiaries.

BASIC SHARED LIVING TRUST
Husband and wife's shared property.

TRUST 1
(irrevocable)
Husband's share of trust property not left to wife.

TRUST 2
(revocable)
Wife's share of trust property plus trust property left to wife by husband.

Husband's beneficiaries (other than wife).

EXAMPLE 2: TRUST CONTAINS SHARED AND SEPARATE PROPERTY

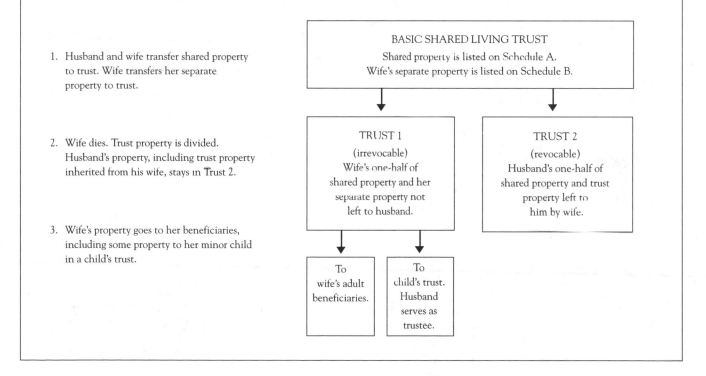

1. Husband and wife transfer shared property to trust. Wife transfers her separate property to trust.

2. Wife dies. Trust property is divided. Husband's property, including trust property inherited from his wife, stays in Trust 2.

3. Wife's property goes to her beneficiaries, including some property to her minor child in a child's trust.

BASIC SHARED LIVING TRUST
Shared property is listed on Schedule A.
Wife's separate property is listed on Schedule B.

TRUST 1
(irrevocable)
Wife's one-half of shared property and her separate property not left to husband.

TRUST 2
(revocable)
Husband's one-half of shared property and trust property left to him by wife.

To wife's adult beneficiaries.

To child's trust. Husband serves as trustee.

E. The Tax-Saving AB Trust

If you and your spouse have a large enough estate, you may well want to avoid estate taxes with an AB trust. This type of trust works by maximizing the use of the personal estate tax exemption, which means having each spouse take full advantage of it.

To remind you, the personal estate exemption allows a set amount of property to pass free of federal tax. The amount depends on the year of death.

1. The Federal Estate Tax

You've undoubtedly heard that Congress has "repealed" the estate tax. Actually, it passed a law that's much more confusing than a simple repeal. Here's a summary of the current federal estate tax law. The law:

- increases the personal exemption from $1.5 million in 2004 and 2005 to $3.5 million in 2009, as shown below

- repeals the estate tax entirely for one, and only one, year—2010

- revives the estate tax, with an exemption of $1 million, for 2011 and thereafter, and

- greatly restricts the "stepped-up" basis rules for inherited property in 2010. (Stepped-up basis rules are discussed in Chapter 3, Section L.)

THE PERSONAL ESTATE TAX EXEMPTION		
Year	Estate tax exemption	Highest estate tax rate
2004	$1.5 million	48%
2005	$1.5 million	47%
2006	$2 million	46%
2007	$2 million	45%
2008	$2 million	45%
2009	$3.5 million	45%
2010	Estate tax repealed	Top individual income tax rate for gift tax only
2001	$1 million unless Congress extends repeal	55% unless Congress extends repeal

For both technical and political reasons, Congress could not flat-out repeal the estate tax law. The law it passed is a mess, in estate planners' opinions. So how can anyone with substantial assets sensibly engage in long-range estate tax planning? It would be extremely difficult to create three different plans—one if you die before 2010, another if you die in 2010 and yet another if you die in 2011. Worse, even if you could prepare a tri-part plan with the help of experts, it couldn't cover what you should do if Congress revises the estate tax law, which it is likely to do. It's the consensus of estate tax experts that Congress will have to revise the law before 2010. It's ridiculous to repeal the estate tax law in one year, and bring it back the next year with an exemption reduced to $1 million. Among the other oddities of that situation, it could make wealthy elderly people quite nervous in 2010, when their inheritors would have a huge financial interest in them dying during that year.

How Congress might revise the estate tax law is uncertain. It will depend upon political and economic realities that cannot be predicted now. For instance, Congress could decide in 2005 to keep the exemption at $1.5 million, and eliminate both further increases and the repeal.

For now, what you can sensibly do is devise a plan that makes sense through 2009. You need to understand that you will likely have to revise your plan:

- if you have the good fortune to live to 2009, or

- if Congress revises the estate tax law.

You can find up-to-date estate tax rules by visiting Nolo's website www.nolo.com.

DEFINITION: MINIMUM AMOUNT OF PROPERTY SUBJECT TO ESTATE TAX

Let's begin with the truly obvious: no one can know, in advance, the year of their death. Since the amount of the personal exemption depends on the year of death, no set dollar figure can define the worth of an estate that can be left tax-free under the personal estate tax exemption. Rather than repeat this table each time I refer to the personal exemption, I use the term "**estate tax threshold**" to mean the amount of this exemption in any and all years. It refers to the various exempt amounts, ranging from $1.5 million to $3.5 million.

UNMARRIED COUPLES

An unmarried couple can use an AB trust if it fits their needs. As with a basic shared trust, when describing an AB trust, I refer to husbands, wives, and spouses, but no exclusion of unmarried couples is implied. In my experience, it's not common for an unmarried couple to want to use this type of trust, but it's certainly possible.

Suppose Anne and Frank—or Anne and Sylvia—have been an unmarried couple for a long while and have a child they both deeply love, whether both are biological parents or not. If this couple has a combined estate large enough to trigger estate taxes, they can use an AB trust and reap exactly the same benefits of probate avoidance and estate tax reduction as a married couple in a similar situation.

2. Why Worry About Federal Estate Taxes?

Under U.S. tax law, a spouse can leave any amount of property, no matter how much it is worth, to the surviving spouse free of estate tax (unless that spouse is not a citizen—see Chapter 15, Section C). This is called the "marital deduction."

⚠ No marital deduction for unmarried couples. There is no exemption similar to the marital deduction for partners or "significant others" or whatever other name unmarried couples, whether gay or heterosexual, use for their mates. Quite simply, the estate tax laws are written to encourage and reward traditional relationships. (Don't blame me; I didn't write the laws.)

COMMON LAW MARRIAGES

The marital deduction is available for couples in legal common law marriages. Such marriages may be created in Alabama, Colorado, District of Columbia, Georgia (only before Jan. 1, 1997), Idaho (only before Jan. 1, 1996), Iowa, Kansas, Montana, New Hampshire (for inheritance only), Ohio (only before Oct. 10, 1991), Oklahoma, Pennsylvania (but a September 2003 court ruling stated that common law marriages could no longer be created; *PNC Bank Corp. v. Workers' Compensation Appeals Board (Stamos)*, 831 A.2d 1269), Rhode Island, South Carolina, Texas, and Utah. If a couple creates a common law marriage in one of these states and then moves to another state, they are still legally married.

So what's the tax worry? After all, under the marital deduction, no tax will be assessed against any amount of property one spouse leaves another. In a nutshell, here's the problem: if a spouse leaves most, or all, of his or her property to the surviving spouse, the estate of the survivor can total more than the estate tax threshold. If this happens, estate taxes will have to be paid when the surviving spouse dies.

Estate planners call a tax due on the death of the surviving spouse the "second tax." The result of the second tax is to reduce the amount of money available to a couple's final inheritors, usually their children.

Example

Sven and Ingrid have a shared combined estate of $3 million. Each leaves his or her property to the surviving spouse. Eventually, when the second spouse dies, they want everything to go to their child Heidi.

Sven dies in 2004. No estate taxes are due, because his property is left to his wife. (Even if he'd left his property to someone else, no taxes would be due because his estate equals the $1.5 million personal exemption for 2004.)

After Sven's death, Ingrid's estate is worth $3 million. It has the same value when she dies in 2007. The personal exemption for that year is $2 million. So $1 million is subject to estate tax. This is the "second tax." The tax owed is $225,000—money Heidi doesn't get.

It is this second tax that an AB trust is designed to eliminate. The diagram below shows what happens without a tax-saving AB trust, for a couple with a combined estate worth $2.8 million, with deaths in 2004 and 2008.

HOW THE SECOND ESTATE TAX CAN COST YOUR FAMILY MONEY

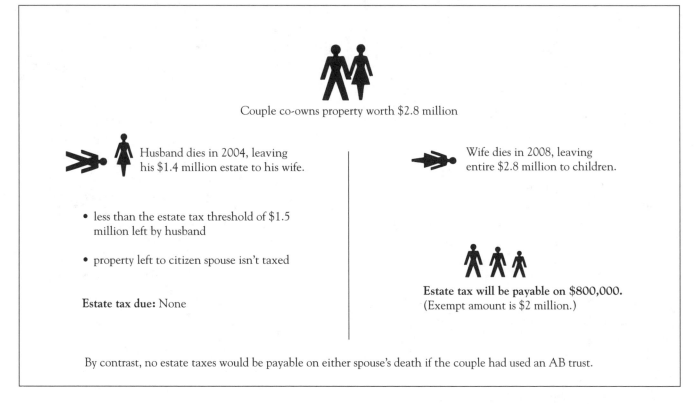

Couple co-owns property worth $2.8 million

Husband dies in 2004, leaving his $1.4 million estate to his wife.

- less than the estate tax threshold of $1.5 million left by husband

- property left to citizen spouse isn't taxed

Estate tax due: None

Wife dies in 2008, leaving entire $2.8 million to children.

Estate tax will be payable on $800,000. (Exempt amount is $2 million.)

By contrast, no estate taxes would be payable on either spouse's death if the couple had used an AB trust.

3. How an AB Trust Can Solve the Second Tax Problem

Couples who each have an estate over the estate tax threshold and who want to leave most or all of their property to each other often have a clear estate planning goal: the surviving spouse will have access to the deceased spouse's property if needed, but the surviving spouse never becomes the legal owner of that property. Happily, with an AB trust, you can achieve this goal. It's one of the rare times in life when you really can have it both ways—well, pretty much.

With an AB trust, spousal estates are never combined. Rather, for tax purposes, each estate is kept separate. So each spouse's estate is subject to tax when that spouse dies. If each estate is under the estate tax threshold, no tax will be paid.

Example

Sam and Cynthia, an elderly couple, have an estate worth $2.3 million, owned equally. If each leaves his or her half, worth $1,150,000, outright to the other, the survivor's estate will be taxed unless the survivor dies in 2009 or 2010. Before 2009, the combined estate of $2.3 million will be over the estate tax exemption. And the combined estate is obviously well over the exempt amount of $1 million for 2011 and thereafter.

Sam and Cynthia create an AB trust, so each spouse leaves his or her property separately. Sam dies in 2004. His trust property is worth $1,150,000. (For the time being, we'll assume an estate does not grow between the time an AB trust is prepared and when it goes into effect.) The personal exemption for 2004 is $1.5 million, so no tax is due.

Cynthia's estate at her death in 2007 is also worth $1,150,000. Her estate is not combined with Sam's, so her estate is also under the estate tax threshold of $2 million in 2007.

Another way to look at the tax benefit of an AB trust is that it allows each spouse to use the personal estate tax exemption. By contrast, if the estates are combined, only one spouse, the second to die, can use this exemption—and, as we've seen, it will be applied to a much larger estate than if the estates hadn't been combined.

With an AB trust, the surviving spouse can be given substantial rights to the trust property, without becoming the legal owner of it. Specifically, under IRS rules, the surviving spouse can have the rights to use the trust property, to receive all income from it, and to spend trust principal for "support, health, education, or maintenance in accord with his or her accustomed manner of living." So with an AB trust, the surviving spouse is most definitely not left out in the cold from the deceased spouse's property.

HOW AN AB TRUST CAN SAVE YOUR FAMILY MONEY

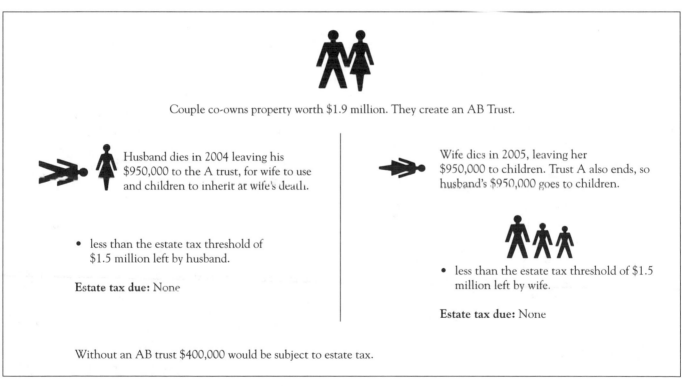

Couple co-owns property worth $1.9 million. They create an AB Trust.

Husband dies in 2004 leaving his $950,000 to the A trust, for wife to use and children to inherit at wife's death.

- less than the estate tax threshold of $1.5 million left by husband.

Estate tax due: None

Wife dies in 2005, leaving her $950,000 to children. Trust A also ends, so husband's $950,000 goes to children.

- less than the estate tax threshold of $1.5 million left by wife.

Estate tax due: None

Without an AB trust $400,000 would be subject to estate tax.

Here's a summary of how an AB trust actually works. Nolo's version of an AB trust is explained in Section F, below, and in more depth in Chapter 5.

Both spouses create a shared living trust like the one described in Section D of this chapter, with one crucial difference. (Sorry if I sound like a nudge, but please be sure you read Section D carefully if you're considering an AB trust.) What's different is that as part of their living trust, each spouse creates a separate AB trust—a trust within a trust. Actually, each AB trust contains two separate trusts, Trust A and Trust B.

Each spouse leaves all, or at least the bulk, of his or her property to Trust A, instead of outright to the survivor. As long as both spouses live, the couple's property remains in the living trust, which can be revoked or changed. When the first spouse dies, the living trust property is split into two separate trusts: Trust A, the deceased spouse's trust, which now becomes irrevocable, and Trust B, the surviving spouse's revocable living trust.

Each spouse names the other as what's called the "life beneficiary" of his or her Trust A. This means that the surviving spouse can use and benefit from the Trust A property for the rest of his or her life, with certain restrictions, but is not given outright ownership of it.

Each spouse also names the "final beneficiaries" of his or her AB trust. Final beneficiaries receive the Trust A property after the surviving spouse dies, and also receive the Trust B property after this spouse dies.

Any trust must have a trustee to supervise and manage trust property. With an AB trust, each spouse normally names the other as trustee. So the surviving spouse is both the life beneficiary and trustee of Trust A.

Only one of the couple's A trusts will become operational—that of the first spouse to die. The surviving spouse now has no use for his or her own A trust, since by definition there's no other spouse. (If the surviving spouse remarries, however, a new AB trust can then be prepared.) The surviving spouse's property, to repeat, goes

into Trust B. The reason each spouse prepares an individual AB trust (within the one overall living trust document) is that when they're setting up their estate plan they can't know which spouse will be the first to die. So each spouse must have an A trust, though only one will ever go into effect.

When the first spouse dies, the survivor gets only a "life estate" interest in all property of the deceased spouse that goes into Trust A. Because of this limited interest, the Trust A property is not entitled to the marital deduction. Rather, the Trust A property is subject to estate tax when the first spouse dies. If this property is worth less than the amount of the personal exemption for the year of death, no federal estate taxes are assessed. When the second spouse dies, the Trust A property is not subject to tax.

HOW AN AB TRUST WORKS

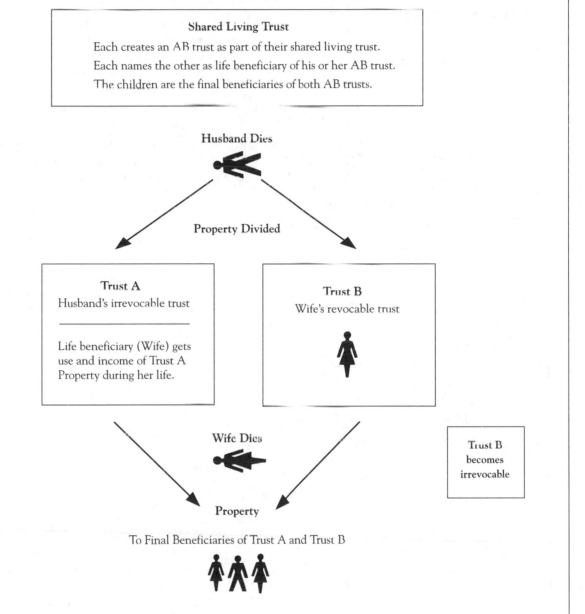

Shared estate of $2,100,000. Each has $1,050,000. Three children.

Shared Living Trust

Each creates an AB trust as part of their shared living trust.

Each names the other as life beneficiary of his or her AB trust.

The children are the final beneficiaries of both AB trusts.

Husband Dies

Property Divided

Trust A

Husband's irrevocable trust

Life beneficiary (Wife) gets use and income of Trust A Property during her life.

Trust B

Wife's revocable trust

Wife Dies

Trust B becomes irrevocable

Property

To Final Beneficiaries of Trust A and Trust B

F. Nolo's AB Trust

This book offers one version of an AB trust, which is explained in detail in Chapter 5. Here you'll learn the basics of Nolo's AB trust, so you can determine whether you want to look deeper into using it.

1. The Size of Your Estate

Because the amount of the personal estate tax exemption depends on the year of death, how do you know whether you can benefit from using Nolo's AB trust?

First, start by looking at some tax figures. At the low end, Nolo's AB trust can be beneficial for a couple whose combined estate is over the personal exemption for the year the first spouse dies. Second, with Nolo's AB trust, you can shield from estate tax a combined estate worth up to double the personal exemption for the year of the first spouse's death (assuming each spouse owns half the property). The table below shows you the amounts for each year.

HOW MUCH NOLO'S AB TRUST CAN SHIELD FROM ESTATE TAX		
Year of First Spouse's Death	Personal Exemption	Maximum Shielded
2004	$1.5 million	$3 million
2005	$1.5 million	$3 million
2006	$2 million	$4 million
2007	$2 million	$4 million
2008	$2 million	$4 million
2009	$3.5 million	$7 million

From the table above, we can see that a combined estate worth $1.8 million could benefit from an AB trust if both spouses died before 2006.

Example

Thalia and Tyrone, an elderly couple, prepare a Nolo AB trust. Their combined estate is worth $1.8 million. Each spouse owns half. Tyrone dies in July 2004, and Thalia dies in November of 2005. If they had not used an AB trust, but each left their property outright to each other, Thalia would have wound up

with an estate of $1.8 million. The personal exemption for 2005 is $1.5 million. So $300,000 would be subject to tax. Surely Thalia and Tyrone would prefer that this money go to their final inheritors rather than the U.S. treasury.

As the personal exemption increases, the size of an individual estate and a combined estate that can use Nolo's AB trust without being subject to tax also rises.

Life is unpredictable—If you're old enough to investigate estate planning, you've certainly learned that. Since you can't predict how long you or you spouse will live, how can you determine whether your estate is within the guidelines for using Nolo's AB trust? The conservative approach is to assume that your AB trust will become operational in the year that you prepared it. In other words, assume a spouse will die in that year. (Of course, this is gloomy thinking, and I wish you, as well as myself, a long and healthy life, but lawyers are paid to consider the practical consequences of gloomy possibilities.) Following the cautious approach, to be safe:

1. Each spouse must have an estate under the personal exemption for that year.

2. The combined estate must be between the amount of the personal exemption and the maximum Nolo's AB trust can shield for that year.

So, if you prepare a Nolo AB trust during 2004, your individual estates should be under $1.5 million and your combined estate under $3 million.

Example

Annette, married to Jacob, has separate property worth $350,000. Their shared property is worth $950,000, so each has a half share of $475,000. In 2004, Annette's total estate is worth $825,000. The personal exemption for that year is $1.5 million, so she and Jacob can safely use Nolo's AB trust.

Should you bother with Nolo's AB trust if your combined estate is unlikely to be subject to tax in a few years? Suppose you and your spouse have a combined shared estate of $1.6 million. Only if both spouses die in 2004 or 2005 could the combined estate be subject to tax; the exemption rises to $2 million in 2006. Unless you're very old, very ill, or very cautious, why prepare an AB trust you won't need in two years?

There are several good reasons to prepare an AB trust, if your combined estate is worth over $1 million:

- As of now, the exemption will be reduced to $1 million for 2011 and thereafter. By preparing an AB trust, you've got a plan in place if this reduction does take affect.

- The estate tax law will almost surely be revised by Congress sometime during the next few years. It is very unlikely that the exemption will ever be reduced to less than $1 million. But if the exemption for any part of 2004-2009 is rolled back to $1 million, you've again got a plan in place.

- As I explain in depth in Chapter 5, with Nolo's AB trust a surviving spouse can obtain any amount of the deceased spouse's trust principal if the surviving spouse needs that money for medical care or other basic needs, so there is little risk to preparing the trust.

- Nolo's AB trust should not be burdensome to establish or maintain.

ESTIMATING THE VALUE OF YOUR ESTATE FOR AB TRUST PURPOSES

To decide whether you want to use Nolo's AB trust, you'll need a rough estimate of the net value of your estate. You don't need to obtain precise appraisals. You simply want a ballpark figure to see if your estate is likely to be over the estate tax threshold when you die.

You can use the Property Worksheet in Chapter 6, Section E, if you want to itemize your property and make written estimates of its worth.

But what about the fact that the worth of your estate will surely change by the time you die? For planning purposes, this doesn't really matter. To try to guess what your estate will be worth at some unknown date in the future is so speculative that it's pointless. Also, even if the worth of your estate increases, so does the amount of the personal exemption. How could you possibly guess whether the value of your estate will increase faster than the exempt amount? You can't, so the sane thing to do is base your planning on the value of your estate now.

---

2. Your Personal Situation

Nolo's AB trust can work well for you if you meet all three of the following criteria:

- you want to leave all or the bulk of your estate to your spouse

- you and your spouse have a combined estate which is likely to be subject to estate tax, and

- you want your spouse to have the maximum possible rights to the trust property, without being the legal owner of the property. (This is discussed further in Section 4, below.)

Nolo's AB trust follows the basics discussed above in Section E. You and your spouse each set up a separate AB trust, as part of your shared living trust. You each name the other spouse as life beneficiary and trustee of your A trust. You each name your final beneficiary or beneficiaries, leaving your property however you want. When the first spouse dies, the living trust property is divided into the irrevocable Trust A and the revocable Trust B (the surviving spouse's continuing living trust).

From a personal point of view, Nolo's AB trust works best when all involved—both spouses and all final beneficiaries—understand and agree on the purposes of the trust, which is to save on estate taxes and, at the same time, give the surviving spouse maximum rights to use Trust A money and property. Without this understanding, serious conflicts between the surviving spouse and the final beneficiaries may develop.

Nolo's AB trust is designed for families where:

- The final beneficiaries understand that all property in Trust A morally, albeit not legally, belongs to the surviving spouse. It is available for her basic needs, such as to pay for health care or to support her in her accustomed manner of living.

- The final beneficiaries understand that taking the trouble to create Nolo's AB trust is a generous act by parents, who do this not to benefit themselves, but their inheritors. After all, the estate tax savings benefit only the final beneficiaries, who receive more (usually much more) of the couple's combined estate than they would if the spouses had left property outright to the other.

- Family members are sufficiently trusting of each other so that it's reasonable to believe they can resolve any inheritance conflicts without lawsuits (or bloodshed).

- The final beneficiaries can be trusted to support the surviving spouse if he (as trustee) decides he needs to spend trust principal for reasons authorized by the IRS and listed in the trust document—that is, "support, health, education, or maintenance in his or her accustomed manner of living." They won't question these expenditures (if there are any) in an effort to preserve the largest possible amount for themselves.

If there is any potential for conflict between the surviving spouse and the final beneficiaries of the trust (often the couple's children), an AB trust may provoke or aggravate it. After all, in theory at least, there is an inherent possibility of conflict of interest between the life estate beneficiary and the final beneficiaries. These final beneficiaries may want all the trust principal conserved, no matter what the needs or wishes of the surviving spouse.

Another problem can arise if the surviving spouse becomes ill and can no longer serve as trustee. If a child who stands to eventually receive trust assets takes over as successor trustee, it's possible the child might be more concerned with preserving principal than with a parent's medical or other needs. I've heard of instances where it seemed to other family members and friends that a child, acting as trustee of Trust A, disregarded his parent's basic needs to protect the trust principal for himself.

Conflicts can also occur if the final beneficiaries believe the surviving spouse, as trustee, is not managing the trust property sensibly—for example, he is investing in very speculative stocks or real estate. If this situation arises, there can be real trouble, possibly even a lawsuit.

Having doubts? See a lawyer. If you have doubts about these personal matters, Nolo's AB trust is not for you. See a lawyer to work out a more individualized trust.

3. What Happens If the Trust A Property Is Over the Personal Exemption in the Year the First Spouse Dies?

If the value of the estate of the first spouse to die (the value of the Trust A property) turns out to exceed the estate tax threshold in the year of death, under Nolo's AB trust, estate taxes must be paid on the overage. Nolo's AB trust allows no other options.

Example

In 2003, Helene and Wesley created a Nolo AB trust for their combined estate of $3.2 million. Helene's half share is worth $1.6 million. Helene dies in 2004. The personal exemption is $1.5 million. Estate tax must be paid on the overage of $100,000.

Also, if the combination of separate property and shared property in one spouse's estate is over the personal exemption in the year of that's spouse's death, with Nolo's AB trust the overage will be taxed. This is true even if the couple's combined estate is under the maximum that can normally be shielded by a Nolo AB trust.

Example

Lisa and Paul prepare a Nolo AB trust for their combined estate of $1.8 million. Lisa has $1.4 million of separate property, and the couple's shared property totals $400,000 (each owns $200,000). So Lisa's total estate is $1.6 million.

Lisa dies in 2005; her property goes into her Trust A. The personal exemption is $1.5 million. There is a taxable overage of $100,000.

Getting help with a possible tax overage. If it's likely that there will be a taxable overage if you use Nolo's AB trust, there are legal devices and methods you can use to prevent or delay any tax from being paid. You can have a trust prepared that directs any overage in the Trust A property be given outright to the surviving spouse. No tax is paid on this overage because it qualifies for the marital deduction. Or you can establish what's called a "QTIP" trust, which delays any tax payment until after both spouses die. On the other hand, you may conclude that the overall tax picture is better if payment is made on any overage when the first spouse dies. Choosing between these and other possible options is complicated. You need the help of a lawyer.

4. The Surviving Spouse's Rights Over Trust A Property

Under the law, there's no one standard that must be used when defining the rights a surviving spouse has over the property in Trust A. The spectrum runs from the maximum permitted by the IRS (any more and the surviving spouse would become the legal owner of the trust property, exactly what you don't want) to fairly rigid restrictions and controls placed on how the surviving spouse can use the property.

As I've said, Nolo's AB trust gives the surviving spouse the maximum rights IRS regulations allow over Trust A property. The survivor:

- receives all interest or other income from the trust property

- is entitled to use and control the property—for example, she can live in a house that's owned by the trust, or sell it and buy another house or do other things with the profits of the sale, such as buy a retirement condo or conserve the profits in a trust account, and

- can spend (invade) any amount of Trust A property (principal) for her health, education, support, or maintenance in her accustomed manner of living.

Example

Mabel and Anthony, who together own property worth $1.8 million, create a Nolo AB trust. Each names the other as the life beneficiary and trustee of Trust A. They have one child, Walter, who has two grown children, Rose and Tim. Mabel and Anthony each name all three as final beneficiaries: Walter to receive 60%, and Tim and Rose each 20%.

Mabel dies in 2004. Her estate, worth $900,000, goes into her Trust A. Her estate is below the estate tax threshold. Anthony's same-sized estate, also below the threshold, goes into his revocable Trust B.

During 2005, Anthony suffers both major financial disasters and grave health problems. To continue his style of living, and pay medical bills, Anthony spends a total of $160,000 of Trust A principal. He also spends all the income from Trust A property. He does not become legal owner of the Trust A property even though he's spent a portion of the principal on himself. When Anthony dies in 2006, the amount remaining in Trust A is $740,000, which is turned over to the final beneficiaries.

So, with a Nolo AB trust, the surviving spouse has the right to spend part or all of the Trust A principal for what really concerns most couples, particularly older ones—the surviving spouse's health care and other basic needs. (The rights of the surviving spouse are discussed in more detail in Chapter 5, Section D.)

The surviving spouse has no power to change the final beneficiaries of Trust A. (The surviving spouse can change the beneficiaries of her own, revocable trust.) The final beneficiaries of Trust A were named by the deceased spouse when the AB trust was originally prepared.

5. Couples Who Are Unlikely to Want Nolo's AB Trust

Should all married couples who might face estate taxes use this kind of trust? No. Aside from couples whose estate is too large to safely use Nolo's AB trust, it is generally not advisable for:

- Younger middle-aged couples—roughly, couples in their 40s, perhaps 50s. In this age group, you probably won't want to tie up assets in a trust, which may last for many years or decades, if one spouse dies prematurely. The surviving spouse could live for decades and be seriously burdened by the hassles and restrictions of the trust. (See Section 6, below.)

Many younger couples create a basic shared living trust to leave each other all or most of their property. Then, once they're older—say in their late 50s or 60s—they revoke their old trust and create an AB trust. After all, before then, if one spouse unexpectedly dies, the survivor will inherit everything estate-tax free, no matter what the amount, because of the marital deduction. That surviving spouse will probably have years to use the money—and years to arrange for other methods of reducing any possible estate tax. (See Chapter 15, Sections C and E.)

- Couples where one spouse is considerably younger than the other and presumably will live much longer. Again, generally there's no need to burden the surviving spouse with a trust designed to save estate taxes when he or she is likely to live for many years. (Of course, such couples may well sensibly decide to use a basic shared living trust, to avoid probate.)

- Couples who don't want to leave the bulk of their property for use of the surviving spouse, but want instead to leave substantial amounts of property directly to other beneficiaries. If you want to make many specific gifts, outside the AB trust property, that add up to a substantial amount of money—as a rough rule, over $50,000 to $100,000—you can simply use a basic shared living trust. After all, if you won't leave most of your property for the benefit of your spouse, there's little reason to bother with an AB trust.

- Many couples in second or subsequent marriages. With Nolo's AB trust, each spouse can name his or her own children from prior marriages as final beneficiaries of his or her A (and B) trust. However, as I've stated, Nolo's AB trust gives the surviving spouse the maximum rights allowed by law over the property in Trust A. Often one or both spouses in a second marriage don't want the other spouse to have such broad rights to consume trust principal or to manage trust property. For example, they want to eliminate or restrict the surviving spouse's authority, as sole trustee, to use trust principal for her or his "health, education, support, or maintenance." Or they may want one of their children to serve as co-trustee, or even to be the only trustee. Other concerns can include: Does the surviving spouse have the authority to sell trust property? What reports and accountings must be given to the children, the final beneficiaries?

In sum, there are often worries about conflicts between the surviving spouse and the deceased spouse's children—how best to allocate rights and powers between them? If relations could become strained between your children and your spouse, you may very well not want to set things up so that they essentially share ownership of property for many years.

Resolving personal issues. Many individual family concerns must be dealt with when setting up an AB trust for couples in second or subsequent marriages. You need to see an experienced estate planning lawyer to draft a trust specifically geared to your situation and desires. (These issues are discussed further in Chapter 15, Section F.)

6. Drawbacks of an AB Trust

Before deciding to use an AB trust, both spouses should understand what they're getting into. Once one spouse dies, that spouse's Trust A becomes irrevocable. The trust imposes limits and burdens on the survivor that cannot be changed.

Here are some possible drawbacks of an AB trust:

a. Restrictions on the Surviving Spouse's Use of the Property in Trust A

As you know, with Nolo's AB trust, the surviving spouse has the right to any income generated by Trust A property and fairly broad rights to use the property for health, education, and support. But he or she cannot spend trust property freely on whatever he feels like. Except for legally permitted expenditures, that property must be held in trust for the final beneficiaries.

b. Administrative Expenses

When one spouse dies, an estate lawyer or accountant is commonly needed to determine how to best divide the couple's assets between the irrevocable Trust A and Trust B. Each item of the couple's shared property does not have to be divided 50/50 between the two trusts. The only requirement is that the shared property in both trusts must be of equal total value. There can be considerable flexibility in allocating assets between the two trusts. It usually takes an expert to decide on the best division. (See Chapter 14, Section B.)

c. Trust Tax Returns

The surviving spouse, as trustee of Trust A, must obtain a taxpayer ID number for this trust. Also, the surviving spouse must file an annual trust income tax return for that trust. This usually isn't a momentous hassle, but like any tax return, it'll require work.

d. Record Keeping

The surviving spouse must keep two sets of books and records, one for his own property (which remains in the surviving spouse's revocable living trust) and one for the property in Trust A, which (as you know by now) is legally separate from property owned by the surviving spouse.

e. No Gifts From Trust A Principal

The surviving spouse has no rights, either as trustee of Trust A or as that trust's beneficiary, to make gifts of the Trust A property to any other person. For instance, a surviving spouse may sensibly want to give some of the Trust A principal to a child, to help her purchase a home, or for other needs. But such a gift is not legal under IRS rules. As I've said, the principal can be spent only for the surviving spouse's needs for "health, education, support, or maintenance."

To end this chapter on a note of optimism, despite the possible drawbacks and limits, Nolo's AB trust has worked very well for many thousands of couples and families. If it fits your situation and needs, it will work just fine for you and save your children or other final inheritors a bundle. For most surviving spouses, the drawbacks amount to no more than relatively minor accounting and record keeping hassles, which they feel are well worth conserving tens or even hundreds of thousands of dollars worth of their property for their beneficiaries. ■

chapter 5

NOLO'S TAX-SAVING AB TRUST

$\mathcal{C}$ouples use Nolo's AB trust for three primary purposes:

1. To save on estate taxes, increasing the amount that can be conserved for their children or other final beneficiaries.

2. To make the deceased spouse's property available for use by the surviving spouse to the extent legally permitted.

3. To avoid probate.

Do not use Nolo's AB trust if you want to restrict the surviving spouse's rights. Nolo's AB trust allows the surviving spouse to have as much right to the deceased spouse's trust property as IRS regulations permit. You may want to limit the surviving spouse's rights. For instance, some couples in second or subsequent marriages decide that the surviving spouse will have no right to spend the deceased spouse's trust principal, no matter what his or her needs. The desire is to make sure the principal remains intact for the deceased spouse's final inheritors, often including children from prior marriages. (See Section D, below, and Chapter 15, Section F.) To prepare an AB trust, many individual questions must be resolved, and you will need a lawyer's help.

This chapter takes a deeper look at how Nolo's AB trust works. First, let's review the tax rules.

A. The Size of Your Estate

Because the tax figures are so important, let me summarize what was discussed in Chapter 4, Section F, regarding federal estate tax law and Nolo's AB trust.

You can safely use Nolo's AB trust if your individual estates are under the amount of the personal estate tax exemption for the year you prepare the trust, and your combined estate is less than twice that amount. The tax table below shows how much the Nolo AB trust can shield from estate tax.

HOW MUCH NOLO'S AB TRUST CAN SHIELD FROM ESTATE TAX

Year of First Spouse's Death	Personal Exemption	Maximum Shielded
2004	$1.5 million	$3 million
2005	$1.5 million	$3 million
2006	$2 million	$4 million
2007	$2 million	$4 million
2008	$2 million	$4 million
2009	$3.5 million	$7 million

Estate tax due on first spouse's death. With Nolo's AB trust, if the estate of the first spouse to die (Trust A) is over the exempt amount for the year of death, a federal estate tax return must be filed and the tax due paid within nine months. If you want to explore ways to avoid paying tax when the first spouse dies, see a lawyer.

B. Should You Do It Yourself?

Before we plunge into details of how Nolo's AB trust works, I again want to give you a serious warning: AB trusts come in a variety of forms, having different tax, legal, and practical consequences. This book presents one type of AB trust, useful for many couples. As long as this trust is right for you, don't hesitate to use it. But if you conclude that your family and monetary situations are different than those discussed summarized below, this trust is not advisable for you.

Beyond having a combined estate that's large enough to trigger concern about estate tax, here's a summary of the basic requirements you should meet to use Nolo's AB trust:

- You want to leave the bulk of your property for the use of your spouse during her or his lifetime, if that spouse survives you.

- Neither you nor your spouse wants to leave more than three gifts directly to other people or institutions.

- You and your spouse want to eventually leave your property to your children (or other people or institutions) in a way that avoids estate tax.

- Key family members understand and approve of the fact that Nolo's AB trust allows the surviving spouse broad powers over Trust A property.

- You are confident that there will be no conflict between your spouse and your final beneficiaries over your trust property.

The comforting truth is that Nolo's AB trust works fine for many couples. If you're among this group, you'll find that the technical aspects of preparing your trust (covered in Chapters 10 and 11) are not onerous, and you can safely prepare this trust yourself, saving yourself at least a thousand dollars—and probably a good deal more—in attorney fees.

C. How Nolo's AB Trust Works

Here we'll focus on precisely how Nolo's AB trust works.

1. Creating the Trust

To create your AB trust, use Form 3 in Appendix B or on the CD-ROM. (Specific, step-by-step instructions for completing this form are in Chapter 10.) In general, the process is as follows:

- Both spouses together create one overall shared living trust and transfer their property to it.

- Within this living trust, each spouse creates an AB trust. This part of the trust document provides that when the first spouse dies, the living trust property will be split into Trust A and Trust B. Trust A is an irrevocable trust that contains the deceased spouse's property. Trust B contains the property that is owned by the surviving spouse.

- Each spouse names the other as the life beneficiary and trustee of his or her A trust. Each spouse names his or her final beneficiaries (and alternates) to receive his or her trust property after both spouses have died. Spouses can name different final beneficiaries, but couples in a first marriage generally name the same final beneficiaries—their children.

- The spouses name a successor trustee, to take over and distribute the Trust A and Trust B property after both spouses have died.

That's basically all there is to it. (That's enough, no?) All the terms and phrases necessary to create a legal AB trust, following the IRS rules to ensure estate tax savings, are printed in Form 3.

Example

Meredith and Gary have a total estate (all shared property owned equally) of roughly $1,820,000. They use Form 3 to create an AB trust in which:
- Both transfer all property into the living trust.
- Meredith leaves her share of the property in her Trust A. Gary is the life beneficiary, and their children are her final beneficiaries in equal shares.
- Gary leaves his share of the property in his Trust A. Meredith is the life beneficiary, and their children are his final beneficiaries in equal shares.
- Gary and Meredith name their daughter Alice to serve as successor trustee after both spouses die.

In practical, day-to-day terms, so long as Meredith and Gary live, nothing really changes after they've created their AB trust. They can still revoke or amend their living trust, and all trust transactions (such as any sale of trust property, or other income from trust property) are reported on the couple's regular income tax return. But when one spouse dies, the trust really becomes operational.

2. How an AB Trust Becomes Operational

When a couple creates an AB trust, they cannot know (although some couples may be pretty sure) which spouse will be the first to die. So each spouse must create a separate Trust A and Trust B. Only the Trust A of the first spouse to die ever becomes operational.

When one spouse dies (called, for our purpose, the "deceased spouse"), that spouse's Trust A goes into effect. The surviving spouse's Trust A won't become operative, because he or she cannot, by definition, have a spouse survive him or her. (However, if he or she remarries, the surviving spouse and new mate can create a new, separate living trust with a new AB trust.) The surviving spouse's property goes into Trust B, his or her (continuing) revocable living trust. At the second spouse's death, the property in Trusts A and B goes to the final beneficiaries.

Example

Continuing with our example of Meredith and Gary, above, Gary dies in 2004. His half of their property is worth $910,000, and goes into his Trust A. Meredith's half of the property goes into her Trust B. Meredith is the life beneficiary of Trust A, with all rights of the surviving spouse (see Section 3, below). Meredith dies in 2007, and Alice becomes successor trustee. She transfers the property of Trust A and Trust B to the final beneficiaries.

3. The Surviving Spouse's Rights to Property in Trust A

Because this subject is a matter of such vital concern to many couples, I want to stress here, at the risk of some repetition, the rights of the surviving spouse. Nolo's trust allows the surviving spouse the maximum legally permitted rights in Trust A property. The trust uses the specific language required by the IRS so that Trust A property is never legally owned by the surviving spouse. At the same time, the surviving spouse has all of the following rights to Trust A property:

- The right to all income from the trust property. The trust document specifically states that the trustee "shall pay to or spend for the benefit of the surviving spouse the net income of Trust A in quarter-annual or more frequent installments."

- The right to use trust property—for example, to live in a house owned, or partially owned, by the trust.

- The right to sell trust property, reinvest trust funds, or buy new property in the name of the trust, as long as principal is not used up. For example, the surviving spouse, as trustee, can sell a house owned or co-owned by the trust and buy a condo in Florida or North Carolina, but cannot use the proceeds to gamble at Las Vegas.

- The right to use the trust principal for any amount necessary for the surviving spouse's "health, education, support, or maintenance in accord with his or her accustomed manner of living." (IRS Reg. 20.2041-1(c)(2).)

The only practical effect of the IRS limitations is that the surviving spouse cannot spend trust principal any way she wants, say for a painting by Elmer Bischoff or a six-month vacation in Europe.

How would the IRS find out if the surviving spouse were improperly spending money from Trust A? (Please realize that this is mostly a lawyer's theoretical question. Surely the overwhelming majority of couples who create and use an AB trust do so in good faith and want to conserve the trust principal for their children.) Improper spending of Trust A principal might be detected by an IRS audit of the annual trust tax return, or perhaps one of the final beneficiaries would learn of these improper expenses and oppose them. (It might take a lawsuit, though, to actually prevent the spouse from continuing to abuse her position.) But even if the children had no objection to the parent spending the money, if the IRS decided it had been spent for an improper purpose, it could conclude that there was never any intention of creating a bona fide AB trust. In that case, the trust is disallowed, for tax purposes, and all Trust A property is treated as owned by the surviving spouse—exactly what you don't want.

⚠ Don't change a word. The language permitting the surviving spouse to spend Trust A principal for "health, education, support, or maintenance in accord with his or her accustomed manner of living" is crucial. If you add a word like "well-being" or "comfort" to the list, under IRS rules the standard for spending principal becomes "subjective"—a fatal mistake. If a "subjective" standard is used, the Trust A property is legally owned by the surviving spouse and would be included in the surviving spouse's estate. As you know, the whole point of setting up an AB trust is to prevent both estates from being lumped together for estate tax purposes.

The right of the surviving spouse to invade the trust principal for any amount needed for "support, health, education, or maintenance in his or her accustomed manner of living" can be of great importance. If the surviving spouse faces any grave financial need—a costly medical emergency, housing crisis, or other necessity of life—and doesn't have enough other funds or assets to pay them, she's legally authorized, as trustee, to spend any amount needed of trust principal to pay for these needs. If a spouse couldn't use Trust A principal for these needs, AB trusts would be far less popular.

The surviving spouse is not required to use up all her assets before using trust principal to pay for, or help pay for, such costs. For example, a survivor doesn't have to sell her house and spend all the proceeds on medical care before using Trust A property for medical needs. The IRS regulations specifically provide that she's entitled to continue to live in her "accustomed manner of living." What's required here is simply that the surviving spouse's use of trust principal be reasonable, under the circumstances, and for one of the IRS-authorized purposes.

Example

A couple, Kumar and Hari, has assets of $2.6 million—a house worth $600,000 (equity), investments, stocks, and money market funds worth $2 million. They establish an AB trust, with each spouse having the maximum legal rights over the trust's property.

Kumar dies in 2004. His half (worth $1.3 million) goes into Trust A. (Hari's property goes into Trust B.) Hari is both the life beneficiary and trustee of Trust A. The couple's children are the final beneficiaries.

Hari remains in the house. She also receives all the income from the $2 million in investments, stocks, and money market funds—half because she owns half the stocks and money market funds directly, half as Trust A income.

Hari has some major health problems over the next years. The costs of the illness are mostly covered by her insurance and Medicare. But one immense medical bill is not covered, and Hari's income is not sufficient to pay it. Hari, as trustee, can spend some of the Trust A principal to pay this bill.

4. Property Left to Specific Beneficiaries

Nolo's AB trust allows each spouse to leave three specific gifts, in addition to the property left in Trust A or retained in Trust B. (Of course, you don't have to leave any specific gifts. In that case, all the deceased spouse's trust property goes to and is held in Trust A.) Any specific gifts left by the deceased spouse go to the named beneficiaries when that spouse dies. Similarly, specific gifts left by the surviving spouse go to the beneficiaries when that spouse dies.

Legally, with an AB trust you can leave as many specific gifts as you want. However, in my experience, it's rare for someone to want to both leave a number of specific gifts while simultaneously leaving the bulk of property for use of the surviving spouse. Thus our limit of three.

You can leave separate gifts from your separate property (if you have any), from your half of shared property, or some combination of both. If you choose to leave specific gifts, they should be relatively minor, totaling roughly no more than $25,000 to $50,000. After all, a central purpose of an AB trust is to leave the bulk, or all, of one spouse's property for the use of the other spouse during his or her lifetime.

Example

Shauna is married and has an estate worth $916,000. Although she wants to leave the bulk of her estate in Trust A for the use of her husband, Max, she decides to leave some of her separate property heirlooms to her sister and nieces: an old music box to her sister Bernice, an antique clock to her niece Danielle, and several lace dresses to her niece Moira. The total monetary value of these gifts is approximately $7,000. Shauna can sensibly use Nolo's AB trust.

5. Division of AB Trust Property When One Spouse Dies

Eventually, one spouse dies. At this point, the property in the AB trust is divided into Trust A and Trust B. From Trust A property, any gifts the deceased spouse left to specific beneficiaries are distributed; all the rest of his or her property stays in Trust A. If the deceased spouse left no specific gifts, all of her or his property stays in Trust A.

The property in Trust B includes:

- The surviving spouse's 50% share of co-owned trust property. (Each item does not have to be divided 50-50, but the total value of the deceased spouse's share of co-owned property must be the same as the value of the surviving spouse's share.)
- All separate trust property of the surviving spouse.

Dividing the property between Trust A and Trust B is the responsibility of the surviving spouse, as trustee of both trusts. She must decide which property she wants placed in the (irrevocable) Trust A, and which she wants retained in her (revocable) Trust B. All that is legally required is that the total dollar amount of shared ownership property in each trust be equal. Ownership of each individual item of property does not have to be split in half.

If your goals include maximum future income tax savings and estate tax savings (beyond what's automatically saved by using Nolo's AB trust), deciding which property goes where is often neither clear nor simple.

Suppose a couple shares ownership of a house worth $800,000 and stocks, money market accounts, and other investments totalling $1 million, and the husband has separate property worth $100,000. What's the wisest way to divide up this property when the first spouse dies? It depends on the couple's needs and circumstances, as well as trying to see into the future.

First, let's look at the house. If the entire $800,000 value of the house is put in Trust A, it will not be subject to estate tax (even if the husband's $100,000 of separate property is added as well), because the total in Trust A is less than the estate tax threshold, no matter what the year of death. If, over the years, the value of the house rises to $7 million before the surviving spouse dies, this increase is never subject to estate tax. (This property was subject to estate tax only once, when the deceased spouse died and Trust A became operational and irrevocable.) If the house weren't in Trust A, it could be assessed at $7 million for estate tax purposes when the second spouse died.

But it's not a law of nature that house prices always rise. House prices are set by a free market, and the only thing we really know about a free market is that (as Bernard Baruch said of the stock market) "prices will fluctuate." If real estate prices go down or even remain flat, maybe the couple (and the children, as the final inheritors) would be better off if the money market funds were all put in Trust A. Or maybe splitting both the house and the money market funds between Trust A and Trust B will prove wisest.

Further, you can sell your home (once every two years) and not pay capital gains tax on the first $250,000 of profit. (For a couple, $500,000 is exempt from capital gains tax.) But this right is only available to a person, not to an irrevocable trust. How does this play into the decision of where to place the house? Would it be better if the house all went into Trust B, so the surviving spouse retained the option to sell it during her lifetime and obtain the capital gain tax break?

Dividing property between Trust A and Trust B is discussed in more detail in Chapter 14, Section B.

Hiring an expert to determine the wisest property division. Many spouses faced with dividing property between the two trusts have sensibly decided to hire a good accountant or estate tax lawyer to determine the most advantageous division. Since this should cost a few hundred dollars—but not thousands—I believe it's often wise to spend the money. An expert can discuss your situation with you and help you understand the possible tax effects of different allocation decisions.

Some paperwork is required to officially allocate property between the two trusts. All property with documents of title that is placed in Trust A must have new title documents prepared (and recorded, if need be, as with real estate deeds), listing Trust A as owner. Technically, the property is transferred from the trustee of the living trust to the trustee of Trust A of the living trust. Yes, this sounds mushy, but it's important.

Example:

Mike and Samantha Corbin-Pawlowski establish an AB trust. Samantha dies. Her Trust A contains real estate. Mike prepares a deed, transferring the real estate from "The Mike and Samantha Corbin-Pawlowski Trust," to "The Mike and Samantha Corbin-Pawlowski Trust, Trust A." He signs the deed as "Mike Corbin-Pawlowski, as trustee of the Mike and Samantha Corbin-Pawlowski Trust."

Property without title must be listed on a schedule attached to the Trust A document.

No new paperwork is usually required to establish Trust B, the surviving spouse's trust, except that a list of the property in it should be separate and kept with the original trust document. No other paperwork is required. Because Trust B is a revocable trust, no separate tax records need be kept.

The IRS will learn of the existence of Trust A when the first trust income tax return is filed. The IRS insists that there be a clear, legally valid record of what property is in each trust. Because the IRS is familiar with the Trust A and Trust B terminology, captioning ownership documents in those terms removes one source of potential tax hassles.

6. Managing the Property in Trust A

When the deceased spouse's Trust A becomes operational, it exists as a distinct taxable entity. The surviving spouse, as trustee, manages Trust A. The minimum required here is to:

- obtain a federal taxpayer ID number for the trust (this can be done by sending the IRS a simple form)

- keep separate, clear tax records of all Trust A transactions (a checkbook will usually suffice), and

- file a separate trust tax return for Trust A each year.

While all of this requires energy and involves some paperwork hassles, few spouses find it truly onerous, at least not compared to the tax savings they're achieving for their inheritors.

If the gross value of the property in Trust A turns out to exceed the personal exemption for the year of the deceased spouse's death, the surviving spouse, as trustee, is responsible for filing a federal estate tax return and paying any taxes due within nine months of death.

Once Trust A is legally established, the surviving spouse, as trustee, must manage the trust property responsibly. For example, any property taxes due on real estate in Trust A should be paid from funds or property of that trust. If there are no liquid assets—cash, or property that can be turned into cash—in Trust A, the surviving spouse is stuck and must pay them from some other source. But remember, she could always refinance the house, assuming there was some equity in it, to obtain cash.

Legally, as trustee, the surviving spouse has what is called a "fiduciary duty" to the final beneficiaries. That means she must manage the trust property reasonably and protect the final beneficiaries' interest in the trust property (principal), except as otherwise authorized in the Trust A document. With Nolo's Trust A, the surviving spouse has the authority to hire financial advisers or consultants, paid for from trust funds (including principal), if need be. Realistically, the surviving spouse has only to use common sense in managing the trust property; he or she should not make risky investments or spend principal in reckless or rash ways.

With Nolo's AB trust, the surviving spouse has no obligation to provide reports about the property in Trust A to any of the final beneficiaries, except to provide them with copies of the annual trust income tax return. This is a compromise between allowing the final beneficiaries no rights at all to know what is going on in the trust and allowing them extensive rights or controls. Since the surviving spouse must prepare and file an annual trust income tax return for Trust A, it does not seem unduly burdensome or intrusive that she give copies of it to the trust's final beneficiaries.

7. Amending Trust B

Trust B, the surviving spouse's living trust, remains revocable while the survivor lives. The survivor can amend the terms of Trust B, or revoke it entirely, as long as he or she is mentally competent.

Many surviving spouses don't need to name new beneficiaries for some or all of their Trust B property. Commonly, both spouses want to leave their property to their children, who were originally named as both spouses' final beneficiaries. This desire doesn't change after one spouse dies.

Example

Zora and Glenway create an AB trust. Each name their two children as final beneficiaries. Glenway dies, and his Trust A becomes irrevocable. Zora's Trust B is revocable, but that doesn't mean she wants to revoke who she wants her property to go to. She continues to want to it go to her children, so she leaves the designation of her final beneficiaries unchanged.

Normally, it's inadvisable for the surviving spouse to change the successor trustee of her trust, unless there are compelling reasons. That's because when the surviving spouse dies, there would be two trustees involved in transferring the property of the two trusts—Trust A, the marital life estate trust, and Trust B, the surviving spouse's trust—to the same final beneficiaries (assuming the final beneficiaries are the same for both trusts). It seems self-evident that there are risks of conflict and tension between two different trustees for different trusts for what is all, basically, "family" money.

However, if the surviving spouse amends her trust to name new final beneficiaries, it may well make sense to also name a new successor trustee for this trust. When she dies, this new successor trustee will distribute her trust property to her new beneficiaries. And the successor trustee for Trust A will distribute that trust's property to the final beneficiaries named by the deceased spouse in the original living trust document.

8. After the Surviving Spouse Dies

After the death of the surviving spouse, the successor trustee (often one of the couple's children) distributes the Trust A property to that trust's final beneficiaries. In addition, the surviving spouse's own living trust, Trust B, becomes irrevocable on his or her death, and the successor trustee distributes that trust's property as the trust document directs.

This usually involves some paperwork and dealing with financial institutions such as stock brokerage companies and title companies. (See Chapter 14, Section B, for a full discussion of this process.) In addition, the successor trustee manages any children's trusts created by either spouse's trust. Finally, the successor trustee is responsible for handling any other trust-related matters. For example, if the gross value of the surviving spouse's estate exceeded the personal exemption in the year of death, the successor trustee must file a federal estate tax return and pay any tax due from the estate.

Example

Lamont and Iola create an AB trust, with their three children as the final beneficiaries to share equally. Lamont leaves some of his separate-property artworks to his sister, Coreen. He leaves everything else to his Trust A, with his wife as life beneficiary. They name their daughter Thelma as the successor trustee.

When Lamont dies, Iola, serving as trustee of the living trust, divides their shared property in half. Lamont's half and his private property are placed in Trust A. From that trust, Iola transfers the artworks to Coreen, and retains the rest of the property in Trust A. Iola, the surviving spouse, is the trustee and life estate beneficiary of this trust. She receives all income from that trust property and has the right to use it and manage it (as trustee) for the rest of her life.

When Iola dies, Thelma, the successor trustee, transfers the property in Trust A to the three children; they own it together, in equal shares. Since one child, Willie, is only 20 years old, his property stays in a child's trust, managed by Thelma, until Willie becomes 35. (See Chapter 9, Section C.) Thelma also transfers Iola's Trust B property equally among the three children. Again, Willie's share of Iola's trust property is placed in the child's trust, with Thelma as the trustee.

DIVISION AND DISTRIBUTION OF TRUST PROPERTY WHEN EACH SPOUSE DIES

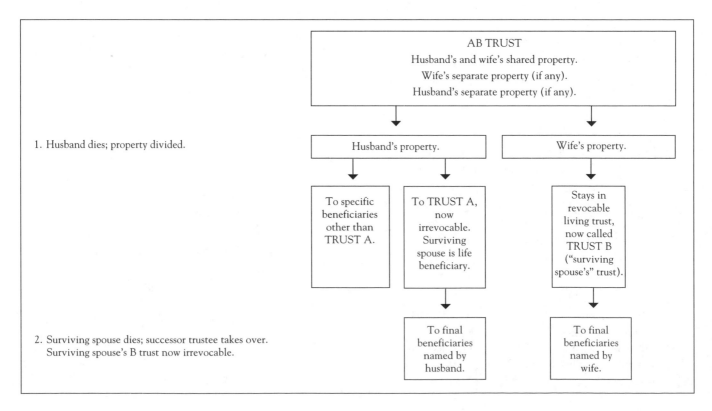

D. Alternatives to Nolo's AB Trust

If you can't safely use Nolo's AB trust, there are a number of methods and devices you can consider to achieve tax savings and other estate planning goals. To use any of these, you'll need to hire a lawyer. Yes, estate planning lawyers are expensive, but remember:

- By studying this book, you'll be better prepared to deal with a lawyer, and can suggest ways to keep fees reasonable (such as you, yourself, transferring assets to your trust rather than paying an attorney $200 or more per hour for what is basically clerical work).

- You are seeing a lawyer to save on overall estate taxes on a combined estate that is worth at least $1.5 million. You can afford to spend some money on legal help.

- Estate tax saving trusts (including more complex versions of an AB trust) can become exceedingly complex and technical. If you don't fully comply with IRS regulations, estate tax savings will be lost.

- Even if your trust qualifies under IRS rules, if it isn't properly geared to your situation, you may not achieve your goals and desires. If you or your spouse or both have children from a prior marriage, for example, you may need a carefully prepared trust to minimize possibilities of family conflict. This can be doubly true if one spouse has far more money than the other, and if you remarried late in life. An AB trust that is technically and legally okay can nevertheless lead to disastrous conflicts if the personal concerns of all involved haven't been addressed and resolved as best they can be.

Now let's look briefly at some of the more widely used sophisticated estate tax saving trusts and devices.

1. A Formula AB Trust

A formula AB trust defines and limits the value of the property placed in Trust A when the first spouse dies. The formula (a series of clauses) specifies that no more than the amount of the personal estate tax exemption in the year of death is placed into the A trust.

Any surplus is dealt with by other methods, to avoid estate tax at this point. It can be left outright to the surviving spouse, exempt under the marital deduction, or it can be left to what is called a "QTIP" trust. (QTIP is jargon for "Qualified Terminal Interest Property." That clears it all up, right?) A QTIP trust allows the surviving spouse to postpone taxes that would otherwise be due on the deceased's estate, while not leaving this property outright to the surviving spouse. (If it sounds tricky, that's because it is.)

Example 1

Molly and Ben have a combined estate worth $4 million, owned equally. In addition, Molly owns separate property worth $300,000. They create a formula AB trust, leaving any amount over the estate tax threshold (in the year the first spouse dies) outright to the other spouse. Molly dies in 2005, when the estate tax exemption is $1.5 million. Molly's total estate is $2.3 million (her $2 million half of the shared ownership property plus her separate $300,000). $1.5 million of Molly's money goes into Trust A. The balance, or overage, of $800,000 goes outright to Ben. No tax is due on the overage because it qualifies for the marital deduction.

Example 2

Damian and Victoria have a combined estate worth $3 million. Damian has separate property worth $400,000. Victoria has separate property worth $850,000. Damian has one child from a prior marriage; Victoria has two children from her prior marriages. Ultimately, each wants his or her property to go to the children. To achieve this, they create a formula AB trust and a QTIP trust for any overage. Damian dies in 2005. His estate is worth $1.9 million. The estate tax exemption for 2005 is $1.5 million. $400,000 is placed in the QTIP trust, where Damian has named his child as the final beneficiary.

A formula AB trust makes sense only where there could be a "surplus" in the deceased spouse's estate—that is, more money than the estate tax exemption in the year of death. In other words, the spouse must have an estate worth more than $1.5 million. If your estate is that large, you have several choices for dealing with the matter (hard to call it a "problem"):

- make tax-free gifts from your property while you live, reducing the size of your taxable estate

- leave any surplus outright to the surviving spouse—that gift is exempt from estate tax because of the marital deduction

- leave all your property in Trust A, understanding that some estate tax will likely be paid at the death of the first spouse (this may result in a lower overall tax than if the surplus had been left to the surviving spouse)

- if one spouse's estate is much larger than the other's, equalize the size of estate by transferring some property while you both live to the spouse who owns less, or

- leave the surplus in a QTIP trust, avoiding any tax until the death of the surviving spouse.

If you are concerned about a possible surplus. Handling a possible surplus enmeshes you in many complexities, including (1) understanding how your various options work, both generally and in your particular case, (2) evaluating the effects of the changes in the annual exemption amounts, and the uncertainty of current estate tax law, on your planning regarding the surplus, (3) choosing which option, or combination of options, you want to use, and (4) drafting the technical legal language to accomplish your goals. All this is far beyond what this book can offer. If you may have, in estate tax terms, a surplus, see an expert lawyer.

2. Limiting the Rights of the Surviving Spouse

As I've mentioned, an AB trust does not have to grant the surviving spouse the broadest powers allowed by law. It's possible to limit, or prohibit altogether, the surviving spouse's right to spend (invade) the Trust A principal. Some AB trusts impose other restrictions on the surviving spouse, such as requiring regular trust reports to trust beneficiaries, or requiring the consent of a specific final beneficiary before spending principal.

Imposing these types of restrictions tends to occur in second or subsequent marriages, where each spouse wants to ensure that his or her children from a prior marriage are protected and will actually receive the principal of Trust A. Because these trusts raise many concerns related to the couple's personal needs and financial circumstances, people who want them should consult a lawyer.

The goal of imposing limits and controls on the property left to the surviving spouse can be combined with estate tax savings, or it can be independent. Even if a couple has no estate tax problems—their combined estate is less than the exempt amount—they may want to create an AB trust to control property left to a surviving spouse. For example, such a trust may be useful if a husband in a second marriage wants to leave his property for the use of his wife during her lifetime, but wants to be

certain that the property eventually goes to his children from his first marriage. (Limiting the rights of a surviving spouse is discussed further in Chapter 15, Section F.)

3. The "5 and 5" Power Trust

Under present IRS rules, the surviving spouse of an AB trust can be given the right to obtain annually, for any reason whatsoever, up to a maximum of 5% of the Trust A principal or $5,000, whichever is greater. Estate planners call this the "5 and 5" power. There can be drawbacks to including this in an AB trust, including adverse tax consequences if the money isn't actually taken annually by the surviving spouse. This "5 and 5" power is not included in this book's AB trust because the surviving spouse already has authority to obtain trust principal in any amount for "health, education, support, or maintenance." In my view, an additional general power for the spouse to use the principal for any reason is unnecessary and possibly unwise.

4. Other Options

There are other high-end devices you may want to consider which are beyond the scope of this book. The most commonly used methods include:

- disclaimers

- charitable remainder trusts, and

- generation-skipping trusts.

These and other methods are briefly summarized in Chapter 15, Section C. ■

chapter 6

CHOOSING WHAT PROPERTY TO PUT IN YOUR LIVING TRUST

Okay, it's time to begin hands-on work. In this chapter, you'll make your initial decisions about what property to put in your trust.

You can place all your property in your living trust, or leave some or even most of it by other means. This chapter tells you when a living trust may not be the best method for transferring your property. Other methods are discussed in Chapter 15.

For many people, deciding what property to transfer to a living trust is not a difficult matter. They have one, or a few, "big ticket" items—for example, a house, some stocks, and a money market account—and they know they want to avoid probate of this property. But for many other people, matters aren't quite so simple. Some have questions about different types of property—say, about personal checking accounts, retirement accounts, or more unusual items such as copyrights or patents. And if you're married, you may need to determine which property is shared in equal amounts and which is the separate property of one spouse.

This chapter:

- discusses types of property you'll probably want to put into your trust

- reviews state marital property laws that can require you to leave property to your spouse, and

- provides a property worksheet you can use to make a thorough inventory of what you own and estimate the net value of your property. You can use this estimate of your net worth to see if your individual, or combined (if you are a couple), estate exceeds the federal estate tax threshold.

Even if you think you know what property you want to put in your trust, read these materials carefully to be sure your decisions pose no potential problems. Of course, you can always revise your decisions before preparing your actual trust document. The point isn't to lock you in now, but to get you started.

A. Listing the Property to Be Put in Your Trust

You must list, in the trust document, each item of property the trust owns. Any property you don't list will not go into your living trust and will not pass under the terms of the trust. It may instead have to go through probate.

A list of trust property is called a "schedule" and is attached to the trust document. (This is explained in detail in Chapter 10, Section D.) A trust for one person has only one schedule. A trust for a married couple (either a basic shared trust or an AB trust) has three schedules: one for shared-ownership property, one for any separate property of the wife, and another for any separate property of the husband. If a spouse doesn't have any separate property, you can simply eliminate the appropriate schedule.

Transferring title to the trustee. You must also prepare separate documents formally transferring legal title to the trust. You do that by placing title in the trustee's or trustees' name(s), "as trustee(s) for the ____[name]____ Trust." Property with a document of title—like a deed to a house, or a stock account—must be transferred by preparing and signing a new document of title. Property without a document of title—such as household goods, jewelry, and clothes—can be transferred simply by listing them on a trust schedule. Preparing these documents is vital, and is explained in detail in Chapter 11. But for right now, your concern is simply to make basic decisions regarding the property you want in the trusts and to write down how you'll list that property.

Many people instinctively think of their trust beneficiaries and property together: The antique dresser goes to Mary; the house will be divided between the kids, and so on. But to be thorough and sure you do the job right, I suggest that you separate these two key elements. Here, list your trust property. Then, in the next chapter, you'll learn about trust beneficiaries and name yours.

ADDING PROPERTY TO THE LIVING TRUST LATER

If you acquire valuable property in your name after you create your living trust, you can easily add it to the trust. Also, once you've set up the trust, if you're buying property you intend to keep for a while, you can simply acquire it in the name of the trustee(s) of your trust. Finally, if you mistakenly leave something out of your trust, you can add it later by amending your trust. (See Chapter 13.)

B. Property That Should Not Be Put in Your Living Trust

You don't automatically need to put everything you own into a living trust to save money on probate. Property that is of relatively low value (the amount depends on state law) may be exempt from probate or qualify for a streamlined probate procedure that's relatively fast and cheap. And in some states, at least some of the property left to a surviving spouse can probably be transferred without a full-blown probate court proceeding.

Generally, it's better not to include the following types of property in your trust:

- **Your personal checking account,** unless you want to pay your bills in the name of the trust. A checking account in the name of a trust can cause raised eyebrows—even refusal to accept the check—by people or institutions who wonder, "Why can't she write the check in her own name? What's this trust business?"

- **Property you buy or sell frequently.** If you don't expect to own the property at your death, there's no compelling reason to transfer it to your living trust. (Remember, the probate process you want to avoid doesn't happen until after your death.)

- **Automobiles.** Some insurance companies won't insure a vehicle owned by a trust. They worry that an unknown number of people could be entitled, under the terms of the trust, to drive the vehicle. Anyway, the value of many people's car or cars isn't so high that they need to worry about transferring them by living trust. Also, most state Departments of Motor Vehicles have special forms that conveniently allow cars to be registered in joint tenancy, a handy way to avoid probate for an auto. And five states, California, Connecticut, Kansas, Missouri, and Ohio, allow "transfer-on-death" vehicle registration, where you name, on your vehicle registration, the person who will receive the vehicle upon your death. No probate is necessary.

But if you own a valuable vehicle, or several, it can be worth your while to seek out an insurance company that will allow you to own and transfer them by living trust. Some insurance companies will insure a vehicle owned by a trust. Indeed, some insurance companies simply list the trust as an "additional insured," with no additional fee or premium.

NAMING YOUR AB LIVING TRUST AS BENEFICIARY OF YOUR RETIREMENT ACCOUNT

If you have substantial assets in an individual retirement account, you may want any funds remaining in that account when you die to help fund Trust A of your AB trust. You can legally do this. However, you need to remember that, except for a Roth IRA, an individual retirement account is a "wasting asset." Once you reach age 70 1/2, you must withdraw a certain percentage of your account each year. The withdrawal percentage is calculated on the basis of the combination of your life expectancy and that of your (oldest) beneficiary. So, if you live a long life, much of the funds in your account will have been withdrawn.

Still, you may understandably be concerned with what happens to your retirement account if you die prematurely, or if, for whatever reason, significant funds remain in the account at your death. You can leave these funds to your AB trust by naming your successor trustee as beneficiary of your account. IRS regulations no longer penalize you for doing this.

You should realize that if you have substantial funds remaining in a retirement account at your death, those funds will probably be withdrawn over a period of years by your successor trustee. If the funds were all withdrawn promptly after your death and placed in Trust A, all this money would be subject to income tax in one year. (Remember, except for Roth IRAs, you paid no income tax when you placed your money in the retirement account, and the IRS will get those income taxes whether you are alive or not.) Therefore, Trust A will likely receive portions of your retirement account funds over a period of years.

By contrast, if you name a living trust as your beneficiary, minimum withdrawals from your retirement account are based on the estimates of how long you and your oldest beneficiary will live. And "oldest beneficiary" includes all contingent beneficiaries, as well as direct ones. Further, if you have named any institution or charity as any type of beneficiary of your living trust, retirement account withdrawals are based solely on your own life expectancy. Finally, special IRS provisions that allow a surviving spouse various favorable rights over deceased spouse's retirement accounts do not apply if a living trust is a beneficiary, even if the surviving spouse is the only primary beneficiary of that trust.

There may be additional paperwork to complete to validly name your AB trust as beneficiary of your retirement plan. For example:

- Federal law requires that all funds in a 401(k) plan be left outright to a surviving spouse, unless that spouse has given a written waiver of that right.
- 401(k) and some other retirement plans must adopt an amendment allowing life expectancy, for withdrawal purposes, to be calculated on the basis of the plan owner and the oldest trust beneficiary. The IRS can supply you with a model amendment form.
- Retirement accounts purchased with community property are co-owned equally by both spouses. If you want all funds in such an account to go to your Trust A, you need a written declaration of gift from your spouse.

A thorough explanation of the applicable laws and rules can be found in *IRAs, 401(k)s & Other Retirement Plans: Taking Your Money Out*, by Twila Slesnick and John C. Suttle (Nolo).

- **Life insurance.** When you buy an insurance policy, you name beneficiaries to receive the proceeds of the policy outside of probate. However, if you have named a minor or young adult as the beneficiary of an insurance policy, you may want to change the beneficiary to your living trust or, more precisely, name the trustee as the beneficiary, as trustee of the child's trust of the living trust. This is covered in detail in Chapter 9, Section D.

- **Joint tenancy property.** Property held in joint tenancy does not go through probate, as is explained in Chapter 15, Section B. So generally there is no need to worry about transferring jointly owned property, including joint bank accounts, into your living trust. However, one possible reason for transferring jointly owned property to the trust is because you cannot name alternate beneficiaries for joint tenancy property. If all owners die simultaneously, each owner's share of the joint tenancy property passes under their will. While you could eliminate this remote possibility by transferring your share to your living trust, making the transfer requires a couple of paper steps that are at least a bit of a hassle (See Chapter 11, Section A.) Most people understandably don't bother with this level of contingency planning.

- **Individual retirement accounts.** Retirement accounts, such as IRAs, 401(k)s, and profit-sharing plans, should not be put in your trust. Indeed, for most individual retirement accounts, it's not legal to do so. You name a beneficiary or beneficiaries in these accounts to receive any money left in them at your death, without probate. While you could name your trust as beneficiary of these accounts, there's generally no reason to do so, unless you'll use an AB trust. If you are preparing an AB trust, consider whether you want to name that trust to receive funds left in the accounts when you die. (See the sidebar above.)

- **Pay-on-death bank accounts.** With these accounts, you name a beneficiary or beneficiaries to receive directly, without probate, all funds in the accounts when you die. (See Chapter 15, Section B.)

- **Community property with right of survivorship.** Alaska, Arizona, California, Nevada, and Wisconsin expressly authorize spouses to own community property in this manner. Thus, spouses in these states can retain the benefits of community property (see Section D, below) and simultaneously obtain the probate avoidance plus of joint tenancy.

- **Employee stock options.** Some businesses give, or allow employees to purchase, options to buy stock of the company for a set price. Often the company imposes restrictions or prohibitions on employee transfers of the options. Even if the company allows transfer to a living trust, complex IRS rules govern the exercise of this type of stock option and subsequent sale of the stock. Because of these rules, it is normally not a good idea to transfer employee stock options to your living trust. By contrast, you can transfer stock options bought on a recognized stock exchange—for instance, the right to buy 1,000 shares of Apple Computer for a set price. This contractual right may be transferred to your living trust by Notice of Assignment. (See Chapter 11, Section G.) Indeed, if you trade frequently in publicly traded options, you can open an option account in the trust's name.

If you decide you must transfer employee stock options to your trust. If you want to transfer employee stock options to your living trust, you'll need a lawyer who's up to date on the complex tax rules, including capital gains tax, that govern the transaction.

- **Contaminated real estate.** Do not transfer to your trust any real estate you know, or suspect, has been chemically polluted. (See Chapter 3, Section I.)

- **Income or principal from a trust.** If you are the beneficiary of an established trust and have the right to leave any of your interest in this trust to someone else, you cannot do that in your own living trust. The reason is that you cannot transfer title of the trust that benefits you into your own living trust, because you are not the owner of the trust. And as I've emphasized, your trust cannot give away what it doesn't technically own. You can leave your rights to this type of trust income property by your will. (See Chapter 16.)

C. Property You Can Put in Your Living Trust

Whatever type of trust you create with this book, one primary goal is avoiding probate fees. As a general rule, the more an item is worth, the more it will cost to probate it. That means you should transfer at least your most valuable property items to your living trust—or use some other probate-avoidance device to leave them at your death. Think about including:

- houses and other real estate
- small business interests, including stock in closely held corporations
- money market accounts
- other financial accounts
- stocks, bonds, and other security accounts held by brokers
- royalties, patents, and copyrights
- valuable jewelry, antiques, furs, and furniture
- precious metals
- valuable works of art
- valuable collections of stamps, coins, or other objects.

Property on which you owe money. Some items of property are commonly not owned free and clear. The most obvious example is a house with a mortgage. When you use your living trust to leave that house to a beneficiary, he or she will receive it subject to the mortgage. Similarly, if you give someone a car subject to a loan and lien, those debts go with the car.

If you have sufficient assets, it's legally possible to use your trust to provide that these debts be paid off. That way, the beneficiary receives a house, car, or other previously debt-encumbered property free and clear. See a lawyer to arrange this.

1. Real Estate

The most valuable thing most people own is their real estate: their house, condominium, or land. Other types of real estate include property such as a boat marina dock space or a timeshare interest in a piece of property, like a vacation house used twice a year. You can save your family substantial probate costs by transferring your real estate through a living trust.

If you own real estate in joint tenancy or tenancy by the entirety, however, you've already arranged to avoid probate for that property, so there's much less reason to transfer it to a living trust. (See Chapter 15, Section B.) One advantage of owning real estate in a living trust is that, in a living trust, you can provide for who will receive the real estate in the event of simultaneous death—both owners die at the same time. You cannot provide for this with real estate owned in joint tenancy. Another reason for transferring joint tenancy real estate into a living trust is if you use an AB living trust and want the real estate to be part of the Trust A property.

IF YOU'RE NOT SURE HOW YOU HOLD TITLE

If you own real estate with someone else but aren't sure how the title is held, look at the deed. It should say how title is held:

- in joint tenancy (sometimes abbreviated JT or JTWROS, for "joint tenancy with right of survivorship")
- tenancy in common
- community property (in community property states); in a community property state, if the deed says the property is owned "as husband and wife," that means community property
- community property with right of survivorship
- tenancy by the entirety.

If you own real estate with someone else, you can transfer just your interest in it to your living trust.

Co-op apartments. If you own shares in a co-op corporation that owns your apartment, you'll have to transfer your shares to your living trust. You may run into difficulties with the corporation; some are reluctant to let a trust, even a revocable living trust completely controlled by the grantor, own shares. Check the co-op corporation's laws and rules, then do some good lobbying, if necessary.

Retirement co-ops. Occasionally, an unfortunate technicality is used to deny transfer to a living trust. For instance, some co-op retirement units restrict ownership to people over a certain age, say 65 or 70. In a few instances, co-op boards have interpreted these rules to prohibit transfer to a trustee of a living trust, claiming that the trust doesn't have an age. While correct, this should be irrelevant. As you know by now, it is not the trust that is the technical owner, but the trustee of the trust. Here, that's the grantor, the person over 65 or 70 who lives in the co-op. If the IRS can understand that the living trust has no independent legal existence as long as the person who created it is alive, co-op officials should be able to comprehend that, too.

Mobile homes. The rules on when an attached mobile home becomes "real estate" vary in different states. If this matters to you, see a lawyer or look up your state's law in the law library. (Legal research is discussed in Chapter 17, Section D.)

Timeshares. A timeshare is usually an interest in a vacation property, often a condominium. The timeshare gives the owner the exclusive right to stay in the property for specific time periods. Technically, ownership of a timeshare may be held by deed, contract, or lease. If the ownership is by deed, a new deed needs to be prepared transferring the interest to your trust. (See Chapter 11, Section E.) If ownership of the timeshare is held by contract or lease, that contract or lease should be assigned to the trust.

Leases on real estate. If you're the owner of a lease on real estate (you've leased a store for five years, say, and the lease has two years to run), that lease is generally considered an interest in real estate. You can transfer it to your living trust if you wish.

HOMEOWNER'S INSURANCE

Don't bother notifying your homeowner's insurance company that you have placed your home in your living trust. As I've explained, as long as you live, you personally are, for all real world purposes including the IRS and homestead rights, the owner of your home. Your homeowner's policy will still cover your home. But if you tell your insurance company about the transfer, they might raise problems and questions that you'll have to waste time answering. Don't risk the hassles.

---

2. Small Business Interests

The delay, expense, and court intrusion of probate can be especially detrimental to an ongoing small business. Using your living trust to transfer business interests to beneficiaries quickly after your death is almost essential if you want the beneficiaries to be able to keep the business running, or even to be able to sell it for a fair price.

Controlling management of a business. If you want to impose controls on the long-term management of your business, a revocable living trust is not the right device. See an estate planning lawyer to draft a different kind of trust, with provisions tailored to your situation.

Different kinds of business organizations present different issues when you want to transfer your interest to your living trust.

Sole proprietorships. If you operate your business as a sole proprietorship, with all business assets held in your own name, you can simply transfer your business property to your living trust as you would any other property. You should also list the business's name itself on a trust schedule; that transfers the customer goodwill associated with the name.

Partnership interests. If you operate your business as a partnership with other people, you can probably transfer your partnership share to your living trust. If there is a partnership certificate, it must be changed to show the trust as owner of your share.

Some partnership agreements require the people who inherit a deceased partner's share of the business to sell that share to the other partners if they want it. But that happens after death, so it shouldn't affect your ability to transfer the property through a living trust.

It's not common, but a partnership agreement may limit or forbid transfers to a living trust. If yours does, you and your partners may want to see a lawyer before you make any changes. If the other partners won't agree to revise your partnership agreement to allow this transfer, you're stuck.

Solely owned corporations. If you own all the stock of a corporation, you should have no difficulty transferring it to your living trust. All you need do is prepare the appropriate corporate papers—for example, Notice of Meeting of Shareholders, and Resolution of Shareholders (there's only one, remember)—authorizing the transfer of the shares of stock to the living trust. The precise corporate paperwork needed depends on what's required by your articles of incorporation and the bylaws of your corporation.

Closely held corporations, including limited liability companies (LLCs). A closely held corporation is a corporation that doesn't sell shares to the public. A limited liability company is akin to the closely held corporation, except that it is treated as a partnership for tax purposes. All shares or ownership interests are owned by a few people who are usually actively involved in running the business. Normally, you can use a living trust to transfer your interest in an LLC or shares in a closely held corporation by listing the interest or stock in the trust document. With the stock, the certificates must be reissued in the trustee's name.

You'll want to check the corporation's bylaws and articles of incorporation to be sure that if you transfer the shares to a living trust, you will still have voting rights in your capacity as trustee of the living trust; usually, this is not a problem. If it is, you and the other shareholders should be able to amend the corporation's bylaws to allow it.

There may, however, be legal restrictions on your freedom to transfer your shares to a living trust. Check the corporation's bylaws and articles of incorporation, as well as any separate shareholders' agreements or, for LLCs, the operating agreement.

One fairly common rule is that surviving shareholders or LLC owners have the right to buy the shares of a deceased shareholder or owner. In that case, you can still use a living trust to transfer the shares or LLC interest, but the people who inherit them may have to sell them to the other shareholders or owners.

Subchapter S or professional corporations. Special IRS rules apply if you want to transfer shares in a Subchapter S corporation to a living trust. The trust must contain special provisions that make it a "Qualified Subchapter S Trust" under the IRS regulations. You must see a lawyer to draft the appropriate provisions for your trust. Also see a lawyer if your business is a professional corporation, such as one for lawyers, doctors, or architects.

3. Money Market and Bank Accounts

Money market funds can be readily transferred into your trust. Often, these money market funds contain substantial amounts of cash, so it's wise to place them in your living trust.

It's not difficult to hold bank accounts or credit union accounts (aside from your personal checking account) in your living trust. But you may well decide that you don't need to, because there's another easy way to avoid probate of the funds. In what's called a "pay-on-death" account (or Totten Trust, or sometimes a revocable trust account), you can designate a beneficiary for the funds in a bank account. The beneficiary receives whatever is in your account at your death, without probate.

A living trust, however, offers one advantage that most pay-on-death arrangements do not: If you transfer an account to a living trust, you can always name an alternate beneficiary to receive the account if your first choice as beneficiary isn't alive at your death. The lack of an alternate may not be a problem if you use a pay-on-death account and name more than one beneficiary to inherit the funds, however; if one of the beneficiaries isn't alive, the other(s) will inherit the money.

CERTIFICATES OF DEPOSIT

Do not put existing CDs in your living trust. For even technical ownership of a CD to change, it must mature. A CD can be redeemed early only by paying a penalty. If you decide that you want to put an existing CD into your living trust, wait until it matures, and then promptly change ownership of the CD when you roll it over. You can simply purchase new CDs in the trust (trustee's) name.

---

4. Stocks and Securities

Stocks and stock accounts are commonly held by living trusts. Brokerage companies are familiar with living trusts; you can readily transfer an existing stock brokerage account into your living trust, or create a new trust account. Once your account is in your trust's name (technically, in your name as trustee for your trust) all stocks in that account become owned by the trust, so you can trade as often as you want without additional trust paper work.

In your living trust, you can leave your brokerage accounts however you desire—all to one person, divided by percentage between several people, or specific stocks to specific people.

If you have personal possession of individual stock certificates, you need to get new certificates issued, listing the new owner as trustee of your trust. (See Chapter 11, Section G.)

5. Cash

It's common for people to want to leave cash to beneficiaries—for example, to leave $5,000 to a relative, friend, or charity. However, there's no way to transfer cash to a living trust—you can't put a stack of dollar bills into a document. Nor does listing $5,000 on a trust schedule work by itself. "Where is this $5,000?" the successor trustee would ask.

You can, however, easily transfer ownership of a cash account—a savings account, money market account, or certificate of deposit, for example—to your living trust. (Don't transfer a pay-on-death account, since the beneficiary for it is already named.) You can then name a beneficiary to receive the contents of the account or any specified sum from it. So if you want to leave $5,000 to cousin Fred, you can put this amount in a bank or money market account, transfer it to your living trust, and name Fred, in the trust document, as the beneficiary. Or you could put an account with a larger amount in your trust, leave $5,000 from it to Fred and the balance to another beneficiary.

Example

Michael would like to leave some modest cash gifts to his two grown nephews, Warren and Brian, whom he's always been fond of. He puts $25,000 into a money market account and then transfers the account into his living trust. In his trust document, he names Warren and Brian as beneficiaries of $5,000 each from that, with whatever is left to go to Michael's wife. After Michael's death, the two nephews will each receive $5,000 from the trust.

If you don't want to set up an account to leave a modest amount of cash to a beneficiary, think about buying a savings bond and leaving it to the beneficiary.

6. U.S. Treasury Notes or Bonds

You can place U.S. Treasury notes or bonds—such as series EE, H, or HH bonds—in your living trust. There are no adverse tax consequences. The federal government requires that a specific form be used to make the transfer into the trust. (See Chapter 11, Section G.)

7. Royalties, Copyrights, and Patents

You can transfer your right to future royalties, or copyrights and patents you own, to your living trust. Simply list the royalty, copyright, or patent in your trust property schedule and then transfer your interest in a copyright, patent, or royalty, to the trust, using the proper legal form. (Instructions are in Chapter 11, Sections K, L, and M.)

Oil, gas, or mineral interests. If you want to transfer one or more of these interests to your living trust, see a lawyer. Complicated matters, such as possible assignment of leases or handling depletion allowances, can arise that require profession attention.

8. Other Valuable Property

You need special forms to transfer some types of valuable property to your trust. Because all airplanes must be registered with the FAA, you transfer an airplane to your trust by complying with appropriate FAA regulations and forms. Similarly, for large boats registered with the Coast Guard, you need to complete that agency's forms. And for powerboats registered with a state agency, you need the appropriate state form. Less valuable boats—unregistered ones, like a rowboat or canoe—do not have documents of title and can simply be assigned to your trust. (See Chapter 11, Section H.)

Many other types of valuable property can also be placed in your trust, including valuable jewelry, antiques, furs, furniture, precious metals, works of art, and collectibles—from Depression china to antique soldiers to old dolls to stamps to whatever objects people will pay money for.

The common denominator of all these types of property is that none of them has any formal ownership papers, like a deed for real estate. Some may have papers authenticating them, but these are not documents of title, and don't need to be changed. So you can transfer any of these valuables to your trust simply by listing them on the trust schedule. You may also want to prepare an "assignment" form for this property, as is explained in Chapter 11, Section A.

D. Marital Property Laws

If you are married, you need to know what property is owned by each spouse separately, and what property is held in shared ownership, to properly complete your trust. Whether you make separate trusts (because most or all of each spouse's property is owned separately) or a shared trust (either the basic shared trust or a living trust with marital life estate), you need to clarify which spouse owns what to know which schedule—basically "ours," "his," and "hers"—to list the property on. Each spouse controls, in the trust document, who will inherit his or her own trust property.

To figure out who owns what, you need to know a little about the law of the state where you live (and of any other state in which you own property) regarding marital property. Marital property laws can be divided into two basic groups: community property states and common law states.

1. Community Property States

Alaska (if spouses prepare a written community property agreement)

Arizona	Nevada	Washington
California	New Mexico	Wisconsin
Idaho	Texas	

SEPARATE PROPERTY

In these states, the general rule is that spouses own everything acquired during the marriage 50-50, unless the spouses agree otherwise. It doesn't matter whose name is on the title slip.

There are a few important exceptions to the general rule. Property acquired before marriage is not community property; it is the separate property of that spouse. Likewise, property given to one spouse, by gift or inheritance, is separate property.

COMMUNITY PROPERTY BASICS

Community property includes:
- money either spouse earns during marriage
- things bought with that money, and
- separate property that has become so mixed (commingled) with community property that it can't be identified.

Separate property includes:
- property owned by one spouse before marriage
- property given to just one spouse, and
- property inherited by just one spouse.

Married couples don't have to accept these rules. They can sign a written agreement that makes some or all community property the separate property of one spouse or have separate property become community property.

Typically, most property owned by spouses is community property, especially if they have been married for a number of years. For example, if while married you bought real estate with money you earned during marriage, your spouse legally owns a half interest in it, unless you both signed an agreement keeping it separate.

Sometimes it's not obvious who owns what. For example, are life insurance proceeds shared property or the separate property of the deceased spouse? The answer depends on the source of the funds used to pay for the insurance and the intention of the couple. If the insurance was paid for with shared marital property, the proceeds are co-owned. Similarly, if the couple agreed (in writing) that the proceeds were shared property, no matter who paid for them, that agreement controls. But if the policy was paid for from the separate property of the deceased, with no agreement that it was a shared ownership policy, the proceeds are the separate property of the deceased.

husband

SEPARATE PROPERTY

Marital property agreements. If you and your spouse have complex property holdings, and there's any question whether any of your property is community or separate, it's wise to prepare a written marital property agreement, defining the nature of each major item of your property. Of course, to prepare the document, you two have to agree how your property should be classified. If you need help with that, see a lawyer or an accountant.

If you move from a common law state to California, Idaho, or Washington, some of your property may be reclassified as community property. In these states, the rule is that property acquired by a couple during marriage, no matter who owned it in a common law state, is treated as community property, owned equally by each spouse, if it would have been community property had the couple acquired it in one of these states. The legal term for such property is "quasi-community property." This means each spouse owns half of this property and can leave only that

share at death. Wisconsin has a similar concept, called "deferred marital property." When one spouse dies, the survivor is entitled to half the value of deferred marital property owned by both spouses.

Example

Cora and Eric Gustafson live in Florida, a common law state. Cora buys some stocks with money she earned while married. She owns the stocks in her own name and is free to leave them by will or trust to whomever she pleases, subject to state law on the inheritance rights of spouses.

Later, Cora and Eric move to California. Because the stocks, had they been bought in California, would have been Cora and Eric's community property, they are now "quasi-community property." At death or divorce, the stocks will be treated as community property, owned 50-50 by each spouse. Cora now owns only half and can leave only half in her trust or will.

If you move from a community property state to a common law state, your ownership rights in the property already acquired stay the same. The new state's law applies only to property acquired in the new state.

Separate property may, however, turn into community property if it is mixed ("commingled") with community property. For example, if you deposit separate property funds into a joint bank account and then make more deposits and withdrawals, making it impossible to tell what part of the account is separate money, it's all considered community property.

Example

Roberto and Celia live in Nevada, a community property state. They have been married for 20 years. Except for some bonds that Celia inherited from her parents, virtually all their valuable property—house, stocks, car—is owned together. The money they brought to the marriage in separate bank accounts has long since been mixed with community property, making it community property too.

In community property states, there are restrictions on one spouse's freedom to transfer community property. Especially in the case of real estate, the consent of both spouses is necessary for either to sell or give away his or her half-interest in the property. Each spouse can, however, leave his or her half-interest in the property through a will or living trust.

If you live in a community property state, and you and your spouse create a living trust together, property you transfer to the trust will stay community property, even though it is technically owned by the living trust. Separately owned property (property of only one spouse) will also remain separate property. That means that community property transferred to a living trust is still eligible for the favorable tax treatment given community property at one spouse's death. (Both halves of community property left to the surviving spouse get a "stepped-up basis" for income tax purposes; see Chapter 15.)

It also means that if either spouse revokes the living trust, ownership of the property will go back to the spouses as it was before the property was transferred to the living trust. Community property goes back to both spouses equally, and separate property goes to the spouse who owned it before ownership was transferred to the trust.

2. Common Law Property States

Alabama	Kentucky	North Dakota
Alaska	Maine	Ohio
Arkansas	Maryland	Oklahoma
Colorado	Massachusetts	Oregon
Connecticut	Michigan	Pennsylvania
Delaware	Minnesota	Rhode Island
District of Columbia	Mississippi	South Carolina
Florida	Missouri	South Dakota
Georgia	Montana	Tennessee
Hawaii	Nebraska	Utah
Illinois	New Hampshire	Vermont
Indiana	New Jersey	Virginia
Iowa	New York	West Virginia
Kansas	North Carolina	Wyoming

In a noncommunity property state, it's usually fairly easy for spouses to keep track of who owns what. The spouse whose name is on the title document—for example, the deed, brokerage account paper or title slip—owns it. In these states, if the property doesn't have a title document, it belongs to the spouse who paid for it or received it as a gift. It's possible, though, that if there were a dispute about ownership, a judge could determine,

based on the circumstances, that a spouse whose name is not on the title document might own an interest in the property.

It's increasingly common for couples, especially if they are older and have children from a prior marriage, to sign an agreement (before or during the marriage) to own property separately. Or they may not make a formal agreement, but carefully avoid mixing their property together.

If you want to co-own property equally, you can do that simply by taking title to property in both names, for new property, or preparing a new ownership deed for previously owned property, listing the new owners as both of you. You should also state you own the property "equally, as tenants in common," if you intend to place the property in your living trusts. (For married couples, no state taxes will be assessed because of any transfer of title, because any transfer of property between spouses is free of tax.)

In common law states, see a lawyer if you don't want to leave at least half of your living trust property to your spouse. This matter is discussed further in Chapter 8, Section H.

E. Completing the Property Worksheet

On the worksheet in this section, you can list your property. This groundwork should make preparing your actual trust document easier. But completing it is not mandatory; use it if you think it will help you.

Even if you plan to leave everything to your spouse or children, you need to describe your property sufficiently on a trust schedule so that it is readily identifiable. In other words, every item (or group of items, in some circumstances) must be specifically described and listed as part of the trust document. (Examples are given in Chapter 10.) Also, you can use the worksheet to estimate your net worth to see if you are near the federal estate tax threshold.

Remember, this worksheet is purely for your convenience. It can be as messy or as neat as you care to make it. Pencil is recommended (unless you're the type who does the *New York Times* crossword puzzle in ink).

1. Section I: Assets

Column 1—Property Description

Here you write out what you own. How specific you should be depends in part on how you plan to leave your property (who your beneficiaries are), which you'll pin down in Chapter 8, "Choosing Your Beneficiaries." For example, if you're going to leave all your books to your daughter, there's no need to list them individually. But if you own several rare first editions, which you'll leave to separate beneficiaries, list each book.

Column 2—Net Value of Your Ownership

In Column 2, estimate the net value of each item listed. Net value means your equity in your share of the property—the market value of your share, less your share of any debts on that share, such as a mortgage on a house or the loan amount due on a car.

If you're a couple, "your share" means the value of both of your interests. For estate tax purposes, it's the value of what you both own that really counts.

Obviously, listing net values for your property means making estimates. That's fine; there's no need to burden yourself with seeking precise figures. After all, your death taxes, if any, will be based on the net value of your property when you die, not its current worth. For example, if you think the net worth of your house, after you subtract the mortgage, is about $200,000, your car $5,000, and your stamp collection would fetch $2,000 if you put an ad in a philatelist's journal, use those numbers.

If you own property with someone other than a spouse or mate, simply estimate the worth of your share of that property.

Example

Paul owns a house with a market value of $250,000 as a tenant in common with his sister Ava; each owns half. Paul computes the net value of his share by first subtracting the amount of mortgages, liens, and past due taxes from the market value to arrive at the total equity in the property. There's a $100,000 mortgage and a $10,000 lien against the property. The total equity, then, is $250,000 minus $110,000, or $140,000. The net worth of Paul's half of the property is $70,000.

With some common sense, you can probably safely make sensible estimates yourself. Only with more complex types of property, such as business interests, might you want expert help.

Example

Stacey is sole owner of the Maltese Falcon Restaurant, a successful business she has run for 20 years. She has only a vague notion of its market value since she has never been interested in selling it. Making a reasonable estimate of the worth of the business is difficult, since the market value of her restaurant includes the intangible of "good will." Stacey talks to an accountant to help her arrive at a sensible estimate of the worth of the restaurant.

Column 3—Who Owns It

Because you need to identify which property is shared and which is separate, indicate that here. Use whatever symbols you want to identify the ownership—for example, O (ours); H (Husband); W (Wife) or S (shared); M (Mary); N (Neil).

Column 4—Transfer to Trust

In Column 4, indicate whether or not you want to transfer this item of property to the trust. For each item you'll put in the trust, put a "T."

2. Section II: Liabilities

Here, list any liabilities (debts) you haven't already taken into account in Section I. For example, list any significant personal debts—the $10,000 loan from a friend or $5,000 unsecured advance on a line of credit. Also list all other liabilities, such as tax liens or court judgments, and add up all these liabilities.

3. Section III: Net Worth

Here's where you calculate your net worth by subtracting your total liabilities (Section II.D) from the total net value of your assets (Section I.E).

Property Worksheet

I. ASSETS

Description of Your Property	Net Value of Your Ownership	Who Owns It	Transfer to Trust?

A. Liquid Assets

1. cash (dividends, etc.)

_____ _____ _____ _____
_____ _____ _____ _____
_____ _____ _____ _____
_____ _____ _____ _____

2. savings accounts

_____ _____ _____ _____
_____ _____ _____ _____
_____ _____ _____ _____
_____ _____ _____ _____

3. checking accounts

_____ _____ _____ _____
_____ _____ _____ _____
_____ _____ _____ _____

4. money market accounts

_____ _____ _____ _____
_____ _____ _____ _____
_____ _____ _____ _____

5. certificates of deposit

_____ _____ _____ _____
_____ _____ _____ _____

6. treasury bills or notes

_____ _____ _____ _____
_____ _____ _____ _____
_____ _____ _____ _____

Description of Your Property	Net Value of Your Ownership	Who Owns It	Transfer to Trust?

B. Other Personal Property
  (all your property except liquid assets, business interests, and real estate)

1. listed (private corporation) stocks and bonds

_____ _____ _____ _____
_____ _____ _____ _____
_____ _____ _____ _____
_____ _____ _____ _____

2. unlisted stocks and bonds

_____ _____ _____ _____
_____ _____ _____ _____
_____ _____ _____ _____
_____ _____ _____ _____

3. government bonds and securities

_____ _____ _____ _____
_____ _____ _____ _____
_____ _____ _____ _____
_____ _____ _____ _____

4. automobiles and other vehicles, including
    planes, boats, and recreational vehicles

_____ _____ _____ _____
_____ _____ _____ _____
_____ _____ _____ _____
_____ _____ _____ _____

5. precious metals

_____ _____ _____ _____
_____ _____ _____ _____
_____ _____ _____ _____

6. household goods

_____ _____ _____ _____
_____ _____ _____ _____
_____ _____ _____ _____
_____ _____ _____ _____

7. clothing

_____ _____ _____ _____
_____ _____ _____ _____
_____ _____ _____ _____

Description of Your Property	Net Value of Your Ownership	Who Owns It	Transfer to Trust?
8. jewelry and furs			
9. artworks, collectibles, and antiques			
10. tools and equipment			
11. valuable livestock/animals			
12. life insurance proceeds			
13. money owed you (personal loans, etc.)			
14. retirement accounts, including IRAs, 401(k)s, profit-sharing plans			
15. other valuable personal property			

Description of Your Property	Net Value of Your Ownership	Who Owns It	Transfer to Trust?

C. Miscellaneous Receivables
   (mortgages, deeds of trust, or promissory notes held by you; any rents due from income property owned by you; and any payments due for professional or personal services or property sold by you that are not fully paid by the purchaser)

D. Real Estate

1. address

2. address

3. address

4. address

5. address

E. Total Net Value of Your Assets $_____

II. LIABILITIES

To Whom Debt Is Owed   Amount

A. Personal Property Debts

　　1.　personal loans (banks, major credit cards, etc.)

_____　　　_____

_____　　　_____

_____　　　_____

_____　　　_____

_____　　　_____

_____　　　_____

_____　　　_____

　　2.　other personal debts

_____　　　_____

_____　　　_____

_____　　　_____

_____　　　_____

_____　　　_____

_____　　　_____

_____　　　_____

B. Taxes (include only taxes past and currently due;
do not include taxes due in the future or estimated estate taxes)

_____　　　_____

_____　　　_____

_____　　　_____

_____　　　_____

_____　　　_____

C. Any Other Liabilities (legal judgments, accrued child support, etc.)　　　_____

_____

_____

_____

D. Total Liabilities (excluding those liabilities already deducted in Section I)　　　$_____

III. NET WORTH (Total Net Value of Your Assets, from Section I.E above,
minus Total Liabilities, from Section II.D above)　　　$_____

■

chapter 7

TRUSTEES

*T*o be legally valid, your living trust must have a trustee—someone to manage the property in the trust. Indeed, as I've said, the trust property is held in the trustee's name. When you create a trust from this book, you are the initial trustee. If you create a basic shared living trust or AB trust, you and your spouse are cotrustees.

When the initial trustee, or both trustees, have died, the "successor trustee" takes over. This person is responsible for transferring trust property to the beneficiaries and handling any other matters required by the trust—such as managing a child's trust or filing federal or state estate tax returns. Technically, the executor of your will is responsible for filing tax returns, but normally, the executor and successor trustee are the same person. In any case, the executor and successor trustee will have to work together.

For many people, the decision of who to name as successor trustee is clear, but for others, complexities and uncertainties can arise.

A. The Initial Trustee

A key to how a living trust works is that you, or you and your spouse, are the initial trustees. Grasping this point is essential to understanding what a living trust is—a device that allows you to absolutely control your own property while you are alive, and at the same time avoid probate of the property after you die.

Naming someone else as initial trustee. If you want to name someone besides yourself to be your initial trustee because you don't want to, or cannot, continue to manage your own assets, see a lawyer; don't use the trust forms in this book. When you make somebody else your initial trustee, you create a more complicated trust, often necessitating much more detailed controls on the trustee's powers to act. In addition, under IRS rules, if you aren't the trustee of your own living trust, separate trust records must be maintained, and a fiduciary trust tax return (Form 1041) filed each year.

1. Your Responsibilities as Trustee

You won't have any special duties as trustee of your trust. As a day-to-day, practical matter, it makes no difference that you now manage your property as trustee, rather than in your own name. You do not need to file a separate income tax return for the living trust. As long as you are trustee, any income the trust property generates must be reported on your personal income tax return, as if the trust did not exist. (IRS Reg. § 1.671-4.) Likewise, you don't have to obtain a trust taxpayer ID number or keep separate trust records.

As explained in Chapter 3, you have the same freedom to sell, mortgage, or give away trust property as you did before you put that property into the living trust. (Thus, one spouse does not have rights over the other spouse's separate property.) Normally, the only difference is that you must now sign documents in your capacity as trustee. It's that easy.

Example

Celeste and Angelo want to sell a piece of land that is owned in the name of their living trust. They prepare a deed transferring ownership of the land from the trustees of the trust to the new owner. They sign the deed as "Celeste Tornetti and Angelo Tornetti, trustees of the Celeste Tornetti and Angelo Tornetti Living Trust dated February 4, 2002."

If you make a shared living trust (either a basic shared trust or an AB trust), it's important to realize that once shared property belongs to the trust, either trustee (spouse) has authority over it. Legally, either spouse can sell or give away any of the shared trust property. In practice, however, both spouses will probably have to consent (in writing) to transfer shared real estate out of the living trust. Especially in community property states, buyers and title insurance companies usually insist on both spouses' signatures on transfer documents.

Naming only one spouse as trustee. If you want only one spouse to be the original trustee of a basic shared living trust or an AB trust, there's an unusual—and unequal—distribution of authority over shared property, and you should see a lawyer.

2. Naming a Cotrustee

If you think you'll want or need someone else to manage your trust property for you, but don't want the hassles of having a separate trustee, you can consider naming yourself and another person to both be the initial trustees of your trust. Both of you would have authority to act on the trust's behalf. No fiduciary trust tax return is required, since *one* of the trustees is the original grantor.

Example

Beatrice is in her 80s. She doesn't want to abandon control over her property but has difficulty managing things—keeping track of bills and payments, for example. So she creates a living trust, naming herself and her daughter Polly as initial cotrustees. Either trustee can act for the trust. Because Beatrice is one of the initial trustees, she does not have to keep separate records or file a trust tax return. And as a practical matter, Polly can handle most trust transactions on her own.

Get help if you want initial cotrustees. If you want to have a cotrustee to serve with you, it's best to see a lawyer, so the authority of the trustees is clearly defined and specifically geared to your situation. Don't rely on the forms in this book.

B. The Trustee After One Spouse's Death or Incapacity

If you create a basic shared living trust or an AB trust, when one spouse dies or becomes incapacitated and unable to manage his or her affairs, the other becomes sole trustee.

Using the trust forms in this book, a spouse's physical or mental incapacity must be certified in writing by a physician. If that occurs, the other spouse, as sole trustee, takes over management of both spouses' trust property. That's the extent of his or her authority; he or she has no power over property of the incapacitated spouse not owned by the living trust, and no authority to make health care decisions for the incapacitated spouse. For this reason, it's also wise for each spouse to create documents called durable powers of attorney and health care directives, giving the other spouse authority to manage property not owned in the name of the trust and to make health care decisions for an incapacitated spouse. (See Chapter 15.)

The duties of a surviving spouse as trustee are summarized below. They are discussed in more detail in Chapters 4 and 5.

THE SURVIVING SPOUSE'S TRUSTEE DUTIES

With a basic shared trust:
- The surviving spouse, as trustee, is responsible for distributing the trust property of the deceased spouse as the trust document directs. Trust property left by the deceased spouse to the surviving spouse does not require any actual distribution, since the trust form specifies that such property remains in the revocable living trust. So no further steps need to be taken to legally transfer this property to the surviving spouse.
- The surviving spouse manages, as sole trustee, the ongoing revocable trust that contains his or her property, including trust property inherited from the deceased spouse.

With an AB trust:
- The surviving spouse divides the living trust property between the "A" trust, containing the deceased spouse's property, and the "B," or surviving spouse's, trust.
- The surviving spouse distributes any specific gifts made by the deceased spouse.
- The surviving spouse leaves all remaining property of the deceased spouse in the "A" trust.
- As trustee, the surviving spouse legally establishes and manages the "A" trust (obtains a federal taxpayer ID number, keeps trust records, etc.).
- The surviving spouse manages the "B" trust, as an ongoing revocable trust that contains his or her property.

With either type of trust, the surviving spouse may have long-term duties if the trust document creates a child's trust for trust property inherited by a young beneficiary, since the surviving spouse may have to manage this property for many years. (See Chapter 9, Section D.)

C. The Successor Trustee

Your trust document must name a successor trustee. The successor trustee takes over after you have died, or, for a basic shared trust or an AB trust, after both members of the couple have died. The successor trustee also takes over if you, or both you and your spouse, become incapacitated and are unable to manage the trust property.

Incapacity means the inability to manage your affairs. The trust forms in this book require that incapacity be documented in writing by a physician before the successor trustee can take over management of the trust property. For a basic shared trust or AB trust, the successor trustee has no authority to act if one spouse is alive and capable of managing trust property.

Picking your successor trustee is an important decision. Not only must you pick someone you trust who can do the job and is willing to do it, you also probably don't want to ruffle any family feathers when making your choice. You can name successor cotrustees, if this fits your needs.

When you decide on your successor trustee, your job isn't done. You should also name an alternate successor trustee, in case the successor trustee dies before you do or for any other reason can't serve. If you named two or more successor trustees, the alternate won't become trustee unless none of your original choices can serve.

1. The Job of the Successor Trustee

Obviously, when you choose your successor trustee, it helps for you both to understand what he or she will need to do. The primary job of the successor trustee is to turn trust property over to the beneficiaries you named in the trust document. This is normally not difficult if the property and beneficiaries are clearly identified. Still, some effort is required.

Usually, the successor trustee obtains several certified copies of the death certificate of the grantor. Then she presents a copy of the death certificate and a copy of the living trust document, along with proof of her own identity, to financial institutions, brokers, and other organizations that have possession of the trust assets. They will then release the property to the beneficiary. If any documents of title (ownership) must be prepared to transfer trust property to the beneficiaries, the successor trustee prepares them. For example, to transfer real estate owned by a living trust to the beneficiaries after the death

of the grantor, the successor trustee prepares, signs, and records (in the local land records office) a deed from herself, as trustee of the living trust, to the specified beneficiaries. No court or agency approval is required.

What happens if an institution won't cooperate with the successor trustee? Happily, such problems are unlikely. Institutions that deal with financial assets—from title companies to county land records offices to stock brokers—are familiar with living trusts and how they work.

NO GOVERNMENT FILING REQUIRED

A successor trustee who takes over because the original grantor(s) have died doesn't need to file any documents to establish his or her authority with any court or governmental agency. Of course, if a trust is ongoing, such as an AB trust or child's trust, the successor trustee must contact the IRS and maintain proper tax records.

It's even easier for the trustee to distribute trust assets that don't have documents of title—household furnishings, jewelry, heirlooms, collectibles—to the appropriate beneficiaries. The trustee just turns the property over to the beneficiaries.

When all beneficiaries have received the trust property left to them in the trust document, the successor trustee's job is over, and the trust ends.

In some situations, additional tasks may be required of the successor trustee.

- **Managing trust property if the trust grantor or grantors become incapacitated.** With all Nolo living trusts, if the grantor (or grantors) become incapacitated and can no longer manage the trust property, the successor trustee manages the trust until the grantor dies or regains capacity. The term "incapacity" is not defined in the trust document. In common-sense terms, it means that the grantor has become mentally or physically unable to handle his or her financial affairs. In our society, doctors normally determine whether someone has become incapacitated. If the determination is disputed, a court must resolve the matter.

With Nolo's marital trusts, either a shared trust or an AB trust, the successor trustee could wind up managing both spouses' trusts if both spouses are alive but incapacitated. Further, with an AB trust, if one spouse has died, the successor trustee could be called upon to manage two trusts—Trust A of the deceased spouse and Trust B of the surviving, incapacitated spouse.

When a successor trustee takes over for an incapacitated grantor, the job is basically financial. The successor trustee must become (rapidly) familiar with the grantor's financial resources and needs and handle all money matters and problems as they arise.

- **Preparing and filing death tax returns.** If a death tax return (state, federal, or both) must be filed after a grantor's death, and death taxes paid, the successor trustee is responsible for these tasks. Also, a final income tax return must be filed for the deceased grantor. The executor you name in your back-up will (see Chapter 16) shares legal responsibility for filing these tax returns. Usually, the same person is appointed as the successor trustee and executor.

- **Managing children's trusts.** The trust forms in this book allow you to leave trust property to young beneficiaries (under 35 when you die) in simple children's trusts. (See Chapter 9, Section D.) If you die before any child reaches the age you've specified, your successor trustee will manage trust property left for the benefit of that child until she reaches that age. Thus, the successor trustee can have ongoing management responsibilities for a child's trust. Annual trust income tax returns are required for each operational child's trust, and are the responsibility of the successor trustee.

- **Amend an AB trust if both spouses are incapacitated.** If— or when—Congress revises the estate tax law during the next few years, it could be desirable to amend an existing AB trust to take best advantage of the new law. (See Chapter 4, Section E.) If both spouses are alive but incapacitated when a new law takes effect, it could be very important to the trust's final beneficiaries that the successor trustee be allowed to amend the trust. The AB trust form in this book provides that the successor trustee can amend the trust to take best advantage of the current estate tax law. The successor trustee has this power only if both spouses are incapacitated when the need arises. With your AB trust, you do not have to grant your successor this power; you can eliminate the provision if you want to. (See Chapter 10, Section D, Step 5A.).

2. The Successor Trustee's Authority

The trust forms in this book spell out the specific powers granted to the successor trustee.

a. The Successor Trustee's Powers

The living trust forms in this book give the successor trustee all powers permitted under state law. The forms also spell out certain specific powers—for example, that the trustee has authority to buy and sell real estate and stocks. Some banks, title companies, stock brokerage companies, or other financial institutions demand this level of detail before approving a trust transaction, even though such authority is clearly included in a general grant of power under state law.

The living trust forms also give the successor trustee broad authority to manage any child's trust, including the power to spend any amount of each child's trust income or principal for that child's "health, support, maintenance, or education." As long as you trust your successor trustee, defining the power to manage young beneficiaries' trust property in this broad way is the best approach.

Once in a while, a financial institution gets quirky and demands that a trust specifically authorize some relatively unusual transaction the trustee wants to engage in. For example, a brokerage company may claim that some sophisticated maneuver isn't authorized by the Trustee's Power clause in your trust. The simple solution here is to learn exactly what wording the institution wants in your trust, and then add it to the Trustee's Power clause of your trust. See Chapter 13, Section F.

b. The Successor Trustee's Duty to Act Responsibly

The successor trustee must manage any trust property, including any property in a child's trust, in a "prudent manner." Practically, this means the trustee must always act honestly and in the best interests of the beneficiary. For example, the trustee must not make risky investments with trust property.

Legally, the trustee cannot personally profit or benefit from a transaction (this is called "self-dealing"). Basically, this means personally profiting or benefiting from a transaction involving trust property, such as buying a house from the trust. But remember, legal restrictions can only be enforced by a lawsuit. As successor trustee, be sure you have someone you trust, to minimize the possibility of litigation.

The successor trustee has authority to get professional assistance if necessary and pay for it with trust money. For example, the successor trustee might want to pay a tax preparer for help with the child's trust income tax return, or consult a financial planner for investment advice.

c. Payment of the Successor Trustee

Typically, the successor trustee of a basic probate-avoidance living trust isn't paid. This is because the successor trustee's duty is simply to distribute the deceased grantor's trust property, which is not normally an arduous job. Also, the successor trustee is usually a major beneficiary of the trust. For these reasons, the trust forms in this book provide that no compensation be paid to the successor trustee, with two exceptions:

* managing any trust when the grantor or grantors have become incapacitated, and

* managing an ongoing children's trust.

The trust forms provide that, in these situations, a successor trustee is entitled, without court approval, to "reasonable" compensation for services. The successor trustee decides what is reasonable and takes it from the appropriate trust property, in either the child's trust or the "A" trust.

In these situations, the successor trustee might have to actively manage the trust property for some time, so some pay for that work seems fair. The duties and burdens of a successor trustee who manages a child's trust can be substantial. The trust can last for decades and entail extensive financial responsibilities. If you have more than one trust, the job can become even more demanding.

Similarly, a successor trustee who takes over an A (marital life estate) trust for an incapacitated spouse will be required to do all the paperwork and other chores needed to keep the trust valid in the eyes of the IRS. Again, it seems fair to provide for reasonable compensation for this work

d. Notifying Trust Beneficiaries

In a number of states, a successor trustee of a living trust is specifically required by statute to provide basic information about the trust to trust beneficiaries. (See Chapter 14, Section B.) This duty includes notifying trust beneficiaries that the trust has become irrevocable. In all states, it's wise for the successor trustee to give this information to beneficiaries, even if the law does not compel it. The specific information required can vary depending on the state, as is discussed in Chapter 14, Section B. The point here is that a successor trustee should understand and accept this responsibility. The good news is that it shouldn't be hard to do—a simple letter setting out basic trust information should suffice.

Restricting the trustee's authority. Consult a lawyer if you are uneasy about:

* the broad grant of powers to the successor trustee

* the successor trustee's authority to sell trust property, regardless of the desires of other beneficiaries

* the lack of specific restrictions on the successor trustee

* the successor trustee's authority to manage and invest trust funds, or

* allowing open-ended compensation for managing a child's trust or Trust A.

Such a concern may well indicate potential serious problems, which require careful professional attention.

Also, if you decide that you want your successor trustee to be compensated for tasks entailed in transferring trust property to adult beneficiaries, see a lawyer. Compensation might be appropriate if your estate is a large one, and federal estate tax returns will have to be filed.

3. Choosing Your Successor Trustee

Clearly, your successor trustee will play a vital role in carrying out the aims of your living trust.

In most situations, the successor trustee does not need extensive experience in financial management; common sense, dependability, and complete honesty are usually enough. A successor trustee who may have long-term responsibility over a young beneficiary's trust property probably needs more management and financial skills than a successor trustee whose only job is to distribute trust property. But as I've said, the successor trustee does have authority, under the terms of the trust document, to get any reasonably necessary professional help—from an accountant, lawyer, or tax preparer, perhaps—and pay for it out of trust assets.

Your successor trustee should be whoever you feel is most trustworthy to do the job, who's willing to do it, and can actually do it. Often a major beneficiary, such as a spouse or adult child, is named as successor trustee. However, you aren't compelled to name a beneficiary as trustee. If you believe the beneficiary (much as you love him or her) will be troubled by having to handle the practical details and paperwork, it is preferable to name someone else, often another family member. Or as a last resort, consider naming an institution as trustee. (See Section C7, below.)

If you are married and create a basic shared trust, keep in mind that the successor trustee does not take over until both spouses have died (or become incapacitated). That means that after one spouse's death, the surviving spouse may have time to amend the trust document and name a different successor trustee if he or she wishes.

The situation is different with an AB trust. The A trust becomes irrevocable upon the death of the first spouse. Therefore, the successor trustee for the A trust cannot be changed by the surviving spouse, so your choice here is particularly important. The surviving spouse remains free, of course, to amend or revoke her own B surviving spouse's trust and name a new successor trustee for it.

AVOIDING CONFLICTS BETWEEN YOUR TRUST, YOUR WILL, AND OTHER DOCUMENTS

Your living trust, will (see Chapter 16), and durable power of attorney for finances (see Chapter 15, Section E) all give someone the authority to make decisions about your property if you can't. If you choose different people to act for you in these different documents, each will become involved in case of your incapacity, and when you die. Clearly, you don't need three heads here. Pick the same person for all three tasks.

If for some reason you want to name different people to be your successor trustee, executor of your will, and to act for you in your durable power of attorney for finances, see a lawyer.

Obviously, you should confer with the person you've chosen to be your successor trustee to be sure your choice is willing to serve. If you don't, you risk creating problems down the line. No one can be drafted to serve as a successor trustee. The person you've chosen may not want to serve, for a variety of reasons. And even if the person would be willing, if he or she doesn't know of his or her responsibilities, transfer of trust property after your death could be delayed.

4. Naming More Than One Successor Trustee

Legally, you can name as many successor cotrustees as you want, to serve together with power divided among them as you specify. However, as a general rule, because of coordination problems and possible conflicts among multiple trustees, it's generally best to name just one successor trustee. This isn't invariably true, however. For example, a parent may not want to be seen to favor one child over others, and to avoid this could name two or more children as successor cotrustees. This can be especially appropriate if the children are equal beneficiaries of the trust. If the children all get along, it rarely causes a problem.

When appointing successor cotrustees, you must decide how authority is shared among them—whether each can act separately for the trust, or all must agree in writing to act for the trust. Consider giving each the power to act for the trust without the formal written consent of the others. Especially if they live far away from one another or travel often, this could speed up the eventual property transfer process, avoiding delays that might otherwise be caused if one cotrustee were temporarily unavailable.

But what is most important is that you have complete confidence that all your successor trustees will get along. Do be cautious here. Power and property can lead to unexpected results (ask King Lear). If the cotrustees are prone to conflict, you may well create serious problems (and are doing none of them a favor) by having them share power as trustees.

If the cotrustees can't agree, it could hold up the distribution of trust property to your beneficiaries. In extreme situations, the other trustees might even have to go to court to get a recalcitrant trustee removed, so that your instructions can be carried out. The result might be much worse, and generate much more bad feeling, than if you had just picked one person to be trustee in the first place and let the chips fall as they will.

Having more than one successor trustee is especially risky if the successor trustees may be in charge of property you have left to a young beneficiary in a child's trust. The trustees may have to manage a young beneficiary's property for many years, and will have many decisions to make about how to spend the money—greatly increasing the potential for conflict. (Children's trusts are discussed in Chapter 9, Section D.)

If you name more than one successor trustee, and one of them can't serve, the others will serve. Only if none of them can serve will the alternate successor trustee you name take over.

Handling conflicts between successor cotrustees. If you're naming successor cotrustees and fear potential conflicts, see a lawyer. Such situations are too touchy to resolve without careful individual analysis. For this reason, the trust forms in this book don't contain clauses for resolving conflicts between successor cotrustees. A lawyer may recommend requiring the trustees to submit disputes to arbitration or mediation, or providing that if there is a dispute, one identified trustee gets to make the call.

5. Naming a Sole Beneficiary as Successor Trustee

It's perfectly legal to name a beneficiary of the trust as successor trustee. In fact, it's common.

Example

Santiago names his only child, Jaime, to be his sole trust beneficiary. Santiago also names Jaime as successor trustee. So when Santiago dies, Jaime's only task is to turn the trust property over to himself.

6. Naming an Out-of-State Trustee

Your successor trustee does not have to live in the same state as you do. But if you are choosing between someone local and someone far away, think about how convenient it will be for the person you choose to distribute the living trust property after your death. Someone close by will probably have an easier job, especially with real estate transfers. But for transfers of property such as securities and bank accounts, it usually won't make much difference where the successor trustee lives.

7. Naming a Bank or Trust Company as Successor Trustee

In my experience, it is almost always a bad idea to name a bank as successor trustee. I've heard some horror stories involving the indifference or downright rapaciousness of banks acting as trustees of family living trusts. Institutional trustees also charge hefty fees, which come out of the trust property and leave less for your family and friends. And banks probably won't even be interested in "small" living trusts—ones that contain less than several hundred thousand dollars worth of property.

Your successor trustee is your link with the ongoing lives of your loved ones. You want that link to be a human being you trust, not a corporation dedicated to the enhancement of its bottom line. However, if there is no person you believe will act honestly and competently as your successor trustee, you'll need to select some financial institution to do the job. Probably the best choice here is a private trust company. These companies generally offer more humane and personal attention to a trust than a bank or other large financial institution. Also, they can be more reasonable about fees charged to wind up a living trust.

For a very large living trust, another possibility is to name a person and an institution as successor cotrustees. The bank or trust company can do most of the paperwork, and the person can keep an eye on things and approve all transactions. ◼

chapter 8

CHOOSING YOUR BENEFICIARIES

*𝒜*fter deciding what property you'll put in your trust and who will be your successor trustee, your next step is to decide who will be your trust's beneficiaries. Who gets what? Obviously, this is the heart of preparing your living trust.

This chapter raises some important concerns about choosing beneficiaries and provides a worksheet where you can list each beneficiary and what property you want to leave him or her.

Even if you believe your beneficiary decisions are cut-and-dried and you are tempted to skip this chapter, please read at least Sections A through G. They contain important information you should take into account even if you have already decided who will inherit your property. For instance, you may initially think you don't want to bother naming alternate beneficiaries, to cover the contingency that a primary beneficiary will die before you do. But to make that decision sensibly, you should understand how alternate beneficiaries are used in living trusts, and why it's often wise to name them.

A. Kinds of Trust Beneficiaries

Several different classes of trust beneficiaries are used in trusts in this book.

1. Individual or Basic Shared Trusts

When you make a simple probate-avoidance living trust, you can name three kinds of beneficiaries:

- *Primary beneficiaries*, whom you name to receive specific property. Primary beneficiaries include individuals, institutions, and groups who receive property together.

- *Alternate beneficiaries*, whom you name to receive property left to a primary beneficiary if that primary beneficiary predeceases you.

- *Residuary beneficiaries (and alternate residuary beneficiaries)*, who receive all trust property not left to primary or alternate beneficiaries (including when both predecease you). You can, if you choose, leave all trust property to your residuary beneficiary, and not name any primary or alternate beneficiaries.

KEEP IT SIMPLE

Some living trust books argue:

- You cannot be trusted to choose your beneficiaries without professional help.

- You need to create all sorts of complex beneficiary provisions, to cover all sorts of contingencies, such as providing for what happens if a child's needs change long after you die, or a spouse remarries.

It's not hard to dream up future contingencies, often rather remote, about beneficiaries. While this certainly makes work for lawyers, it isn't what most people want. Most are wise enough to understand that it's rarely sensible to try to impose post-death controls over property given to beneficiaries.

"My life has been full of misfortunes, most of which never happened." —Mark Twain

This book assumes you'll leave property outright, with no strings attached (except for gifts to minors or young adults, discussed in Chapter 9, or property in an AB trust, discussed in Chapter 5).

Conditions on gifts. If you do want to impose conditions on gifts—for instance, providing for partial distributions, such as distributing money in three installments, or varying the amount left a beneficiary, depending on future needs—see a lawyer.

---

2. AB Living Trusts

If you and your spouse create a Nolo AB trust to save on estate taxes, you each will name:

- *The life beneficiary*. This beneficiary is always the surviving spouse.

- *Final beneficiaries*. Each spouse names these for his or her trust property. Eventually, the final beneficiaries are those (1) named by the deceased spouse to receive the property in the A trust when the surviving spouse dies; (2) named by the surviving spouse to receive the property in the surviving spouse's B trust.

- *Specific beneficiaries.* If you wish, you can name up to three beneficiaries who will inherit specific gifts left by the deceased spouse. You do not have to name any specific beneficiaries.

B. Naming Your Primary Beneficiaries

For single people, or couples using a basic shared living trust, choosing your primary beneficiaries is often the heart of making your trust. Deciding on your primary beneficiaries is, of course, entirely up to you. Your beneficiaries can include a spouse, mate, friends, young adults, children, or charitable or other institutions.

⚠ **Disinheriting a spouse or child.** If you are married and live in a common law state and you don't plan to leave at least half of what you own to your spouse, consult a lawyer experienced in estate planning. (See list of common law states, in Section H, below.) Whatever your wishes, state law entitles your spouse to some of your estate, including some of the property in your living trust. In most circumstances, you don't have to leave anything to your children. But if you want to disinherit a child, you should state that expressly in your will. (See Section H, below.)

PROPERTY RECEIVED BY BENEFICIARIES IS NOT SUBJECT TO INCOME TAX

Beneficiaries who inherit property are not liable for any federal income tax on that property. Of course, large estates may have had to pay estate taxes, but once they've been paid, the recipient of a gift is not subject to income tax on its value. If that gift generates income in the future, the beneficiary is responsible for paying income tax on it.

---

1. Individual Trust

Naming beneficiaries here is simple. Just list on the worksheet, and later on Form 1, whomever you want to receive your trust property. That's it!

2. Basic Shared Living Trust

Each spouse names beneficiaries separately, because each spouse's share of trust property is distributed when that spouse dies. When the first spouse dies, that spouse's trust property is distributed to the beneficiaries he or she named in the trust document. If property is left to the other spouse, it stays in the ongoing revocable trust of that spouse. When the second spouse dies, all the property in his or her trust is distributed to the second spouse's beneficiaries.

Example 1

Roger and Marilyn Foster create a basic shared living trust. Each puts shared, equally owned property and separately owned property in the trust. When Roger dies, Marilyn takes over as sole trustee. The property Roger left to Marilyn stays in the trust. Marilyn distributes the trust property Roger left to other beneficiaries. When Marilyn dies, her trust property will be distributed by her successor trustee to her beneficiaries.

Example 2

Marcia and Perry transfer all the property they own together into their basic shared living trust. Marcia names Perry as the beneficiary of all her interest in the trust property. Perry names Marcia to inherit all of his half except his half-interest in their vacation cabin, which he leaves to his son from a previous marriage, Eric. If Perry dies first, Perry's half-interest in the cabin will go to Eric, who will co-own it with Marcia.

3. AB Trust

If you use an AB trust, you have much less concern with specific beneficiaries. The bulk of your property is left in Trust A, with the surviving spouse as life beneficiary. While with this book's AB trust form each spouse can name up to three specific beneficiaries to receive gifts outside of the trust property, such individual gifts are relatively minor. (See Chapter 5.) Each spouse can also name alternate beneficiaries for any specific beneficiaries.

As discussed in Chapter 5, the property in trust A is left for the surviving spouse to use during his or her lifetime. Each spouse names final beneficiaries—the people who will eventually inherit the life estate trust property when the second spouse dies. It's best for each spouse to name the same final beneficiaries. This is commonly done when the couple are in their first marriage and both want their property eventually to go to their children. When each member of a couple wants to name different final beneficiaries, that's usually because each has children from prior marriages.

Each spouse can name different final beneficiaries using Nolo's AB trust, but as I've urged, be cautious. As a general rule, there's likely to be less tension and conflict if a surviving spouse and final beneficiaries have a parent-child relationship than if they do not. But if you feel secure that all people involved trust each other and will cooperate and get along, you can name different final beneficiaries.

You can also name alternate final beneficiaries, in case a final beneficiary predeceases you.

Both spouses create an A trust, on paper, since you can't know which spouse will die first. However, the surviving spouse's Trust A never goes into effect (because there's no spouse for the surviving spouse to leave property to). Still, both spouses need to name final beneficiaries for their trust property to ensure their property ends up going to those whom they want to get it. (See Chapter 10, Section D.)

SOME THOUGHTS ABOUT GIFTS

Before plunging into technical concerns about how to name beneficiaries or shared gifts, let's pull back for a moment and consider what gifts are. In our predominantly commercial culture, gifts are special, whether they are made during life or at death. Gifts are free, voluntary transfers of property, made without any requirement or expectation of receiving anything in return. The essence of gift-giving is generosity, an open spirit. To say one makes gifts "with strings attached" is not a compliment.

Much of the real pleasure of estate planning comes from contemplating the positive effects your gifts will have on those you love. Sometimes, these pleasures are focused—you know how much Judith has always liked your mahogany table, and now she'll get to enjoy it. Others are more general—your son will be able to buy a house with the money you leave him, which will relieve some of the financial pressure that has been weighing on him.

I mention the spirit of giving here because it's easy to get entrapped by the mechanics of preparing a living trust and lose sight of your real purpose. So, if technicalities and legalities start to get to you, take a break and remember whom you're giving your property to, and why. And if you wish to explore in profound depth what gift-giving is, or can mean, read Lewis Hyde's *The Gift* (Vintage/Random House), a brilliant exploration of how gifts work in many cultures.

C. Simultaneous Death Clauses

I address the issue of simultaneous death early on in this chapter because it's a real concern to many couples. The statistical probability of simultaneous death is very low, but still it's one of the first things many couples ask about when preparing a shared living trust or an AB trust: What happens if we're both killed in a plane crash?

If you leave all your trust property directly to your spouse or in an AB trust, and your trust document doesn't have a clause to cover simultaneous death, and you and your spouse die in circumstances that make it difficult to tell who died first, your property could pass to your spouse or mate, and then immediately to your spouse's inheritors. That might not be the result either of you want.

The forms in this book (the basic shared living trust or AB trust, and the will for a member of a couple) contain a simultaneous death clause to prevent this. These clauses are worded slightly differently depending on the form, because the trust is a joint form used by both spouses and the will is a separate form for each spouse. But each clause works the same: If both spouses die simultaneously, or if it's difficult or impossible to tell who died first, the property of each spouse is disposed of as if he or she had survived the other.

Example

In their shared living trust, Edith and Archie leave much of their property to each other. However, Archie wants his property to go to his daughter from his first marriage if Edith dies before he does. Edith wants her property to go to her sister if Archie dies before she does. Edith and Archie are killed in a car crash. Under the living trust's simultaneous death clause, Archie's property would go to his daughter, and Edith's to her sister.

You may ask, "How, logically, can simultaneous death clauses work? How can I be presumed to have outlived my spouse when she's also presumed to have outlived me?" Yes, it is a paradox, but it does work. Under the law, each person's trust and will property is handled independently of the other. This allows both spouses to achieve the results each wants in the event of simultaneous death. (As Oliver Wendell Holmes put it, "The life of the law has not been logic, it has been experience.")

D. Cobeneficiaries

You can name more than one beneficiary (primary, alternate, residuary, or final) to inherit any item of trust property. People frequently want to make shared gifts to their children, for example.

When making a gift to be shared by two or more beneficiaries, always use the beneficiaries' actual names; don't use collective terms such as "my children." It's not always clear who is included in such descriptions. And there can be serious confusion if one of the people origi-

nally included as a beneficiary dies before you do; the law may give the beneficiary's children the right to inherit their parent's share, which may not be the result you intend.

Obviously, if you name cobeneficiaries for a piece of property that can't be physically divided—a house, for example—give some thought to whether or not the beneficiaries are likely to get along. If they are incompatible, disagreements could arise over taking care of property or deciding whether or not to sell it.

You need to resolve these important questions before naming cobeneficiaries:

1. What percentage of ownership will each beneficiary receive?

2. What happens down the line if the cobeneficiaries can't agree on how to use the property?

3. What happens if one cobeneficiary dies before you do?

The rest of this section discusses these concerns.

1. Percentage of Ownership

The key here is to say in your living trust document how ownership is to be shared between the beneficiaries. If you don't specify shares of ownership, it's generally presumed that you intended equal shares, but this rule isn't ironclad, and there's no good reason to be silent on this matter. If you want a gift shared equally, say so.

Here are two examples of what the language in your trust document might look like:

"The grantor's three children, Anne Pasquez, Rob Pasquez, and Tony Pasquez, shall be given the house at 1123 Elm St., Centerville, in equal shares."

"The grantor's daughters, Maxine Jones and Simone Jones, shall be given all stock accounts, in equal shares."

The beneficiaries can share ownership any way you want. For instance:

"The grantor's spouse and children shall be given all the grantor's interest in the grantor's house and real estate known as 111 57th St., Muncy, Iowa, in the following shares:

　　　50% to the grantor's spouse, Mary
　　　25% to the grantor's son, Jon
　　　25% to the grantor's daughter, Mildred."

2. Conflict

Conflict between beneficiaries is the basic risk with shared ownership. Suppose the people to whom you've left property disagree about how to use it. In most states, any co-owner can go to court and force a partition and sale, with the net proceeds divided by percentage of ownership. Let's say, for example, you leave your house to your three children. Suppose two want to sell it, and one doesn't. The house would be sold even if one child wanted to live in it.

If you are apprehensive, discuss it with the proposed beneficiaries. If there's genuine agreement among them, potential problems are less likely to become real ones. If you conclude there's no risk of conflict, you can simply make the shared gift without any conditions or directions, leaving it up to the beneficiaries to resolve any problems.

It's possible to put provisions governing the issue of what the shared owners can do in your trust document, but I don't recommend it. For instance, you could state, "The house cannot be sold unless all three of my children agree on it." But often other problems follow. If two want to sell the house, but one doesn't, who manages the house? Does it have to be rented at market value? Can the child who wants to keep the house live in it? If so, must that child pay the others rent? And what happens if one child dies? The difficulties of dealing with these types of complications are why it's usually more sensible not to specify details of long-term control of property you leave beneficiaries. Let them work it out. If you don't think the beneficiaries can work out any such problems, a shared gift probably isn't appropriate.

Imposing controls on cobeneficiaries. If you fear conflict between cobeneficiaries and want to impose controls on the use of the property they inherit, see a lawyer.

3. What Happens If One Cobeneficiary Dies Before You Do

You can name alternate beneficiaries for each cobeneficiary. See Section F, below.

E. Some Common Concerns About Beneficiaries

Here are some common concerns and choices you may face when choosing your beneficiaries.

1. One Primary Beneficiary

Unless you make an AB trust, you can name only one person (or one institution) as your primary beneficiary. For instance, many people want their spouse or mate to receive all their trust property. You can name one person as your primary beneficiary either by listing that person as a sole primary beneficiary or by leaving everything in your residuary clause to your residuary beneficiary.

With an AB trust, to repeat again, most or all of each spouse's property must be left to the Trust A itself.

2. Married Beneficiaries

When you leave property to someone who's married, the gift is that person's individual or separate property if you make the gift only in his or her name. For example, suppose your trust document says: "Mary Kestor shall be given the antique clock," or "Mary Kestor shall be given the grantor's interest in the house at 279 18th St., San Francisco." Mary would be entitled to keep the entire gift if she divorces, assuming the gift had been kept separate, not commingled (mixed) with shared marital property so that the gift could no longer be separately identified.

If you want to emphasize your wishes, you could say: "Mary Kestor shall be given the grantor's antique clock as her separate property." But if Mary later commingles the gift with shared property, it may lose its separate property status. Proof once again that you have only limited control over what happens to your property after you die.

If you want to make a gift to a member of a couple and have it remain that person's separate property, note that on the beneficiary worksheet, to remind you that when you prepare your living trust in Chapter 10, you should expressly state that.

By contrast, if you wish to make a gift to a married couple, simply make it in both their names. For example: "Edna and Fred Whitman shall be given the grantor's silver bowl." Again, you can provide clarity by expressly stating your intent: "Edna and Fred Whitman shall be given the grantor's silver bowl as co-owners."

3. Children From Prior Marriages

If you or your spouse have children from a prior marriage, you have a number of alternatives for leaving gifts to them—and you also have the right to disinherit the children:

- You can leave them gifts outright, using either a basic shared living trust (Form 2) or an AB trust (Form 3).

- You can use Nolo's AB trust to create a life estate for your spouse, and name children from a prior marriage as final beneficiaries. Often each child is left a set percentage of the remaining trust property when your spouse dies.

Conflict between a surviving spouse and children. If there is a risk of conflict after your death between your surviving spouse and your children, see a lawyer.

- You can create a trust that imposes more restrictions on the power of the surviving spouse to use and spend trust principal than Nolo's AB trust does. As previously explained, Nolo's AB trust gives the surviving spouse the maximum powers over trust principal allowed by the IRS. (See Chapter 5, Section C.) Some spouses in second or subsequent marriages want to limit the surviving spouse's power to use or spend trust principal, in order to be sure that the principal is preserved for their children.

Example

Marshall, age 67, and Lisa, age 71, marry. Lisa has a son, Nick, age 32, from a prior marriage. Lisa owns a paid-for house that she and Marshall will live in, and has $280,000 worth of other assets. She creates a trust that allows Marshall to live in the house if she dies before him, but doesn't allow him to sell it, rent it, or borrow against it. Nick will receive the house free and clear when Marshall dies.

Drafting a life estate trust restricting the rights of your spouse. Creating this kind of trust is discussed further in Chapter 15, Section F. As explained there, many individual questions need to be resolved to set up such a trust, which must be prepared by a knowledgeable lawyer.

4. Minors or Young Adults

If a beneficiary you name is a minor (under 18) or a young adult who can't yet manage property without adult help, you can arrange for an adult to manage the trust property for the beneficiary. The management will take effect only if the beneficiary is still too young to sensibly manage property when she inherits it. (See Chapter 9.)

5. Your Successor Trustee

It's very common and perfectly legal to leave trust property to the person you named to be successor trustee—the person who will distribute trust property after you (or if you are making a trust with your spouse, you and your spouse) die.

Example

Nora and Sean name their son Liam as successor trustee of their basic shared living trust. Each spouse names the other as sole beneficiary of his or her trust property, and both name Liam as alternate beneficiary. When Nora dies, her trust property goes to Sean and stays in the trust. Unless Sean amends the trust document to name someone else as successor trustee, after Sean's death, Liam, acting as trustee, will transfer ownership of the trust property from the trust to himself.

6. Pets

As a part of their estate planning, many pet owners arrange informally for a friend or relative to care for a pet. But you can make more formal arrangements. Here are a few things to keep in mind:

- You can use your living trust (or will) to leave your pets, and perhaps some money for expenses, to someone you trust to look out for them. But don't make the gift of an animal a surprise—make sure the people you've chosen are really willing and able to care for your pets.

- You can't leave money or property outright to a pet. The law says animals are property, and one piece of property simply can't own another piece. In most states, if you do name a pet as a beneficiary in your will or living trust, whatever property you tried to leave it will probably go, instead, to the residuary beneficiary (the person who gets everything not left to the beneficiaries named in the will or trust). If there's no residuary beneficiary, the property will be distributed according to state law.

- Consider making arrangements for emergency care for your animals in case you suddenly can't care for them.

- In 22 states, you can establish a trust for your pet. The trust is a legally independent entity, managed by a trustee you name. In the trust document, you direct how your pet is to be cared for. Pet trusts can be desirable if you'd prefer not to leave your pet outright to someone. But creating a pet trust is more costly and complicated than simply leaving your pet outright.

STATES THAT ALLOW TRUSTS FOR PETS

Alaska	Missouri	Oregon
Arizona	Montana	Tennessee
California	Nebraska	Utah
Colorado	Nevada	Washington
Florida	New Jersey	Wisconsin
Iowa	New Mexico	Wyoming
Kansas	New York	
Michigan	North Carolina	

 You'll need an attorney to prepare a pet trust. You'll need to hire an attorney to get the document drafted.

These issues are discussed in detail in *Dog Law*, by Mary Randolph (Nolo).

7. People Who Cannot Legally Inherit

Some felons, and anyone who unlawfully caused the death of the grantor of the living trust, cannot legally inherit property.

F. Naming Alternate Beneficiaries

You can name an alternate beneficiary, or beneficiaries, for each gift made to a primary beneficiary. The alternate beneficiary receives the gift if the primary beneficiary pre-

deceases you and you haven't amended your trust to name a new primary beneficiary for that gift.

Naming alternate beneficiaries can be sensible, for a number of reasons. Perhaps you've left property to older people, or ones in poor health. Or you're just a cautious person. Or you don't want the bother of redoing your trust document if the unlikely occurs and a beneficiary does die before you. Or you're concerned that you might not have time, before your own death, to revise your estate plan after a beneficiary dies.

On the other hand, some people decide they don't want the morbid bother of worrying about their beneficiaries dying before they do. They leave their property—as many people do—to those considerably younger than they are. If the unlikely occurs and a beneficiary dies before the grantors, normally they'll be able to modify the trust to name a new beneficiary.

Here are two examples of how alternate beneficiaries are named in a trust document:

"Mike McGowan shall be given the grantor's outboard motor and boat. If he doesn't survive the grantor, they shall be given to his son, Pat McGowan."

"The grantor's children, Bert Wemby and Cherrie Wemby, shall be given the grantor's interest in the house at 221 Maple Avenue, Winton, New York. If one beneficiary doesn't survive the grantor, the house shall be given to the other. If neither survives the grantor, the house shall be given to Kamal Abram."

You don't have to name an alternate for a charity or other institution you name as a beneficiary. If the institution is well established, it seems safe to assume that it will still exist at your death.

1. Basic Shared Trust

With a basic shared living trust, each spouse makes his or her own separate gifts, and each spouse has the right to name his or her own alternate beneficiaries. They do not need to be the same as the other spouse's.

Example

Larry and Louisa create a basic shared trust. Each leaves a one-half interest in their house to the other. Larry names his two children from a previous marriage as alternate beneficiaries for his half-interest in the house. Louisa names her sister as her alternate beneficiary for her gift.

2. AB Trust

Alternate beneficiaries play a different role with an AB trust. If you do make gifts to specific beneficiaries, outside the ongoing Trust A, you can name alternates for those beneficiaries.

As you know, the surviving spouse is always the life beneficiary of the property that remains in Trust A when the first spouse dies. You do not name an alternate beneficiary for the surviving spouse. Instead, each spouse names final beneficiaries, and can name alternates for those final beneficiaries.

When both spouses die the property in both Trust A and Trust B goes to each trust's final beneficiaries. If a beneficiary is deceased, the property goes to the deceased beneficiary's alternate. Often, in a first marriage, both spouses name the same alternate final beneficiaries, commonly grandchildren.

Example

Vittorio and Sophia create an AB trust. Each names their two children, Luigi and Anna, as final beneficiaries. Vittorio and Sophia also each name the same alternate final beneficiaries: for Luigi the alternate beneficiary is his child Alfonso; for Anna, the alternate beneficiaries are her children Gina, Carmela, and Marcello, in equal shares.

As you know, the surviving spouse's B trust remains revocable during his or her life. Of course, as long as she is competent, the surviving spouse can amend this trust to name new (final) beneficiaries, and alternates, disposing of the trust property any way she chooses. Only when she dies does Trust B become irrevocable.

3. Naming Alternate Cobeneficiaries

You can name more than one person or institution as alternate beneficiaries. If you do, you must define how these co-alternate beneficiaries will share the property.

Example 1

Rosa names her husband Ramon as beneficiary of her interest in their house, which they have transferred to their basic shared living trust. As alternate beneficiaries, she names their three children, Miguel, Constanza, and Guillermo, to share equally.

Ramon dies just before she does, leaving his half of the house to Rosa. Under the terms of the trust document, it stays in the living trust. At Rosa's death, the house goes to the three children, because Ramon is not living. All three own equal shares in all of it. If they sell the property, each will be entitled to a third of the proceeds.

Example 2

Benjamin names Bela, his wife, as his primary beneficiary of his interest in their house. He names their children, Susan and Zelda, as alternate beneficiaries. However, Benjamin and Bela have paid many thousands of dollars to help Zelda through medical school. Susan has been self-supporting since she left college. So Benjamin and Bela decide to leave Susan 75% of the house and Zelda 25%, and state this in the trust document when naming them as alternate beneficiaries.

4. Naming Alternate Beneficiaries for Cobeneficiaries

Things become complicated if you decide to move on to the next level of contingencies—naming alternate beneficiaries for a shared gift. Say you want to leave your house to your three children. What are your options if you want to name alternate beneficiaries?

- You can specify that a deceased child's share is to be shared by the remaining beneficiaries.

Here's a clause specifying that the other beneficiaries of a shared gift share the interest of a deceased beneficiary:

"Mollie Rainey, Allen Rainey, and Barbara Rainey Smithson shall be given the grantor's house at 1701 Clay St., Peoria, IL. If any of them fails to survive the grantor, his or her interest in the grantor's house shall be shared equally by the survivors."

- You can provide that a deceased child's share is to be shared equally by that beneficiary's own children, and, if there are none, then between the remaining beneficiaries.
- You can name an "outside" alternate beneficiary (a friend or other relative) to receive the interest of any child who dies before you do.
- You can name three separate alternate beneficiaries, one for each child—for example, each of their spouses.

Before plunging into complexities about alternate beneficiary provisions for a shared gift, consider whether or not you really want to worry about this contingency. Some people don't like to consider the possibility of one of their children dying before them (and you can always revise your trust if that remote possibility occurs). And once you get started worrying about these kinds of possibilities, where do you stop? You could also worry about what happens if all your alternate beneficiaries, as well as your beneficiaries themselves, die before you. There's no total security, no matter how many levels of alternate beneficiaries you name.

5. Imposing a Survivorship Period

Some people want to impose what is called a "survivorship period" on gifts made to primary and/or alternate beneficiaries. This means that the beneficiary must outlive the grantor by a set period of time, defined in the living trust, to receive the gift. If the beneficiary doesn't live this long, the gift goes to the alternate beneficiary.

The trust forms in this book do not impose a survivorship period. Many people (including me) think they are unnecessarily cautious. And people who do want them differ widely as to how long the period should be.

If you decide you do want to impose a survivorship period on your primary beneficiaries, you can add one to the trust document. (See Chapter 10, Section D.) I recommend a relatively short period, between 15 and 45 days. Imposing a longer period normally just unnecessarily delays distribution of gifts to the primary beneficiaries.

Example

In Laura's basic shared living trust, she imposes a 15-day survivorship requirement on all her beneficiaries.

Laura leaves all her trust property to her husband Juan-Carlos, and names her daughter from a previous marriage as alternate beneficiary. Laura and Juan-Carlos are seriously injured in a car accident; Juan-Carlos dies four days after Laura does. Because Juan-Carlos did not survive Laura by at least fifteen days, the trust property he would have inherited from Laura goes to Laura's daughter instead.

If there had been no survivorship requirement, Laura's trust property would have gone to Juan-Carlos. When he died four days later, it would have gone to beneficiaries he had named in the trust document.

G. Residuary Beneficiaries

Residuary beneficiaries are the person, persons, or institutions you name to receive trust property that isn't given, for whatever reason, to a primary beneficiary or an alternate. For example, if a primary beneficiary predeceases you or can't be located, and you didn't name an alternate, the property would go to the residuary beneficiary.

1. Individual or Basic Shared Living Trusts

With these trusts, you must name a residuary beneficiary. With a living trust for one person, you should always name a residuary beneficiary and an alternate residuary beneficiary, who will inherit if the residuary beneficiary dies before you.

With a basic shared living trust, each spouse names his or her own residuary beneficiary and alternate residuary beneficiary. They may name different people.

Example

Peter leaves a house to his wife Jane, or if Jane dies before him, to Jane's sister Carolyn. He names his sister Julie as residuary beneficiary. Jane and Carolyn are killed in a car crash three days before Peter dies. Because the primary and alternate beneficiaries are dead, the house goes to Julie. (Pretty cheerful example of how living trusts can work, huh?)

You can name co-residuary beneficiaries, and co-alternate residuary beneficiaries as well. But if you do, you must handle all the potential problems of naming cobeneficiaries (discussed in Section D, above).

For instance, a person could split the bulk of her estate among her children by leaving it all to the children as residuary beneficiaries. For example, she could name as her residuary beneficiaries: "Henry McCormick, Aaron McCormick, and Joanne Guiliam, in equal shares."

Another approach is to make a few relatively minor gifts and leave the bulk of your property to your residuary beneficiary.

Example 1

Jennifer wants to leave her two Tiffany lamps to her friend Linda, $5,000 in a money market account to her niece Martha, and her car to her sister Joan. She wants to leave all the rest of her extensive estate—houses, stocks, limited partnerships—to her long-time partner, Paul. She can simply name Paul as her residuary beneficiary, after listing the three specific gifts. She names Joan as her alternate residuary beneficiary.

Example 2

Claudia and John are in their second marriage. They have no children together. Each has children from their first marriages—Claudia's are Wendy and Linus, John's are Krystin, Phil, and Gary. Claudia and John each name the other as residuary beneficiary. But as alternate residuary beneficiaries, Claudia names Wendy and Linus. John names Krystin, Phil, and Gary.

The residuary beneficiary of a living trust for a single person, or of one person's portion of a basic shared living trust, will receive:

- any trust property for which both the primary and alternate beneficiaries you named die before you do
- any trust property that you didn't leave to a named beneficiary (this could include property you transferred to the trust later but didn't name a beneficiary for, and trust property that was owned by your spouse, which he or she left you)
- any property you leave to your living trust through a "pour-over" will (because property left through a pour-over will doesn't avoid probate, there's usually no reason to use one; see Chapter 15), and
- any property that you actually transferred to your living trust but didn't list in the trust document.

2. AB Trusts

With this type of living trust, residuary beneficiaries have no role. Aside from any specific gifts left to specific beneficiaries or alternates, all property of a deceased spouse goes into Trust A. After the death of the surviving spouse, this trust property is distributed to the final beneficiaries. Likewise, property in Trust B goes to that trust's final beneficiaries. If both a specific beneficiary and alternate for a specific gift predecease a grantor, and the trust is not amended to name a new beneficiary for the gift, that gift becomes part of the Trust A property, or part of the property in the surviving spouse's Trust B left to his or her final beneficiaries.

H. Disinheritance

You can disinherit most people simply by not leaving them anything in your living trust or will. If you don't leave someone any of your property, he has no rights to it, period. However, when it comes to your spouse, no disinheritance is possible except in the eight community property states. And, when it comes to your children, you should either leave them something or expressly disinherit them in your will.

1. Disinheriting a Spouse

Whether or not you can legally disinherit a spouse (not that many people want to) depends on whether you live in a community property state or common law state.

a. Community Property States

In community property states (listed below), the general rule is that spouses together own all property that either acquires during the marriage, except property one spouse acquires by gift or inheritance. Each spouse owns a half-interest in this "community property."

Alaska (if spouses prepare a written community property agreement)

Arizona	Louisiana	Texas
California	Nevada	Washington
Idaho	New Mexico	Wisconsin

You are free to leave your separate property and your half of the community property to anyone you choose. Your spouse—who already owns half of all the community property—has no right to inherit any of your half.

UNMARRIED COUPLES

Unmarried couples living together have no right to inherit any of each other's property (except, as previously mentioned, lesbian and gay couples in California, Hawaii, and Vermont who register with the state). In short, each person can leave his or her property to anyone he or she wants to. However, if the couple has created a valid contract that gives each one the specific right to inherit specific property, that contract will normally be enforced if the person who feels cheated goes to court.

---

b. Common Law States

If you live in one of these 41 common law states or the District of Columbia, you cannot exclude your spouse from receiving some of your property after your death.

Alabama	Kentucky	North Dakota
Alaska	Maine	Ohio
Arkansas	Maryland	Oklahoma
Colorado	Massachusetts	Oregon
Connecticut	Michigan	Pennsylvania
Delaware	Minnesota	Rhode Island
District of Columbia	Mississippi	South Carolina
Florida	Missouri	South Dakota
Georgia	Montana	Tennessee
Hawaii	Nebraska	Utah
Illinois	New Hampshire	Vermont
Indiana	New Jersey	Virginia
Iowa	New York	West Virginia
Kansas	North Carolina	Wyoming

In a common law state, a surviving spouse who doesn't receive one-third to one-half of the deceased spouse's property (through a will, living trust, or other method) is entitled to insist upon a set share of the property. The exact share depends on state law. So, a spouse who doesn't receive the minimum he or she is entitled to under state law (the "statutory share") may be able to claim some of the property in your living trust. To be safe, give your spouse at least half your property in your trust (except, of course, in an AB trust, where he or she receives only a life interest in the Trust A property).

Even property given away before death may legally belong to the surviving spouse under these laws. For example, take the case of a man who set up joint bank accounts with his children from a previous marriage. After his death, his widow sued to recover her interest in the accounts. She won; the Kentucky Supreme Court ruled that under Kentucky law, a spouse is entitled to a half-interest in the other spouse's personal property (everything but real estate). Her husband had not had the legal right to give away her interest in the money in the accounts. (*Harris v. Rock*, 799 S.W.2d 10 (Ky. 1990).) Most noncommunity property states have similar laws, called "dower" or "curtesy" laws.

State law may also give your spouse the right to inherit the family residence, or at least use it for his or her life. The Florida constitution, for example, gives a surviving spouse the deceased spouse's residence, no matter what the deceased spouse's will says. (Fla. Const. Art. 10, § 4.)

Disinheriting your spouse. If you live in a common law state and you want to leave your spouse less than half of your property from a basic shared trust, see a lawyer.

2. Disinheriting a Child

With rare exceptions, it is legal to disinherit a child. (The Florida constitution prohibits the head of a family from leaving his residence to anyone except his spouse or child, if he has either (Fla. Const. Art. 10, § 4).)

You do not have to leave your child anything in your living trust. But to completely disinherit a child (or the children of a deceased child), your state laws require you to do so in your will, even if you transfer all your property by a living trust.

There are two ways to disinherit a child in a will. One is to expressly disinherit the child in the will, by stating that you aren't leaving him anything. The other is to leave the child a minimal amount, which ensures the child cannot successfully claim to have been overlooked or accidentally omitted. If you don't mention a child in your will, state law may give him or her the right to a certain share of your property.

The will forms in this book require you to list all your children. The forms then state that if you haven't left any property to a listed child, that failure to do so is intentional. So, if you leave a child nothing (by will or otherwise), this functions as a disinheritance clause.

3. Children Born After a Will or Trust Is Prepared

Some state laws protect offspring who were born after a parent's will was prepared. Although these laws mention only wills, not living trusts, it's possible that a court could apply them to a living trust, reasoning that the living trust is serving the function of a will. And as living trusts become more widespread, state legislatures may expand their laws to include children not mentioned in living trusts.

These laws presume that the parent didn't mean to disinherit a child who is born after the parent's will has been signed, and thus is not mentioned in a parent's will. (Such children are called "pretermitted heirs," in legalese.) The law assumes that the parent simply hadn't yet gotten around to writing a new will. Such a child is legally entitled to a share (the size is determined by state law) of the deceased parent's estate, which may include property in a living trust.

The easy answer to this problem is to amend your living trust after a child is born. Most parents want to provide for a new child, so it's simply a matter of getting the work done. Amending your trust to provide for a new beneficiary is not difficult. (See Chapter 13, Sections D and F.)

4. Grandchildren

Grandchildren have no right to inherit from their grandparents unless their parent has died. In that case, the grandchildren essentially take the place of the deceased child and are entitled to whatever he or she would have been legally entitled to.

5. General Disinheritance Clauses

You may have heard that some lawyers recommend leaving $1 to close relatives in your trust or will. This is not legally necessary and it's a bad idea. There's no need to mention anyone but your spouse and perhaps your children in your trust. No one else has a legal right to any of your property. Moreover, your successor trustee must track down each beneficiary to whom you leave a dollar and procure an acknowledgment that the beneficiary received the dollar. That's a lot of work, especially when there's no point to it.

Lawsuits contesting a living trust are very rare. A relative could conceivably try to contest your trust by claiming that you, the grantor, were mentally incompetent when you prepared your trust, and were duped by someone to leaving most or all of your property to them, while you really wanted to leave it to this relative.

Heading off contests by relatives. If you think a relative might try to contest your trust, you might leave that relative $1, to make it absolutely clear you did consider that person and wanted to give no more. But before you settle on that option, see a lawyer to determine the wisest course of action.

6. No-Contest Clauses

A "no-contest clause" in a living trust (or a will) is a device used to discourage beneficiaries of your trust or will from suing to void the trust or will and claiming they are entitled to more than you left them. Under a no-contest clause, a beneficiary who challenges a living trust or will and loses forfeits all his inheritance under that document. Without a no-contest clause, someone left property from a living trust can sue, lose, and still collect the amount given him in the trust.

Example

Pip leaves his daughter Estelle $10,000 in his living trust, and includes a no-contest clause in that document. If Estelle challenges the trust and loses, she does not receive the $10,000.

No-contest clauses can be sensible if there's a risk a beneficiary might challenge your estate plan. On the other hand, many people do not like to include a no-contest clause in their estate planning documents, because it seems to imply a suspicion of their beneficiaries that they don't actually feel. The trust and will forms in this book do not contain no-contest clauses.

Adding a no-contest clause. If you think you may need a no-contest clause, that's an indication of a potential serious problem. See a lawyer to discuss how to handle the risk of a court fight; often, a no-contest clause is just one part of a larger strategy.

I. Putting Conditions on Beneficiaries

Occasionally a person wants to make a gift with restrictions or conditions on it. If done thoughtfully, this is usually a complex task. The trust forms in this book do not allow you to make conditional gifts. (You can, however, appoint someone to manage trust property inherited by a minor child or young adult. See Section E, above.)

Example

Ravi wants to leave money to a nephew, Monir, if he goes to veterinary school, but, if he doesn't, to his niece Sheela. This sounds simple, but here are just a few problems inherent in this approach: How soon must Monir go to veterinary school? What happens if he applies in good faith but fails to get in? Who decides if he's really studying? What happens to the money before Monir goes to veterinary school? What happens if Monir goes to veterinary school but drops out after a year and says he'll go back eventually? What happens if he graduates but doesn't become a vet?

Imposing restrictions and controls on beneficiaries is sometimes called "dead-hand control." The obvious risk of dead-hand control is that circumstances can change, so you must try to anticipate what is likely—or even possible—to occur in the future, and provide for it. This, at best, is complex work, and helps to enrich estate planning lawyers.

Long-Term Trusts. Except for an AB trust or child's trust, you cannot create long-term trusts using this book. Some major types of long-term trusts are discussed in Chapter 15. You'll need a lawyer's help if you want to prepare one.

J. Property You Leave in Your Trust That You No Longer Own at Your Death

If you make a gift of specific property in your trust, but then remove that property from your trust before you die—that is, you sell it or give it to someone—the beneficiary for that gift is simply out of luck, and is likely to be quite upset (if he knew he was supposed to get it). So if you do transfer property from your trust, be sure to amend your trust document and formally delete the provision that left it to a beneficiary. (Chapter 13, Section F, shows how to amend your trust document.)

K. Beneficiary Worksheets

On one of the following worksheets, you'll list your beneficiaries and the property you want to leave to each.

- Use Worksheet 1 for an individual living trust.
- Use Worksheet 2 for a basic shared living trust. Each spouse names beneficiaries separately.
- Use Worksheet 3 for an AB trust. Each spouse can name at most three beneficiaries of specific gifts, aside from the surviving spouse and final beneficiaries.

To get started, go back to the Property Worksheet in Chapter 6, where you listed what items you will transfer to your trust. On these worksheets, you will name a beneficiary for each item. If you're making a gift to co-beneficiaries and naming alternate cobeneficiaries, you need to decide what share each cobeneficiary receives.

If you need more space than the worksheet provides, attach additional sheets (or scribble in the margins, for that matter). Also, if you think you may do a substantial amount of revising, photocopy the blank worksheet before you begin filling it out.

Beneficiary Worksheet 1: For an Individual Trust

1. Specific Gifts

_____
Item of Property

_____
Primary Beneficiary

_____
Alternate Beneficiary

_____
Item of Property

_____
Primary Beneficiary

_____
Alternate Beneficiary

_____
Item of Property

_____
Primary Beneficiary

_____
Alternate Beneficiary

_____
Item of Property

_____
Primary Beneficiary

_____
Alternate Beneficiary

_____
Item of Property

_____
Primary Beneficiary

_____
Alternate Beneficiary

_____
Item of Property

_____
Primary Beneficiary

_____
Alternate Beneficiary

_____
Item of Property

_____
Primary Beneficiary

_____
Alternate Beneficiary

_____
Item of Property

_____
Primary Beneficiary

_____
Alternate Beneficiary

_____
Item of Property

_____
Primary Beneficiary

_____
Alternate Beneficiary

_____
Item of Property

_____
Primary Beneficiary

_____
Alternate Beneficiary

2. Residuary Beneficiary or Beneficiaries

_____
Residuary Beneficiary(ies)

_____
Alternate Residuary Beneficiary(ies)

Beneficiary Worksheet 2: A Basic Shared Living Trust

WIFE'S BENEFICIARIES

1. Specific Gifts

Item of Property
_____

Primary Beneficiary
_____

Alternate Beneficiary
_____

Item of Property
_____

Primary Beneficiary
_____

Alternate Beneficiary
_____

Item of Property
_____

Primary Beneficiary
_____

Alternate Beneficiary
_____

Item of Property
_____

Primary Beneficiary
_____

Alternate Beneficiary
_____

Item of Property
_____

Primary Beneficiary
_____

Alternate Beneficiary
_____

Item of Property
_____

Primary Beneficiary
_____

Alternate Beneficiary
_____

Item of Property
_____

Primary Beneficiary
_____

Alternate Beneficiary
_____

Item of Property
_____

Primary Beneficiary
_____

Alternate Beneficiary
_____

2. Residuary Beneficiary or Beneficiaries

Residuary Beneficiary(ies)
_____

Alternate Residuary Beneficiary(ies)
_____

Beneficiary Worksheet 2 (continued)

HUSBAND'S BENEFICIARIES

1. Specific Gifts

Item of Property

Primary Beneficiary

Alternate Beneficiary

Item of Property

Primary Beneficiary

Alternate Beneficiary

Item of Property

Primary Beneficiary

Alternate Beneficiary

Item of Property

Primary Beneficiary

Alternate Beneficiary

Item of Property

Primary Beneficiary

Alternate Beneficiary

Item of Property

Primary Beneficiary

Alternate Beneficiary

Item of Property

Primary Beneficiary

Alternate Beneficiary

Item of Property

Primary Beneficiary

Alternate Beneficiary

Item of Property

Primary Beneficiary

Alternate Beneficiary

2. Residuary Beneficiary or Beneficiaries

Residuary Beneficiary(ies)

Alternate Residuary Beneficiary(ies)

Beneficiary Worksheet 3: AB Trust

1. Wife's Specific Beneficiaries

_____
Item of Property

_____
Primary Beneficiary

_____
Alternate Beneficiary

_____
Item of Property

_____
Primary Beneficiary

_____
Alternate Beneficiary

_____
Item of Property

_____
Primary Beneficiary

_____
Alternate Beneficiary

2. Wife's Final Beneficiaries

_____

_____

_____

_____

3. Wife's Alternate Final Beneficiaries

_____

_____

_____

_____

4. Husband's Specific Beneficiaries

_____
Item of Property

_____
Primary Beneficiary

_____
Alternate Beneficiary

_____
Item of Property

_____
Primary Beneficiary

_____
Alternate Beneficiary

_____
Item of Property

_____
Primary Beneficiary

_____
Alternate Beneficiary

5. Husband's Final Beneficiaries

_____

_____

_____

_____

6. Husband's Alternate Final Beneficiaries

_____

_____

_____

_____

chapter 9

PROPERTY LEFT TO MINOR CHILDREN OR YOUNG ADULTS

*I*f any of the beneficiaries you've named (including alternate, residuary, or final beneficiaries) might inherit trust property before they are ready to manage it responsibly, you'll want to arrange for an adult to manage that beneficiary's property.

If your young beneficiaries won't inherit anything of great value—that is, if you're leaving them objects that have more sentimental than monetary value—you don't need to arrange for an adult to manage the property.

Here are the beneficiaries you should arrange management for:

- **Any beneficiary now under 18.** Children under 18 cannot, by law, directly manage substantial amounts of money—roughly, anything over $2,500 to $5,000, depending on state law.

  If a minor inherits valuable trust property, and you have not arranged for the property to be managed by an adult, a court-appointed guardian will have to manage the property. Contrary to what you might expect, a child's parent does not automatically have legal authority to manage any property the child inherits. A child's parent will have to ask the court to grant them that authority, and will be subject to the court's supervision. If neither of the beneficiary's parents are alive, there may be no obvious person for the court to appoint as property guardian. In that case, it may be even more important for you to name someone in your living trust.

  Reminder. If you have a child under age 18, you must nominate a personal guardian—the adult responsible for raising the child—in your will. You can't do this in your living trust.

- **Any beneficiary over 18 you believe is not mature enough to responsibly handle your gift.** If a beneficiary is over 18 when he or she inherits trust property, you do not need, legally, to have anyone manage the property on the beneficiary's behalf. If you don't make any arrangements, the beneficiary will get the property with no strings attached. But with the forms in this book, you can arrange for property management to last until a young adult beneficiary turns any age up to 35—that is, you can choose any age between 19 and 35 when the young adult receives the property outright.

WHY 35?

We've created a rule that any beneficiary must receive a gift made from a Nolo living trust outright by age 35 at the latest. We've chosen 35 for the cut-off age because it seems reasonable to conclude that an adult who can't manage financial matters responsibly by that age may never be able to do so. If you want someone else to manage the trust property of a beneficiary who's over 35, you'll probably want to see a lawyer to create a special type of trust, usually called a "spendthrift trust," and resolve specific problems, such as who will be the trustee many years down the line if the beneficiary survives to old age.

Obviously, whether or not you want to provide for management of property inherited by a young adult beneficiary is a personal decision. Some young adults are fully capable of managing money at age 21, while others at the same age might indulge recklessly, even disastrously, if they received a large inheritance outright.

A. Property Management Options

If you want to provide for property management for a gift to a minor or young adult beneficiary, you have several options.

- **Leave the property directly to an adult to use for the child.** Many people don't leave property directly to a child. Instead, they leave it to the child's parent or to the person they expect to have care and custody of the child if neither parent is available. There's no formal legal arrangement, but they trust the adult to use the property for the child's benefit.

- **Create children's trusts.** You can establish "children's trusts" in your living trust. Technically, a children's or child's trust is a subtrust of the overall living trust. If you do establish children's trusts, your successor trustee will manage the trust property you left each child or young adult and spend it for that child's education, health, and other needs. If you create a shared living trust or an AB trust, the surviving spouse would manage property left to minors by the deceased spouse; the successor trustee would act only after both spouses die. Each child's trust ends at whatever age you designate for that child (between 18 and 35), and any remaining property is then turned over to the beneficiary outright.

- **Name a custodian under the Uniform Transfers to Minors Act (UTMA).** This is a model law written by a national panel of experts. All but two states (South Carolina and Vermont) have adopted this law, sometimes with minor modifications. In states with the UTMA, you can use your living trust to name a "custodian" to manage property you leave a child, until the child reaches 18 or 21, depending on state law (up to 25 in some states). If you don't need management to last beyond the age your state law allows, a custodianship is often preferable to a child's trust.

Children with special needs. These property management options are not designed to provide long-term property management for a child or young adult with serious disabilities. You'll need to see a lawyer and make arrangements geared to your particular situation.

B. Which Method Is Better for You: Children's Trust or Custodianship?

Both a child's trust and a custodianship are safe, efficient ways of managing trust property that a young person inherits. Under either system, the person in charge of the young beneficiary's property has the same responsibility to use the property for the beneficiary's support, education and health. For example, you can leave a gift of life insurance by using a child's trust or by naming a custodian under the UTMA, and in either case, the proceeds will be held in trust by an adult for benefit of the child you name to be the beneficiary. So use whichever method works best for you, but don't get hung up worrying about technicalities or puzzling over possible legal intricacies.

The most significant difference between a child's trust and an UTMA gift is that a child's trust can last longer than a custodianship, which must end at age 18 to 21 in most states (but can last up to 25 in some states). For that reason, a child's trust is a good choice when it's con-

ceivable that a young person could inherit a large amount of property, and you want the money handled by a more mature person, at least through the child's middle 20s.

STATES THAT HAVE ADOPTED THE UTMA

State	Age at which minor gets property
Alabama	21
Alaska	18-25
Arizona	21
Arkansas	18-21
California	18-25
Colorado	21
Connecticut	21
Delaware	21
District of Columbia	18-21
Florida	21
Georgia	21
Hawaii	21
Idaho	21
Illinois	21
Indiana	21
Iowa	21
Kansas	21
Kentucky	18
Maine	18-21
Maryland	21
Massachusetts	21
Michigan	18-21
Minnesota	21
Mississippi	21
Missouri	21
Montana	21
Nebraska	21
Nevada	18-25
New Hampshire	21
New Jersey	18-21
New Mexico	21
New York	21
North Carolina	18-21
North Dakota	21
Ohio	21
Oklahoma	18
Oregon	21-25
Pennsylvania	21-25
Rhode Island	21
South Dakota	18
Tennessee	21-25
Texas	21
Utah	21
Virginia	18-21
Washington	21
West Virginia	21
Wisconsin	21
Wyoming	21

An UTMA custodianship is usually preferable to a child's trust if the beneficiary will inherit roughly $50,000 worth of property (or perhaps up to $100,000 or so if the child is quite young). That amount is likely to be used up for living expenses by the time the child reaches age 18, let alone 21. And if your state allows the UTMA gift to be kept in custodianship until the child is 21 or older, amounts up to $100,000 can surely be consumed by four years of college costs. In these situations, there's probably no need to create a children's trust to last beyond the UTMA cutoff age.

A custodianship can have other advantages as well:

- Handling a beneficiary's property can be easier with a custodianship than with a trust. A custodian's powers are written into state law, and most institutions, such as banks and insurance companies, are familiar with the rules. Trusts, on the other hand, vary in their terms. So before a bank lets a trustee act on behalf of a beneficiary, it may demand to see and analyze a copy of the trust document.

- You can name whomever you wish to be a custodian, and you can name different custodians for different beneficiaries. So if you want to arrange custodianships for grandchildren, for example, you could name each child's parent as custodian. A child's trust is not so flexible: The surviving spouse, or the successor trustee, will be the trustee of all child's trusts created for your young beneficiaries.

- A custodianship may offer better income tax rates than a trust. A trust is taxed at 28% on retained income over $1,500 annually, with the top rate reaching 39.6% on income over $7,500. By contrast, property managed by an UTMA custodian is taxed as income paid directly to the child, often a lower rate than paid by a trust. (This can get complicated, because income paid to a child under 14 is taxed at the child's parents' tax rate.)

C. Tax-Saving Educational Investment Plans

Beyond leaving property to children, you should know that federal law provides two different plans you can use to save for the educational expenses of children. These plans could affect your living trust planning because if you establish one of these plans for your own children,

you should have less worry about future educational expenses draining your estate.

1. 529 Plans

A 529 plan is an investment account established to pay for the higher education of a named beneficiary. The beneficiary must be a "family member," who can range from your own children to cousins. Income accumulates in a 529 plan free of taxes. More importantly, no income tax is assessed on money paid from a 529 plan for the beneficiary's tuition, books, fees, supplies, and equipment necessary to attend college, graduate school, or approved vocational institutions. Authorized expenses can also include special needs services for a disadvantaged student.

You can give up to $11,000 per year free from gift tax to a 529 account for any one beneficiary. (Contributions can be made only in cash.) A couple can give up to $22,000 per year. Any amount over those limits given to one account within a year is subject to federal gift tax. (See Chapter 15, Section C.)

These plans are called "529" plans because they were created by that section of the Internal Revenue Code. (They are also sometimes called "qualified tuition programs.") Under federal law, you can invest only in a state-authorized plan. Each state now has its own separate plan, managed by an investment company or companies selected by that state. Managers range from TIAA-CREF to Vanguard to J. P. Morgan to various lesser-known financial institutions.

Some state plans allow you to invest only if you live in that state. Also about half the states allow residents to deduct 529 contributions from their state income tax, which could be a major incentive to buy a home-grown 529 plan. On the other hand, the majority of 529 plans allow anyone to invest in them. Indeed, you could invest in more than one. If you're seeking the best plan for your investment needs and beliefs, you have a rather bewildering array of plans to choose from.

However you choose to invest in a 529 plan, you are basically investing in securities—stocks and bonds—that come with the stock market pitfalls we've all become aware of. But some state's 529 managers have a far more aggressive (risky) investment strategy than do managers of other state's plans. So you'll need to do quite a bit of homework before selecting a 529 plan that's right for you.

If a beneficiary does not attend college, you can name a new beneficiary from the eligible family group. But if you wind up taking money out of a 529 plan for non-educational purposes, taxes and penalties apply.

2. Coverdell Accounts

With a Coverdell account (formerly called an Educational IRA), you can contribute up to $2,000 per year, though contribution amounts phase out for folks with six-figure incomes. Further, this $2,000 limit is the total amount that can be set aside in any one year for any one beneficiary. In other words, different family members cannot each contribute $2,000 per year for one beneficiary. Combined, they can contribute no more than $2,000.

Contributions are not tax-deductible when you make them. But money in the account is not taxed when (or if) it grows, and no tax is due when you make qualified withdrawal from the account to pay for a child's education expenses.

The $2,000 limit definitely decreases the appeal of a Coverdell account, and more parents use 529 plans to save for their children's education. But a Coverdell account can still be useful in the right circumstances. For example, a grandparent or other relation could establish Coverdell accounts for your children, while you invest in a 529 account or save in other ways for higher education costs.

D. Children's Trusts

As I've said, if you leave any trust property to minors or to young adults who cannot responsibly manage property, you can create, within your living trust, a separate child's trust for each such beneficiary. Your surviving spouse or successor trustee manages all child's trusts.

1. How a Child's Trust Is Created

The first step is to make your gifts in your living trust document, including gifts left to any children or young adults. One common example is life insurance proceeds made payable to your living trust. You name your child or children as beneficiaries for all proceeds turned over to the trust. Then you complete another clause in your trust document, the children's trust clause, where you list each child's name and the age (from 18 to 35) at which this beneficiary is to receive his or her trust property outright. If at your death the beneficiary is younger than the age you specified, a trust will be created for that beneficiary. If the beneficiary is older, he or she gets the trust property with no strings attached, and no trust is created. (Leaving life insurance through your trust is discussed in more detail in Section 4, below.)

Example

In their basic shared living trust, Roger and Victoria each leave their trust property to the other. They name their daughters, who are 22 and 25, as alternate beneficiaries, and arrange for any trust property they may inherit, including their life insurance proceeds, to stay in children's trusts until each daughter reaches 30. They name Victoria's sister, Antoinette, as successor trustee.

Roger and Victoria die in a car accident when one daughter is 28 and the other is 31. The 28-year-old's half of the trust property stays in a children's trust, managed by Antoinette, until she turns 30. The 31-year-old gets her half outright; no trust is created for her.

HOW A CHILD'S TRUST WORKS

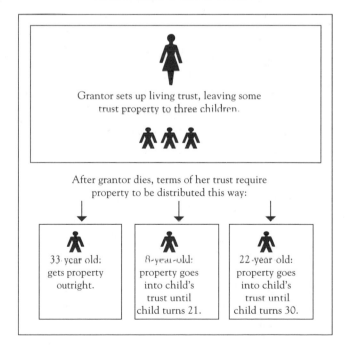

If a child's trust becomes operational, your successor trustee (or surviving spouse, if you made a trust together) must obtain a separate trust taxpayer ID number for each child's trust, file separate tax returns, and keep separate accountings and records for each trust. The successor trustee must manage each trust individually. So an operational child's trust is both a component of the overall living trust and a distinct entity. If light can be both a wave and a particle, surely this kind of duality is acceptable. And indeed it is, in the real world of the IRS, banks and trust beneficiaries.

Example

In his individual living trust, Stanley names his 14-year-old son Michael as beneficiary of $75,000 worth of stock. He specifies that any stock Michael inherits when Stanley dies should be kept in a trust until Michael is 28, subject to the trustee's right to spend it on Michael's behalf.

Stanley dies when Michael is 19. The stock goes into a children's trust for him, managed by the successor trustee of Stanley's living trust. The trustee is free to use the stock (and the income it produces) to pay for Michael's education and support. Michael will receive what's left of the stock when he turns 28.

You will create a separate children's trust for each young beneficiary you list. If these children's trusts ever become operational, Nolo's living trust forms provide that each one is given the name of its particular beneficiary. This allows each child's trust to be readily identified and managed in the real world.

Example

Leo Goldstein's living trust creates children's trusts for his grandchildren, Janet and John Ronninger, which are to last until each is 30. Leo dies while Janet and John are minors. Leo's successor trustee manages the children's trusts, one of which is called "The Leo Goldstein Living Trust, The Janet Ronninger Child's Trust" and the other of which is called "The Leo Goldstein Living Trust, The John Ronninger Child's Trust." Thus these trusts are identified as independent entities, while technically they are part of the original living trust as well.

With an AB trust, children's trusts are also possible. You can use your AB trust to make up to three specific gifts and name alternate beneficiaries for each gift. If any of these beneficiaries is a minor or young adult, you can create a child's trust.

2. The Trustee of Children's Trusts

The trustee for each child's trust is your successor trustee or, if you made a shared or AB trust with your spouse, then your spouse. After both spouses are deceased, the successor trustee takes over any operational children's trusts. The trust forms in this book do not allow you to name another person to be a trustee for a child's trust.

The reason is that naming separate trustees creates serious paperwork and practical problems. Which trustee gets the original of your living trust document? Do you create several originals? Besides, it's usually hard enough to find one competent person who'll serve as trustee for all children's trusts. If you really want to name someone other than your successor trustee to be custodian for a gift to a minor, in all but two states you can use the UTMA. (See Section E, below.)

Choosing someone else to be trustee of a child's trust. If you want to have children's trusts managed by someone other than your surviving spouse or your successor trustee, see a lawyer.

3. The Duties of a Trustee of a Children's Trust

The trustee's powers and responsibilities are spelled out in the trust document. The trust trustee must:

- Manage each trust's property until that trust's beneficiary reaches the age set out in the trust document—which can take years.

- Use each trust's property or income to pay for that trust beneficiary's expenses, such as support, education, and health care.

- Keep separate records of trust transactions and file income tax returns for each trust.

- A very few states require periodic reports to the beneficiary of a child's trust. However, in most cases, it doesn't matter whether or not it's done, since everything is within the family.

If the trust trustee needs to hire an accountant, tax lawyer, or other expert to help manage a trust, he or she can use that trust's assets to pay a reasonable amount for the help.

The trust document also provides that the trustee of a children's trust is entitled to reasonable compensation for his or her work as trustee. The trustee decides what is a reasonable amount, without court approval; the compensation is paid from the assets of the particular trust involved.

When the beneficiary reaches the age designated by the trust document, up to 35, the trustee must give the beneficiary what remains of that child's trust property.

4. Leaving Children Life Insurance Proceeds Through a Children's Trust

If you name minor children as beneficiaries, or alternate beneficiaries, of your life insurance, you need to create some type of adult management for the proceeds. You may also want mature adult management while the children are younger adults.

A sensible way to accomplish this is to name your living trust as the beneficiary of your life insurance. Then in the trust document, you name each child as a beneficiary of the proceeds, specifying the percentage or amount each child is to receive. Finally, within your living trust, you create a separate child's trust for each child.

Your living trust does not become the owner of the life insurance policy. You remain the owner. If you die while the child or children are under the age you specified in your living trust, the money will be managed for the child by your successor trustee until the child is old enough to receive the money outright.

Another possible approach for life insurance with child beneficiaries is to create a custodianship for each child, and name each child's custodian as beneficiary in specified portions for the insurance. (See Section E, below.) A problem with this approach is that in most states, the custodian must turn over all property to the child when he or she reaches 21; in a number of states, the age is 18. With a child's trust, you can extend the age the child must reach before gaining unfettered control of the property.

Technically, passing the proceeds of a life insurance policy through your living trust is a bit more complicated than leaving other property this way. You must take two steps:

1. Name the trustee, as trustee of the child's trust of the living trust, as the beneficiary of your life insurance policy. Your insurance agent will have a form that lets you change the beneficiary of the policy. Tell the agent what you want to do and make sure you've got forms that are acceptable to the insurance company.

2. When you list property items in the living trust document (that is, property owned by the trust), list the proceeds of the policy, not the policy itself. (Chapter 10, Section D, contains an example of how to list beneficiaries for insurance proceeds left to your trust.)

E. Custodianships

As noted, creating a custodianship for a gift under your state's Uniform Transfers to Minors Act (UTMA) may be a preferable alternative to creating children's trusts.

1. How a Custodianship Is Created

After you make all your gifts in your living trust, in a separate section of the trust form you can create as many custodianships as you want for minor or young adult beneficiaries. You do this by identifying the property and the beneficiary it is left to and appointing a custodian to be responsible for supervising that property. The form provides that the custodian is to act "under the [your state] Uniform Transfers to Minors Act." You can also name an alternate custodian in case your first choice can't do the job. Finally, you list the age at which the minor is to receive the property outright, using the list in Section B as your guide. In most states, you have no choice and must list the age that state's UTMA decrees. In a few states, you can choose an age in a set range.

The custodian manages any trust property the young beneficiary inherits until the beneficiary reaches the age at which state law says the custodianship must end. (See Section B, above.)

OTHER TYPES OF TRUSTS FOR MINORS OR YOUNG ADULT BENEFICIARIES

In some situations, you may want a different type of child's trust than the individual trusts you can create with this book's living trust forms. Consult a lawyer if you want to:

- place extensive controls over the use of property in the trust—for example, you place real estate in the trust and you want it managed in a specific way

- provide for special care for a disadvantaged child

- create a trust for any beneficiary who is already over age 35, or

- combine property for different children into a single trust (often called a "family pot" trust). In this type of trust, the trustee doles out money to different children as he sees fit, according to their needs. Establishing this sort of trust may not be a good idea. The trust doesn't end until the youngest child reaches the designated age (the older ones can't get their share outright before this), and the trustee may prefer one child's needs over another's, setting up the possibility of conflict, or at least resentment. On the other hand, for young children in a family group, this sort of trust may be sensible, so that the trustee can spend, as a parent would, according to the children's needs.

Example

Sandra and Don make a basic shared living trust. Sandra leaves 100 shares of Nike stock to her niece Jennifer Frankel. She names Hazel Frankel, Jennifer's mother, as custodian under the Illinois Uniform Transfers to Minors Act.

At Sandra's death, Jennifer is 13. So Don, as trustee of the living trust, turns the stock over to the custodian, Hazel. She will manage it for Jennifer until Jennifer turns 21, the age Illinois law says she must be given the property outright.

As discussed, in some states, you can specify—within limits—the age at which custodianship will end. If your state allows this, you must state the age at which the custodianship will terminate.

Example

Alexis and Jonathan, who live in New Jersey, make a basic shared living trust. They leave most of their trust property to each other and leave some property to their young children, Ian and Noel. They both specify, in the trust document, that any trust property the children inherit should be managed by the other spouse as custodian, under the New Jersey Uniform Transfers to Minors Act, until the boys turn 21. Under New Jersey law, they could have specified any age from 18 to 21. As alternate custodian, both name Jonathan's mother.

Alexis and Jonathan die simultaneously in an accident. Jonathan's mother, as custodian, takes over management of the trust property left to her grandchildren. When each boy turns 21, he will receive whatever of his property hasn't been used for his support or education.

HOW A CUSTODIANSHIP WORKS

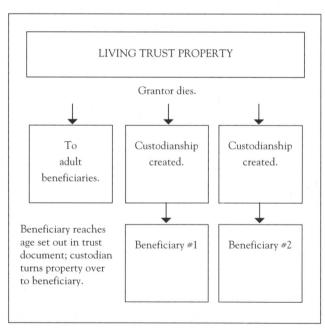

2. Changes in State Law

States are free to change their rules about the age at which custodianships terminate. If your state does this after you make your living trust, it could affect any custodianships you have set up, though not in any drastic way.

- If your state raises the age at which custodianships terminate, the new age will determine when your beneficiary's custodianship ends.

- If your state adopts a flexible scheme allowing you to choose the age at which the custodianship ends, you can amend your living trust document to designate an age. If you don't amend it, the custodianship will end when the beneficiary reaches the youngest age allowed under the law—in most cases, 18.

3. If You Move

If you move to South Carolina or Vermont, states that haven't adopted the UTMA, it may be necessary to revise your living trust by creating children's trusts for any gifts previously made using a custodian. However, if the beneficiary of the gift, or the custodian for it, remains in a state that has an UTMA, you can still use that law for your gift. Finally, if you move from one UTMA state to another, you can keep your UTMA clause as it is, unless you've moved to a state that has a lower age for turning over the gift to the minor than the age allowed in your old state. If this is the case, you'll have to amend your trust to establish a new age for the gift to be turned over to the child.

4. The Custodian's Responsibilities

A custodian has roughly the same responsibility as the trustee of a child's trust: to manage the beneficiary's property wisely and honestly. The custodian's authority and duties are clearly set out by the Uniform Transfers to Minors Act, as enacted by your state. No court directly supervises the custodian.

The custodian must:

- Manage the property until the beneficiary reaches the age at which, by law, he or she gets the property out-

right. If the child is quite young at your death, this can be a number of years.

- Use the property or income to pay for the young beneficiary's support, education, and health care.

- Keep the property separate from his or her own property.

- Keep separate records of trust transactions. The custodian does not have to file a separate income tax return; income from the property can be reported on the young beneficiary's return. (By comparison, the trustee of a child's trust must file a separate tax return for the subtrust.)

A custodian who needs to hire an accountant, tax lawyer, or other expert can use the property to pay a reasonable amount for the help.

If state law allows it, the custodian is entitled to reasonable compensation and reimbursement for reasonable expenses. The payment, if any is taken, comes from the property the custodian manages for the beneficiary. If this concerns you, check out your state's laws or see a lawyer. (See Chapter 17, Section D.)

5. Choosing a Custodian

In most cases, you should name as custodian the person who will have physical custody of the minor child. That's almost always one of the child's parents. If the beneficiary is your child, name the child's other parent, unless you have serious reservations about that person's ability to handle the property for the child.

Only one person can be named as custodian for one beneficiary. You can, however, name an alternate custodian to take over if your first choice is unable to serve. And you can name different custodians for different beneficiaries.

Example

Elaine, in her living trust, leaves property to two young nephews, Jerry and Mark, and one young niece Reyna. She names Jerry and Reyna's mother, Alice, as custodian for their gifts. She names Mark's mother, Angela, as custodian for his gift. ∎

chapter 10

PREPARING YOUR LIVING TRUST DOCUMENT

$\mathcal{N}$ow it's time to actually prepare your living trust document. This chapter explains how to do it, step-by-step, when you use one of the trust forms in this book.

Please read this entire chapter carefully so you understand the choices you will make. Take your time and reread as much as you need to.

**CHECKLIST FOR PREPARING
YOUR LIVING TRUST DOCUMENT**

1. Using a tear-out form in Appendix B

- Remove the form you need from Appendix B.
- Fill in the form by following the step-by-step instructions in this chapter.

2. Using a form on the CD-ROM

For instructions on how to use the forms CD that comes with this book, see Appendix A. Then:

- Open the form file you need.
- Fill in the form by following the step-by-step instructions in this chapter.
- Use your word processor's "Save As" command to rename and save your completed document.
- Print out and proofread your final document.

3. Finalizing your document

- Type or word process the completed form, and proofread the final version.
- Sign your trust document in front of a notary public in the state where you live.
- Store your trust document in a safe place. (See Chapter 12.)

A. Choosing the Right Trust Form

Appendix B and the CD-ROM contain three fill-in-the-blanks living trust forms:

- **Form 1:** Basic probate-avoidance living trust for one person.
- **Form 2:** Basic probate-avoidance shared living trust for a couple (married or not) with shared ownership property.
- **Form 3:** AB trust for a couple (married or not) who want to save on overall estate taxes and avoid probate.

Generally, you should use only one trust. However, in a few special situations you may decide it's preferable to use more than one living trust. (See Chapter 4 for a discussion.)

B. Getting Started

Once you've selected the appropriate trust form, you may want to photocopy it, so you have a clean copy (or several) to use if you need to prepare more than one draft. One draft is all many people need make before they type up their final document. But having extra copies of the form certainly can't hurt, and may be useful if you make many corrections or changes.

Use a pencil to make corrections easier, and go through the form slowly and carefully, filling in the blanks, or crossing them out if the information required doesn't apply to you.

C. Making Changes to a Trust Form

These Nolo trusts are intended to be used as printed, except for minor, commonsense variations, or where the directions specifically allow you a choice of what to include. Generally, it's risky to make changes to the trust forms, particularly Form 3, the AB trust. Changes create the possibility of confusion and even contradictions regarding what you intend with your trust. If you want to make many changes to the form, this should alert you to the fact that our form does not suit you, and you need to see a lawyer.

As previously discussed, you may need to make minor word changes. If you want to name co-successor trustees, you'll need to change the word "trustee" to "trustees" at various places in the form. Just be clear on your draft form what minor changes you've made.

 Be very cautious about making changes. You will have to use your common sense to decide whether or not changes in the form are needed. But do be very careful. Don't stray far from the language of the form, especially with an AB trust. You certainly don't want to risk making a change that could cost you your estate tax savings. Be sure you understand the effect of any changes you make.

D. Step-by-Step Instructions

Important: *These instructions are keyed to numbers on the trust forms. For example, Step 1 tells you how to fill in your name(s) and how to name your living trust. On the trust form, each time your name, or names, are called for, you'll see a ①.* (If you prepare your trust using the CD-ROM, the numbers will appear in parentheses rather than in a circle.)

The steps are set out in the most logical order. However, the circled numbers on the forms do not always proceed sequentially; for example, number ①, the name of your trust, appears at the beginning of the form and also later, after other circled numbers. This is because the information called for is needed in more than one place in your trust form. Other numbers appear out of sequence because the information called for is necessary only for that one form, so the number given comes after the numbers and information common to all forms. Just remember the basic principle: The circled number refers you to the specific step in this section that explains how to fill in this blank.

Some simple information you must fill in is not keyed to a circled number because no instructions seem necessary. For instance, where you see a blank and "he/she" printed underneath, put in either "he" or "she," depending on whether the person referred to (which will be clear in the context) is male or female. Similarly, where you see a blank with "your state" printed underneath, fill in the state where you live.

When you have completed the form, proofread it carefully. Then proceed, as explained in Sections E through G, below, to finish your trust document.

For couples. For the most part, the same decisions must be made whether you're preparing a living trust for one person or for a couple, so the instructions are just about the same. However, some instructions apply only to the two shared living trusts. They are identified by this symbol:

SPECIAL INSTRUCTIONS FOR UNMARRIED COUPLES

Forms 2 and 3 are written in terms of a married couple. Therefore, an unmarried couple will need to change some wording in these forms. For example, the printed forms use the terms "spouse" or "surviving spouse" and, in Form 3, "Surviving Spouse's Trust." You can use "mate," "surviving mate," "partner" or whatever words seem most suitable to you. Once you have selected a word or words, stick with them throughout the trust. And, of course, be sure you've read the trust document carefully, to make all the necessary substitutions.

Aside from words like "spouse" in the text, you'll see a number of blank lines to be filled in, with words below the line, such as

_____

wife's name

or

_____

husband's name

You will delete the words that appear below the lines from your final trust. But of course, you need to fill in the appropriate member of the couple's name, not a (nonexistent in your case) wife's or husband's name.

Though making these word changes does require some extra work, it's really just a matter of cross-outs and substitutions, which you shouldn't find difficult or onerous.

Step 1: Name Your Living Trust

You must give your living trust a name. Normally, you simply use your own name—for example, "The Denis Clifford Living Trust." It's legal to use more inventive names, for reasons ranging from a desire for privacy to nostalgia. (I once had a client who created the "Rue de Rivoli Trust.") Also, if you create more than one trust, you will want to distinguish them. One way to do this is to use numbers, particularly Roman numerals, to prevent any confusion in a basic shared trust, which splits into

Trust #1 and Trust #2 on the death of a spouse. For example, "The Denis Clifford Living Trust #I," "The Denis Clifford Living Trust #II," and so on. Generally, however, it's preferable to sign the trusts on different days and identify each trust by the date signed—for example, "The Denis Clifford Living Trust, 3/19/1996"; "The Denis Clifford Living Trust, 4/7/1996."

Use only one name per person; don't enter various versions of your name joined by "aka" (also known as).

If you go by more than one name, be sure that the name you use for your living trust is the one that appears on the ownership documents for property you plan to transfer to the trust. If it isn't, it could cause confusion later, and you should change the name on your ownership documents before you transfer the property to the trust.

Example

You use the name William Dix for your trust, but own real estate in your former name of William Geicherwitz. You should prepare and sign a new deed, changing the name of the real estate owner to William Dix, before you prepare another deed to transfer the property from you (William Dix) to your living trust.

Married couples who make a basic shared living trust or an AB trust normally use both their names to identify their trust—for example, "The Kay and Ornette Lewison Living Trust" or "The Cynthia Duffy and Mike O'Mally Living Trust." As with a trust for an individual, a couple can give their shared trust a fanciful name.

Unmarried couples can simply use both their names—for example, "The Natalia Williams and Andrew Johnson Living Trust" or "The Lillian Perry and Sandra Bick Living Trust."

If you use your name or names for your trust, insert it every time there is a ① on the living trust form.

If you don't use your own name, you'll need to determine, each time you see a ①, whether your own name or the trust's name is required. For example, when naming the original trustees, you'll put in your own name(s), not the trust's name.

Step 2: Decide How Many Property Schedules Your Trust Needs

By this time, you should have decided which items of your property you will place in your living trust and which you will leave by other means. (See Chapter 6.) Now you need to list all property that you will transfer to the trust on a "schedule" or "schedules," which will be attached to your trust document. How to list the property on a trust schedule is explained in Step 3.

As you can see by looking at the trust forms, a trust schedule is nothing more than a blank sheet of paper. For an individual trust, there's only one "Schedule A." For a couple, there are these:

- "Schedule A, Shared Property Placed in Trust";
- "Schedule B, Wife's Separate Property Placed in Trust"; and
- "Schedule C, Husband's Separate Property Placed in Trust."

First, you must decide how many trust schedules you want to use. If you're creating a trust for one person (Form 1), you will use only one schedule, "Schedule A," even if several—or many—different types of property will be transferred to the trust.

Example

Mrs. Johnson wants to transfer her house, two cars, stock accounts, and jewelry to her living trust. She lists all this property on one trust schedule, Schedule A.

The shared trust form (Form 2) and Nolo's AB trust (Form 3) have three schedules, A, B and C. Schedule A is for the couple's shared ownership property. On Schedule A, you need to identify the character of shared ownership property such as "community property" or "tenants in common." (This is discussed in detail in Step 4, below.) Schedule B is for the wife's separate property, and C is for the husband's separate property. If you have shared property and each spouse has separate property, you will use all three schedules.

Example

Mrs. and Mr. Andrezly, in their 60s, have been married for 15 years. Each has children from a former marriage. When they got married, each owned property which they agreed would remain each one's separate property. Since they married, they have acquired shared property, including a home. In their basic shared living trust, each wants his or her separate property to go to the children from the first marriage; their shared property goes to the surviving spouse.

They list their property in the basic shared living trust by using three schedules: Schedule A for the shared property, Schedule B for Mrs. Andrezly's separate property, and Schedule C for Mr. Andrezly's separate property.

If the Andrezlys created three separate trusts—a basic shared living trust for the shared marital property and two individual living trusts for each spouses' separate property—they would use only Schedule A of the shared trust for their shared marital property.

If one, or both, spouses does not have separate property, you won't use Schedule B, Schedule C, or both of them. You'll also need to delete references in the trust document to that spouse's (or both spouses') separate property. The paragraphs you may need to change are listed below.

Example

Tau and Lien Yu prepare a basic shared living trust. They own shared property. Lien has separate property; Tau does not. So they omit Schedule C from their draft trust and edit the trust form following the instructions below.

CHANGES TO TRUST FORMS 2 OR 3 IF SEPARATE PROPERTY NOT INCLUDED

If either spouse doesn't transfer separate property to the trust, you'll need to make appropriate changes on Form 2 or 3 by deleting the irrelevant material from the following sections:

- Section II, Paragraph A, refers to Schedules A, B, and C. Thus, if neither spouse has separate property, delete "B and C." If a wife has separate property and her husband does not, this would become "Schedules A and B."
- Section II, Paragraph B(1), refers to the wife's separate property.
- Section II, Paragraph B(2), refers to the husband's separate property.
- Section II, Paragraph D(2), refers first to the wife's separate property on Schedule B and the husband's separate property on Schedule C.
- Section IV refers to Schedules A, B, and C.
- In Form 2, Section V (B) refers to Schedules A, B, and C.

Below I show a sample draft Form 2 where one spouse owns separate property, and one does not. This draft shows the changes that are necessary to prepare the final draft when Schedule C is not used.

Step 3: List Your Trust Property on the Trust Schedule(s)

After you've decided how many schedules to use, list your trust property on them. Listing the trust property on a schedule does not give that property to beneficiaries. You list the property to make clear what property you have transferred to the trust and is owned by the trust. Then, in your trust document, you name your beneficiaries—that is, specify who will inherit the trust property after your death (Step 7, below).

Example

This is Form 2, Sections II (D)1 and II (D)2 from the "Tau and Lien Yu Shared Living Trust." Lien has separate property; Tau does not.

(D) Character of Property Placed in Trust

While both grantors are alive, property transferred to this trust shall retain its original character. If the trust is revoked, the trustee shall distribute the trust property to the grantors based on the same ownership rights they had before the property was transferred to the trust, as specified below.

1) Shared Property

All trust property listed on Schedule A was shared property:

④   owned as community property of the grantors and shall retain that

<u>identify the character of shared property listed in Schedule A</u>

character after being transferred to this trust. If the trust is

revoked, this property shall be returned to the grantors as their

community property.

(2) Separate Property

The trust property listed on Schedule B shall retain its character as the separate property of

Lien Yu   . ~~The trust property listed on Schedule C~~

wife's name

~~shall retain its character as the separate property of~~ _____.

~~husband's name~~

⚠ **Transferring property to the trust.** To complete the transfer of property to the trust, you also must reregister title to that property in the trustee's or trustees' name(s). This absolutely essential process is explained in detail in Chapter 11.

When listing trust property on a trust schedule, generally you can use the same wording you used on the worksheet in Chapter 6. Just describe each item clearly enough so that the surviving spouse or successor trustee can identify it and transfer it to the right person. No magic legal words are required. Remember, this isn't a document that will be picked over by lawyers and courts. It's a document for the real world; what's important is

that your successor trustee, family, and other inheritors are clear on what you've done and what you want.

Think about who will ultimately inherit the property. If you're leaving everything to one person, or a few major items to be parceled out among a few people, there's less need to list property in great detail. But if there will be a number of trust beneficiaries, and objects could be confused, be more precise about each one. When in doubt, err on the side of including more information.

When you name the beneficiaries for the trust property in your trust document (Step 7), your gifts must, of course, be consistent with the property listed on the schedule. You can't leave someone something that isn't listed on a trust property schedule. But the schedule does not have to be as detailed as your gifts. For example, on a schedule you could list "the house, furnishings, and personal possessions at [street address]." You can leave all this property to one beneficiary, or you could divide it, naming one beneficiary for the house and another for the furnishings and possessions, or break it down still further into many separate gifts.

IDENTIFYING OWNERSHIP OF TRUST PROPERTY

Don't use "my" or "our" when listing trust property on a schedule. For example, don't enter "my books" or "my stereo system." That's because once the property is in the living trust, technically it doesn't belong to you anymore—it belongs to the living trust, and is held in the name of the trustee.

If you need to refer to yourself or your property in a trust schedule, do so in the third person, by calling yourself "the grantor" or "grantors" rather than using "I" or "we." Sometimes, to clarify what property is owned by the trust, it helps to state on the schedule that identified property was "formerly" or "previously" owned by the grantor.

For example, on a trust schedule, you list: "The 3/4-carat diamond bracelet formerly owned by the grantor."

A variation of this is to identify and list property "in the possession of the grantor," for example, "All compact discs and videos in the possession of the grantor."

---

1. Real Estate

A house can be listed by its street address—for example, "The house and real estate at 10001 Lakeway Drive, Seaview, Florida." Similarly, unimproved property can usually be listed by its common name: "The lots previously owned by the grantor on 50 to 80 Alligator Road, Seaview, Florida."

Usually, the street address is enough. It's not necessary to use the "legal description" found on the deed, which gives a subdivision plat number or a metes-and-bounds description. But if the property has no street address or common name—for example, if it is undeveloped land, off-road, out in the country, you need to designate exactly what land you're referring to. So carefully copy the full legal description, word for word, from your deed.

If you own a house and several adjacent lots, it's a good idea to indicate that you are transferring the entire parcel to your living trust by describing the land as well as the house.

Example

The house at 390 Normal Road, Montclair, New Jersey, and all unimproved land between 390 Normal Road and 320 Normal Road.

Real estate often contains items that are properly classified as personal property. For instance, farms are often sold with tools and animals. If you intend to leave both real estate and personal property together to a beneficiary, make clear what this "together" consists of. It's best to specify the large-ticket items (tractor, cattle) and refer generally to the rest of the items as "personal property."

- *"240-acre truck farm on Route 11, in Whitman County, Iowa, with all tools, animals, tractors, threshers, and other machines and all other personal property located there."*

- *"Fishing cabin on the Wild River in Washington County, Maine, with all the fishing gear, furniture, tools, and other personal property found there."*

- *"The house at 442 Wanaha Bay Road, Island of Hawaii, Hawaii, and all personal possessions and household furnishings in the house."*

- *"The mobile home permanently located at E-Z motor camp, Kalispell, Montana, and all possessions and furnishings contained in it."*

If you own real estate with someone else and are transferring only your share to the trust, you don't need to specify how big a share you own. Just describe the property. The trust schedules then state that you are transferring all your interest in the property, whatever share that is, to the living trust.

Examples

Rhea owns a one-fifth interest in an apartment house located in Atlanta, Georgia. She prepares a deed transferring her one-fifth interest to her living trust's name. On the trust schedule, she simply writes *"The interest in the apartment house at 434 Madison Street, Atlanta, Georgia, previously owned by the grantor."*

Timeshares. A timeshare in a house or apartment is real estate and can be transferred to the trust like any other real estate. You can describe your interest as: *"the grantor's share in ___(address)___,"* or *"the grantor's right to three weeks per year use of ___(address)___."*

2. Furnishings and Household Items

Household furnishings can be generally listed:

- *"The house and real estate at 12 High St., Chicago, Illinois, and all household furnishings and personal possessions in it."*
- *"All the grantor's household goods and personal possessions located at 82 West Ave., Chicago, Ill."*

Or you can get more specific:

- *"All the furniture normally kept in the house at 44123 Derby Ave., Ross, KY."*
- *"All furniture and household items normally kept in the house at 869 Hopkins St., Great Falls, Montana."*

You can also list individual items, if you plan to leave them separately.

- *"The antique brass bed in the master bedroom in the house at 33 Walker Ave., Fort Lee, New Jersey."*
- *"Daumier print captioned 'Les beaux jours de la vie.'"*
- *"Two Victorian rocking chairs in the living room at 75 Washington Street, Jefferson, Montana."*

3. Bank and Money Market Accounts

You can list bank accounts by any means sufficient to identify them. Generally, it makes sense to list the account number:

- *"Bank account # 78-144212-8068 at Oceanside Savings, Miami, Florida, Market St. Branch."*
- *"Savings Account No. 9384-387, Arlington Bank, Arlington, MN."*
- *"Money Market Account 47-223 at Charles Schwab & Co., Inc., San Francisco, CA."*

4. Cash

You cannot transfer cash to a living trust simply by stating a dollar figure on the schedule. For example, if you list "$25,000" on Schedule A, this doesn't transfer that amount of cash to the trust, because no source for these funds is given. Instead, list a specific source of cash. You can then make specific cash gifts from this source when you name your trust beneficiaries. Here are some examples:

- *"Bank account #33-931007-6214 at Bonanza Thrift, Miami, Florida."*
- *"$25,000 from the grantor's stash in his desk."* (This is obviously risky. If the money is moved from the desk, technically it is no longer owned by the trust.)

5. Securities

Securities, including mutual fund accounts, need to be listed clearly so there is no question what property is referred to:

- *"Mutual fund account #6D-32 2240001, at International Monetary Inc., Chicago, Illinois."*
- *"All stock and any other assets in account #144-16-4124, at Smith Barney & Co., New York City, branch at 58th St./6th Ave."*

- *"100 shares of General Motors common stock."*
- *"Mutual funds in account # 55-144-2001-7, Calvert Social Responsibility Fund, Boston, MA."*

6. Sole Proprietorship Business Property

With a sole proprietorship business that has not been incorporated, the proprietor is the legal owner of all assets of the business, including the business name and any "good will." So you can simply list all assets of that business as a single item of trust property.

- *"All assets of the grantor doing business as Mulligan's Fish Market, 44 Wellington St., Wymouth, Kentucky."*
- *"All assets of the grantor doing business as Fourth Street Records and CDs, 10 Piper's Lane, Hoboken, NJ."*
- *"All assets of the grantor doing business as Jim Pine Plumbing, 477 Market Street, Fort Lauderdale, Florida."*

You can also divide up the business assets if you're leaving different parts to different people. For example:

- *"All accounts receivable of the business known as Garcia's Restaurant, 988 17th St., Atlanta, GA."*
- *"The business name, goodwill, lease, and all food and food preparation and storage equipment, including refrigerator, freezer, hand mixers, and slicer used at Garcia's Restaurant, 988 17th St., Atlanta, GA."*

7. Shares in a Closely Held Corporation

- *"The stock of ABC Hardware, Inc., formerly owned by the grantors."*

8. Partnership Interest

Because a partnership is a legal entity that can own property, you don't need to list items of property owned by the partnership. Just list your partnership interest:

- *"All the grantor's interest in the Don and Dan's Bait Shop Partnership, Belmore, Oregon."*

9. Shares in a Solely Owned Corporation

- *"All shares in the XYZ Corporation."*
- *"All stock in Fern's Olde Antique Shoppe, Inc., 23 Turnbridge Court, Danbury, Connecticut."*

10. Membership Interest in a Limited Liability Company

- *"The grantor's membership interest in the Goat-Cheese-Wine LLC."*

11. Miscellaneous Items of Personal Property

There are various ways you can list items of personal property on a trust schedule, depending primarily on whether you want to leave separate items to different beneficiaries, or all of one type of item to a sole (or group of) beneficiaries.

For items of significant monetary or sentimental value, you may want to list them individually.

- *"The Macintosh computer (serial number 129311) with keyboard (serial number 165895)."*
- *"The medical textbooks in the grantor's office at 1702 Parker Towers, San Francisco, CA."*
- *"The photograph collection usually kept at 321 Glen St., Omaha, NE."*
- *"The collection of European stamps, including [describe particularly valuable stamps], usually kept at 440 Loma Prieta Blvd., #450, San Jose, CA."*
- *"The Martin D-35 acoustic guitar, serial number 477597."*
- *"The signed 1960 Ernie Banks baseball card kept in safe deposit box 234, First National Bank of Augusta, Augusta, IL."*
- *"The Baldwin upright piano kept at 985 Dawson Court, South Brenly, Massachusetts."*
- *"Gold earrings with small rubies in them, purchased from Charles Shreve and Co. in 1971."*

If you are like most people, you have all sorts of minor personal possessions you don't want to bother itemizing. To deal with them, you can group a number of items in one category:

- *"all tools"* (or *"all carpenter's tools, including power saws, in possession of the grantor"*),
- *"all dolls"*
- *"baseball cards"*
- *"records, tapes, and compact discs,"* or
- *"machines and equipment."*

Of course, some items without large monetary value can have great emotional worth to you and your family: a photo album, an old music box, a treasured chair. These can be separately listed as you desire.

If you're leaving all these groups of personal items to one beneficiary, there's no need to separately list them, even as groups. You can simply conclude your list with one catch-all item, such as "all personal property previously owned by the grantor."

Sample Schedule A for Shared Property

Below is a sample of a draft Schedule A for shared property for Form 2, a basic shared trust. When the final trust form is typed, the schedule is likewise typed, eliminating the printed instructions on the form. The final typed schedule is attached to the trust document.

$Sample$

SCHEDULE A

Shared property placed in trust:

The house and real estate at 428 Dubuque Drive, Alameda, California.

All shares of stock in the Mo-To Corporation, Alameda, California.

The grand piano located at 428 Dubuque Drive, Alameda, California.

The Diebenkorn painting located at 428 Dubuque Drive, Alameda, California.

All other household possessions and furnishings located at 428 Dubuque Drive, Alameda, California.

Money market account #7033372, Working Assets, Boston, MA.

Certificate of Deposit No. 10235, Lighthouse Savings and Loan Association, Oakland, CA.

All copyrights and rights to royalties previously owned by the grantors in these books, currently published by Fly High Press, Berkeley, California:

Dunk It: How You Can Learn to Dunk a Basketball

Winning Through Whining, a Self-Help Guide

Watch It! How to Survive Urban Life

Step 4: Identify the Nature of Shared Trust Property (Forms 2 and 3 only)

If you and your spouse are creating a trust together, you should state in the trust document that all shared property transferred to the trust (listed on Schedule A) retains the legal character it had before. That means that it stays community property if you live in a community property state. If you live in a common law state, all shared property transferred to the trust should be owned equally by the couple as tenants in common, not as joint tenants or tenants by the entirety. (See Chapter 11, Section A. Also see Chapter 6, for a discussion of community property states and common law states.)

If you don't share ownership 50-50, be sure to list each person's percentage of ownership.

If you are an unmarried couple who owns property together, you can likewise state that shared ownership property on Schedule A be returned to you two in the percentages of ownership you define in the schedule, and in this clause, if the trust is ever revoked.

To define the nature of shared trust property, insert one of the following clauses in the living trust form where you see: "All trust property listed on Schedule A was shared property," followed by a line with ④:

- **If you live in a common law state:**

  "co-owned equally by the grantors as tenants in common and shall retain that character after being transferred to this trust. If the trust is revoked, this property shall be returned to the grantors as co-owned equally by them as tenants in common."

- **If you live in a community property state:**

  "owned as community property of the grantors and shall retain that character after being transferred to this trust. If the trust is revoked, this property shall be returned to grantors as their community property."

- **If you are an unmarried couple:**

  "co-owned equally by the grantors as tenants in common. Any power reserved to the grantors to alter, amend, modify, or revoke this trust, as to the property listed in Schedule A, must be exercised by both grantors, in writing, to be effective. If this trust is revoked, this property shall be returned to the grantors as co-owned equally by them as tenants in common."

If you are married, you can change ownership of trust property without any possible gift tax consequences—for example, to convert one spouse's separately owned property to shared or community property or vice versa.

Step 5A: Decide Whether You Want Management of Trust Property If You Become Incapacitated (All Forms)

Form 1 provides that the successor trustee takes over management of the trust if you (the grantor) become incapacitated and unable to manage trust property. These provisions eliminate any need for court proceedings to appoint a guardian or custodian for trust property if you become incapacitated.

The basic shared trust (Form 2) and an AB trust (Form 3) provide that if both spouses become incapacitated, or if the survivor becomes incapacitated after one spouse dies, the trust property is managed by the successor trustee for the grantor's benefit.

It's sensible and standard to provide for management of trust property if you become incapacitated. If you want this, simply leave the clause where you see ⑤Ⓐ as is. If for some very unusual reason you don't want this, delete the clause where you see the ⑤Ⓐ. Be aware that if you delete the clause, you might later be the subject of court financial custodianship proceedings if you become incapacitated.

Allowing your successor trustee to step in and manage trust property doesn't give your successor trustee legal authority over property that's not in your living trust. To give someone that power, you need a document called a durable power of attorney for finances.

If you don't prepare a durable power of attorney and you become incapacitated, property not transferred to your living trust will need to be managed by a court-appointed conservator or guardian.

For this reason (and because you may receive other property or income in the future that doesn't make it into the trust), I strongly suggest that you also create a durable power of attorney for finances. See Chapter 15, Section E.

Step 5B: Decide Whether Your Spouse or Successor Trustee Is Permitted to Amend Your AB Trust If You Are Incapacitated and the Estate Tax Law Changes (Form 3 Only)

The trust forms in the book do not allow either spouse to amend a trust if one spouse is incapacitated. Nor do the forms allow a successor trustee to amend a trust (though you can change this. See Chapter 13, Section E.) If you prepare an AB trust and the estate tax law changes, it may become desirable to amend the trust to take full advantage of the new tax law. (See Chapter 4, Section E for a discussion.) It's wise to consider what will happen if you are incapacitated and this need arises. Here you can give your spouse, or the successor trustee, the authority to amend your AB trust for the narrow and specific purpose of taking advantage of any new estate tax law.

Realistically, this situation will rarely occur. The provision would take effect only if both of the following things happen:

- Both spouses are still alive and one or both are incapacitated. If one spouse has died, the AB trust has already been split into Trust A and Trust B. Trust A, the estate tax saving trust, has become irrevocable. It was subject to tax under the estate tax law that existed when the spouse died, and so cannot be affected by subsequent changes in that tax.

- Congress changes the estate tax law in ways that make it desirable to change the existing AB trust.

If you want your spouse and successor trustee to have authority to amend your AB trust if these two criteria are met, simply leave the provision found in Section VII (B) of Form 3, where you see the ⑤Ⓑ. This provision reads:

"If both grantors are alive and one is incapacitated, and Congress changes the estate tax law, the competent spouse shall have authority to amend this AB trust in order to take best advantage of the new tax law. If both grantors are alive and both are incapacitated, and Congress changes the estate tax law, the successor trustee shall have authority to amend this AB trust in order to take best advantage of the new tax law."

To use this provision in your AB trust, it is absolutely essential that you fully trust your successor trustee. Of course, that's already absolutely essential, but here even more so. If you have any worries that your successor trustee might somehow abuse this power, do not use this provision. It's understandable that you might not want to risk anyone else being able to alter your AB trust. You could sensibly decide that the risk of undesired change outweighs the possibility of need for change if the estate tax law is revised. If you feel this way, simply delete the provision from your trust before preparing your final trust document.

If You Want More Control. You could try to pin down more precisely what circumstances would authorize your successor trustee to amend your trust. For instance, you could speculate on changes Congress might make, and provide rules for each possibility. Or you could require that the successor trustee get the agreement of another key beneficiary before being able to make the changes. If you want to try for this kind of control, see a lawyer for help with drafting your provision. But be advised that it may turn out to be both complicated and costly. Also, the very fact that you want more control means you have some doubt about your successor trustee, at least in this situation. That alone suggests you'd be wise to talk with an attorney about your concerns.

Step 6: Name Your Successor Trustee

In the blanks with the ⑥ on the trust forms, name your successor trustee and your alternate successor trustee. (Choosing your successor trustee is discussed in Chapter 7.) You've already named yourself as the original trustee.

Example

Using Form 3, the AB trust, a couple completes Section III(E), Successor Trustee, as follows:

"Upon the death or incapacity of the surviving spouse, or the incapacity of both spouses, the successor trustee shall be Vicki J. Benoit. If she is unable to serve or to continue serving as successor trustee, the next successor trustee shall be B.J. Benoit."

1. Naming Co-Successor Trustees

If you name more than one successor trustee or more than one alternate successor trustee, you need to specify in your trust document how the authority of the cotrustees is to be shared. Clearly, this is your personal decision, depending on how well the cotrustees get along and whether or not you think it's safe to let any of them act individually for the trust. So, depending on your needs, immediately after you name your successor trustees and alternate successor trustees, you'll insert one of the following clauses from the form:

- *"Any of the successor trustees has full and independent authority to act for and represent the trust."*

or

- *"All the successor trustees must agree in writing to any transaction involving the trust or trust property."*

If you have only one successor trustee and don't use co-successor trustees, you'll need to delete all this material from the form.

LISTING SPECIFIC TRUSTEE POWERS

The trust forms provide that the trustee has "all authority and powers" your state's laws allow. But the trust forms also list specific powers, including the power to sell trust real estate, buy or sell stocks, and several other detailed powers. All of these specific powers are normally included in the general authority conferred on a trustee under state law. But banks, title companies, stock brokerage companies, and other financial institutions frequently insist that a trustee be specifically authorized by the trust document to engage in a transaction involving their institution. So spelling out these powers often makes the successor trustee's work much easier in the real world.

2.　Bond

The forms provide that no trustee has to post a bond. A bond is basically an insurance policy guaranteeing that a person will honestly carry out his or her duties; it pays off up to a stated amount if he or she doesn't. Bonding companies, which are normally divisions of insurance companies, issue a bond in exchange for a premium, usually about 10% of the face amount of the bond.

If you select a trustworthy successor trustee, there's no reason for a bond. In almost all situations, the question never comes up. Since the successor trustee handles the trust outside any court system, there's no forum where a demand for a bond could be raised. But just in case the question is somehow raised in a lawsuit (very unlikely), it's sensible to have waived any bond requirement. The cost of a bond would have to be paid for by your estate, and your beneficiaries would then receive less. Also, it's difficult for an individual to even get a bond in many states.

Requiring a successor trustee's bond. If you do want your successor trustee to post a bond, see a lawyer.

Step 7:　Name the Primary and Alternate Trust Beneficiaries

Now you enter the names of your trust beneficiaries, naming who gets what.

With a trust for an individual (Form 1) or a basic shared living trust (Form 2), insert their names, and descriptions of property given them, in the blanks where you see ⑦. You can make as many separate gifts as you need to. The forms have spaces for five; if you have more, use another sheet of paper.

Reminder for Unmarried Couples: If you are an unmarried couple and use either Form 2 or 3, you'll need to change the printed form's references to spouses. Thus "Husband's Beneficiaries" or "Wife's Beneficiaries" must be changed to the appropriate individual's name. Example: "Al Smith's Beneficiaries" instead of "Husband's Beneficiaries."

With an AB trust (Form 3), each spouse can make up to three separate gifts to specific beneficiaries, outside of the AB trust property, and can list alternates for these gifts. Of course, it isn't required that you make such gifts; many couples simply leave everything to each other. (See Chapter 5, Section C.)

With Form 3, each spouse will also name his or her final beneficiaries, to receive the marital trust property after the surviving spouse dies, and alternate final beneficiaries. See Step 8B, below.

1.　Changing Forms 2 or 3 If You Don't Leave Specific Gifts

If you, your spouse, or both of you choose not to leave any specific gifts, but instead leave all trust property to each other, you'll need to eliminate the provisions in Forms 2 and 3 for making specific gifts, and also make any necessary revisions to the Beneficiaries Section.

With Form 2, this may involve deleting Section IV(A)1 and/or Section IV(B)2:

Example 1, Form 2

Lola and Malcolm Decamp use Form 2. Lola leaves two specific gifts, Malcolm leaves none. They revise the Beneficiaries Section of the form as shown below.

This example shows how to revise a trust form only if you do not want to leave specific gifts. Some portions of the trust forms in the back of this book have been omitted from the following example.

IV. BENEFICIARIES

(A) Husband's Primary and Alternate Beneficiaries

Upon the death of _____, trust property
husband's name

owned by _____, as his share of the trust property
husband's name

listed on Schedule A and any separate property listed on Schedule C, shall be distributed as specified to the beneficiaries named in this section.

1. Husband's Specific Beneficiaries

a. ⑦ _____ shall be given
beneficiary's name(s)

_____.
property identified

If _____ does not survive _____ ,
beneficiary　　　　　　　　　　　　husband's name

that property shall be given to _____ .
alternate beneficiary

[All specific husband beneficiary provisions deleted]

A 2. Husband's ~~Residuary~~ Beneficiary

The ~~residuary~~ beneficiary of any trust property owned by _____ Malcolm Decamp _____
husband's name

as his share of the trust property listed on Schedule A or any separate property listed on Schedule C, ~~and not specifically and validly disposed of by Section IV, Paragraph (A)1,~~ shall be

⑦A Lola Decamp _____ . If _____ Lola Decamp _____
~~residuary~~ beneficiary　　　　　　　　　　　~~residuary~~ beneficiary

does not survive _____ Malcolm Decamp _____ , that property shall be given to
husband's name

⑦A Ted and Linda Decamp, in equal shares _____ .

(B) Wife's Primary and Alternate Beneficiaries

Upon the death of _____Lola Decamp_____, trust property

wife's name

owned by _____Lola Decamp_____ _____, as her share of the trust property

wife's name

listed on Schedule A and any separate property listed on Schedule B shall be distributed as specified to the beneficiaries

named in this section.

1. Wife's Specific Beneficiaries

a. ⑦_____Susan Fergis_____ shall be given

beneficiary's name(s)

_____all trust gold jewelry formerly owned by Lola Decamp_____.

property identified

If _____Susan Fergis_____ does not survive _____Lola Decamp_____,

beneficiary   wife's name

that property shall be given to _____Jean Fergis_____.

alternate beneficiary

b. ⑦_____John Fergis_____ shall be given

beneficiary's name(s)

_____the autographed photo of Willie Mays_____.

property identified

If _____John Fergis_____ does not survive _____Lola Decamp_____,

beneficiary   wife's name

that property shall be given to _____the residuary beneficiary_____.

alternate beneficiary

c. ⑦_____ shall be given

beneficiary's name(s)

_____.

property identified

If _____ does not survive _____,

beneficiary   wife's name

that property shall be given to _____.

alternate beneficiary

[All other wife specific beneficiary provisions deleted]

2. Wife's Residuary Beneficiary

The residuary beneficiary of any trust property owned by _____ Lola Decamp _____
_{wife's name}

as her share of the trust property listed on Schedule A or any separate property listed on Schedule B, and not specifically and validly disposed of by Section IV, Paragraph (B)1, shall be

(8A) _____ Malcolm Decamp _____ . If _____ Malcolm Decamp _____
_{residuary beneficiary}   _{residuary beneficiary}

does not survive _____ Lola Decamp _____ , that property shall be given to
_{wife's name}

(8A) _____ Ted and Linda Decamp, in equal shares _____ .
_{alternate residuary beneficiary}

If you use Form 3, you may need to delete
Section IV(A) and/or Section IV(B) and make selective
deletions in Section V(B)2 and Section VI(C)2:

Example 2, Form 3

Scott and Margie Vasquez create an AB Trust, using Form 3. Neither makes any specific gifts. Each leaves all their trust property to the other. They revise Form 3 as shown below.

IV. Beneficiaries

(A) Wife's Specific and Alternate Beneficiaries

Upon the death of _____, trust property
_{wife's name}

owned by _____, as her share of the trust property
_{wife's name}

listed on Schedule A and any separate property listed on Schedule B shall be distributed as specified to the beneficiaries named in this section.

(7)1. _____ shall be given
_{beneficiary's name(s)}

_____ .
_{property identified}

If _____ does not survive _____ ,
_{beneficiary}   _{wife's name}

that property shall be given to _____ .
_{alternate beneficiary}

[All Wife's Specific Beneficiary Provisions deleted]

Preparing Your Living Trust Document

(B) Husband's Specific and Alternate Beneficiaries

Upon the death of _____, trust property owned by

_____, as his share of the trust property listed on Schedule A and

husband's name

any separate property listed on Schedule C shall be distributed as specified to the beneficiaries named in this section.

⑦1. _____ shall be given

beneficiary's name(s)

_____.

property identified

If _____ does not survive _____,

beneficiary   husband's name

that property shall be given to _____ .

alternate beneficiary

[All Husband's Specific Beneficiary provisions deleted]

~~(C) Remaining Trust Property~~

~~Except as provided by Section IV, Paragraph (A) or (B),~~ all ~~other~~ trust property of the deceased spouse shall be transferred to, and administered as part of, Trust A, The Marital Life Estate Trust, defined in Section V.

V. Creation of Trust A, the Marital Life Estate Trust, on Death of Deceased Spouse

(B) Division of Trust Property on Death of Deceased Spouse

1. Upon the death of the deceased spouse, the trustee shall divide the property of The

① _____ Scott and Margie Vasquez _____ Living Trust listed on Schedules A, B, and C

your names

into two separate trusts, Trust A and Trust B.

2. All trust assets of the deceased spouse, as defined in Section V, Paragraph (A)2, shall be placed in a trust known as Trust A, the Marital Life Estate Trust, ~~after making any specific gifts provided for in Section IV, Paragraph (A) or (B), subject to any provision in this Declaration of Trust that creates childrens' subtrusts or creates custodianship under the Uniform Transfers to Minors Act.~~

VI. Trust B: The Surviving Spouse's Trust

~~(C) Distribution of Property in Trust B~~

1. Upon the death of the surviving spouse, Trust B becomes irrevocable.

2. ~~The trustee shall first distribute any specific gifts of the surviving spouse to the beneficiaries named in Section IV, Paragraph (A) or (B).~~ The trustee shall ~~then~~ distribute all ~~remaining~~ property of Trust B to ~~his or her~~ the final, or alternate final, beneficiaries, as named in Section V, Paragraph (C)3 or (C)4.

2. How to Enter Beneficiaries' Names

Many people worry that some precise, technical language must be used in living trusts to identify their beneficiaries, or their gifts won't be legally binding. Fortunately, this isn't true. You simply need to give the name that clearly identifies a beneficiary, so that your successor trustee understands to whom the gift is to be made. You don't have to worry about using a person's "legal" name, such as the full name on her birth certificate. Nor do you need to list the beneficiary's address or Social Security number.

If you name an institution (charitable or not) to inherit property from your trust, enter its complete name. It may be commonly known by a shortened version, which could cause confusion if there are similarly named organizations. Call to ask if you're unsure. (An institution that stands to inherit some of your money will be more than happy to help you.) Also, be sure to specify if you want a specific branch or part of a national organization to receive your gift—for example, a local chapter of the Sierra Club.

3. Identifying Property Left to Beneficiaries

There are three basic approaches to identifying property in a beneficiary clause:

1. Use exactly the same words you used on your property schedule. For example, if you listed "Money Market Account #60-32 2240001 at International Money Inc., Boston, MA" on your schedule, use exactly the same words in the beneficiary clause.

2. Group items left to a certain beneficiary. If you listed and specifically identified a number of similar items on a schedule (for example, five bank accounts, ten valuable paintings, four automobiles) and you wish to leave all

items in a particular group to the same beneficiary, it's sufficient to say "all bank accounts listed on Schedule A" or "all paintings listed on Schedule A."

3. Be more specific than your trust schedule. For example, suppose on Schedule A you listed "all books in possession of the grantor," to indicate that ownership of all your books is transferred to your living trust. However, you don't wish to leave all these books to one beneficiary. When making gifts, you could state:

- *"Beth Ruveen shall be given all books by F. Scott Fitzgerald in the possession of the grantor."*

- *"John Advale shall be given all books in French in the possion of the grantor."*

- *Jim Horton shall be given all books in the possession of the grantor, except those left or given by this trust document to Beth Ruveen and John Advale."*

Shared property. On Forms 2 and 3, each spouse can give away only his or her half-interest in shared property, not all of it. So, when naming a beneficiary or beneficiaries for property listed on Schedule A of a shared living trust, it must be clear that each spouse is giving away only his or her share of the co-owned property. To accomplish this, when you leave a gift from property on Schedule A, add an identifying phrase to the beneficiary clause. Here are two examples; the language you must add is in italics:

If property left to one beneficiary:

Karen Zombanski shall be given _all Lonnie Zombanski's_
beneficiary

interest in the house listed on Schedule A.
property identified

If property left to more than one beneficiary:

Charles Berry shall be given _50%_, and
beneficiary

Le Petit Richard and _B. Diddly_
beneficiary   beneficiary

each shall be given _25% of all Jackson Smith's interest in_

the stock account at Smith Barney, NYC, #177-4N-2044,

as listed on Schedule A.

4. Naming Children or Young Adults as Beneficiaries

You name a child or a young adult as a beneficiary exactly as you do an adult beneficiary, entering the child's name and identifying the trust property left to him or her.

Later in the trust document, you can arrange for an adult to manage property left to a young beneficiary. (See Steps 10 and 11.)

5. Leaving All Trust Property to One Beneficiary or Group of Beneficiaries

If you are using Form 1 or 2 and you want to leave all of your trust property to one person or to be shared by several, you can use just one beneficiary clause. Here are some examples:

- For a basic shared trust:

  All property to your spouse: _"John Andrews shall be given all grantor Mary Andrews's interest in the property listed on Schedule A and Schedule B."_

- For an individual trust:

  All property equally to children: _"Steve Cronin, Elizabeth Cronin, and Roarke Cronin shall be given all property listed on Schedule A in equal shares."_

6. Leaving Property to Several Beneficiaries to Share

You may want to leave an item of trust property to be shared among several beneficiaries. This is fine, as long as you use language that clearly identifies what share each beneficiary is to receive. This is best done by using percentages. If you use one of the marital trusts (Form 2 or 3), be sure you are clear that you're giving away only your own interest in any property you share with your spouse. (Shared gifts are discussed in detail in Chapter 8, Section D.)

Example

From a stock account transferred to his shared living trust (Form 2), Jim Denniston makes the following gifts:

- _"Melinda Denniston shall be given 20% of Jim Denniston's interest in the trust's stock account #660134-N, Dean Witter Co."_
- _"Mike Denniston shall be given 30% of Jim Denniston's interest in the trust's stock account #660134-N, Dean Witter Co."_
- _"Roger Denniston shall be given 5% of Jim Denniston's interest in the trust's stock account #660134-N, Dean Witter Co."_
- _"Margo Denniston shall be given 35% of Jim Denniston's interest in the trust's stock account #660134-N, Dean Witter Co."_
- _"Cerrita Gibbs shall be given 10% of Jim Denniston's interest in the trust's stock account #660134-N, Dean Witter Co."_

7. Naming Beneficiaries of Proceeds from a Life Insurance Policy

If you have named your living trust as the beneficiary or alternate beneficiary of a life insurance policy, you can simply name, within the trust, a beneficiary, or beneficiaries, for any insurance proceeds payable to the trust. Remember, you don't need to list the policy on a trust schedule, because the trust never owns the policy; it is simply the beneficiary of it.

Example

"The grantor's children, Zack Philson and Zelda Philson, shall be given, in equal shares, all life insurance proceeds on the grantor's life paid to the trust."

If the beneficiaries you name are minors or young adults, you can arrange for someone to manage property, including insurance proceeds that they inherit while still young. (See Steps 10 and 11.)

8.   Explanations and Commentary Accompanying a Gift

There are times, particularly in family situations, when explaining the reasons for your gifts can help avoid hurt feelings or family fights. If you wish, you can provide a brief commentary when making a gift. There are two ways to do it: in the trust document itself, or in a separate letter.

In the trust document. You'll need extra space for your comments. For your rough draft, you can simply write out your comments on a separate piece of paper and attach it to the trust form, with a note about where they should be inserted in the trust document. When you prepare your trust, you can integrate your comments into the trust form.

Examples

- *"The grantor's business associate, Mildred Parker, who worked honestly and competently with her over the years, and cheerfully put up with her occasional depressions, shall be given $40,000 from the Money Market Fund #166-SJ-4111, Parnassus Mutual Funds, San Francisco, California."*

- *"The grantor's best friend, Hank Salmon, whom the grantor enjoyed fishing with for so many years, shall be given the cabin and boathouse on Lake Serene and the boat and outboard motor in the boathouse."*

- *"Theodore Stein shall be given 40% of Alfred Stein's interest in the house at 465 Merchant St., Miami, Florida.*

   "Sandra Stein Rosen shall be given 40% of Alfred Stein's interest in the house at 465 Merchant St., Miami, Florida.

   "Howard Stein shall be given 20% of Alfred Stein's interest in the house at 465 Merchant St., Miami, Florida.

   "I love all my children deeply and equally. I give 20% to Howard because he received substantial family funds to go through medical school, so it's fair that my other two children receive more of my property now."

- *"Matt Jackson shall be given the bank account #41-6621-9403 at First Maple Bank.*

"I love all my children deeply and equally. I leave more of my property to Matt than my other children because Matt is physically disadvantaged and is likely to need special care and attendants throughout his life."

Notice that in your explanations, you can refer to yourself in the first person, as "I," not "the grantor." It just sounds too awkward to express deep feelings as "the grantor." Besides, this type of wording isn't making a gift, but explaining it, so it's hard to imagine that any trouble could possibly arise from referring to yourself as "I" when speaking of your love for your kids.

In an accompanying letter. Another approach is to write a letter stating your views and feelings and attach it to your living trust document. Many people prefer this approach because it allows personal sentiments to be kept private. The living trust will have to be shown to people in various institutions, from banks to title companies to brokerage offices to county records offices. Many people don't want their personal feelings exposed to strangers in the business world. A letter can simply be removed from the trust document when showing the trust to any outsider. Also, if you have a lot to say, a letter is generally better than trying to express all your sentiments in the trust document itself.

Your letter isn't a legal part of your trust document, and it has no legal effect. It is prudent for you to state in your letter that you understand this, to eliminate any possibility someone could claim you intended the letter to somehow modify the terms of your trust.

The scope of your remarks is limited only by your imagination, short of libel. (If you write something so malicious (and false) that you libel someone, your estate could be liable for damages.) Some writers have expressed, at length and in their own chosen words, their love for a mate, children, or friend. By contrast, Benjamin Franklin's will left his son William, who was sympathetic to England during our Revolution, only some land in Nova Scotia and stated, "The fact he acted against me in the late war, which is of public notoriety, will account for my leaving him no more of an estate that he endeavored to deprive me of."

9.   Imposing a Survivorship Period

When you leave property to a primary beneficiary, you can specify that if the beneficiary doesn't survive you by some specified period of time, the gift will go to the alternate beneficiary, if you name one, or the residuary beneficiary if you don't name an alternate. The pros and cons of survivorship periods are discussed in Chapter 8, Section F.

If you want to add a survivorship period, simply insert a specific time period before naming the alternate beneficiary.

Example

"_____*Hester Dinsdale*_____ *shall be given the grantor's*
        primary beneficiary's name

interest in the antique doll collection located at

61 Hawthorn Lane, Gabels, Massachusetts .
                    property

"*If* _____*Hester Dinsdale*_____ *doesn't survive the grantor*
                beneficiary

by 30 days, *that property shall be given to* ____*Pearl Dinsdale*___."

(added survivorship clause)   alternate beneficiary

10. Naming Alternate Beneficiaries

As discussed, you are not required to name an alternate beneficiary for a gift. Some people, understandably, don't wish to contemplate the chance of an inheritor, usually someone younger, dying before they do. But most people name an alternate beneficiary for each gift to a primary beneficiary. After all, there is always the chance that the primary beneficiary may not survive you, and you won't be able to amend your trust in time to leave the gift to someone else.

With Form 1 or Form 2, if you don't name an alternate, the property that beneficiary would have received will be distributed to the person or institution you name as your "residuary beneficiary." (See Step 8A, below.)

With an AB trust (Form 3), you can name alternate beneficiaries only for any specific gifts you make (up to three). If the primary beneficiary and alternate predecease you, that gift becomes part of the A or B trust property.

You can name more than one person or institution as alternate beneficiaries. These "co-alternate beneficiaries" share the property equally, unless you specify otherwise.

Example

Sherry names her husband as beneficiary of her interest in their house, which they have transferred to their basic shared living trust. As alternate beneficiaries, she names their three children, Sean, Colleen, and Tim, to share equally.

Sherry's husband dies just before she does, leaving his half of the house to Sherry. Under the terms of the trust document, it stays in the living trust. At Sherry's death, because her husband (the primary beneficiary) is no longer alive, the house goes to the three children. All three own equal shares in all of it.

For shared gifts, it's easiest to name the other surviving beneficiaries to receive a deceased beneficiary's share. You can accomplish this by using or adapting the following language, which may require some minor changes in the printed portion of a beneficiary clause:

"*Gwen Riordan, Richard Riordan, and Martha*

*Riordan Ling*_ *shall be given* _____*Jack Riordan's*_____
    beneficiaries   grantor's name

interest in the house at _41 Sussex Road, Needles, Arizona_,
in equal shares. If any of these beneficiaries doesn't survive
_____*Jack Riordan*_____, *the deceased beneficiary's interest shall be shared equally by the surviving beneficiaries.*"

You can also name different alternates for each beneficiary of a shared gift. For example, an older person who leaves a shared gift to his children may list each child's children (or spouse) as alternate beneficiaries for that child's share of the gift.

"_Gwen Riordan, Richard Riordan and Martha Riordan Ling_ *shall be given all Jack Riordan's interest in* _the house at 41 Sussex Road, Needles, Arizona_ .

"*If Gwen Riordan doesn't survive Jack Riordan, her children, Mike Riordan James and Tracy Riordan James, shall be given the interest in the property she would have received.*

"*If Richard Riordan doesn't survive Jack Riordan, Richard's child, Sean Riordan, shall be given the interest in the property he would have received.*

"*If Martha Riordan Ling doesn't survive Jack Riordan, her husband, Patrick Ling, shall be given the interest in the property she would have received.*"

Step 8A: Name Your Residuary Beneficiary (Forms 1 and 2 only)

If you are preparing an AB trust (Form 3), skip to Step 8B. If you are preparing a trust for one person (Form 1) or a basic shared living trust (Form 2), the next step is to name your residuary beneficiary or beneficiaries.

You must name one or more residuary beneficiaries for your living trust, where you see the ⑧Ⓐ.

The residuary beneficiary of your living trust is the person or organization who will receive:

- any trust property designated for primary and alternate beneficiaries who die before you do
- any trust property that you didn't leave to a named beneficiary (this could include property you transferred to the trust later but didn't name a beneficiary for)
- any property you leave to your living trust through a pour-over will (because property left through a pour-over will doesn't avoid probate, there's usually no reason to use one; see Chapter 16, Section D), and
- any property that you actually transferred to your living trust but didn't list in the trust document.

Sometimes the residuary beneficiary of a basic living trust doesn't inherit anything from the trust, because all trust property is left to primary beneficiaries, with alternates. In this situation, naming a residuary beneficiary can be just a back-up measure, to guard against the extremely small chance that both a primary and alternate trust beneficiary do not survive you.

You may, however, deliberately leave the residuary beneficiary trust property by:

- Not naming specific beneficiaries for most trust property. Everything not left to a specific beneficiary will go to your residuary beneficiary. It's common, for example, for a grantor to leave much of his estate to his children as residuary beneficiaries.
- Adding property to the trust later and not amending your trust document to name a specific beneficiary to receive it after your death.
- Using a pour-over will to leave property to your living trust and not naming a specific beneficiary in the trust document to receive property that passes through the will. (See Chapter 16, Section D.)

Co-residuary beneficiaries. If you name more than one residuary beneficiary (or alternate residuary beneficiary), you need to state, in the clause, what portion or percentage each residuary beneficiary will receive. It's common, especially if one's children are the residuary beneficiaries, to state that they each receive an equal share.

Example

"The residuary beneficiaries…shall be Rachel Weinstock and Alan Weinstock, each to receive 50% of all trust property not specifically and validly disposed of…."[by earlier gifts]

Of course, you can also specify that residuary beneficiaries receive unequal shares. In that case, you must specify what percentage of the property each residuary beneficiary will receive.

Example

Zane Jilconty names three siblings—Lucy, Jill, and Warren—as his residuary beneficiaries. For several reasons, he wants to leave them unequal amounts. So he provides, in his residuary clause, that his residuaries are: *"Lucy Jilconty, 50% of the residuary property; Jill Jilconty Jackson, 30% of the residuary property; and Warren Jilconty, 20% of residuary property."*

Alternate residuary beneficiaries. You should also name an alternate residuary beneficiary, or beneficiaries, to be sure you have one final backup to receive trust property if all other beneficiaries, including your residuary beneficiary, predecease you and you can't amend your trust in time. (True, this is a remote possibility, but remote possibilities are lawyers' stock-in-trade, and even we at Nolo can't bring ourselves to completely jettison concern for such unlikely contingencies.)

Step 8B: Name Your Final Beneficiaries (Form 3 Only)

If you are preparing an AB trust, it's vital that each spouse name a final beneficiary or beneficiaries, and normally alternate final beneficiaries, where you see ⑧Ⓑ. Each spouse names his or her own final beneficiary or beneficiaries. Often these are the same people for both spouses, most commonly their children. But spouses can name different final beneficiaries if they want to. (See Chapter 5, Section C.)

Example

Cara and Hugh O'Neill create an AB trust. Each wants to name their four children as final beneficiaries. They complete Section V(C)3 and V(C)4 of Form 3 as follows:

"If Cara O'Neill is the deceased spouse, the final beneficiaries shall be: Paula O'Neill, Patrick O'Neill, Olivia O'Neill, and Moira O'Neill.

"If Hugh O'Neill is the deceased spouse, the final beneficiaries shall be: Paula O'Neill, Patrick O'Neill, Olivia O'Neill, and Moira O'Neill."

The final beneficiaries will receive all property remaining in the A trust after the surviving spouse (the life beneficiary) dies. (See Chapter 5, Section C.) The final beneficiaries might also receive any of the specific gifts the deceased spouse made, if both the specific beneficiary and the alternate beneficiary for a specific gift predecease that spouse (a remote possibility, surely, but not unheard of). In that case, the specific gift becomes part of the Trust A property.

Each spouse's final beneficiaries also serve as the primary beneficiaries of Trust B, the surviving spouse's trust. As you know, after one spouse dies, the surviving spouse's trust remains revocable. But if he or she does not amend that trust and name new beneficiaries, the property in that trust (again, except for up to three specific gifts) will go to the final beneficiaries he or she named in the original trust document.

Charities as final beneficiaries. If you name a charity as a final beneficiary, and federal estate taxes are due, the IRS will take all the taxes from other gifts you've made. This may diminish the value of these gifts substantially, or even wipe some out. To avoid this, you can specify that any proportion of taxes on your estate be paid out of property left for the charity. Then the charity gets whatever is left. The math calculations here can get complex and confusing because the size of the charitable contribution depends on the amount of estate taxes, and vice versa. If you want to work out the exact figures, see a knowledgeable estate tax accountant or lawyer.

Step 9: Provide for Payment of Debts and Taxes

There are two ways to handle payment of debts and taxes after your death:

- leave it up to the successor trustee, or
- designate that certain trust assets be used.

For many people, payment of debts and taxes is not a serious concern. Their estates are now well under the minimum estate tax threshold, so they don't expect that federal taxes will be due, and their debts are relatively minor—perhaps a few personal bills, credit card charges, household utilities, and any unpaid bills from the last illness or funeral/burial costs.

Complex Debt or Tax Problems. If your estate is likely to face difficult debt or tax problems, see an attorney to discuss how to handle this. A good lawyer can help you draft specific provisions for payment of these obligations. Similarly, if much of the value of your estate will be transferred by methods other than your living trust, do not rely on the debt and tax payment options presented here, which do not apportion payment between trust and non-trust assets.

1. Leave the Decision to the Trustee

You do not have to decide what assets will be used to pay your debts and taxes. Many people prefer to leave this decision to their successor trustee, who will know what the real financial situation is when these debts must be paid. You can, at best, make only a reasonable guess now. If you direct that a specific asset or assets be used to pay any debts or estate taxes, it can cause problems later on. If you've also left the asset to a specific beneficiary, the provision for payment of debts and taxes takes priority, so that beneficiary may receive little or nothing from your gift. Also, if the property you identified isn't sufficient to pay all your debts and taxes, your successor trustee will still have to decide how to pay any balance due.

If allowing the trustee to make the decision makes sense to you, for an individual trust, where you see the ⑨, delete all language after the first sentence of this section, as shown in the example below.

DECIDING ABOUT DEBTS AND TAXES

(C) Payment by Trustee of the Grantor's Debts and Taxes

The grantor's debts and death taxes shall be paid by the trustee. ~~The trustee shall pay these from the following trust property:~~

⑨ _____

_____

_____.

If the property specified above is insufficient to pay all the grantor's debts and death taxes, the trustee shall determine how such debts and death taxes shall be paid from trust property.

With a basic shared living trust (Form 2) or Nolo's AB trust (Form 3), each spouse can choose how his or her debts are to be paid. If both spouses want their successor trustee to decide this, there's a little more crossing out to do. With Form 2, make deletions like those shown above for "Wife's Debts and Taxes," Section VIII C (1), and "Husband's Debts and Taxes," Section VIII C (2). Then delete all of the next provision, "If Specified Property In-sufficient," Section VIII C (3). With Nolo's AB trust, make these same deletions. The section numbers for the AB trust are IX C (1), IX C (2), and IX C (3). Finally, if for some unusual reason one spouse wants to choose how debts and taxes are paid but the other does not, simply make deletions like those shown in the above example for the spouse leaving the decision to the trustee.

2. Designate Specific Assets

If you decide you want to make specific provisions for payment of your debts and taxes from trust property, write in the specific items you want used to pay them in the blank where you see the ⑨ on the trust forms. And do your best to be sure these assets will actually be sufficient to pay all your debts and taxes.

Example

"The grantor's debts and death taxes shall be paid by the trustee from the following trust property:

- *First, from the bank account #99-8062144, Wells Fargo Bank, Berkeley, California.*

- *Second, from stock account #82-304, Smith Barney & Co., San Francisco, California."*

Remember that any property you specify to pay your debts and taxes must be owned by your trust. That means you must list it on a property schedule and transfer title into the trustee's name. (That process is explained in Chapter 11.)

In a basic shared living trust or an AB trust, each spouse can specify the property to be used to pay his or her debts and death taxes.

Example

Sid and Ellen Wall want each one's debts and taxes paid from a shared stock account. In their basic shared living trust, they provide:

"*1. Wife's Debts*

"*Ellen Wall's debts and death taxes shall be paid by the trustee from the following trust property: her interest in stock account #0014463, Smith Barney & Co.*

"*2. Husband's Debts*

"*Sid Wall's debts and death taxes shall be paid by the trustee from the following trust property: his interest in stock account #0014463, Smith Barney & Co.*"

With an AB trust, the property a spouse specifies to be used to pay debts and taxes will normally be part of Trust A. So primarily what's accomplished by specifying assets to pay debts is to protect the specific gifts from being used to pay any debts and taxes.

Step 10: Create Children's Trusts (If Desired)

In the blank with the ⑩ on the trust forms, you establish children's trusts by listing each person (minor or young adult) you want to name as beneficiary of a child's trust. This may include minors and young adults you've named as alternate beneficiaries. Be sure not to list as children's trust beneficiaries any persons you want to make gifts to using the Uniform Transfers to Minors Act. You'll do that in Step 11. You cannot leave a gift to a minor by both the Uniform Transfers to Minors Act and a child's trust.

For each trust beneficiary you list where you see the ⑩, you also state the age at which you want that beneficiary to receive his or her trust property. If you die before the beneficiary reaches the age you specify, the beneficiary's property will be retained in a child's trust until the age is reached. (See Chapter 9, Section B.) If you don't specify an age, each listed beneficiary will receive the trust property outright at the age of 35.

Step 11: Create Custodianships Under the Uniform Transfers to Minors Act (If Desired)

If you want to make a gift to a child using your state's Uniform Transfers to Minors Act (UTMA), complete the custodianship clause where you see an ⑪. The form con-

tains three blank clauses for individual beneficiaries, but you can add as many additional clauses as you want.

IF YOU DO NOT CREATE A CHILD'S TRUST OR MAKE GIFTS USING THE UNIFORM TRANSFERS TO MINORS ACT

If you do not create a child's trust or make any gifts under the Uniform Transfers to Minors Act, simply cross out the blank section(s) before your final trust is typed. These clauses have been placed at the end of the trust form so that you do not have to renumber other trust clauses if you delete both of them.

If you create children's trusts but do not make gifts under the Uniform Transfers to Minors Act, simply delete that later clause. Again, no renumbering of clauses is required.

However, if you do not create any children's trusts but do make gifts under the Uniform Transfers to Minors Act, you must delete the children's trust clause and renumber the Uniform Transfers clause. To do this, simply change the clause number for gifts under the Uniform Transfers to Minors Act:

- From "X" to "IX" in the Living Trust for One Person
- From "XI" to "X" in the Basic Shared Living Trust
- From "XII" to "XI" in the AB trust.

To complete the UTMA clause, begin by listing the state where you live (after doublechecking the list in Chapter 9, Section B, to be sure your state has adopted the UTMA). Then, to make an individual gift, you fill in the beneficiary's name, the custodian's name, and the age the beneficiary will receive the property outright. You can also use an UTMA clause to leave gifts to other minors, such as grandchildren, if they live in a state that has an UTMA law.

The age a child will receive the gift outright depends on state law; Chapter 9, Section B, lists each state's termination age. In some states, you are given a limited choice of when the custodianship ends. For example, you can choose any age from 18 to 21 in Maine, and 18 to 25 in California. But most states allow you no choice. The gift must end at the age set by the state. So to complete the age provision of an UTMA gift clause in states where you have no choice, all you need do is fill in the age from the list in Chapter 9.

Examples

In California, where you can choose an age between 18 and 25:

"*All property Ned Clark becomes entitled to under this trust document shall be given to Mary Clark as custodian for Ned Clark under the California Uniform Transfers to Minors Act until Ned Clark reaches age 24.*"

In New Hampshire, where a custodianship must end at age 21:

"*All property Luisa Brookside shall become entitled to under this document shall be given to Nancy Curtis as custodian for Luisa Brookside under the New Hampshire Uniform Transfers to Minors Act until Luisa Brookside reaches age 21.*"

Step 12: Decide About Reports to Final Beneficiaries (Form 3 Only)

You have a choice regarding reports the surviving spouse (as trustee) must give the final beneficiaries about an operational Trust A.

The trust form provides, where you see the ⑫ (in Section V(C)6), that the surviving spouse doesn't have to provide any accountings, except that the spouse must give the final beneficiaries copies of the trust's annual federal income tax return.

Some couples, understandably, feel that even providing tax returns is an intrusion into their financial privacy—that just because they've established a trust to save on estate taxes for their children is no reason they must reveal details of their finances to them yearly. If you feel this way, simply delete the final portion of this accounting clause, so that it reads:

"*No accounting of the Trust A shall be required of the trustee.*"

Another version is to provide that no accounting is required as long as the surviving spouse serves as trustee, but when the successor trustee takes over, accountings are required. If you decide on this approach, here is the clause to use when you see the ⑫ (Part V(C)6):

"*No accounting of Trust A shall be required as long as the surviving spouse serves as trustee. When any successor trustee serves as trustee of Trust A, the final beneficiaries shall be provided with copies of the annual trust income tax return.*"

Unless the surviving spouse becomes incapacitated and cannot serve as trustee for a while, the successor trustee will take over only when the surviving spouse dies.

So usually, this last clause will require the successor trustee to provide only the one final trust income tax return to the beneficiaries. The trust property should be rapidly transferred to the final beneficiaries, and the last trust income tax return is just one part of closing down the trust.

E. Prepare Your Final Trust Document

When you have completely filled in the trust form, proofread it carefully. Check to be sure you have:

- included all property you want to leave through the trust

- clearly and accurately identified all property (doublecheck account and serial numbers, for example)

- included all beneficiaries to whom you want to leave property

- spelled beneficiaries' (including alternate and residuary beneficiaries) names correctly and consistently, and

- made adequate arrangements for management of trust property that young beneficiaries might inherit.

When preparing the final trust, you want a document that looks as much like a conventional lawyer's living trust as possible. So don't include any of the following material from your draft form in your final version:

- The top caption of the form, such as "Form 2, Basic Shared Living Trust." You can leave the heading of the trust schedules as printed. For example, if you use a Schedule C, "Schedule C, Husband's Separate Property Placed in Trust," this does not need to be crossed out or changed.

- Instructions

- Circled numbers

- Any printed material on the form that doesn't apply to you. This may include:

  - blank beneficiary clauses, if you don't have as many beneficiaries as the forms provide space for

  - the alternate beneficiary provision of a beneficiary clause, if you decided not to name alternates for a specific gift

  - all material relating to trusts for minor beneficiaries, if you didn't create any

  - all material relating to the Uniform Transfers to Minors act, if you didn't make any gifts using it.

Cross out all material you want to eliminate before the final trust document is typed.

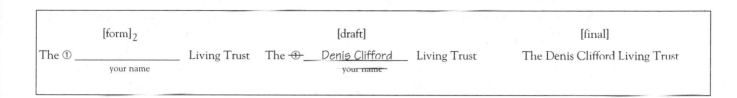

Once you're satisfied that your trust form is fully completed, prepare the final document from your draft, including all trust schedules. You can either type it (or have it typed) or use a word processor. The final version should be prepared on good quality (bond) 8½" x 11" typing paper. Although not required by law, obviously it makes sense to use non-erasable paper.

Be sure the pages of the final document are consecutively numbered correctly. You may have to change the numbering from that on the form. For instance, if you add material (such as commentary about gifts), or have quite a number of primary beneficiaries—say 16—you'll have to renumber the pages of your final document. Similarly, if you deleted material (such as the sections on children's trusts or gifts under the Uniform Transfers to Minors Act), you'll need to renumber the pages of your final document.

After the final trust document has been typed, carefully proofread it.

F. Consider Having Your Work Checked by a Lawyer

Once you are sure your final trust document is clear and correct, consider whether or not you want to look for a lawyer who can review your work. This can sound like a good idea that shouldn't cost much, but the reality is that it is often difficult to find a lawyer willing to do the job; most want a full fee for preparing a trust from scratch and won't accept review work. (See Chapter 17, Section A.)

Before setting off to try to find a lawyer, take stock of whether you are really likely to benefit by employing one. If your desires are clear and straightforward, and you've conscientiously followed the forms and instructions in this book, your trust should work just fine. On the other hand, if you have an estate large enough to be liable for estate taxes, or other complex property or beneficiary concerns, this book has surely referred you to a lawyer already.

G. Sign Your Living Trust in Front of a Notary

It is essential that you sign your trust document and have your signature notarized by a notary public in the state where you live, even if you work in another state. Normally, no witnesses watch you sign a living trust. Because of this, it's always possible that after your death someone could claim that the signature wasn't genuine. As you won't be around to verify it then, you should do it now. The best way to remove any question of whether or not the signature on the document is authentic is to sign it in front of a notary.

Special Florida requirements. In Florida, it is customary, though not legally required, to have your living trust witnessed by two witnesses. It's safest to go along with this custom. Since the notary counts as one, you must have at least one other. Use the special Florida Witness Statement, Form 4, in Appendix B.

The signature line on the trust form is preceded by a provision entitled "Certification by Grantor(s)." Here you state that you've read the trust document and approve of it. This is a bit of legalese, included to make your trust look more like ones with which most financial institutions are familiar.

A notarization form is included with each living trust form in Appendix B. If your notary prefers to use a different form, fine—the important thing is to get the notarization done.

Finding a notary shouldn't be a problem; many advertise in the Yellow Pages. Or check with your bank, which may provide notarization as a service to customers. Real estate offices and title companies also have notaries.

Both spouses must sign a basic shared trust or AB trust, and both spouses must appear before a notary.

⚠ **Don't rely on a bank guarantee for your signature.**
Some banks provide guarantees for customers' signatures on bank and other important documents. Some readers have asked whether they can use a bank guarantee for their living trust, in place of notarization. The answer is no. After your death, it's vital that your living trust be accepted by many institutions, from title companies to county land records offices to stockbrokers. These institutions are not used to seeing living trust signatures validated by a bank guarantee. If any institution refuses to accept your living trust for this reason, there is little or nothing your successor trustee will be able to do about it. Getting a bank guarantee may, for some people, be easier than locating a notary. Unfortunately, this convenience is irrelevant. You must have your signature notarized.

⚠ **Don't stop now.** Even after your trust document is signed and notarized, you're not done. You must transfer the property you listed in the trust schedules into the name of the trust. Do it as soon as possible. Chapter 11 shows you how. ∎

chapter 11

TRANSFERRING PROPERTY TO YOUR TRUST

*A*fter you sign your living trust document, you have a valid living trust. But the trust is of absolutely no use to you until the property you listed in the trust document (on the property schedules) is actually transferred into the trust. Lawyers call this "funding" the trust.

Transferring your property to your living trust is crucial, and takes some time and paperwork, but it's not difficult. You should be able to do it yourself, without a lawyer.

WE'RE COUNTING ON YOU: MAKE SURE YOU DO IT

Many lawyers who prepare living trusts insist on doing all the property transfer work themselves, because they claim their clients cannot be trusted to do this work themselves. In other words, lawyers get paid hundreds of dollars per hour to do paperwork and won't allow their clients to do it.

Both this book and Nolo rest on the belief that people can be trusted to understand basic legal forms and do the work required to make the forms work. It is absolutely essential that you do the work necessary to formally transfer your property to your trust. If you don't, your trust will not work and, perhaps worse, you'll be proving that those lawyers who say people just can't be trusted to do basic tasks correctly are, sadly, sometimes correct. So, study this chapter carefully and be absolutely sure you've properly transferred all trust property into the trust's name.

A. Paperwork

Each item of property listed on your trust schedule(s) must be transferred to the trust. How much paperwork is required depends on whether or not the property has a document of title—a formal ownership paper—such as a real estate deed, securities account registration form, or boat registration.

1. Property Without a Document of Title

Property without a document of title includes most furniture, clothing, books, appliances, and other household goods, as well as some more valuable items, like jewelry, artworks, furs, promissory notes, or loans owed to you, precious metals, electronic and computer equipment, and most farm equipment and livestock. For property without a document of title (ownership document), in almost all states you don't need to do anything but prepare your trust document and list the property on a trust schedule.

You can prepare a written "Assignment of Property" of these kinds of property to your trust by using Form 5 or 6. Form 5 is an assignment form for a one-person trust. It is also for a member of a couple who assigns separately owned property to a shared trust or an AB Trust. Form 6 is for a couple to assign shared ownership property to a shared trust or an AB trust.

In most all states, a written notice of assignment for property without documents of title is not required. However many lawyers use it to provide additional written proof that these items of property have been transferred. Certainly it can't hurt

New York residents must prepare a notice of assignment for property without documents of title. New York law now requires you to prepare a separate Notice of Assignment for property without documents of title transferred to your trust (N.Y. Est. Powers and Trusts Law §7-1.18). Simply listing such property on a trust schedule is not sufficient. If there's no Notice of Assignment, the property is not validly placed in the trust. However, the Notice can simply repeat the listing of such property as used in a trust schedule. (Use Form 5 or 6 from Appendix B or the CD-ROM.)

2. Property With a Document of Title

For items that have a title document that shows ownership, you will have to prepare new documents to establish that the trust owns the property. This chapter shows you how to accomplish this. Technically, you transfer your property to yourself, as trustee of your living trust. You'll see how this works when you come to actually preparing title transfer documents, starting with Section E, below.

For certain types of property without a title document, but that seem to require formal transfer because they are property owned in paper form—such as promissory notes or deeds of trust—you can use an assignment form to make absolutely clear that this property is transferred to the trust. Assignment forms are Forms 5 and 6 in Appendix B.

Finally, trademarks, patents, and copyrights have special transfer forms and are discussed in Sections K, L, and M, below.

⚠ Don't delay. Formally transferring property to your trust is so vital, I'll give you one more warning, at the risk of redundancy. Failing to transfer property to the trust is the most serious mistake people can make when creating a living trust. If you don't get around to preparing, signing, and filing (where required) these new documents, your trust document will have no effect on what happens to any of your property after your death. Instead, that property will go to the residuary beneficiary named in your back-up will. (See Chapter 16.) If you don't have a will, that property will go to certain close relatives, according to state law. Either way, it will probably go through probate.

⚠ TRANSFERRING JOINT TENANCY PROPERTY IF YOU LIVE IN A COMMON LAW STATE OR ARE NOT MARRIED

If you are a couple and live in a common law state—that is, any state except Arizona, California, Idaho, Louisiana, Nevada, New Mexico, Texas, Washington, Wisconsin, or Alaska (if agreed to in writing by both spouses)—transfers of property held in "joint tenancy" or "tenancy by the entirety" require one more step than transfers of other shared property. Also, if you are an unmarried couple, in any state, you must go through the additional step described here to transfer joint tenancy property into a shared or AB living trust. If your deed or title document lists you as "tenants-in-common owners" (or lists ownership as "tenants in common"), you can safely go ahead and prepare a deed or title document transferring the property from you to the trust. But if you are listed as "joint tenants" or as holding the property "in joint tenancy" or "tenancy by the entirety," you'll have to do more work. Also, if your deed simply lists your names, and makes no mention of what type of ownership you two share, you need to either take this extra step, or check with a local lawyer regarding real estate ownership rules for your state. In some states, any deed to a husband and wife by itself creates a tenancy in the entirety, even if the document does not specifically state that.

Before you transfer joint tenancy property to your trust, you'll need to prepare and execute an additional deed or title document, transferring that property from you as "joint tenants" (or tenants by the entirety) to you as "tenants in common, in equal shares." Then you prepare a second deed or document of title, transferring the property from you as "tenants in common" into the trust.

Why is this rigmarole necessary? Because some lawyers argue that joint tenancy property transferred to a living trust in common law states (somehow) retains its character as joint tenancy property, even if the trust declares otherwise. Worse, the IRS could argue the same. You do not want any risk of having joint tenancy property in your trust. Joint tenancy property must go to the surviving joint tenant, your spouse. This may be what you want; indeed, if it is, consider leaving the property in joint tenancy rather than putting it in your trust. (See Chapter 15, Section B.) But if you want to leave some of that property to someone other than your spouse, or you want to name alternate beneficiaries for your share of the property, you should be sure no one can assert, after a spouse dies, that the trust property is, in legal reality, still joint tenancy property.

With an AB trust, you could face even worse problems. If the joint tenancy property had to go to the surviving joint tenant, the surviving spouse, Trust A might have relatively little money or property in it. Most property of the deceased spouse would be owned outright by the surviving spouse—exactly what you don't want.

So, to be absolutely safe, prepare the extra deed or document of title wherever your present ones list you as owning the property as "joint tenants" or as "tenants by the entirety," or simply lists your two names.

B. Technical Ownership

To transfer ownership of property with a document of title to your living trust, list the new owner(s) as your name, or names, followed by "as trustee(s) for the [your name(s)] Trust." It's common to include the date the trust was signed and notarized.

Example 1

Denis Clifford creates a living trust and transfers real estate to it. On a new real estate deed, he lists the new owner as "Denis Clifford, as trustee of the Denis Clifford Living Trust, dated July 10, 2001."

Example 2

Denise and Fred Gulekston create a shared living trust and transfer their home, a money market account, and a stock brokerage account to the trust. On each title document, they name the new owners as "Denise and Fred Gulekston, as trustees of the Denise and Fred Gulekston Living Trust, dated October 14, 2002."

Formally, the property is owned by the trustee(s), not the trust itself. The reason for holding technical ownership in the trustee(s)' name(s), and not the trust's, is that some title companies and a few other financial institutions have been known to insist that the trust itself cannot own property. This position is at best dubious, but why risk a quarrel between your beneficiaries and some financial company? It makes sense to hold your trust property in the technical form least likely to bother financial institutions.

Including the date your living trust was signed and notarized isn't necessary, but may make your documents appear more lawyer-like, and therefore more acceptable to banks, title companies, and other financial institutions. (It also avoids confusion over subsequent trusts with the same name, if there are any.)

Another form of dating a living trust is to include the letters "UTD" (for Under Trust Dated) and then give the date. For example, "Denis Clifford, as trustee of the Denis Clifford Living Trust, UTD 7/10/2000."

1. Property You Acquire Later

If, after your trust has been created, you acquire property you want to be part of the trust, you can simply take ownership in the trustee's name directly. There's no reason to buy the property in your personal name and then transfer it to you as trustee.

Example

Mr. and Mrs. Siqueiros buy a new house. They take title in their names, listing the new owners as "Juan and Luisa Siqueiros, as trustees of The Juan and Luisa Siqueiros Living Trust, dated September 20, 2000."

2. Problems With Financial Institutions

I've received a few reports, from readers of other Nolo books and from lawyers, that some banks, mutual funds, or other financial institutions (usually in more remote parts of the country) have balked at re-registering trust property in the trustee's name. People have been told, "You can't do that. Only our trust department does that," or "You need a federal tax ID number."

If this happens to you, simply insist that it is absolutely legal, and essential, for you to re-register your property in the trustee's name, and that this can be done without a new taxpayer ID. If you have to, go higher up in the institution's bureaucracy until you find someone who understands what the law is now, not what it may have been 20 years ago (when a federal tax ID number was required).

C. An Abstract of Trust

An abstract of trust, sometimes called a "certification of trust," is a kind of shorthand version of the trust document. You may find one useful when actually transferring property to your trust. County records offices, banks, or other institutions may require proof that the trust exists. The purpose of an abstract of trust is to establish that the trust exists, without revealing the heart of it—that is, what property is in it and who will inherit. Some people do not want to reveal this core information to institutions that require proof of the trust's existence, so they submit an "abstract of trust," rather than a copy of the entire trust.

In most states, there's no one set form for an abstract of trust. Ask first, to see what's wanted. Some institutions accept a copy of the first and last (signature) pages of the trust. Another method is simply to remove the property and beneficiaries provisions from a copy of the trust and call what's left an abstract. You do not need to re-sign or re-notarize this document. A photocopy of the original signature(s) and notarization suffices. Or, you can sign a statement swearing you created the trust. However an abstract of trust is prepared, the following points are usually shown:

- that the trust was created (the first page of the trust document will do)
- who the original trustees are
- the date the trust was created (the date the trust document was signed)
- what the trustees' powers are (this can be quite a bit of verbiage)
- the signature of the grantor(s), and
- the notarization of the trust document.

You will find an example of a general form for an abstract of trust on the next page. The signature and notarization are simply copies from the original trust.

⚠️ **Some states have their own forms.** The states listed below have adopted statutes that certain basic information be included in an abstract of trust. (More legislative tinkering, more work for lawyers.) If you live in one of these states, do not use or adapt the general form shown on the next pages. You can always choose

not to bother with an abstract and submit a copy of the entire trust, or you can do any of the following instead:

- check with the financial institution involved to see what they'll accept
- look up your state's law and get the precise form for your state, or
- see a lawyer to get your state's form.

If you want to look up your state's statute, go to the Legal Research Center at www.nolo.com. You can also find them in a local law library.

State	Statute sections on certification of trust
California	Cal. Prob. Code § 18100.5
Idaho	Idaho Code § 68-115
Iowa	Iowa Code § 633.4604
Kansas	Kan. Stat. § 58a-1013
Michigan	Mich. Comp. Laws Ann. § 565.432
Minnesota	Minn. Stat. Ann. § 501B.56
Mississippi	Miss. Code Ann. § 91-9-7
Nevada	Nev. Rev. Stat. Ann. § 164.410
Ohio	Ohio Rev. Code § 5301.01
Oklahoma	Okla. Stat. tit. 60, § 175.6
Oregon	Or. Rev. Stat. § 128.236
Rhode Island	R.I. Gen. Laws § 34-4-27
South Dakota	S.D. Codified Laws § 55-4-42
West Virginia	W. Va. Code § 36-1-4a

ABSTRACT OF TRUST
THE NORINE AND PAUL LOMBARDI
DECLARATION AND INSTRUMENT OF TRUST

I. TRUST NAME

This trust shall be known as The Norine and Paul Lombardi Trust.

II. TRUST PROPERTY

(A) Norine and Paul Lombardi, wife and husband, called the "grantors" or the "trustees," declare that they have set aside and hold in The Norine and Paul Lombardi Trust, all their interest in that property listed in attached Schedules A and B. The trust property shall be used for the benefit of the trust beneficiaries, and shall be administered and distributed by the trustees in accordance with this trust document.

. . . .

IX. TRUSTEE'S POWERS AND DUTIES

(A) Powers Under State Law

To carry out the provisions of this Declaration of Trust and to manage the trust property of The Norine and Paul Lombardi Living Trust, The Marital Life Estate Trust and The Surviving Spouse's Trust, and any child's trust created under this Declaration of Trust, the trustee shall have all authority and power allowed or conferred under New York law, subject to the trustee's fiduciary duty to the grantors and the beneficiaries.

(B) Specified Powers

The trustee's powers include, but are not limited to:

1. The power to sell trust property, and to borrow money and to encumber property, specifically including trust real estate, by mortgage, deed of trust, or other method.

2. The power to manage trust real estate as if the trustee were the absolute owner of it, including the power to lease (even if the lease term may extend beyond the period of any trust) or grant options to lease the property, to make repairs or alterations and to insure against loss.

3. The power to sell or grant options for the sale or exchange of any trust property, including stocks, bonds, debentures, and any other form of security or security account, at public or private sale for cash or on credit.

4. The power to invest trust property in property of any kind, including but not limited to bonds, debentures, notes, mortgages, and stocks.

5. The power to receive additional property from any source and add to any trust created by this Declaration of Trust.

6. The power to employ and pay reasonable fees to accountants, lawyers, or investment experts for information or advice relating to the trust.

7. The power to deposit and hold trust funds in both interest-bearing and non-interest-bearing accounts.

8. The power to deposit funds in bank or other accounts uninsured by FDIC coverage.

9. The power to enter into electronic fund transfer or safe deposit arrangements with financial institutions.

10. The power to continue any business of either grantor.

11. The power to institute or defend legal actions concerning the trust or the grantors' affairs.

12. The power to execute any documents necessary to administer any trust created in this Declaration of Trust.

13. The power to diversify investments, including authority to decide that some or all of the trust property need not produce income.

. . . .

Certification by Grantors

We certify that we have read this Declaration of Trust and that it correctly states the terms and conditions under which the trust property is to be held, managed, and disposed of by the trustee and we approve the Declaration of Trust.

Dated: July 6, 20xx

Norine Lombardi
_____
Norine Lombardi

Paul Lombardi
_____
Paul Lombardi
Grantors and Trustees

State of New York

County of Dutchess

On July 6, 20xx, before me, _____Ilana Weinstock_____, a notary public for the State of New York, personally appeared Norine Lombardi and Paul Lombardi, known to me to be, or proved to me on the basis of satisfactory evidence to be, the trustees and grantors of the trust created by the above Declaration of Trust, and to be the persons whose names are subscribed to the Declaration of Trust, and acknowledged that they executed it as grantors and trustees.

IN WITNESS WHEREOF, I have set my hand and affixed my official seal the day and year first above written.

/s/_____Ilana Weinstock_____
NOTARY PUBLIC

D. Property That Names the Living Trust as a Beneficiary

If you have named your trust (technically, your trustee) as beneficiary of a life insurance policy or retirement plan, you do not re-register title to the policy or plan. For example, if you want your living trust to receive the proceeds of your life insurance policy at your death, all you need to do is designate your trust as the beneficiary of that policy. You do not transfer ownership of the policy into the trust's name.

While you live, the trust is not the legal owner of the insurance policy; you personally remain the legal owner. The trust is simply the entity you've named to receive the life insurance proceeds payable on your death. Because the trust never owned the insurance policy, this asset was not listed on a trust schedule. You do, of course, name one or more beneficiaries and alternate beneficiaries for the proceeds in the trust document. For example, a wife could name her husband as beneficiary, and her two minor children as alternate beneficiaries. If the children received the proceeds while minors, the money would be held in children's trusts.

E. Real Estate

The term "real estate" includes land, houses, condominiums, cooperatives, most "timeshares," and any other interest in what lawyers call "real property." To transfer title of a piece of real estate to a living trust, you prepare and sign a deed listing the trustee or trustees of the trust as the new owner. You can fill out the new deed yourself; it's not difficult. Then you sign the deed in front of a notary public and record a copy of it with the county land records office. You don't have to prepare a second document transferring your mortgage; that liability follows the asset, the real estate. Nor do you need to notify the mortgage holder (the bank) of the transfer. (See Chapter 3, Section I.)

Co-op apartments. If you own a co-op apartment, you can't simply use a deed to transfer your shares in the co-op. You will have to check the co-op corporation's rules to see if the transfer is allowed. Some co-ops resist such transfers because they are afraid a living trust isn't a proper shareholder in the corporation. You can probably overcome any resistance you encounter by reminding the powers that be that, for all practical purposes, you and the trust are the same—you have the same tax identification number, for example.

Mobile homes. Whether or not a mobile home is treated as real estate depends upon the law of the state where it is located, and, in some states whether it is permanently affixed to land or not. You'll have to check with the state agency that handles mobile home registrations to learn how to transfer title to your trust.

Timeshares. A timeshare is an ownership interest in a vacation property. Each owner has the right to exclusive use of the property for set time periods. Ownership can be held by real estate deed, lease, or contract. If a deed is used, the timeshare must be transferred to your living trust by a deed. If ownership is by lease or contract, you can use a simple assignment form.

1. Preparing the Deed

First, locate your existing deed. Then get a deed form in common use in the state where the real estate is located. The technical requirements for real estate deed forms vary from state to state, so it is essential that you get one from the appropriate state.

FINDING DEED FORMS AND INSTRUCTIONS

Generally, you can use either a quitclaim or warranty deed form. Technically, a quitclaim deed doesn't make the promises of full and clear ownership that a grant or warranty deed does. In Texas, it appears that a warranty deed is required. In other states you can use any deed form; after all you are merely transferring the property from yourself under one hat to yourself under another.

Deed forms vary from state to state. If you're in California, you can find deed forms and instructions for filling them out in *Deeds for California Real Estate*, by Mary Randolph (Nolo). Much of the book's information is valid in other states as well, but it's best to use a deed form that's in common use in your area.

In many places, you can find blank deed forms in stationery or office supply stores, or perhaps from a local title company. If you live in a small town and can't find a deed in a local store, try calling a stationery store in a major city, because deed forms are the same throughout a state. Or go to a local law library; look for books on "real property" that have deed forms you can photocopy.

Although deed forms vary somewhat, they all require the same basic information. Using a typewriter, fill out your deed like the sample shown below. Type in:

- **The recording information, at the top left of the document.**

- **The date.**

- **The current owners' names.** If you are the sole owner, or if you and someone else co-own the property and you are transferring just your share, only your name goes here. If you are transferring only a portion of ownership, you can specify what portion (for example, "1/3 ownership of …" or simply state "all his/her interest in…"). If you and your spouse own the property together and are transferring it to a shared marital trust or an AB trust, type in both of your names. Use exactly the same form of your name as is used on the deed that transferred the property to you and you used in your living trust document.

As you can see from the sample completed document, you may have to type in the correct ending of some printed words, like "part…." If you are a couple, you add "ies" to make this "parties." If you are a single person, you add a "y" to make it "party."

IF YOUR NAME HAS CHANGED

If your name has changed since you bought real estate, how do you sign the transfer deed? Simply sign using both names: the name you used when you originally bought the property, and the name you use now.

- **The new owner's name.** Fill in the trustee's name or trustees' names and add the date of notarization of the trust if you wish. (See Section B, above.)

- **The "legal description" of the property.** This is usually something like, "From a point 12 degrees South of… Map 4, Book 6," etc. Copy the description exactly as it appears on the previous deed.

Depending on the form you use, you may need to cross out, as shown in the sample deed, inappropriate printed language, such as words stating the transfer is "forever," or that the property is also transferred to the second party's (here, the trust's) "assigns, etc."

After everything is filled in, sign and date the deed in front of a notary public for the state in which the property is located. Everyone listed as a current owner, who is transferring his or her interest in the property to the trust, must sign the deed.

Below is a completed quitclaim deed transferring a home to a living trust. As you'll see, this deed contains bunches of legalese ("…appurtenances thereunto belonging or appertaining…"). I'm no fan of the legalese it uses, but it's typical of a deed you're likely to get at a stationery store.

OUT-OF-STATE REAL ESTATE

If you own real estate located in another state, you face a few problems transferring that property to your trust:

- Tracking down the deed form for that state, and getting a blank deed. Often the easiest way to get the correct deed is to call a title company in the state where the real estate is located.

- Making sure your notarization of the deed is acceptable in the other state. Generally, deeds can be notarized in the state you live in, even for out-of-state real estate.

- Learning whether any other paperwork is required for a valid transfer. One example of this is California's Preliminary Change of Title Report, discussed in the sidebar *California Property Taxes*, below.

- Properly recording the deed.

Transferring out-of-state real estate. Transferring out-of-state real estate can be a real hassle. If it becomes one for you, you might decide to hire a lawyer to do just this one task. And if you own real estate in another country, you must hire a lawyer familiar with that country's laws. (See Section E7, below.)

Sample Deed

Quitclaim Deed

This Indenture made the ......twenty-first................................. day of
.......April......................... one thousand nine hundred and ...eighty-eight...............

Between ....Jane and Gordon McCann.............................
.... the part..ies of the first part,
and Jane and Gordon McCann, as trustees of the Jane and Gordon McCann Living Trust, ..
.......dated April 12, 1988..................................... the part..y... of the second part,

Witnesseth: That the said part..ies.... of the first part,XX XXXXXXXXXXXXXX XXXXX
ofXXXXXXXXXXXXXXXXXXXXXXXXXXXXXXXXXXXXXXXXXXXXXXXXXXXXXXdoXXX,
lawful moneyXX the United States of America,XXXXXXXXXXXXXXXXXX to bepaid byXXe
part XXXXXX of the second part,XXXXXXXX whereof XX hereby acknowledged do .... hereby
release and foreverQUITCLAIM unto the part y........ of the second part, andXX XXXXX heirs
and assignsXall that........ certain lot........., piece .... or parcel .... of land situate in
the ..City .of .Chicago............................ County of ....Cook...............................
State of ......Illinois..................................., and bounded and described as follows, to-wit:

Commonly known as 47 Greene Street, and more particularly described as:

(Legal description, exactly as given in previous deed)

Together with the tenements, hereditaments, and appurtenances thereunto belonging
or appertaining, and the reversion and reversions, remainder and remainders, rents, issues,
and profits thereof.

To have and to hold the said premises, together with the appurtenances, unto
the part .y........ of the second part, XXXXXXXXXXXXXXXXX heirs and assigns forever.

In Witness Whereof the part ..ies.... of the first part have....... executed this
conveyance the day and year first above written.

Signed and Delivered in the Presence of

_____ _Jane McCann_____

  [notarized]   _Gordon McCann_____

2. Recording the Deed

After the deed is signed and notarized, you must "record" it—that is, put a copy of the notarized deed on file in the county office that keeps local property records. Depending on the state, the land records office is called the County Recorder's Office, Land Registry Office, or County Clerk's office.

Just take the original, signed deed to the land records office. (You can probably mail it in, if you wish. Call the land records office to find out the correct procedure.) For a small fee, a clerk will make a copy and put it in the public records. You'll get your original back, stamped with a reference number to show where the copy can be found in the public records.

3. Transfer Taxes

Very rarely, if ever, will you have to pay a state or local transfer tax when you transfer real estate to a revocable living trust. Most real estate transfer taxes are based on the sale price of the property and do not apply when no money changes hands. Others specifically exempt transfers where the real owners don't change—as is the case when you transfer property to a revocable living trust you control.

To be absolutely safe, before you record your deed, get information on any possible transfer tax from the county tax assessor, county recorder, or state tax officials.

CALIFORNIA PROPERTY TAXES

In California, transferring real estate to a revocable living trust does not trigger a reassessment for property tax purposes. Similarly, transfers from the trustee back to the original owner don't cause reassessments. (Cal. Rev. & Tax. Code § 62(d).) You may, however, have to file a form called a Preliminary Change of Title Report with the county tax assessor. If you do, you sign this form with your name, as trustee for your trust.

EXAMPLE

Erin Quake signs a Preliminary Change of Title Report as "Erin Quake, Trustee, the Erin Quake Living Trust dated November 7, 20xx."

---

4. Due-on-Sale Mortgage Clauses

Many mortgages contain a clause that allows the bank to call ("accelerate") the loan—that is, demand that you pay the whole thing off immediately—if you transfer the mortgaged property. Fortunately, in most instances lenders are forbidden by federal law to invoke a due-on-sale clause when property is transferred to a living trust. The lender can't call the loan if the borrower is a trust beneficiary and the transfer is "unrelated to occupancy" of the premises. (Garn-St. Germain Act, 12 U.S.C. §§ 1464, 1701.) Also, it's doubtful that the transfer of any real estate to your trust is the type of transfer that would legally permit a bank to call a loan. (See Chapter 3, Section I.)

5. Insurance

Your insurance policies should not be changed simply because your home has been placed in your living trust. You do not need to notify your insurance company (or any title company) of the transfer of real estate property. (Why disturb a bureaucracy if you don't have to?)

6. Transferring Deeds of Trust

One type of real estate asset is called a "deed of trust." It is similar to a mortgage. If you lend money to someone, you may receive a deed of trust, making real estate collateral for a loan—that is, if the borrower defaults, you can foreclose on the real estate to collect what's owed you. Because a deed of trust is an interest in real estate, it should be recorded.

To transfer a deed of trust to your living trust, you can prepare a "Notice of Assignment" transferring it from you to your trust. You then record that document. Use Form 5 or 6 in Appendix B.

7. Real Estate Outside the United States

There is no reason to transfer foreign real estate to a U.S. living trust. That property wouldn't go through U.S. probate anyway, and U.S. courts don't have authority to order transfer of real estate in another country.

Each country has its own rules and laws regarding real estate. (When I lived in Ireland, I had to visit a lawyer—a "solicitor"—and sign a fancy legal document to rent an apartment.) If this is important to you, hire someone in that other country to learn what you can do. After all, if you own real estate in a foreign country, that's fortunate, so spending a little money to learn how to transfer that property after your death isn't a disaster.

F. Bank Accounts and Safe Deposit Boxes

It should be simple to re-register ownership of a bank account in your name(s) as trustee(s) of your living trust or open a new account in the trustee's name. Just ask the bank what paperwork you need to submit.

The bank will be concerned with the authority granted to the trustees to act on behalf of the trust. Depending on the kind of account, the bank may want to know whether or not the trustees have the power to borrow money, put funds in a non-interest-bearing account, or engage in electronic transfers. (The trust forms in this book include all these powers.)

To verify your authority, the bank may want to see a copy of your trust document or have you fill out its own form, often called a Trust Certification.

If you want to transfer title to a safe deposit box to your trust, you'll have to re-register its ownership, too. The bank will have a form for you to fill out.

Estate planning note. Instead of transferring a bank account to a living trust, you may want to turn the account into a pay-on-death account. It's another, even easier, way to avoid probate of the money in the account. (See Chapter 15.)

G. Securities

How you transfer stocks, bonds, mutual funds, and other securities to your living trust depends on whether or not you hold your stocks in a brokerage account or keep the actual certificates yourself. (For stocks in closely-held corporations, see Section 13, below.)

1. Brokerage Accounts

If, like most people, you hold your stocks, bonds, or other securities in a brokerage account, either change the account to the trustee's name or open a new account in the trustee's name. Simply ask your broker for instructions.

The brokerage company may have a straightforward form that you can fill out, giving information about the trustees and their authority.

Tell them you want the account to keep the same account number as when it was in your name. If they don't want to, insist (politely). If they still refuse, you've got a technical problem, because the account number listed in your trust document isn't the same as the new number of that account in the trustee's name. You'd have to revise a trust schedule to get the new account number in it. So, you can see why you want to insist the account keep your original number.

If the brokerage company doesn't have its own form, you will probably need to send the broker:

- a copy of the trust document or an "abstract of trust," and

- a letter instructing the holder to transfer the brokerage account to the trustee's name or open a new account in the trustee's name.

After you've submitted your request, get written confirmation that the account's ownership has in fact been put in the trustee's name.

2. Stock Certificates

If you have the actual stock certificates or bonds in your possession—most people don't—you must get new certificates issued, showing the trustee as owner. Ask your broker for help. If the broker is unwilling or unable to help, write to the "transfer agent" of the corporation that issued the stock. You can get the address from your broker or the investor relations office of the corporation. The transfer agent will give you simple instructions.

You will probably have to send in:

- your certificates or bonds

- a form called a "stock or bond power," which you must fill out and sign

- a copy of the trust document or an "abstract of trust," showing your notarized signature, and

- a letter requesting that the certificates be reissued in the trustee's name.

The stock or bond power may be printed on the back of the certificates; if not, you can probably find a copy at a stationery store.

3. Government Securities

To transfer government securities—for example, Treasury bills or U.S. bonds—you need to complete Form PD 1851 and mail it to the U.S. Treasury. You can get the form through your stockbroker if you have one, or you can contact the local Federal Reserve Bank. Also, local banks may have the necessary transfer forms.

4. Mutual Fund Accounts

Mutual funds should be re-registered in the name of the trustee of your living trust by communicating with the company and meeting its requirements. You'll probably just need to send a letter of instructions (or a form the company provides) and a copy of the trust document.

5. Stock Options

You can transfer publicly traded stock options by using a Notice of Assignment (Form 5 or 6 in Appendix B). Private, employee stock options often cannot be transferred to a living trust. (See Chapter 6, Section B.)

H. Vehicles, Boats, and Planes

Most people don't transfer vehicles such as cars or trailers to a living trust, for reasons discussed in Chapter 6, Section B. (A mobile home may be considered real estate rather than a vehicle. See Section E, above.)

If you want to put a vehicle in trust, you must fill out a change of ownership document and have title to the vehicle reissued in the trustee's name. The title certificate to your vehicle may contain instructions. If you have questions, call your state's Motor Vehicles Department.

Transferring a large boat to your living trust requires you to re-register title with the Coast Guard. The paperwork is handled by the U.S. Department of Transportation's National Vessel Documentation Center (800-799-8362). The forms and information needed to transfer a boat into a trust are contained in the "Exchange Packet," available without charge. You need to complete Form CG-1340 (a "Bill of Sale") and form CG-1258 and pay the appropriate fee.

To transfer larger, motorized boats registered with a state agency, you must prepare a state new registration form, listing the trust—that is, you as trustee—as the new owner. Transferring small boats, such as rowboats or canoes, can be done simply listing them on a trust schedule, and, if you wish, by preparing a Notice of Assignment for them.

If you own an airplane, you must contact the FAA to obtain a new certificate of registration in the trustee's name.

I. Business Interests

How you transfer small business interests to your living trust depends on the way the business is owned.

TRADEMARKS AND SERVICE MARKS

If you have a registered trademark or service mark, you must re-register ownership in the name of the trustee of the living trust. For sample forms, see *Trademark: Legal Care for Your Business & Product Name* by Steve Elias (Nolo).

---

1. Sole Proprietorships

An unincorporated business that you own by yourself is the easiest to transfer to a trust. First, you list the business, by name, as an item of property on a trust schedule—for example, "De Tach Restaurant." That transfers the name and whatever customer goodwill goes with it, to your living trust.

Because you own the business assets in your own name (a sole proprietorship, unlike a corporation, is not an independent entity that can own property), you transfer them to your living trust like you would any other valuable property. For many businesses, this simply means listing those business assets on the appropriate trust schedule—for example, "…all property and assets used in the grantor's business Jim Dimes Hardware." Because there is no ownership document for the business, nothing further is required.

2. Solely Owned Corporations

If you own all the stock of a corporation, you shouldn't have any problem transferring it to your living trust. Follow these steps:

Step 1. Fill out the stock transfer section on the back of the stock certificate.

Step 2. Mark the certificate "canceled" and place it in your corporate records book.

Step 3. Reissue a new certificate in the name of the trustee of the living trust.

Step 4. Show the cancellation of the old certificate and the issuance of the new certificate on the stock ledger pages in your corporate records book.

3. Closely Held Corporations and Limited Liability Companies

Normally, you can transfer your shares in a closely held corporation or interest in a limited liability company (LLC) to your living trust by following corporate bylaws or an LLC operating agreement and having the ownership document reissued in the name of the trustee of the trust. But first, check the corporation's bylaws and articles of incorporation, as well as any separate shareholders' agreements or the LLC operating agreement, to see if there are any restrictions on such transfers. If an agreement limits or forbids transfers, it will have to be changed before you can put your shares in your living trust.

4. Partnership Interests

To transfer your partnership interest to your living trust, you must notify your business partners and modify the partnership agreement to show that your partnership interest is now owned by the trustee of your living trust. If there is a partnership certificate, it must be changed to substitute the trustee as owner of your share.

Revising a partnership agreement. You can revise your partnership agreement by using *The Partnership Book*, by Denis Clifford and Ralph Warner (Nolo).

J. Limited Partnerships

Limited partnerships are a form of investment, governed by securities laws. Contact the partnership's general partner to find out what paperwork is necessary to transfer your interest to a living trust.

K. Copyrights

If you want to transfer your interest in a copyright to your living trust, list the copyright on a trust schedule. Then sign and file, with the U.S. Copyright Office, a document transferring all your rights in the copyright to the trustee of the living trust. Sample transfer forms are in *The Copyright Handbook*, by Stephen Fishman (Nolo).

L. Patents

If you own a patent and want to transfer it to your living trust, you should prepare a document called an "assignment" and record it with the U.S. Patent and Trademark Office in Washington, DC. There is a small fee for recording. Assignment forms and instructions are in *Patent It Yourself*, by David Pressman (Nolo), available as a book or software.

M. Royalties

Your rights to receive royalties—from sales of a book, copies of photos, residuals for TV ads, whatever—can be transferred to your trust with technical ownership held by the trustee. It's best to transfer any royalty rights by preparing an Assignment of Property (Form 5 or 6), although legally, just listing these rights on a trust schedule would suffice. But with an assignment form, you can clearly specify, in a separate, distinct document, exactly what royalty rights are transferred to the trust.

It is sensible to give a copy of the assignment form to whatever company pays you the royalty rights. Let them know, of course, that they are to keep making payments to you while you live. It can help get these payments to your beneficiaries without great hassles if you give the company some warning that your royalty rights will be transferred by your successor trustee out of your living trust when you die. ∎

chapter 12

COPYING, STORING, AND REGISTERING YOUR TRUST DOCUMENT

*a*fter you've completed your living trust and signed all documents necessary to transfer property to the trust, you're almost done. There are just a couple of minor tasks left to accomplish.

A. Making Copies

You will probably need some copies of your completed trust document. Some lawyers advise stamping or writing the word "COPY" on each duplicate, so none can ever be mistaken for an original. While you can certainly do this, it seems a bit overcautious to me. Photocopies of your original trust are different from the original—your signature is not in ink on the copy, nor is the notary stamp original. But then again, that's not always so easy to determine these days, with better and better quality photocopying, so if you want maximum security, go ahead and write or stamp "COPY" on each copy, or even on each page of each copy.

You may well need copies to transfer certain types of property—stocks, for example—to your trust. (See Chapter 11, Section G.) If a broker, bank, or other institution wants to see your trust document, use a photocopy of the original.

You may want to give a copy of your trust document to your successor trustee so that person knows what is in your trust well in advance of actually serving as trustee. Keep the original, which your successor trustee will need after your death or incapacity.

Finally, you should instruct your successor trustee to give copies after your death to any custodian you named for trust property inherited by a young beneficiary.

There's no requirement that you give copies to any beneficiaries. Indeed, there can be drawbacks to this. If you later revoke or amend the trust but don't collect all the old copies, there will be outdated copies of your trust document floating around. Someone who is given less (or nothing) in the new document may cause trouble later on. Also, the property in the trust may substantially change later if the trustee must dip into or even deplete the trust because of a grantor's illness or other unexpected expenses. Why set up expectations that may not be fulfilled even with the best of intentions?

On the other hand, if you doubt the trust property will change much, and if there are only a few beneficiaries and you trust them all—as is true for many families—why not let your beneficiaries know now what they'll receive? What's wrong with revealing your generosity?

⚠️ **Sign only one trust document.** It is important not to prepare another "original" document—that is, to sign a second copy of your living trust form. This is because each trust document you actually sign becomes, legally, a distinct trust document (even if it isn't notarized). If you revoke or change one original, that does not revoke or change other originals. Clearly, you don't want any duplicate original trust documents floating around.

B. Storing the Trust Document

Store your living trust document where you keep other important papers, such as your financial records, will, or durable power of attorney. A fireproof box in your home or office is fine. If you want to be extra careful, a safe deposit box is a good choice, but only if the successor trustee has access to it. Many people keep their living trust document in a locked drawer in a home desk or file cabinet. (After all, it's very unlikely anyone would steal a trust document, since it has no value to anyone but you. But this doesn't deal with the risk of fire or other disaster.)

Make sure your successor trustee (or spouse, if you made a basic shared living trust or a living trust with marital life estate) knows where the original trust document is and can get hold of it soon after your death or incapacity. The new trustee will need it to manage or distribute trust property. (The new trustee will also need to know the information in Chapter 14, "After a Grantor Dies," to carry out his or her duties.)

C. Registering the Trust

STATES THAT PROVIDE FOR REGISTRATION OF LIVING TRUSTS	
Alaska	Michigan
Colorado**	Mississippi
Florida*	Missouri
Hawaii	Nebraska*
Idaho	North Dakota
Maine	

*Not mandatory.

** Registration of a revocable living trust not required until the grantor's death; no registration required if all trust property is distributed to the beneficiaries then.

Some states require that the trustee of a trust register the trust with the local court. But there are no legal consequences or penalties if you don't, which, in effect, means this is an optional requirement. (The only exception is that if a court demands that a trustee register a trust, and the trustee refuses, the trustee can be removed.)

Registration of a living trust doesn't give the court any power over the administration of the trust, unless there's a dispute. Registration serves to give the court jurisdiction over any disputes involving the trust—for example, if after your death a beneficiary wants to object to the way your successor trustee distributed the trust property. But if you don't register your trust, the result is the same: the court still has jurisdiction if a disgruntled relative or creditor files suit.

To register a revocable living trust, the trustee must file a statement with the court where the trustee resides or keeps trust records. The statement must include at least the following:

- the name(s) of the grantor(s)
- the name(s) of the original trustee(s)
- an acknowledgment of the trusteeship (that is, a written acceptance by the trustees of their role), and
- the date of the trust document.

A trust can be registered in only one state at a time. ■

chapter 13

LIVING WITH YOUR LIVING TRUST

*T*his chapter discusses what you need to know after your living trust is up and running, and how to change your trust document if your circumstances change.

As a day-to-day, practical matter, it makes no difference that your property is now owned by your revocable living trust. As you know by now, you have no special paperwork to prepare, tax forms to file, or other duties to perform as the trustee of your own revocable living trust. Nor do you have any legal responsibilities to any of the beneficiaries you named in the trust document. They have no rights over any trust property while you are alive.

Some lawyers urge you to have your trust reviewed and updated by a lawyer every year. There's no need for this whatsoever. Indeed, there's no need for you to review your trust yourself every year. Review your trust if something major has changed, or you want to make a major change. But for many, probably most, people who create a living trust, there's very little or no change that affects the trust from the time they create it to the time it goes into effect.

A. If You Move to Another State

Your living trust remains valid if you prepare it in one state and then move to another. When you prepare a trust using the forms in this book, you declare the state of your legal residence and state that the law of this state applies to any disputes about disposition of the property as long as you live in that state. If you move to a new state, that new state's laws will govern property disputes. Still, no matter where you are living at your death, your successor trustee generally will only have to deal with one state's law. However, you may need to amend your trust if you move, for one or more reasons explained in Section D, below.

B. Adding Property to Your Living Trust

The living trust forms in this book specifically give you the right to add property to your trust. If you acquire valuable items of property after you create your living trust, you should promptly add them to the trust so that they won't have to go through probate at your death.

There are four steps to adding property to your trust:

Step 1. Type a revised Property Schedule A, B, or C of your trust document, adding the new property. (If you made an individual trust, you have only one schedule, Schedule A. If you and your spouse made a basic shared living trust or an AB trust, Schedule A lists your co-owned property, Schedule B lists the wife's separate property, if any, and Schedule C lists the husband's separate property, if any.)

Step 2. Remove the old schedule from your trust document and attach the new one.

Step 3. Place title of the property in the trustee's name. If, acting in your capacity as trustee, you originally purchased the property in the trustee's name, you don't need to bother about this, because, obviously, you've already done it. But if you acquire the property in your own name—for example, an inheritance—you need to prepare the appropriate title document. (See Chapter 11.)

Example

Rose and Michael prepare an AB trust. Later on, they buy a new house, and they want it to be in their living trust. So, on the deed, they take title in the name of "Rose Morris and Michael Morris, trustees of the Rose Morris and Michael Morris Living Trust, dated January 13, 20xx." They then type a revised Schedule A (which lists shared property) of their trust document and replace the old Schedule A.

Step 4. Amend the trust document if you need to name a beneficiary for the new property. You won't need to amend the trust document if you've left all your trust property to one person or if you want the property to go to your residuary beneficiary.

Example

Mercedes adds a new money market account to her living trust. She wants to leave this account to her brother, Neil, who is not her residuary beneficiary. Mercedes must prepare an amendment of her trust, listing Neil as the beneficiary for this new property. (See Section F, below.)

Usually, you won't need to amend the trust document of an AB trust if you put new property in the trust. That property will be subject to the trust provisions creating the AB trust. Only if you want the new property to go to someone other than Trust A, for the benefit of your spouse and then to your final beneficiaries, do you need to amend the trust.

C. Selling or Giving Away Trust Property

You have complete control over the property you have transferred to the living trust. If you want to sell or give away any of it, go ahead, using your authority as trustee. This means you (or you and your spouse, if you made a basic shared marital trust or AB trust) sign ownership or transfer documents (the deed, bill of sale or other document) in your capacity as trustee of the living trust.

Example

Martin transfers ownership of his house to his living trust, but later decides to sell it. He transfers the house to the buyer by signing the new deed as "Martin Owens, trustee of the Martin Owens Living Trust dated June 18, 20xx."

If you and your spouse made a basic shared living trust or an AB trust, either trustee (spouse) has authority over trust property. That means that either spouse can sell or give away any of the trust property—including the property that was co-owned or was the separate property of the other spouse before it was transferred to the trust. In practice, however, both spouses will probably have to consent to transfer real estate out of the living trust. Especially in community property states, buyers and title insurance companies usually insist on both spouses' signatures on transfer documents.

If for any reason you want to take property out of the trust but keep ownership of it, you can transfer the property to yourself. So if Martin, in the previous example, wanted to take his house out of his living trust but keep ownership in his own name, he would make the deed out from "The Martin Owens Living Trust dated June 18, 20xx, Martin Owens, trustee" to "Martin Owens." He would sign the deed "Martin Owens, trustee of the Martin Owens Living Trust, dated June 18, 20xx."

Unless this change will be for a brief period (for example, only for the time necessary to obtain refinancing of your home loan), you should modify the property schedule of your trust document to reflect the change. If you don't, the schedules will still show that the property is owned by the trust. Legally, the trust no longer owns it, and the discrepancy could be confusing to the people who carry out your wishes after your death.

Example

Wendy and Brian, a married couple, made a basic shared living trust several years ago. Wendy transferred a valuable antique dresser, which she inherited from her grandfather before she was married, to the living trust. It's listed on Schedule B of the trust document. The trust document provides that the dresser will go to her son at her death. But she's changed her mind and decided to give the dresser to her daughter while she's alive.

After Wendy gives the dresser to her daughter, she prepares two documents. First, she prepares a new Schedule B, deleting the dresser from the list of property, and replaces the old Schedule B attached to her trust document. Second, she prepares a Trust Amendment, stating that the paragraph that left the dresser to her son is no longer in effect. (See Section F, below.)

D. When to Amend Your Living Trust Document

One of the most attractive features of a revocable living trust is its flexibility: you can change its terms, or end it altogether, at any time. This section discusses several events that should be red flags, alerting you that you may need to amend your living trust.

In most circumstances, you will want to amend your living trust document, not revoke it. At first glance, it might seem easier to revoke it and start again, as is usually done with a will. But if you revoke your living trust and create another one, you must transfer all the trust property out of the old living trust and into the new one. This means preparing new documents of title and all the other paperwork required to transfer property to your original trust. (Section G, below, discusses when it is advisable to revoke your living trust and make another.)

As explained in Section C, above, you may need to amend your trust document if you sell or give away property from your trust. Following are other events that normally require amendment of a trust.

1. You Marry or Have a Child

If you get married or have a child, you'll almost certainly want to amend your trust document to provide for your new spouse or offspring. And remember that your spouse or minor child may be entitled, under state law, to a certain portion of your property. (See Chapter 8, Section H.)

2. You Move to Another State

Although your living trust is still valid if you move to another state, you may want to change your living trust in response to your new state's laws. Here are several aspects of your trust, and overall estate plan, that may be affected by a move to a new state.

a. Registering Your Trust

Your new state may require you to register your living trust document. (See Chapter 12, Section C.)

b. Marital Property Laws: Who Owns What

As previously discussed, if you are married and move from a common law state to California, Idaho, or Washington, property you acquired during marriage may become "quasi-community property," and so owned by both spouses, however it was originally owned. Wisconsin has a similar rule. See Chapter 6, Section D. You'll need to review your property disposition to make sure it complies with your new state's laws.

c. Property Management for Young Beneficiaries

Your state's law determines the choices you have when it comes to arranging for property management for young trust beneficiaries. In all states, you can create a child's trust for any beneficiary who might inherit trust property before he or she is 35. And, to repeat, in all states but South Carolina and Vermont, you can appoint an adult custodian to manage the child's property. The age at which the child receives the property outright can vary from state to state, between the ages of 18 to 25. (See Chapter 9, Sections B and D.)

If you made a gift using your old state's version of the Uniform Transfers to Minors Act (UTMA) and you move to South Carolina or Vermont, you may need to amend your trust, deleting the UTMA gift and creating a child's trust for it. Or, if you move to a state that has a lower UTMA age for turning over the property to the minor, you'll have to amend your trust to set the new age for the child to receive the gift. (See Chapter 9, Sections C and D.)

d. Rights of a Surviving Spouse to Inherit

Different states entitle surviving spouses to different shares of a deceased spouse's estate. If you prepare a shared basic living trust and you plan to leave at least one-half of your total estate to your spouse, you don't

have to worry about this. And, as previously mentioned, this doesn't apply to an AB trust. But if you want to leave your spouse less than one-half, and you're concerned that your spouse might challenge your estate plan and demand the "statutory share" of your property after your death, you'll need to know what your new state's laws allow. (See Chapter 8, Section H.)

e. State Death Taxes

If you move to a new state, that state's laws, including its law on death taxes, will govern all your property, except for out-of-state real estate. (See Chapter 15, Section D.)

3. You Change Your Name

If you change your name, for whatever reason—marriage, divorce, desire for a new identity, whimsy—your existing legal trust remains valid. If you want, you can amend your trust to formally replace your old name with your new one, but you don't have to. As long as it's clear who you are when you die, your trust will function properly.

4. Your Spouse Dies

If you and your spouse made a basic shared living trust, when one spouse dies the other will probably inherit some, if not all, of the deceased spouse's trust property. The surviving spouse may want to amend his or her trust to name beneficiaries for that property.

If you and your spouse made an AB trust, the surviving spouse cannot amend Trust A, which is created when the first spouse dies. And there's often no reason the surviving spouse needs to amend his or her trust, which remains revocable. (This is explained in Chapter 5.) The surviving spouse could amend her Trust B if she now wants to change it—for example, by revising her beneficiary plan or changing her successor trustee.

5. A Major Beneficiary Dies

If you left much or all of your trust property to one person, and that person dies before you do, you may well want to amend your trust document. If you named an alternate beneficiary for the deceased beneficiary, there's not an urgent need; the alternate will inherit the property. But it still makes sense to amend the trust so that you can name another alternate beneficiary, who will receive the property if the former alternate (now first in line) dies before you do.

Example

Maria and Carlos make a basic shared living trust together. Maria leaves all her trust property to Carlos, but he dies before she does. Because she named her daughter Teresa as alternate beneficiary for her husband, she has already planned for the possibility of Carlos's death. But it still makes sense for her to amend her trust to name Teresa as the beneficiary and then to name an alternate beneficiary for Teresa.

Remember that your trust document has another back-up device built into it: the residuary beneficiary. If both the primary and alternate beneficiary die before you do, the residuary beneficiary will inherit the trust property.

With an AB trust, if a final beneficiary dies before either spouse dies, the spouses can amend their trust to name a new final beneficiary, or they can leave the trust as is, allowing the alternate(s) named for the deceased final beneficiary to inherit that beneficiary's share of the AB trust property. (If they were cautious, the couple might still amend the trust, to name new alternate final beneficiaries, since the previous alternates for the deceased final beneficiary have become the final beneficiaries themselves.)

Also, as I've frequently stated, with an AB trust, the surviving spouse can amend her own revocable surviving spouse's trust to name a new final beneficiary, if she desires to, as long as she is competent.

6. You Want to Change Ownership of Trust Property

Sometimes couples decide, for various reasons, to change shared property into property owned separately by one spouse or the other. Or a spouse may decide to change his or her separate property into shared ownership property. The legal term for this is "transmutation of property."

If after you've placed property in a trust you want to make this type of change, you'll need to:

- Prepare the appropriate transfer documents for a change of ownership. If real estate is involved, new deeds reflecting the changed ownership must be prepared. If it's property without documents of title, you need a (reverse) assignment. A reverse assignment is simply a document transferring property from the trust

(technically, you as trustees back to yourself as a couple).

- Revise the appropriate trust schedules, so the changed property is deleted from the old schedule and placed on the correct one.

Example

Soon after they get married, Felicity and Russell Jones create a basic shared living trust. They live in a home in New Jersey that is Felicity's separate property, and is listed as such on Schedule B of their trust. After several happy years together, Felicity decides she wants to place the house in shared ownership with Russell. So she lists the house on Schedule A, the shared property schedule of their trust, removing it from Schedule B. As trustee, Felicity executes a deed transferring the house to herself, as her separate property. She then executes a second deed, identifying the property as co-owned equally between her and her husband. The house is now owned by the couple as trustees of their trust.

Since each spouse owns half the house, they'll need to revise their beneficiary provisions, unless each simply left all his or her property to the other spouse.

E. Amending a Living Trust Document

Who can amend the terms of a living trust document depends on the kind of trust you created.

1. Individual Living Trusts

If you created an individual living trust, you (the grantor) can amend any of its provisions at any time, as long as you are mentally competent.

2. Basic Shared Living Trusts and AB Trusts

While both spouses are alive, both must agree to any changes in the provisions of the trust documents—for example, to change a beneficiary, successor trustee, or the management set up for a young beneficiary.

After one spouse dies, a basic shared living trust is split into two trusts. The deceased spouse's trust can no longer be amended. The surviving spouse can, of course, amend his own revocable trust.

The same rules apply to Nolo's AB trust. Both spouses must agree to any amendment unless it is a situation where one spouse is incompetent and the other is permitted to amend the trust if the estate tax rules change. (See Chapter 10, Section D, Step 5A.) When a spouse dies, the AB trust splits into two distinct new trusts. Trust A, containing property of the deceased spouse, becomes irrevocable. The surviving spouse cannot change it. She cannot, for example, name a new successor trustee for Trust A. But again, the surviving spouse can amend or revoke her own trust, Trust B, as long as she remains alive and competent.

3. Someone Acting on Your Behalf

A trust document created from a form in this book cannot be amended by someone acting on a grantor's behalf, except in a situation where you have permitted the successor trustee of an AB trust to amend the trust if both spouses are alive and incapacitated, and the estate tax law changes. If a successor trustee uses this authority to amend an AB trust, she would have to modify the appropriate trust amendment (Form 8), to specify that it is the successor trustee, and not the grantors, who amend the trust.

Granting someone else the power to amend your trust under other circumstances is inherently dangerous. You've gone to considerable trouble to set up your estate plan and living trust. Normally, those plans shouldn't change when you are incapacitated. Therefore, the trust forms in this book do not authorize amendment by others if you become incapacitated, with the sole exception of amending an AB trust to take advantage of any new tax law.

To allow someone else to amend your living trust if you become incapacitated, you need to do two things:

- **Expressly authorize amendments in your living trust.** To accomplish this, add a new provision to the trustee powers' clause of your trust. The wording of this new provision varies, depending on the type of trust. For Form 1, the Basic Living Trust for One Person, you'd need something like:

   "If the original trustee of this trust becomes incapacitated, the acting successor trustee shall have authority to amend this trust."

   For Forms 2 or 3, you might use something like the following:

   "If one spouse becomes incapacitated, the other spouse can amend this trust. If both spouses become incapacitated, the surviving trustee can amend this trust."

   If you want to allow others to amend your trust. The above provisions are only examples, not actual clauses for your trust. If you want to allow others to be able to amend your trust, see a lawyer. You could impose a variety of different limits on the power to amend.

- **Prepare a durable power of attorney for finances.** In this document, you name a person to handle your financial matters if you are incapacitated and cannot handle them yourself. This person is called your "attorney-in-fact" or your "agent." To avoid conflicts, you should name the same person to be both your attorney-in-fact under a durable power of attorney and your successor trustee under your living trust. And to make your intention absolutely clear, in your power of attorney, you should expressly authorize your attorney-in-fact to amend your living trust. (See Chapter 15, Section E for more information about durable powers of attorney.)

F. How to Amend Your Trust Document

It's simple to amend your trust document to change a beneficiary, successor trustee, or custodian named in it, or change any other provision. Simply complete the appropriate amendment form from Appendix B or the CD-ROM, sign it, and have the form notarized, and then attach it to your original trust document. If you have an individual trust, use Form 7; if you have either a shared living trust or an AB trust, use Form 8.

You can subsequently refer to your trust by the date of the amendment.

Example

"The Jane and Werner Kopf Trust, as amended September 3, 2001"

With an AB trust, you can't change the life beneficiary (the other spouse) while both spouses are alive. To do so defeats the whole point of this kind of trust. Otherwise, any term of the trust can be changed while both spouses live.

A sample draft amendment of an AB living trust, ready for final typing, is shown below.

Sample Form 8: Amendment to Basic Shared Living Trust or AB Trust

AMENDMENT TO LIVING TRUST

This Amendment to The ① __Jim and Toni Nance_____ Living Trust

<small>your names</small>

dated _____July 1,_____, _20xx_, is made this _30th_ day of ____November_____ ,20xx___,

<small>date Declaration of Trust signed</small>

by _____Toni Nance and Jim Nance_____, the grantors and trustees of the trust. Under the power

<small>your names</small>

of amendment reserved to the grantors by Section II, Paragraph (F), of the Declaration of Trust, the grantors

amend the trust as follows:

1. The following is added to the Declaration of Trust:

   _in Section IV, Paragraph A(1), Aaron Nance shall be given all Jim Nance's interest___

   _in the Wyche Co. stock_____

2. The following is deleted from the Declaration of Trust:

   _in Section IV, Paragraph A(1), Eileen Nance Jones shall be given all Jim Nance's__

   _interest in the Wyche Co. stock_____

[Repeat as needed]

In all other respects, the Declaration of Trust as executed on _____July 1_____, _20xx_, by

the grantors is hereby affirmed.

Executed at _____Fairview_____, _____Ohio_____, on

<small>city   state</small>

_November 30_____, _20xx_ .

<small>date</small>

_____

Grantor and Trustee

_____

Grantor and Trustee

Example

Jim and Toni created their AB trust three years ago. Jim named his sister Eileen as a specific beneficiary for some stock in the Wyche Co. (he named no alternate beneficiary) that Jim transferred to the trust. But since then, Jim and his sister have had a falling out. He wants to amend the trust document to leave the stock to his brother Aaron.

All Jim and Toni need to do is use Form 8 to prepare a trust amendment. The amendment deletes the paragraph in the Declaration of Trust that left the stock to Eileen. It also adds a paragraph leaving the stock to Aaron and stating that if Aaron doesn't survive him, that it should go to his nephew David.

If they eliminated Eileen as a beneficiary but didn't name a new beneficiary for the stock, it would eventually become part of Trust A or the surviving spouse's Trust B (if Toni predeceases Jim).

Their draft trust amendment form (before typing, with appropriate cross-outs in the form) is shown on the preceeding page.

Similarly, you can amend your trust document if you change your mind about who you want to serve as:

- **Successor trustee.** The person who handles the trust, and any children's trusts, after your death or the surviving spouse's death if a shared trust was created.

⚠️ **Do not change the original trustees of your living trust.** You (and your spouse, if you made a basic shared living trust or AB trust) must be the original trustees of your living trust. If you aren't, the tax treatment of the trust changes. (See Chapter 7, Section A.)

- **Alternate successor trustee.** The person who takes over as trustee if your first choice can't serve.

- **Custodian of a child's property.** The person who manages a young beneficiary's property under the terms of the Uniform Transfers to Minors Act, if it's available in your state.

- **Alternate custodian.** The person who serves as custodian if your first choice can't serve.

Example

Geoffrey creates a living trust and names his brother as successor trustee. His brother moves to Europe two years later, so Geoffrey prepares a Trust Amendment to his trust document, naming his friend Brad as successor trustee instead.

⚠️ **If you have registered your trust.** If you live in a state where you can register your trust with a government agency, and have chosen to do so, you should file a copy of any amendment (or revocation) with that agency. (See Chapter 12, Section C for a list of states that authorize registration of living trusts.)

G. Revoking Your Living Trust

You can revoke your living trust at any time, but you probably won't want to. After all, the reasons you established a trust won't go away, and revoking a living trust (unlike revoking a will) requires some work. The revoked trust ceases to exist and cannot own property. That means you must transfer ownership of all the trust property out of the living trust, back into your own name (or names) or into the name of a new living trust.

1. Who Can Revoke a Living Trust

Who can revoke your living trust depends on the kind of trust you created.

a. Individual Living Trust

If you create an individual living trust, you (the grantor) can revoke it at any time. The trust document does not allow the trust to be revoked by someone acting on your behalf (your attorney-in-fact, for example) unless you have specifically granted that authority in another document. (See Section E, above.)

b. Basic Shared Living Trust or AB Trust

Either spouse can revoke either of these trusts, wiping out all terms of the trust. The trust property is returned to each spouse according to how they owned it before transferring it to the trust.

Example

Yvonne and André make a basic shared living trust. Each transfers separately owned property to the trust. They also transfer their house, which they own together equally, as tenants in common, to the trust. Later Yvonne, anticipating a divorce, transfers the trust property she owned back to herself, and the property her husband owned back to him. The co-owned house goes back to both of them, who own it as tenants in common as before. She then revokes the trust.

The reason either spouse can revoke either a basic shared or AB trust, but it takes both to amend one, is that revocation simply returns both spouses to the status quo. By contrast, in the event of divorce or bitter conflict, it's risky to allow one spouse to amend a trust that governs both spouse's property.

2. When to Revoke Your Living Trust

If you're like most people, amending your living trust will take care of your changing circumstances over the years, and you will never need to revoke your trust. But here are two situations in which you might need to revoke a living trust and start over.

a. You Want to Make Extensive Revisions

If you want to make very extensive revisions to the terms of the trust document, you should revoke it and start fresh with a new trust document. If you don't, you risk creating inconsistencies and confusion.

b. You Get Divorced

If you divorce, you should revoke your living trust, and you and your ex-spouse should make new, separate ones. In a few states, the provisions of your living trust that affect your spouse are automatically revoked by divorce, but you should definitely not rely solely on these laws. They might change. Your own revocation will not.

3. How to Revoke Your Living Trust

To revoke your living trust, you must do two things:

Step 1. Transfer ownership of trust property from the trust back to yourself. Basically, you must reverse the process you followed when you transferred ownership of the property to the trust's name. (See Chapter 11.) You can make the transfer because of your authority as trustee of the trust.

Step 2. Use Form 9 in Appendix B or on the CD-ROM to prepare a simple document called a Revocation of Living Trust. Type the form deleting all extraneous material from the final version. Sign the typed revocation in front of a notary. Then store the revocation in a safe place, with your other vital papers. ■

chapter 14

AFTER A GRANTOR DIES

The benefit of a revocable living trust doesn't come until after a grantor's death, when trust property is transferred to beneficiaries, or placed in an AB trust, without probate. The all-important responsibility of handling that transfer falls to your surviving spouse, if you made a basic shared living trust or an AB trust, or to your successor trustee, if you made an individual living trust.

To transfer property outside of probate, the successor trustee or surviving spouse does not have to file any reports with, or be supervised by, any government agencies or court.

Federal or state estate tax returns. If the value of the grantor's estate is over the estate tax threshold (see Chapter 4, Section F) a federal estate tax return must be filed. The successor trustee (as well as the executor of the deceased's will) is responsible for filing this document. It is a complicated tax form, and an expert lawyer or tax accountant should be hired to do the work.

A. Who Serves as Trustee After the Grantor's Death

With a basic shared marital trust or AB trust, the surviving spouse serves as sole trustee after one spouse's death. With an individual trust, or when the surviving spouse dies, the successor trustee is in charge.

WHO SERVES AS TRUSTEE AFTER GRANTOR'S DEATH?

Individual Living Trust

1. Successor trustee(s)
2. Alternate successor trustee(s)

Basic Shared Living Trust or AB Trust

1. Surviving spouse
2. Successor trustee(s)
3. Alternate successor trustee(s)

---

1. More Than One Successor Trustee

If more than one person is named in the trust document as successor trustee, they all serve together. Whether each must formally agree on any action taken with regard to the living trust property, or they can act independently, depends on the terms of the trust document.

If one of the trustees cannot serve, the others remain as trustees. The person named as alternate successor trustee does not take over unless all the people named as successor trustees cannot serve.

2. If a Trustee Resigns

A trustee can resign at any time by preparing and signing a resignation statement like the one shown below. The ex-trustee should deliver the notice to the person who is next in line to serve as trustee.

NOTICE OF RESIGNATION

I, Lucia Freni, current trustee of The Robert Ambruzzi Living Trust dated March 3, 20xx, resign my position as trustee, effective immediately.

Date: November 19, 20xx

Lucia Freni

[notarization]

Under the terms of Nolo living trusts, any trustee, including the last acting trustee, can appoint someone else to take over if no one named in the trust document can serve.

Normally, it would be the last, or alternate, successor trustee who named someone else to act as trustee if the need arises. The appointment must be in writing, signed and notarized. The trustee making the appointment can prepare a simple document like the one shown below.

APPOINTMENT OF TRUSTEE

I, Lucia Freni, Trustee of The Robert Ambruzzi Living Trust dated March 3, 20xx, appoint Clarence Ryan as trustee, effective immediately. This appointment is made under the authority granted in the Declaration of Trust.

Date: November 19, 20xx

Lucia Freni
_____
[notarization]

3. Removing a Trustee

Very rarely, a beneficiary becomes seriously unhappy with the way a trustee handles trust property. For example, the beneficiary of a child's trust might complain that the trustee isn't spending enough of the trust property's income on the beneficiary's education. If the dispute can't be worked out, the beneficiary can file a lawsuit to try to force the removal of the trustee.

B. The Trustee's Duties

Every trustee must take two steps as soon as he or she assumes responsibility for your living trust: The trustee must execute and record a document establishing that he or she can act for the trust and must obtain an appraisal of the value of major trust assets.

Beyond these basics, a trustee's job depends on whether your state imposes specific requirements on trustees (only a few states do) and on what type of living trust you made: an individual living trust, a basic shared living trust with your spouse, or an AB trust.

1. All Trustees

All successor trustees should take the following steps after assuming responsibility for a living trust.

a. Preparing an Affidavit of Successor Trustee

The trustee may need proof that he or she is entitled to act for the trust, particularly for transactions involving real estate, since there are no court proceedings to officially give the trustee authority. The accepted convention is to record a document called "Affidavit of Assumption of Duties by Successor Trustee" at the county land records office. There is no set form for this affidavit. It should always include:

- the name of the trust
- the date the trust document was signed, and
- the name of the person becoming successor trustee.

A certified copy of the grantor's death certificate should be attached. Certified copies can be obtained from your county or state's vital records department.

A sample draft Affidavit of Assumption of Duties by Successor Trustee, ready for final typing, is shown below. A fill-in-the-blanks version is in Appendix B or on the CD-ROM, Form 12.

Form 12: Affidavit of Successor Trustee

AFFIDAVIT OF ASSUMPTION OF DUTIES BY SUCCESSOR TRUSTEE

State of _____Illinois_____, County of _____Cook_____.

                          state   county

_____Ida Beilengeur_____, of legal age, first being duly sworn, declares:

                successor trustee's name

On _____March 23_____, 19xx, _____Rosa and Vladimir Rostop_____ created

               date   name(s) of grantor(s)

The _____Rosa and Vladimir Rostop_____ Living Trust.

            name(s) of grantor(s)

On _____Sept. 2,_____, 19xx, _____Vladimir Rostop_____ died, as

              date   grantor's name

established in the attached certified copy of the Certificate of Death.

[for a shared or AB trust, add:]

On _____Nov. 3,_____, 20xx, _____Rosa Rostop_____ died, as

              date   second grantor's name

established in the attached certified copy of the Certificate of Death.

The Declaration of Trust creating The _____Rosa and Vladimir Rostop_____ Living Trust

                                  grantor(s) name(s)

provides that upon the death of the grantors, I, _____Ida Beilengeur_____,

                                      successor trustee's name

become the trustee of the trust.

I hereby accept the office of trustee of the trust, and am now acting as trustee of the trust.

Dated: _____

_____
Successor Trustee
        [notarized]

b. Appraising the Value of Significant Trust Assets

The successor trustee should prepare a written statement of the market value of major trust assets as of the date of the grantor's death. (The IRS also permits the trustee to value all the assets as of six months after death. This is an all-or-nothing proposition. The trustee cannot value some assets as of the date of death and others as of six months thereafter.) Because all property of the deceased, including all living trust property, is entitled to a stepped-up basis under current estate tax laws (see Chapter 3, Section L), inheritors need to have hard figures on the market prices of the property when the living trust owner died. If the market value of living trust property is not obtained promptly after the grantor dies, it may be difficult or impossible to obtain reliable evaluations later. This may mean that the IRS will not allow any stepped-up basis when calculating profit, or loss, from any subsequent sale of the property.

Some valuations are easy to obtain. Stock and bond prices are, obviously, printed daily during the week. Other valuations require more work. Real estate needs an appraisal, unless the property is promptly sold. In practice, a broker should be able to make a sensible estimate. Other valuable property, such as jewelry, collectibles, or artworks requires appraisal by an expert in the field.

c. Providing Basic Information to Trust Beneficiaries

Under common (judge-made) law, a successor trustee has a basic, if not always clearly defined, duty to provide essential trust informaion to trust beneficiaries. Doing so is also wise trustee policy—it's not hard to do, and can eliminate conflicts or even lawsuits that could arise if a trustee works in secret.

2. State-Specific Duties

Several states require a successor trustee to take specific action with regard to a living trust. This section sets out the requirements for those states.

a. The Uniform Trust Code

The Uniform Trust Code (UTC) has been adopted in the following states: Connecticut, the District of Columbia, Kansas, Maine, Missouri, New Mexico, Nebraska

(effective Jan. 1, 2005), and Wyoming. Many other state legislatures are considering adopting the UTC.

The UTC essentially requires that a successor trustee keep trust beneficiaries reasonably informed of trust matters. Specific requirements are that within 60 days of becoming the active trustee, a successor trustee must provide all beneficiaries with his or her name, address, and phone number, and must also inform them that the trust has become irrevocable, and that any beneficiary who requests it has a right to a copy of the trust and of any reports that the successor trustee must make.

These are not onerous requirements. Indeed, they seem sensibly designed to reduce or eliminate problems that could arise if a successor trustee kept his management of the trust secret or refused to give a copy of the trust document to beneficiaries.

b. California: Notification of Beneficiaries and Heirs

California law requires the trustee to notify all trust beneficiaries and heirs of the deceased living trust grantor when the trust has become irrevocable. (Cal. Prob. Code § 16061.5 and following sections.)

The notice must be sent within 60 days after the grantor's death and must include:

- the name and date of death of the grantor
- the date of execution (signing) of the trust
- the name, mailing address, and phone number of the trustee
- the address of the "physical location of where the principal place of administration of the trust is located" (usually, this is the successor trustee's home or office)
- notification that the recipient is entitled to a copy of the trust, upon reasonable notification to the trustee, and
- this specific warning in at least 10-point bold type: **You may not bring an action to contest the trust more than 120 days from the date this notification by the trustee is served upon you or 60 days from the day on which a copy of the terms of the trust is mailed or personally delivered to you in response to your request during that 120-day period, whichever is later.**

These requirements cannot be waived by the grantor.

The California statute contains ambiguities. For instance, does "beneficiary" include alternate or final beneficiaries? In terms of Nolo's living trusts, the answer is "no" for alternate beneficiaries, but "yes" for the final beneficiaries of an AB trust. Also, who are the deceased's "heirs?" These, by law, are the people who would inherit if the deceased died without having any valid document leaving his property. Heirs are closest family members—spouse, children—then (if none) up, down, and out the line—parents, siblings, and so on.

The purpose of the statute is to prevent abuse of power by trustees. If you are secure that your family and other beneficiaries will not fight over your property or with your trustee, this statute imposes only some relatively minor paperwork on your trustee. If you worry that a fight might develop, this statute is one more reason you should see a lawyer before preparing your living trust.

c. Ohio: Affidavit for Trust Holding Real Estate

Ohio law requires the successor trustee of a trust holding real estate to file an affidavit with the county auditor and the county recorder where the real estate is located. (Ohio Rev. Code § 5302.171.) The affidavit must be filed "as soon as practical," and must contain the following information:

- the names and addresses of all trustees

- a reference to the deed granting ownership to the trustees, and

- a legal description of the property.

This affidavit is not required if the original trust document, or a "memorandum of trust" that complies with Section 5301.255 of the Ohio Code, has previously been recorded with the county recorder.

d. Tennessee: Notification of AB Trust Beneficiaries

The successor trustee of an AB trust in Tennessee must, within 60 days of assuming his or her duties, notify the life beneficiary and all final beneficiaries of the details of the trust. (Tenn. Code Ann. § 35-50-119.) The successor trustee can provide this notice by sending the beneficiaries a copy of the trust document or an abstract of trust. The requirements for the abstract of trust are numerous and specific; it must include, among other details, "an estimate of the value of the trust at the date of the notice." This information is not required to be in the

trust document itself, so it seems less work to send the trust document, rather than an abstract.

3. Trust-Specific Duties

A successor trustee's job depends primarily on what type of living trust you made: an individual trust, a basic shared trust, or an AB trust.

a. Individual Trust

When the grantor, who is also the trustee, dies, the successor trustee named in the trust document takes over as trustee. The new trustee is responsible for distributing the trust property to the beneficiaries named by the grantor in the trust document.

It is not the trustee's responsibility to sell or manage trust property.

Example

Jamie is Elliot's successor trustee. Elliot's trust leaves his house to his children, Clarence and Grace. Elliot dies. Jamie, as trustee, deeds the house from the trust to Clarence and Grace, who can do with it what they wish—live in it, rent it, or sell it. Jamie does not sell the house and divide the proceeds between the beneficiaries—that's not his decision to make.

Normally, the trust continues to exist only as long as it takes the successor trustee to distribute trust property to the beneficiaries. In many cases, a living trust can be wound up within a few weeks after a grantor's death. No formal termination document is required. Once the trust property has been distributed, the trust ends.

The successor trustee is also in charge of managing any property left to a young beneficiary in a child's trust. A child's trust will exist until the beneficiary reaches the age specified in the trust document, so if there's such a trust, the successor trustee may have years of work ahead. (See Chapter 9, Section D.)

If trust property inherited by a young beneficiary is to be managed by a custodian under the Uniform Transfers to Minors Act, instead of in a child's trust, the person named as custodian will receive that property and be responsible for it. The successor trustee may also have been named as the custodian for a young beneficiary's property.

b.   Basic Shared Living Trust

When a spouse dies, a basic shared living trust automatically splits into two separate trusts:

- Trust 1 contains the deceased spouse's share of trust property, excluding any trust property he or she left to the surviving spouse. The terms of Trust 1 cannot be changed; it cannot be revoked.

- Trust 2 contains the surviving spouse's trust property, including any of the deceased spouse's share of the trust property that is left to the surviving spouse. The surviving spouse remains free to amend the terms of Trust 2, or even revoke it.

The survivor is sole trustee of Trust 1, Trust 2, and any children's trusts set up for the deceased spouse's young beneficiaries.

The two new trusts can be identified by adding "Trust 1" or "Trust 2" to the original basic shared living trust's name.

Example

Debra and Timothy Zeltzer create a basic shared living trust. Timothy dies in 2002. Debra can refer to her trust as "The Debra and Timothy Zeltzer Trust, Trust 2," and to her husband's trust, now irrevocable, as "The Debra and Timothy Zeltzer Trust, Trust 1."

It's the surviving spouse's job to distribute the property in Trust 1 to the beneficiaries the deceased spouse named in the trust document. If, as is common, much of the trust property is left to the surviving spouse, that spouse will have little to do. The trust property he or she inherits is already in the revocable trust (Trust 2), and remains there. The trust document provides that trust property left to the survivor does not go to the surviving spouse in an individual capacity but instead stays in the living trust and becomes part of the property in Trust 2. If it did not contain such a provision, the property would have to be transferred from the living trust to the spouse and then, if the surviving spouse wanted it to avoid probate, back to her living trust again.

When all the property in Trust 1 has been distributed to the beneficiaries, that trust ceases to exist. No formal termination document is required.

Trust 2 contains only the surviving spouse's property and remains revocable. The surviving spouse is free to change it as he or she wishes.

Example

Edith and Jacques create a basic shared living trust. They transfer their house, which they own together, into the trust, and name each other as beneficiaries. Edith names her son as alternate beneficiary.

When Jacques dies, Edith inherits his half-interest in the house. Because of the way the trust document is worded, she doesn't have to change the trust document to name a beneficiary for the half-interest in the house that she inherited from her husband, nor does she have to prepare a new deed for the house. Both halves of the house will go to her son at her death. She may, however, want to amend the trust to make her son the primary beneficiary and name someone else to be alternate beneficiary.

When the second spouse dies, the successor trustee named in the trust document takes over as trustee. The process of winding up the living trust is the same as that for an individual trust. (See Section 1, above.)

Example

Harry and Maude, a married couple, set up a basic shared living trust to avoid probate. They appoint Maude's cousin Emily as successor trustee, to take over as trustee after they have both died. They transfer ownership of much of their co-owned property—their house, savings accounts, and stocks—to the trust. Maude also puts some of her family heirlooms, which are her separate property, in the living trust.

In the trust document, Maude leaves her heirlooms to her younger sister. She leaves her half of the trust property she and Harry own together to Harry.

When Maude dies, Harry becomes the sole trustee. Following the terms of the trust document, he distributes Maude's heirlooms (from Trust 1) to her sister, without probate. Maude's half of the property they had owned together stays in the trust (in Trust 2); no transfer is necessary. After Maude's death, Harry decides to amend the trust document to name his nephew, Burt, as successor trustee instead of Maude's cousin Emily. When Harry dies, Burt will become trustee and distribute the property in Trust 2 according to Harry's written gifts made in the trust document. When all the property is given to Harry's beneficiaries, the trust ends.

THE SURVIVING SPOUSE'S DUTIES: BASIC SHARED LIVING TRUST

- Distribute the deceased spouse's share of the trust property to beneficiaries named in the trust document.
- Manage property left in a child's trust, if any.
- File federal and state estate tax returns, if necessary (this is also the executor's responsibility, if there is a will).
- Amend Trust 2 to reflect changed circumstances, if necessary or desired.

---

c. Nolo's AB Trust

With Nolo's AB trust, both spouses are the original trustees. When a spouse dies, the surviving spouse becomes sole trustee. The living trust splits into two trusts: the irrevocable Trust A (of the deceased spouse) and Trust B, the revocable surviving spouse's trust. A new trust document is not needed, except that new schedules listing the property in Trust A and Trust B must be prepared.

The surviving trustee prepares two new printed or typed schedules. On the first, the trustee lists all property which will be held and owned by Trust A. On the second, the trustee lists all property held in Trust B, property owned by the surviving spouse. The property needs to be described with sufficient clarity so that the IRS can tell what property belongs to Trust A. There is no legal requirement that the new schedules be notarized, but the trustee can have that done if desired. Attach the originals of the two schedules to the original trust document.

The surviving spouse, as trustee, must first distribute any trust property the deceased spouse left to specifically

named beneficiaries. (Remember, each spouse can make specific gifts of trust property to beneficiaries other than the other spouse.) Then the trustee must maintain the rest of that property in the ongoing Trust A.

THE SURVIVING SPOUSE'S DUTIES: AB TRUST

- Create and maintain Trust A. Divide property between this trust and the surviving spouse's Trust B.
- In California and Tennessee, the trustee must notify the final beneficiaries of Trust A that this trust has now become irrevocable. (See Section B, above.)
- Distribute any specific gifts of the trust property made by the deceased spouse.
- Administer Trust A. File trust tax return each year, and, if required by trust document, give copies to final beneficiaries.
- Manage property left in a child's trust, if any.
- File federal and state estate tax returns, if necessary. This is also the executor's responsibility if there is a will. (See Section D, below.)
- Amend the surviving spouse's trust, Trust B, to reflect changed circumstances, if necessary or desired.

Determining the most financially desirable way to divide the living trust property between Trust A and the surviving spouse's Trust B is often not a simple task. Any allocation of equally owned trust property is valid, as long as each trust gets 50% of the total worth. But each item of property does not have to be split, with half going to each trust. For example, stock worth $300,000 can be placed in Trust A, as long as other co-owned property with a total worth of $300,000 is placed in Trust B.

Determining the wisest division of property between the Trusts A and B can be tricky. Hiring an expert financial advisor at this point is a wise investment, resulting in substantial tax savings further down the line. If state property ownership laws allow some flexibility with allocation of shared property, as is particularly true in community property states, you and your advisors can make tax-saving divisions. (For a discussion of some issues that can arise when allocating property between Trust A and Trust B, see Chapter 5, Section C.) Further complexities can arise if each spouse names different final beneficiaries for her or his portion of shared-ownership property. Does that mean that every item of the shared property must be divided 50/50? If not, how can the successor trustee ensure that all final beneficiaries will be treated equally? An expert can help to ensure that property will be divided and distributed as you wish.

Because the IRS might want to know, at some point, the value of the property placed in Trust A and in Trust B, the successor trustee should prepare a list designating the net value of each item of property, as of the date of division.

As I've said, to establish Trust A, the survivor does not need to create a new trust document. But property must be clearly identified as being owned by Trust A or Trust B. This usually requires some reregistering of title of some of the living trust property in the name of Trust A. For example, if you decide that it is wisest to put all of a shared ownership house in the Trust A, a new deed should be prepared to reflect this, listing the new owner as, for example, "The Moira and Joseph O'Sullivan Living Trust, A." The deed is signed by the surviving spouse, as trustee.

In addition to a name, as just described, Trust A needs a federal taxpayer ID number. The surviving spouse must keep appropriate trust financial records and file a federal trust tax return every year. The IRS will want it clear which trust owns what. Annual state trust tax returns may also be required, in states with income taxes.

If the trust document requires it, the trustee is required to give copies of the trust's annual federal trust income tax return to the final beneficiaries.

The spouse as trustee manages the property in Trust A and, as life beneficiary, receives any income it generates.

The surviving spouse's trust, Trust B, goes on as before. Trust B remains revocable and can be changed at any time. No new property documents are required; any property the deceased spouse leaves to the surviving spouse is added to Trust B. No tax return needs to be filed for this trust.

After the death of the surviving spouse, the successor trustee winds up both A and B trusts by distributing all property (except for any specific gifts made by the surviving spouse) of both trusts to each trust's final benefi-

ciaries. The successor trustee must file a final tax return for Trust A. The successor trustee also manages any property left in a child's trust and files a closing income tax return for the second spouse.

C. Transferring Property to Beneficiaries

The procedure for transferring trust property depends on who the beneficiaries are:

- Property of a basic shared living trust left by a deceased spouse to the surviving spouse remains in the trust, and no action is required.

- Property left to Trust A must be clearly identified as Trust A property.

- Property left to Trust B by the deceased spouse remains in the ongoing living trust, and no action is required.

- Trust property left to adult beneficiaries must be actually transferred to them.

- Property left to a young beneficiary in a child's trust stays in that trust until the child reaches the age to receive the trust property outright.

- Property left to a custodian under the Uniform Transfers to Minors Act must be given to the custodian named in the trust document.

To obtain the trust property, the trustee usually needs a copy of the grantor's death certificate (both grantors' death certificates, if both are dead and the trust property was originally co-owned) and a copy of the trust document. (The trustee should be prepared to show the original trust document in case anyone doubts the copy's authenticity.) Frequently an Affidavit of Assumption of Duties by Successor Trustee will also be needed. And finally, in some cases, the trustee will need to prepare some other paperwork, such as a specific form of a brokerage company or a new deed for real estate.

BUREAUCRATS, BUREAUCRATS

In rare instances, the trustee can encounter odd and difficult problems, depending on the narrowness and obstinacy of the bureaucracy holding the property. For example, one successor trustee was told by two institutions that he must obtain a written statement or "certification" from a lawyer or bank that the trust hadn't been modified since it was signed. This was an irrational and unreasonable requirement. No law requires any "certification." The grantor was dead, and no lawyer or bank was involved in preparing his trust. Eventually, after considerable persistence, the trustee succeeded in persuading the institutions that he knew of no amendment to the trust, and it was ridiculous for them to demand impossible proof that no amendment existed. The transfers were allowed.

Moral: Be persevering if you must, and eventually you'll get the transfer approved by the transfer agent.

Specific requirements for transferring property vary slightly from place to place, and the trustee may have to make inquiries at banks, stock brokerages, and other institutions about current procedures, but here are the general rules. A trustee who runs into difficulties has the authority to get help—from a lawyer, accountant, or other expert—and pay for it from trust assets.

Help for California residents. *How to Probate an Estate in California*, by Julia Nissley (Nolo), contains forms and instructions for transferring the property of a deceased person, including living trust property.

Terminology. This section refers to whoever takes over as trustee after a grantor's death as the "trustee." To remind you, if you made an individual trust, the trustee is the person you named as successor trustee. If you made a shared marital trust, or an AB trust, the trustee is the surviving spouse or, after both spouses have died, the successor trustee.

1. Property Without Title Documents

For trust property that doesn't have a title document—furniture, for example—the task of the trustee is quite simple. The trustee must promptly distribute the property to the beneficiaries named in the trust document. If the trustee thinks it's a good idea, it's appropriate to have the recipient sign a receipt. But in many family situations, where all trust each other, this formality isn't necessary.

2. Bank Accounts

It should be simple for the trustee to transfer the funds in a bank or savings and loan account, already held in the name of the living trust, to the beneficiary. Financial institutions are familiar with living trusts and how they work, and the bank probably has the trust document (or a bank form with information about the trust) already on file.

The trustee will need to show the bank or savings and loan:

- a certified copy of the trust grantor's death certificate
- a copy of the living trust document, if the bank doesn't already have one (again, being prepared to show the original trust document, if demanded), and
- proof of his or her own identity, perhaps including an Affidavit of Assumption of Duties by Successor Trustee.

3. Real Estate

The trustee needs to prepare and sign a deed transferring ownership of real estate from the trust to the beneficiary. The trustee signs the deed, in her capacity as trustee.

Example

"Jane Adanski, Trustee of The Robert Whilhite Living Trust, dated October 25, 1992."

The signed and notarized deed should also be filed (recorded) with the county land records office. In most places, recording costs no more than a few dollars per page. It's unlikely, but depending on local and state law, there may be a transfer tax to pay. (Deeds, recording and transfer taxes are discussed in Chapter 11, Section E.)

Example

The deed to Evelyn Crocker's house shows that it is owned by Evelyn Crocker, as trustee of her living trust. The living trust document states that Evelyn's daughter, Amanda, is to inherit the house when Evelyn dies. Amanda is also the successor trustee of the trust.

After Evelyn's death, Amanda prepares and signs a new deed, transferring ownership of the house from the trust to herself. She signs the deed in her capacity as trustee of the trust, and records the deed in the county land records office, along with an Affidavit of Assumption of Duties by Successor Trustee.

A title company, before it will issue title insurance to the new owners, will probably want a copy of the trust document and a certified copy of the death certificate of the trust grantor.

4. Stocks and Bonds

How to transfer stocks or bonds from a trust to the beneficiary depends on whether they were held in a brokerage account or separately. (For information about transferring stock in closely held corporations, see Section 6, below.)

a. Brokerage Accounts

The trustee should contact the broker and ask for instructions. The brokerage company will almost surely already have either a copy of the living trust document or a form that includes relevant information about the trust. (These are necessary to transfer the account to the living trust in the first place.)

If not, the trustee will probably need to send the broker:

- a copy of the trust document or an "abstract of trust" (the first, last and other relevant pages of the trust document, showing the notarized signature—see Chapter 11, Section C, for a sample Abstract of Trust), and
- a letter instructing the holder to transfer the brokerage account to the beneficiary's name.

b. Stock Certificates

If the deceased grantor kept the stock certificates or bonds in his or her possession—most people don't—the trustee must get new certificates issued, showing the beneficiary as the new owner.

The trustee will have to send the securities' transfer agent several documents. It's a good idea to write the transfer agent and ask exactly what is needed. Usually, the name and address of the transfer agent appear on the face of the stock or bond certificate. But because transfer agents change occasionally, the first thing the trustee should do is write or call (or check with a stock brokerage firm) to verify the name and address of the current transfer agent.

The trustee will probably have to send in:

- a certified copy of the grantor's death certificate
- the certificates or bonds
- a document called a "stock or bond power," which the trustee must fill out and sign, with the signature guaranteed by an officer of a bank or brokerage firm (the stock or bond power may be printed on the back of the certificates; if not, stationery stores carry them)
- a copy of the trust document or an "abstract of trust" if the transfer agent did not receive one when the securities were transferred into the trust
- an Affidavit of Domicile (a form available from banks and stock brokers) signed by the trustee, showing what the trust grantor's state of residence was, and
- a letter of instructions requesting that the certificates be reissued in the beneficiary's name.

Also, the trustee may be required to have his signature "guaranteed" by a stockbroker. If neither the trustee nor the deceased grantor have, or had, a stock account with a brokerage company, this too may cause trouble. The trustee will have to locate a broker—maybe one who handles a friend's account—to "guarantee" your signature.

The trustee may be required to produce "certified copies" of the living trust, although the transfer agent isn't sure what agency "certifies" documents. Your best bet here is to file the original document with your local county records office and have them "certify" copies for you.

c. Government Securities

To transfer government securities—Treasury bills or U.S. bonds, for example—the trustee should ask the broker to contact the issuing government agency, or contact the government directly.

5. Mutual Funds or Money Market Accounts

For mutual funds or money market accounts owned in the trust's name, the trustee should ask the company what it requires to reregister ownership of the account in the beneficiary's name. Generally, the trustee must send the company proof of his or her own identity, a copy of the grantor's death certificate, a letter of instructions (or a form that the company provides), and a copy of the trust document.

6. Small Business Interests

How a trustee transfers small business interests owned by a living trust depends on the way the business was organized.

Transferring trademarks. A registered trademark or service mark of a small business must be reregistered in the name of the beneficiary. See *Trademark: Legal Care for Your Business and Product Name*, by Steve Elias (Nolo). Similarly, a website domain name must be reregistered. See *Domain Names: How to Choose and Protect a Great Name for Your Website*, by Steve Elias and Patricia Gima (Nolo).

a. Sole Proprietorships

The trustee must transfer business assets to the beneficiary as he or she would transfer any other trust property. The name of the business itself, if owned by the living trust, does not have a title document, so the trustee doesn't need to do anything to transfer it to the beneficiary.

b. Solely Owned Corporations

Corporation officers must prepare the appropriate corporate records to show that ownership has been transferred to the beneficiary. The specifics depend on the incorporation papers and company bylaws. Often a resolution by the board of directors is required. Additional paperwork may include such documents as "Notice of Special Meeting of Board of Directors" and "Waiver of Notice of Time Requirements to Hold Special Meeting of Board of Directors." Then the trustee must have the stock certificates reissued in the beneficiary's name.

c. Closely Held Corporations and Limited Liability Companies

The stock certificates or ownership interest owned by the trust will have to be reissued in the beneficiary's name. The trustee should contact the officers of the corporation or LLC; the other shareholders or owners may have the right, under the corporation's bylaws or a shareholders' agreement, to buy back the shares or interest. For LLC information, see *Form Your Own Limited Liability Company*, by Anthony Mancuso (Nolo).

d. Partnership Interests

The trustee should contact the deceased grantor's partners, who may have the right to buy out the grantor's share. If the beneficiary wants to enter into the partnership, the partnership agreement must be changed to add the beneficiary. See *The Partnership Book*, by Denis Clifford and Ralph Warner (Nolo).

7. Copyrights

To transfer an interest in a copyright to a beneficiary, the trustee should sign and file, with the U.S. Copyright Office in Washington, DC, a document transferring all the trust's rights in the copyright to the beneficiary. Sample transfer forms are in *The Copyright Handbook*, by Stephen Fishman (Nolo).

8. Patents

To transfer a patent from a living trust, the trustee should prepare a document called an "assignment" and record it with the U.S. Patent and Trademark Office in Washington, DC. There is a small fee for recording. Sample assignment forms and instructions are in *Patent It Yourself*, by David Pressman (Nolo).

9. Other Property With Title Documents

If an item of trust property has a title document that shows ownership in the name of the trust, the trustee must prepare and sign a new title document transferring ownership to the beneficiary. Usually, the trustee will need a copy of the trust document and of the trust grantor's death certificate if the property is in someone else's possession.

If a vehicle was owned by the trust, the trustee should contact the state Department of Motor Vehicles to get the forms required to transfer it to the beneficiary.

D. Preparing and Filing Tax Returns

Depending on the circumstances, the successor trustee may have to file several tax returns:

- federal estate tax return for the deceased grantor, if the value of the estate is over the estate tax threshold for year of death
- state death tax return for the deceased grantor, if state law requires it
- final federal income tax return (and state return, if there's a state income tax) for the deceased grantor, and
- final federal income tax return (and state return, if there's a state income tax) for Trust A after both spouses die.

Legally, filing these returns is the responsibility both of the successor trustee and of the executor named in the deceased grantor's will. The same person usually serves as both executor and successor trustee.

Generally, the state and federal income tax returns are due April 15 of the year following the grantor's death. The federal estate tax return is due nine months after the grantor's death.

The trustee is entitled, by the terms of the trust document, to pay for professional help out of the trust assets. And that help may well be necessary, because tax matters—particularly estate tax matters—can get quite tricky.

Help with tax returns. For assistance with the estate tax return, the successor trustee can get a helpful set of instructions, "Instructions for Form 706," from the Internal Revenue Service. Another useful IRS publication is called "Federal Estate and Gift Taxes" (Publication 448). You can download these materials for free by visiting the IRS website at www.irs.gov.

E. Administering a Child's Trust

If, in the trust document, the deceased grantor set up a child's trust, the trustee will have to manage that property if the beneficiary isn't old enough to receive it outright. A child's trust comes into being only if, at the grantor's death, the beneficiary has not yet reached the age the grantor specified.

Example

Carl sets up a living trust and names his two young children as beneficiaries. He specifies that if either child is younger than 30 when he dies, the property that child is to inherit from the trust should be kept in a separate child's trust.

When Carl dies, one child is 30; the other is 25. The 30-year-old receives her trust property with no strings attached. But a child's trust is created for the 25-year-old. The successor trustee is responsible for managing the property and turning it over to the child when he turns 30.

The trustee's duties when managing a child's trust are explained in Chapter 9, Section D.

F. Administering a Custodianship

Someone who is appointed in the trust document to be the custodian of trust property inherited by a young beneficiary has roughly the same management responsibilities as the trustee of a child's trust. (See Chapter 9, Section E.) The specifics of the custodian's duties are set out in the Uniform Transfers to Minors Act, as adopted by the particular state's legislature. ■

chapter 15

A LIVING TRUST AS PART OF YOUR ESTATE PLAN

revocable living trust can accomplish most people's main estate planning goal: leaving their property to their loved ones while avoiding probate and perhaps saving on estate taxes as well. But it is not, by itself, a complete estate plan. For example, in most states, parents of young children can't use a living trust to appoint a personal guardian to care for their minor children. To do this, you need a will. A living trust also can't take care of property you buy or inherit shortly before you die and don't get around to transferring to the trust.

This chapter provides an overview of estate planning methods that you may want to explore in addition to a living trust. Basically, estate planning includes:

- deciding who will inherit your property when you die

- deciding who will take care of your children and their finances if you die while they are young

- setting up procedures and devices to minimize probate fees at your death

- if your estate is large, planning to reduce federal estate taxes and state death taxes, if your state has them (with the exception of an AB trust, the trust forms in this book don't afford any estate tax savings), and

- arranging for someone to make financial and health care decisions for you in case at some time you can no longer do so yourself.

A. Using a Back-up Will

Even though you create a living trust, you need a simple back-up will, too. Like a living trust, a will is a document in which you specify what is to be done with your property when you die.

Having a will is important for several reasons:

- A will is an essential back-up device for property that you don't get around to transferring to your living trust.

- In a will you can name someone to be the personal guardian of your minor child, in case you and the child's other parent die while the child is still under 18. In most states, you can't do that in a living trust. (A few states' laws can be construed to permit appointing a child's personal guardian in a living trust, but it's prudent to be conventional and appoint the guardian in a will, the normal way.)

- If you want to disinherit your spouse or a child, you must make your wishes clear in a will. (State law may restrict your freedom to disinherit a spouse; see Chapter 8.)

Instructions for preparing a back-up will are in Chapter 16, and sample will forms are in Appendix B and on the CD-ROM (Forms 10 and 11).

B. Other Probate-Avoidance Methods

A living trust is not the only way to transfer some kinds of assets without probate, and it's not the best in all circumstances. For example, it's usually cumbersome to have your personal checking account held in the name of your living trust, because businesses may be reluctant to accept your checks.

Fortunately, you can mix and match probate-avoidance techniques. Just put whatever property you want in your living trust, and choose other transfer methods—ones that also avoid probate—for the rest of your property.

You might, for example, want to put your checking account into joint tenancy with your spouse; at your death, your spouse would automatically take sole ownership of the account. Some helpful probate-avoidance methods are summarized below.

1. Pay-on-Death Financial Accounts

Setting up a pay-on-death account is an easy way to transfer cash at your death, quickly and without probate. All you do is designate, on a form provided by a financial institution, one or more persons you want to receive the money when you die.

OTHER NOLO ESTATE PLANNING RESOURCES

Plan Your Estate, by Denis Clifford and Cora Jordan, covers all the estate planning methods briefly discussed in this chapter, and more. It contains extensive discussion about probate avoidance methods and estate tax reduction techniques from gift-giving to generation-skipping trusts, including estate and gift taxes, and ongoing trusts.

Estate Planning Basics, by Denis Clifford, provides concise, straightforward and easy-to-read explanations of the major components of estate planning.

Quicken WillMaker Plus (software for Windows) enables you to prepare a comprehensive will, including a simple trust for your minor children, allowing you to choose the age at which your children inherit property you leave them. It also lets you make a probate-avoidance living trust, a health care directive, a durable power of attorney for finances, and many other useful legal forms.

Nolo's Simple Will Book, by Denis Clifford, is an in-depth explanation of how to prepare a will that covers all normal needs, including simple trusts for your minor children.

The Quick & Legal Will Book, by Denis Clifford, enables you to prepare a basic will easily and effectively.

8 Ways to Avoid Probate, by Mary Randolph, provides in-depth explanations of all major probate-avoidance methods.

How to Probate an Estate in California, by Julia Nissley, enables Californians to handle a normal probate without an attorney.

Deeds for California Real Estate, by Mary Randolph, explains how to use deeds to transfer real estate for estate planning.

Medical Directives & Powers of Attorney for California, by Shae Irving, provides all the information Californians need to authorize someone to handle medical and financial matters in the event of incapacity.

Choose the Right Long-Term Care: Home Care, Assisted Living & Nursing Homes, by Joseph Matthews, discusses how to finance and choose long-term care.

Social Security, Medicare and Pensions, by Joseph Matthews, is an excellent resource about rights and benefits of older Americans.

Pay-on-death accounts are used primarily for bank accounts, including savings, checking, or certificate of deposit accounts. You can also register ownership of certain kinds of government securities, including bonds, Treasury bills, and Treasury notes, in a way that lets you name a beneficiary to receive them at your death.

Example

Terry opens a savings account in her name, and names Lynn Harris as the pay-on-death (P.O.D.) beneficiary. When Terry dies, whatever money is in the account will go to Lynn.

During your life, the beneficiary has absolutely no right to the money in the account. You can withdraw some or all of the money, close the account, or change the beneficiary, at any time. When you die, the beneficiary can claim the money simply by showing the bank the death certificate and personal identification.

Bank accounts may be frozen. Like other bank accounts, a pay-on-death account may be temporarily frozen at your death, if your state levies death taxes. The state will release the money to your beneficiaries when shown that your estate has sufficient funds to pay the taxes. If you live in a state that imposes death taxes, you might want to check with your bank to learn if your accounts, including any pay-on-death accounts, may be frozen after you die. If so, it's sensible to warn your inheritors that they could face this hassle. (If you don't know if your state has death taxes, ask the bank and see what they say.)

COMMON PROBATE-AVOIDANCE METHODS

Method	Advantages	Disadvantages
Revocable living trust	Flexible, private. Easy to create. You keep control over property during your life.	Some paperwork involved. May need attorney if yours is a complicated estate.
Pay-on-death-financial accounts	Easy to create, using a form provided by the bank or brokerage company.	Limited to bank accounts and securities.
Naming beneficiary of pension plan or retirement account	Easy to do. Beneficiary inherits all funds in the account at your death.	None, unless particular program imposes limits.
Life insurance	Good way to provide quick cash for beneficiaries or to pay estate taxes. Proceeds don't go through probate.	Family members may not need much immediate cash if they don't rely on you to support them, so expense of policy may not be justified.
Joint tenancy with right of survivorship	Easy to create.	Restricted in Alaska to husband and wife. If you don't already own property in joint tenancy, you may not want to add another owner, who could sell his share. (For larger estates, there are negative gift tax consequences, too.) Can be a problem if a co-owner becomes incapacitated. No probate avoidance if all joint owners die at once.
Tenancy by the entirety	Easy to create.	Available only in about half the states; limited to married couples. Can be a problem if one spouse becomes incapacitated.
Community property with right of survivorship	All the benefits of community property ownership plus probate-avoidance when one spouse dies.	Available only to married couples in the following states: Alaska, Arizona, California, Nevada, and Wisconsin.
Gifts of property made while you're alive	Reduces amount of property in your estate, which avoids both probate and estate taxes.	You lose control over property given away while you're alive. Large gifts use up part of your federal gift/estate tax exemption. Insurance policies must be given away at least three years before death, or proceeds are included in your taxable estate.
State laws that allow simplified probate proceedings	Exempts certain property from formal probate.	Applies only to small estates; you may still need an attorney to explain the technicalities of your state's laws.
Transfer-on-death designation for motor vehicles	Easy to do. All you do is name, on your registration form, someone to inherit your vehicle.	Currently available only in California, Connecticut, Kansas, Missouri, and Ohio, but other states are considering similar programs.
Transfer-on-death registration for securities	Easy to do. All you do is name, on the registration form, someone to inherit the securities at your death.	Not available in North Carolina, New York, or Texas. See list in Chapter 6.

Most banks have forms for setting up this kind of account, and they don't charge more for keeping your money this way. Before you open a pay-on-death account, ask your bank if there are any special state law requirements about notifying the beneficiary. In a few states, a pay-on-death provision isn't effective unless you have notified the beneficiary that you've set up the account. Your bank should be able to fill you in on your state's rules.

2. Transfer-on-Death Registration for Stocks and Bonds

In all but a few states, you can register securities (individual stocks or bonds or accounts, including mutual funds) in a transfer-on-death form. The only states that don't yet allow this are New York, North Carolina, and Texas. In every other state, you can designate a beneficiary or beneficiaries to receive the securities outside of probate. Your brokerage company should have a form for opening this kind of account.

3. Retirement Accounts

Retirement accounts such as IRAs, Roth IRAs, and profit-sharing plan accounts weren't designed to be probate avoidance devices, but if you have any money left in such accounts when you die, they can easily be used that way. All you have to do is name a beneficiary to receive the funds still in your pension plan or retirement account at your death, and the funds will not go through probate. If you are considering making your AB trust the beneficiary of your retirement account, see the discussion in Chapter 6, Section B.

Except for a Roth IRA, after age 70½, federal law requires you to withdraw at least a certain amount every year or face a monetary penalty. The amount is refigured every year, based on your current life expectancy and that of your beneficiary.

4. Life Insurance

As insurance agents will be delighted to explain, life insurance is a good way to provide surviving family members with quick cash for debts, living expenses, and, for larger estates, estate taxes. And because you name the beneficiary in the policy itself, not in your will, life insurance proceeds don't go through probate.

The only circumstance in which life insurance proceeds are subject to probate is if the beneficiary named in the policy is your estate. That's done occasionally if the estate will need immediate cash to pay debts and taxes, but it's usually counterproductive. It's almost always a better idea to name your spouse, children, or another beneficiary who can take the money free of probate and use it to pay debts and taxes.

Although the proceeds of a life insurance policy don't go through probate, they are included in your estate for federal estate tax purposes. If you think your estate will be liable for federal estate taxes, you can reduce the tax bill by giving away the policy to the beneficiary, another person or an irrevocable life insurance trust (discussed below in Section C3).

LIFE INSURANCE TO PROVIDE FOR YOUR CHILDREN

If you have young children but not much money, consider buying a moderate amount of term life insurance, which would provide cash to support your children if you died while they were still young. Because term life insurance pays benefits only if you die during the covered period (often five or ten years), it's far cheaper than other types of life insurance. You can stop renewing the insurance when, by the end of the current term, the children will be on their own or your estate would be large enough to support them until they are.

---

5. Joint Tenancy

Joint tenancy is one of the more commonly used probate-avoidance devices. It's an efficient and practical way to transfer some kinds of property in some situations, but for most kinds of property, a living trust is usually a better choice. In many states, married couples can use a special type of joint tenancy called "tenancy by the entirety." (See Subsection 6, below.)

a. How Joint Tenancy Works

Joint tenancy is a way two or more people can hold title to property they own together. It is available in almost all states.

For estate planning purposes, the most important characteristic of joint tenancy is that when one joint owner (called a joint tenant) dies, the surviving joint owners automatically get complete ownership of the property. This is called the "right of survivorship." The property doesn't go through probate court—there is only some simple paperwork to fill out to transfer the property into the name of the surviving owner.

Example

Evelyn and her daughter own a car in joint tenancy. When Evelyn dies, her half-interest in the car will go to her daughter without probate. Her daughter will need only to fill out a simple form to transfer ownership of the car into her own name.

Joint tenancy certainly has the virtue of simplicity. To create a joint tenancy, all the co-owners need to do is pay attention to the way they are listed on the document that shows ownership of property, such as a deed to real estate, a car's title slip, or a card establishing a bank account. In the great majority of states, by calling themselves "joint tenants with the right of survivorship," the owners create a joint tenancy. In a few states, additional specific words are necessary. If you want to set up a joint tenancy and aren't sure how to word a title document, ask a real estate lawyer or someone at a land title company. All joint tenants must own equal shares of the property.

A joint tenant cannot leave his or her share to anyone other than the surviving joint tenants. So even if Evelyn, in the preceding example, left a will giving her half-interest in the car to her son instead of her daughter, the daughter would still get the car.

This rule isn't as ironclad as it may sound. A joint tenant can, while still alive, break the joint tenancy by transferring his or her interest in the property to someone else (or, in most states, to himself, but not as a "joint tenant"). The new owner isn't a joint tenant with the other original owners.

Example

David, Jan, and Loren own property together in joint tenancy. David sells his one-third interest to Paul. Paul is not a joint tenant with Jan and Loren; he is a "tenant in common," free to leave his property to whomever he wants. Jan and Loren, however, are still joint tenants with respect to their two-thirds of the property; when one of them dies, the other will own the two-thirds.

JOINT BANK ACCOUNTS

If you and someone else want to set up a joint tenancy account together, so that the survivor will get all the funds, normally you can do it in a few minutes at the bank. Your bank should be able to tell you about any requirements. In a few states, you may need to comply with certain formalities. Texas law, for example, requires a written agreement—not just a signature card—to set up such an account. A dispute over such an account ended up in the Texas Supreme Court. Two sisters had set up an account together, using a signature card that allowed the survivor to withdraw the funds. When the surviving sister withdrew the funds, the estate of the deceased sister sued and won the funds.

---

b.   When to Consider Joint Tenancy

Joint tenancy often works well when couples (married or not) acquire real estate or other valuable property together. If they take title in joint tenancy, probate is avoided when the first owner dies.

But there are advantages to transferring the property to your living trust, even if you already own it in joint tenancy. First, a living trust, unlike joint tenancy, allows you to name an alternate beneficiary—someone who will inherit the property if the first beneficiary (your spouse) doesn't survive you. If you own property in joint tenancy, and you and your spouse die at the same time, the property will go to the residuary beneficiary named in your will—but it will have to go through probate first.

Second, if you transfer joint tenancy property to a living trust, you will avoid probate both when the first spouse dies and when the second spouse dies. With joint tenancy, probate is avoided only when the first spouse dies. The second spouse, who owns the property alone after the first spouse's death, must take some other measure—such as transferring it to a living trust—to avoid probate.

⚠ Transferring joint tenancy property in common law states. As discussed in Chapter 11, Section A, if you live in a common law state, when transferring joint tenancy property to a living trust, you need first to transfer the property into "tenancy in common, in equal shares" by preparing a new deed, and then transfer the property to your trust.

c. When to Think Twice About Joint Tenancy

Joint tenancy is usually a poor estate planning device when an older person, seeking only to avoid probate, puts solely owned property into joint tenancy with someone else. Doing this creates several potential problems that don't occur with a living trust:

You can't change your mind. If you make someone else a co-owner, in joint tenancy, of property that you now own yourself, you give up half ownership of the property. The new owner has rights that you can't take back. For example, the new owner can sell or mortgage his or her share. And even if the other joint tenant's half isn't mortgaged, it could still be lost to creditors.

Example

Maureen, a widow, signs a deed that puts her house into joint tenancy with her son to avoid probate at her death. Later, the son's business fails, and he is sued by creditors. His half-interest in the house may be taken by the creditors to pay the court judgment, which means that the house might be sold. Maureen would get the value of her half in cash; her son's half of the proceeds would go to pay the creditors.

By contrast, if you put property in a revocable living trust, you don't give up any ownership now. You are always free to change your mind about who you want to get the property at your death.

There's no way to handle the incapacity of one joint tenant. If one joint tenant becomes incapacitated and cannot make decisions, the other owners must get legal authority to sell or mortgage the property. That may mean going to court to get someone (called a conservator, in most states) appointed to manage the incapacitated person's affairs. (This problem can be partially dealt with if the joint tenant has signed a document called a "Durable Power of Attorney," giving someone authority to manage his affairs if he cannot. See Section E, below.)

With a living trust, if you (the grantor) become incapacitated, the successor trustee (or the other spouse, if it's a shared trust) takes over and has full authority to manage the trust property. No court proceedings are necessary.

Gift taxes may be assessed. If you create a joint tenancy by making another person a co-owner, federal gift tax may be assessed on the transfer. This probably isn't a reason not to transfer property; making a gift can be a sound estate planning strategy. But be aware that if gifts to one person (except your spouse) exceed $11,000 per year, you must file a gift tax return with the IRS. (See Section C, below.) There's one exception: If two or more people open a bank account in joint tenancy, but one person puts all or most of the money in, no gift tax is assessed against that person. A taxable gift may be made, however, when a joint tenant who has contributed little or nothing to the account withdraws money from it.

Surviving spouse misses an income tax break. If you make your spouse a joint tenant with you on property you own separately, the surviving spouse could miss out on a potentially big income tax break later, when the property is sold.

When it comes to property owned in joint tenancy, the Internal Revenue Service rule is that a surviving spouse gets a stepped-up tax basis only for the half of the property owned by the deceased spouse. The tax basis is the amount from which taxable profit is figured when property is sold. You may not face this problem if you live in a community property state. If property held in joint tenancy property is actually community property, it will still qualify for a stepped-up tax basis if the surviving spouse can show the IRS that it was in fact community property. But it's up to you to prove it; when one spouse dies, the IRS presumes that property held in joint tenancy is not community property. When the property is later sold, this means higher tax if the property has gone up in value after the joint tenancy was created but before the first spouse died.

If you leave your solely owned property to your spouse through your living trust, however, the entire property gets a stepped-up tax basis

6. Tenancy by the Entirety

"Tenancy by the entirety" is a form of property ownership that is similar to joint tenancy, but is limited to married couples. It is available only in the states listed below.

STATES THAT ALLOW TENANCY BY THE ENTIRETY

Alaska*	Maryland	Oklahoma
Arkansas	Massachusetts	Oregon*
Delaware	Michigan*	Pennsylvania
District of Columbia	Mississippi	Rhode Island
Florida	Missouri*	Tennessee
Hawaii	New Jersey	Vermont
Illinois*	New York*	Virginia
Indiana*	North Carolina*	Wyoming
Kentucky*	Ohio**	

*Allowed for real estate only.

**Only if created before April 4, 1985.

Tenancy by the entirety has almost the same advantages and disadvantages of joint tenancy and is most useful in the same kind of situation: when a couple acquires property together. When one spouse dies, the surviving spouse inherits the property. The property doesn't go through probate.

If property is held in tenancy by the entirety, neither spouse can transfer his or her half of the property alone, either while alive or by will or trust. A living spouse must get the other spouse's consent to transfer the property; at death, it must go to the surviving spouse. (This is different from joint tenancy; a joint tenant is free to transfer his or her share to someone else during his life.)

Example

Fred and Ethel hold title to their apartment building in tenancy by the entirety. If Fred wanted to sell or give away his half-interest in the building, he could not do so without Ethel's signature on the deed.

7. Community Property With Right of Survivorship

Married couples in one of the following community property states—Arizona, California, Nevada, Texas, Wisconsin—have another option that may be useful.

Couples in Arizona, California, Nevada, or Wisconsin can hold title to their community property "with right of survivorship"—meaning that when one spouse dies, the other automatically owns all the property. Several states, including Washington and Texas, let couples make a written agreement that some or all of their community property will have a right of survivorship.

These arrangements offer all the benefits of community property ownership, plus the important advantage that the property doesn't go through probate when one spouse dies. Instead, the surviving spouse owns it automatically.

Wisconsin law goes even further. It lets married couples avoid probate altogether for their marital property. In a "marital property agreement," they can name a beneficiary—a person, trust, or other entity—to inherit their marital property, without probate. And like an AB trust, the agreement can even provide for the disposition of property at the death of the second spouse (though that spouse can amend the agreement after the first spouse's death unless the agreement says otherwise).

8. Gifts

If you give away property while you're alive, there will be less property in your estate to go through probate when you die. But if probate avoidance is your goal, usually it's better to use one of the other methods discussed above, which let you keep control over your property while you're alive, than to give away everything before you die.

Making tax-exempt gifts every year, however, may be a good strategy if you expect your estate to owe federal estate tax after your death, and you want to reduce the eventual tax bite. (See Section C, below.)

9. Probate Shortcuts for Small Estates

Many states have begun, albeit slowly, to dismantle some of the more onerous aspects of probate. Who benefits? As you might guess, one big category comprises people who don't leave much of monetary value—and whose probate cases therefore aren't worth much to lawyers.

Because of the way the laws are written, however, not only small estates can benefit. Many larger estates—worth hundreds of thousands of dollars—legally qualify as "small estates," eligible for special transfer procedures that speed property to inheritors.

Here are the kinds of shortcuts available for small estates:

Claiming property with affidavits—no court required. If the total value of all the assets you leave behind is less than a certain amount, the people who inherit your personal property—that's anything except real estate—may be able to skip probate entirely. The exact amount varies tremendously. The limit in California or Hawaii is $100,000. The highest limit is $150,000 in Wyoming.

If the estate qualifies, an inheritor can prepare a short document stating that he or she is entitled to a certain item of property under a will or state law. This paper, signed under oath, is called an affidavit. When the person or institution holding the property—for example, a bank where the deceased person had an account—receives the affidavit and a copy of the death certificate, it releases the money or other property.

Leaving property to the surviving spouse—no court required. In some states, if a surviving spouse inherits less than a certain amount of property, no probate is necessary.

Simplified court procedures. Another option for small estates (again, as defined by state law) is a quicker, simpler version of probate. The probate court is still involved, but it exerts far less control over the settling of the estate. In many states, these procedures are straightforward enough to handle without a lawyer, so they save money as well as time.

Most people leave property that is worth more than can be passed through these probate shortcuts. In many states, if the value of your entire estate exceeds the maximum set by law for simplified procedures, you cannot use the procedures to pass any property.

Example:

At her death, Jane has an estate worth $300,000. Her major asset is her home, worth $200,000, which she passes to her daughter through a living trust. She also passes $80,000 worth of other property through other probate-avoidance devices. That leaves $20,000 worth of property. In Jane's state, the maximum total estate (including all property transferred by all methods) for streamlined probate procedures is $25,000. So Jane's heirs can't use the simplified procedures for the last $20,000 because Jane's total estate exceeds the limit.

In some states, however, even if your total estate is too large, you can still make use of simplified procedures if the amount that actually goes through probate is under the limit. For example, in California, property worth less than $100,000 transferred by will is exempt from normal probate, no matter how large the total estate. So if Jane lived in California, the $20,000 worth of property left through Jane's will could be transferred out of court or through simplified court procedures.

How to find out about your state's probate shortcuts. Most states have all the shortcuts discussed above; some have just one. You can learn the details of your state's law in *8 Ways to Avoid Probate*, by Mary Randolph (Nolo) or *Plan Your Estate*, by Denis Clifford and Cora Jordan (Nolo).

C. Federal Gift and Estate Taxes

We've already covered the basic estate tax rules in Chapters 4 and 5. Let's summarize them again, and then look a little deeper into taxes and estate planning.

- The personal exemption allows property worth between $1.5 million and $3.5 million, depending on the year of death, to be left free of tax. Further, the estate tax is scheduled to be repealed in 2010, but only for that year. (For a discussion of the uncertainties and oddities of the new estate tax law, see Chapter 4, Section E.)

- The marital deduction exempts from tax all property, no matter how large the dollar value, left by a deceased spouse to a surviving spouse. But if the surviving spouse is not a citizen of the U.S., the marital deduction does not apply.

- The charitable exemption authorizes all property given or left to tax-exempt charities to pass tax-free.

FEDERAL ESTATE AND GIFT TAX EXEMPTIONS

Year	Estate tax exemption	Gift tax exemption	Highest estate and gift tax rate
2004	$1.5 million	$1 million	48%
2005	$1.5 million	$1 million	47%
2006	$2 million	$1 million	46%
2007	$2 million	$1 million	45%
2008	$2 million	$1 million	45%
2009	$3.5 million	$1 million	45%
2010	Estate tax repealed	$1 million	Top individual income tax rate (gift tax only)
2011	$1 million unless Congress extends repeal	$1 million	55% unless Congress extends repeal

Federal estate taxes. A comprehensive explanation of federal estate taxes is contained in *Plan Your Estate*, by Denis Clifford and Cara Jordan (Nolo).

A federal estate tax return must be filed if the gross value of the estate exceeds the exempt amount for the year of death. Estate taxes will be due if the net estate exceeds the amount of all applicable exemptions. The assets in the estate are valued as of the date of death or, as an optional alternative, six months later, if it produces a lesser estate value. An exception is that any asset distributed to beneficiaries or sold at an earlier date must be valued when it is distributed or sold. Tax must be paid within nine months of death.

1.　Federal Gift Taxes

As you can see from the above chart, the federal government also taxes substantial gifts made during life. Congress reasoned that if only property left at death were taxed, people would give away as much property as they could during their lives. Gift tax rates are the same as estate tax rates, to eliminate any tax incentive to gift making.

If you look closely at the chart, you will notice that although the estate tax exemption now exceeds $1 million, the gift tax exemption remains at $1 million. What does this mean? It means that, before 2010, you can give away a total of up to $1 million in taxable gifts, but not pay any tax, because of the gift tax exemption. But if you give away more than $1 million, you are taxed.

Example

In 2006, Franklin makes taxable gifts of $2 million. He must pay tax on $1 million. But in 2006, the personal estate tax exemption is $2 million. If Franklin had left the same amount at his death, his estate would owe no taxes.

As this example demonstrates, the divergence of the gift and estate tax exemption is a matter only for the rich, and immaterial to most people.

More important for regular folks is the federal law that exempts from gift tax a set dollar amount of gifts per year. Currently, you can give up to $11,000 per person per year without owing gift tax. This gift tax exemption is indexed yearly to the cost of living. As the cost of living rises (assuming it does), the gift tax will also rise, in increments of $1,000. In other words, cost-of-living increases must cumulatively raise the current exemption by something more than $1,000 before the gift tax exemption will be raised to $12,000.

Normally, if gift tax is assessed, no tax is actually paid on gifts until your death, when your combined gift and estate tax liability is calculated. However, if you've made nonexempt gifts that total more than the estate tax threshold, gift tax must be paid on an annual basis.

Example

Susan has made taxable gifts totaling $900,000 by 2003. She does not have to pay any gift tax, because her total gifts are under the $1 million gift tax exemption. In 2004, Susan gives away another $300,000 subject to gift tax. Her total lifetime gifts are now $1.2 million, $200,000 over the gift tax exemption. In 2004, she must pay tax on this $200,000.

Other gifts are exempt regardless of amount, including:

- gifts between spouses who are U.S. citizens
- gifts to directly pay someone else's medical bills or school tuition, and
- gifts to tax-exempt charitable organizations.

2. Special Rules for Noncitizen Spouses

The unlimited marital deduction for property one spouse leaves (or gives while living) to another applies only if the recipient spouse is a citizen of the United States. It doesn't matter that a noncitizen spouse was married to a U.S. citizen or is a legal resident. While both are alive, a spouse can, however, give the other, noncitizen, spouse up to $112,000 per year free of gift tax.

The personal estate tax exemption, however, remains available no matter who inherits the property. A citizen can leave a noncitizen spouse property tax-free under this exemption.

Example

Lily Lim, a U.S. citizen, leaves her entire estate worth $1,700,000 to her husband, Choy Lim, a non-U.S. citizen. Lily dies in 2005, when the personal exemption is $1.5 million. $200,000 of her property is subject to estate tax. By contrast, if Choy were a U.S. citizen, all Lily's estate would pass free of tax because of the marital deduction.

Special trusts for noncitizen spouses. Property left by one spouse to a noncitizen spouse in what's called a "Qualified Domestic Trust" is allowed the marital deduction. To create one of these trusts, you'll need to see a lawyer. Indeed, if you're married to a noncitizen and have an estate worth more than the exempt amount, see a lawyer for estate tax planning.

3. Reducing Estate Tax

If your property is likely to be subject to estate tax, even if you use Nolo's AB trust, there are a number of options you can consider. For the very rich, tax avoidance schemes can become extraordinarily twisted. Here we'll briefly look at some more common options.

a. Gifts

If you don't need all your income and property to live on, making tax-exempt gifts from your trust, or indeed from any of your assets, while you're alive can be a good way to reduce eventual federal estate taxes.

Every person can currently give $11,000 to any one person per year, so a couple can give $22,000 per year.

Example

Allen and Julia give their two daughters $22,000 each every year for four years. They have transferred a total of $176,000 without becoming liable for gift tax.

Gifts made within three years of death. The gift tax exemption is not allowed for a few types of gifts made in the last three years of someone's life. The gift itself is valid, but for estate tax purposes the value of the gift is included in the giver's estate. Most importantly, a gift of a life insurance policy is not entitled to the gift tax exemption if made within three years of death.

How to choose property to give away. It's usually wise to give away property that you think will go up in value substantially before your death. That way, you may avoid gift tax now—if the gift is worth less than the gift tax exemption—and you may avoid estate tax later, because the increased value of the property won't be included in your estate when you die. Also, if the recipient (other than a child age 14 or under) is in a lower tax bracket, you may want to give away income-generating property, so that the income will be taxed at the recipient's lower tax rates. Any income over $750 per year received by a child 14 years or under from any gift (whether from parents or anyone else) is taxed at the parents' rate.

You may not, however, want to give away property that has already appreciated greatly in value. Usually, it's wiser to hold onto it until death to take advantage of the stepped-up tax basis rules discussed in Section B, above.

Gifts of life insurance. Life insurance policies you own on your own life and give away at least three years before your death are excellent gifts, from an estate planning view. Your gift tax liability is determined by the current value of the policy, which is far less than the amount the policy will pay off at death. For many policies, the present value will be less than the $11,000 annual gift tax threshold, which means that no gift tax will be assessed.

To give away a life insurance policy, you must comply with some fairly technical IRS rules, which should be available from your insurance company. The process of actually transferring ownership is simple. Insurance companies have forms you can use to make the transfer. You must make an irrevocable gift of the policy. If you keep the right to revoke the gift and get the policy back, the proceeds will be taxed as part of your estate.

If you buy a policy that requires future premium payments, you'll want to make more gifts to the new owner of the policy to cover the payments. As an alternative, you can pay for some kinds of policies all at once; these are called single-premium policies.

Example

Sarah buys three single-premium life insurance policies (that is, she pays the entire premium in advance) for $50,000 each and transfers ownership of the policies to her three children. She must file a gift tax return because the value of the gifts exceeds the $11,000 per person per year tax exemption. The taxable value of all three gifts is $120,000. The gift tax assessed is not due until her death. When Sarah dies, each policy pays $700,000. The total proceeds, $2.1 million, are not included as part of her estate; only the $117,000 that exceeded the gift tax exemption is included in her estate.

b.   Tax-Saving Trusts and Devices

As you know, this book presents one type of estate tax-saving trust: Nolo's AB trust. Other types of tax-saving trusts and devices can be used by couples, or in some cases individuals, with larger estates. Here are some important ones.

- **Property left to spouse.** A married person with an estate worth more than the amount that can be shielded from tax by an AB trust may leave the overage outright to his or her spouse. No tax is due when the first spouse dies, because all property left to a surviving spouse is exempt.

- **QTIP trusts** (for married couples only). A QTIP trust postpones payment of estate taxes that otherwise are due when the first spouse dies. A QTIP trust can be desirable for a spouse with property over the estate tax threshold who wants:

  * to leave all his or her property to the other spouse with no payment of taxes until that surviving spouse dies, and

  * wants to name final beneficiaries of the trust property (that is, doesn't want to leave the property outright to the other spouse).

  One drawback of a QTIP trust is that the federal estate taxes eventually paid on the property of the first spouse to die are assessed against what the property is worth when the surviving spouse dies, not what the property was worth when the first spouse died. Usually, that means higher taxes.

Example

Mary Edna, a widow with three grown children, marries Roberto. Her estate has a net value of $4 million. Roberto has little property beyond his monthly Social Security check. Mary Edna wants Roberto to be able to continue to live in both her houses if she predeceases him. After his death, she wants all her property to go to her children.

If Mary Edna creates an AB trust, with Roberto having a life estate, all of her property will be subject to estate tax when she dies. Some tax probably will have to be paid, because her estate is over the exempt amount for all years except 2010. This could necessitate the sale of one of her houses. So she creates a QTIP trust. No estate taxes will be assessed against her property until Roberto dies. However, if the worth of the property has risen to $6 million when Roberto dies, estate taxes will be based on this value.

- **Generation-skipping trusts** (for individuals or couples). One of the legal devices traditionally used by the very wealthy to minimize estate taxes has been to leave the bulk of their property in trust for their grandchildren, with the income (but not the principal) from the trusts available to their children. This strategy avoids death taxes several times. Without a trust, taxes would typically be paid when the first grandparent died, then again when the second grandparent died, and then when each of their children died.

  Current law imposes a tax on all "generation-skipping transfers" in excess of the amount of the personal estate tax exemption. A generation-skipping trust worth more than the exempt amount is subject to tax on the overage. This tax is assessed against the trust property when the middle (income) generation dies.

Example

Paul establishes a generation-skipping trust for his daughter and her children. He dies in 2005 leaving the maximum tax-free amount in a generation skipping trust. When his daughter dies, the trust property is worth $2 million more than Paul left to the trust. Tax must then be paid on $2 million of the trust property.

Generation-skipping trusts are very complicated. These trusts are designed to have effect for at least two generations after the grantor's life, normally over 50 years, and many contingencies should be considered.

Also, there are IRS requirements regarding the age of the trustee and when estate taxes will be assessed.

- **Disclaimers** (for individuals or couples). Using a disclaimer, someone who's inherited a gift declines to accept it. The gift is then given to an alternate beneficiary originally named by the gift-giver. The beneficiary who disclaims the gift does so to make the overall estate tax picture better. Of course, this means she doesn't need the gift she disclaimed to live on. Any beneficiary has an inherent right to disclaim a gift, but often that right is expressly stated in estate planning documents.

- **Life insurance trusts.** An irrevocable life insurance trust is a legal entity you create for the purpose of owning life insurance you previously owned. It becomes operational during your lifetime. An irrevocable trust, like a corporation or any other trust, is a legal entity, distinct from any human being.

  Transferring ownership of your life insurance policy to a new owner—the trust—reduces death taxes, especially federal estate taxes, by removing the proceeds of the policy from your taxable estate. Why create a life insurance trust, rather than simply transfer a life insurance policy to someone else? One reason is that there may be no one you want to give your policy to. In other words, you want to get the proceeds out of your taxable estate, but you don't want the risks of having an insurance policy on your life owned by someone else. For example, the trust could specify that the policy must be kept in effect while you live, eliminating the risk that a new owner of the policy could decide to cash it in.

Example

Brenda is the divorced mother of two children in their 20s, who will inherit her property. Neither is sensible with money. Brenda has an estate of $750,000, plus life insurance that will pay $500,000 at her death. She wants to remove the proceeds of the policy from her estate. If she doesn't, her estate may be subject to estate tax. However, there's no one Brenda trusts enough to give her policy to outright. With the controls she can impose through a trust, however, she decides it's safe to allow her sister, the person she's closest to, to be the trustee of a life insurance trust for the policy. She creates an irrevocable trust and transfers ownership of the life insurance policy to that trust.

Strict federal requirements govern life insurance trusts. To gain the estate tax savings:

- * The life insurance trust must be irrevocable. If you keep the right to revoke the trust, you will be considered the owner of the policy, and the proceeds will be considered part of your estate upon death.

- * You cannot be the trustee. You must name either an "independent" adult (that is, someone not under your legal control) or an institution to serve as trustee.

- * You must establish the trust at least three years before your death. If the trust has not existed for at least three years when you die, the trust is disregarded for estate tax purposes, and the proceeds are included in your taxable estate.

- **Charitable remainder trusts.** With a charitable remainder trust, you make an irrevocable gift of property to a tax-exempt charity while you're alive. You are entitled to receive certain income from the property as well as continue to use and control it while you're alive, with significant income tax breaks. When you die, the property, of course, must go to the charity—and therefore, no estate tax can be due.

Don't try this on your own. If you want to create any of these kinds of trusts or devices, see an experienced estate planning lawyer.

Plan Your Estate, by Denis Clifford and Cora Jordan (Nolo), discusses these and many other advanced estate planning strategies.

c. Family Limited Partnerships

In the right circumstances, establishing a family limited partnership can produce significant tax savings for inheritors. The first requirement here is that you must have a legitimate business, one that the IRS accepts as genuine. You cannot create a tax-valid family limited partnership (FLP) simply to manage your regular investments, such as your securities or savings accounts.

You, as the original owner of the FLP, transfer, usually by gift, minority interests in the business to your inheritors, normally your children. The value of these minority interests can be "discounted," under IRS rules, from what the value would be if the interests had remained held by the majority owner. The theory is that minority interests, which have no legal control over the business, would be worth proportionally less to a legitimate buyer than a majority interest. The amount of the discount is subjective, and is frequently contested between the IRS and FLP owners.

Example

Olivia owns a successful pet food company. She intends to leave the business equally to her three children, who can maintain it or sell it, as they choose. The business is worth $2 million.

Olivia creates an FLP and transfers the business into it. There are 100 shares of the FLP. So it would seem that each share is worth $20,000. But if Olivia gives one share to each child, that share is worth less than $20,000, for gift and estate tax purposes, because, as a minority interest, it has less value to a buyer. So the gift shares may each be worth $17,000, or $15,000, depending only the discount allowed. Olivia can transfer up to 49% ownership of the FLP to her children, and all those interests will receive minority discounts.

FLPs that save on estate taxes are tricky creatures. The FLP must be operated as a family-owned business, which means that profits must be distributed (roughly) according to legal ownership. If you create a limited partnership but continue to treat the business assets as if they were solely yours, the IRS will include the full value of the business in your estate at your death. In other words, a family limited partnership cannot be run solely as an estate-tax-avoiding shell.

You need a lawyer before giving away minority interests. If you want to explore giving interests in a family limited partnership to family members (or anyone else), you must see a lawyer. This is a difficult and rapidly changing area of the law. The IRS is not fond of discounted gifts of an FLP and tries to scrutinize them. You must be sure you do it right, and that requires working with a lawyer knowledgeable in this subject.

D. State Death Taxes

A few states impose death taxes on:

- all real estate owned in the state, no matter where the deceased lived, and

- all property of residents of the state, no matter where it's located.

In most states that have them, death taxes are called inheritance taxes. In a few, they are called estate taxes. Although theoretically different—one's a tax on the person who inherits, the other a tax on the estate itself—the reality is the same. The tax is paid from the deceased's property.

State tax rules. Death tax rules for states that impose death taxes are summarized in *Plan Your Estate*, by Denis Clifford and Cora Jordan (Nolo). More detailed information is also available from state tax officials.

Because of recent changes in federal and state tax laws, a new type of state estate tax can be a concern for prosperous people. Here's the story.

Before 2002, most states collected only what was called a "pick-up" tax from estates large enough to have to pay federal estate taxes. A pick-up tax didn't increase the overall tax paid by the estate. Rather, the state was entitled, under federal law, to collect a certain percentage of the federal tax due.

Congress changed this system in 2002. Under current federal law, states can claim less of a pick-up tax each year until 2005, when the amount goes down to zero. To make up for this loss of revenue, a number of states have enacted new estate taxes, which are no longer connected to the federal system. Many other states are likely to adopt similar laws soon. The details of these new laws vary between different states. The common denominator is that some estates may have to pay state estate tax even if they are not large enough to pay federal estate tax.

This could be true even if you use an AB trust. If you leave an amount of property that exceeds your state's threshold for state estate tax, your estate will owe state tax, even though no federal tax is assessed.

Example

Roy and Ann, Rhode Island residents, make an AB trust. At Roy's death in 2004, his share of the couple's property is $900,000. That amount goes into Trust A, the deceased spouse's trust. Roy's estate is well under the 2004 federal estate tax threshold of $1.5 million, so it owes no federal tax. However, Roy's estate will owe Rhode Island estate tax, because Rhode Island imposes its own estate tax on estates of $675,000 or more.

These laws are changing fast. If you are concerned about new state taxes, see a lawyer who can bring you up to date.

If you divide your time between a state that doesn't impose inheritance tax (or has a very low one) and one with high death taxes, you'll want to establish your permanent residence in the lower tax state.

To establish your legal residence in a particular state, you should register all vehicles there, keep bank and other financial accounts there, and vote there.

Getting your legal residence established. Establishing residence in a no-tax state can be tricky if you also live in a high-tax one, because the high-tax state has a financial incentive to conclude that you really reside there. If you have a large estate, and a complicated two-or-more-state living situation, consult a knowledgeable tax lawyer or accountant.

E. Planning for Incapacity

A living trust can be a big help if you become unable to manage your own affairs, because your successor trustee (or your spouse, if you make a shared trust) can take over management of trust property. That person, however, has no power over any of your other financial assets or your health care decisions. For that reason, you should prepare a few other documents and coordinate them with your living trust.

1. Durable Power of Attorney for Finances

The best way to plan for the management of property not covered by your living trust is to use a document called a durable power of attorney for finances. Every state recognizes this document. It gives a trusted person you choose, called your "attorney-in-fact," the legal authority to manage your finances (except for property owned by your living trust) on your behalf. The document can be worded so that it becomes effective only if you become incapacitated, as certified in writing by a physician.

Making a durable power of attorney for finances. You can use *Quicken WillMaker Plus*, software from Nolo, to prepare a durable power of attorney for finances that is valid in your state. If you live in California, you can also use the book *Medical Directives & Powers of Attorney for California*, by Shae Irving (Nolo).

2. Medical Care Documents

The increasing use of life-sustaining medical technology has raised fears in many of us that our lives may be artificially prolonged against our wishes. The right to die with dignity and without the agony and expense of artificial life-prolonging procedures has been addressed and confirmed by the U.S. Supreme Court, the federal government, and every state legislature. Every state authorizes individuals to create simple documents setting out their wishes concerning life-prolonging medical care.

There are two basic documents that allow you to do this, both grouped under the broad label "health care directives." You need to prepare both. First, you need a "declaration," a written statement you make directly to medical personnel that spells out the medical care you do or do not wish to receive if you become incapacitated. Your declaration functions as a contract with the treating doctor, who must either honor your wishes for medical care or transfer you to another doctor or facility that will honor them.

Second, you'll want what's usually called a "durable power of attorney for health care." In this document you appoint someone you trust to be your "attorney-in-fact" (sometimes called your "agent" or "health care proxy") to see that your doctors and other health care providers give you the kind of medical care you wish to receive. You can also give your attorney-in-fact greater authority to make decisions about your medical care, including:

- making decisions about any issues you don't cover in your declaration
- hiring and firing medical personnel
- visiting you in the hospital or other facility even when other visiting is restricted
- having access to medical records and other personal information, and
- getting court authorization, if it is required, to obtain or withhold medical treatment if, for any reason, a hospital or doctor does not honor your health care directives.

Several states combine the declaration and durable power of attorney for health care into a single document, usually called an "Advance Health Care Directive."

A HEALTH CARE DIRECTIVE BY ANY OTHER NAME . . .

Depending on the state, your health care documents may be called by one of several different names: Advance Health Care Directive, Medical Directive, Directive to Physicians, Declaration Regarding Health Care, Designation of Health Care Surrogate, or Patient Advocate Designation. A health care declaration may also be called a "living will," but it bears no relation to the conventional will or living trust used to leave property at death.

Making health care directives. You can make a health care directive with *Quicken WillMaker Plus*, software from Nolo. In most states, you can obtain forms from the state medical association. Or, you can get your state's forms from a nonprofit organization called Partnership for Caring, 1620 I Street NW, Suite 202, Washington, DC 20006, 800-989-9455. You can order the forms for a small fee or download them for free from the organization's website at www.partnershipforcaring.org.

F. Long-Term Trusts to Control Property

In certain circumstances, you may want to dictate how your property is to be managed and distributed over many years. You may want to leave property to people who, for one reason or another, may not be able to manage it for themselves, even when they are over age 35. Or you may want to impose strict controls over property left to your spouse for his or her life, to be sure it remains intact to go eventually to your children from a former marriage.

Reminder. For a discussion of how to leave property to a minor or young adult, and have someone manage it until the beneficiary is older, see Chapter 9.

Long-term property management is not a do-it-yourself job. See an experienced lawyer if you want to create one of the property management trusts discussed in this section.

1. AB Trusts Used to Control Property

If you or your spouse have children from a previous marriage, you may want your current spouse to have some of your property during his or her life, but be sure that that property eventually goes to your children. One way to do this is to establish a special type of AB trust that limits the surviving spouse's use, and rights, to property in Trust A. Nolo's AB trust gives the surviving spouse, as trustee of Trust A, maximum freedom over Trust A property. Spouses in second or subsequent marriages often prefer more control over the surviving spouse's rights, to try to insure that their children will eventually receive the bulk of their property.

Example

Ilana and Harvey are both in their 50s. Ilana has a son from her first marriage. Harvey has two daughters from his. Ilana and Harvey purchase, equally, an $800,000 house. If one dies, each wants the other spouse to be able to live in the house for the remainder of his or her life. But after both have died, each wants his or her share of the house to go to the children of their first marriages. So Ilana and Harvey create an AB trust. Each spouse's A trust allows the surviving spouse full use of the house, but not the right to sell it and buy another one. Then half the house goes to Ilana's son, and the other half to Harvey's two daughters.

Many questions need to be resolved in setting up the trust.

- How strict should the controls on the surviving spouse be?

- Can the spouse sell the house to pay for health needs? For any needs?

- Should the spouse be the sole trustee, or is it better to have a child share that job or to have a child be the sole trustee?

- What reports and accountings must be given to the children?

Suppose a wife wants to allow her husband the right to stay in her home while he lives. How specifically does the right need to be pinned down in the trust? Can the husband sell the house and buy another? Can he rent it out? Suppose he needs to go to a nursing home—can the house then be sold? What happens to the profits of the sale? Who gets any income from trust property?

 An AB trust intended to impose controls on trust property must be carefully drafted by a knowledgeable attorney. Inherently, you are dealing with possible conflicts—the basic concern, after all, is that the surviving spouse's desires and interests may be very different from, or directly conflict with, the desires and interests of the deceased spouse's children. To resolve these issues wisely, you need a trust geared to your desires and to the specific realities of your situation.

2. Spendthrift Trusts

If you want to leave property to an adult who just can't handle money, a "spendthrift trust," where an independent trustee can dole out the money little by little, is a good idea. A spendthrift trust keeps the property from being squandered by the beneficiary or seized by the beneficiary's creditors.

3. Trusts for Disabled People

A person with a serious physical or mental disability may not be able to handle property, no matter what his or her age. Often, the solution is to establish a trust with a competent adult as trustee to manage the trust property.

The trust should be carefully prepared by an expert familiar with federal and state law, so that the trust won't jeopardize the beneficiary's eligibility for government benefits.

4. Flexible Trusts

You may want the determination of how your property is spent after your death to be decided in the future by a successor trustee, not by you before you die. The usual way to do this is to create a "sprinkling trust," authorizing the trustee to decide how to spend trust money for several beneficiaries. ∎

chapter 16

WILLS

I urge you to prepare a simple "back-up" will, even if you leave most, or all, of your property by your living trust. Back-up will forms are contained in Appendix B.

A. Why Prepare a Back-up Will?

It's always sensible to prepare a back-up will for one, or probably more, of the following reasons:

- **To name a personal guardian for your minor children.** If you have young children, you need a will to achieve the vital goal of nominating a personal guardian for them. In most states, you can't use your living trust to nominate a personal guardian. Also, in your will you can appoint a property guardian for your children to manage any of their property not otherwise legally supervised by an adult. Younger people with minor children, who don't have much property, may decide that because nominating a personal guardian is the primary thing they're worried about, a simple will is all the estate planning they currently need. (See Section B, below.)

- **To choose a beneficiary for suddenly acquired property.** Anyone may end up acquiring valuable property at or shortly before death, such as a sudden gift, inheritance, or lottery prize. Under the will forms in this book, that property will go to the residuary beneficiary of your will. You may well not get around to, or have time to, transfer the property to your trust. Therefore, it cannot be subject to your trust. And if you didn't have a will, the property would, under your state's "intestate succession" laws, go to your closest relatives.

- **To leave property not transferred by a probate-avoidance device.** If you don't get around to planning probate avoidance for all your property (by placing it in your living trust, for example), a will is a valuable back-up device. If you have a will, the property will go to who you want to have it (your residuary beneficiary), and not pass under the intestate succession laws.

- **To give away property someone left you that is still in probate.** If someone has left you property by will, and that property is still enmeshed in probate when you die, you can't arrange to transfer it by a probate-avoidance device. Since you don't have title to the property, you have no legal right to transfer it. But again, under your will, that property will go to your residuary beneficiary when the probate court releases it.

- **To name your executor.** In your will, you name your executor (and alternate executor), the person with legal authority to supervise distribution of property left by your will and to represent your estate in probate court proceedings. It is a good idea to have an executor even if you have also set up a living trust and named a successor trustee to manage it when you die, because banks and other institutions are often reassured to know an executor exists. Normally, it's best to name the same person as your successor trustee and executor.

- **For married couples, to avoid confusion in case of simultaneous death.** The will for a member of a couple provides that if both members "die simultaneously or under such circumstances as to render it difficult or impossible to determine who predeceased the other," the will writer is conclusively presumed to have outlived the other spouse. This clause works for each spouse, in his or her own will. How can that be, you may ask? Well, the official reason is that each will is interpreted independently from the other. The real reason is that it achieves a desired goal of preventing one spouse's property from going to another's estate if one only lives a few minutes or hours longer than the other.

B. What You Can Do in a Back-up Will

The back-up will forms in this book enable you to:

- Make up to three specific gifts—for example, "I leave my piano to Julia Rhodes." You can leave property that you haven't transferred to your living trust—for example, your personal bank account or car—to whomever you choose.

    You can leave a gift to be shared among several beneficiaries (or alternate beneficiaries) in any percentages you choose. Before doing this in your will, be sure to review Chapter 8, Section D.

- Name alternate beneficiaries for these specific gifts in case the primary beneficiary dies before you do.

- Name a residuary beneficiary and alternate residuary beneficiary to inherit any property subject to your will that is not specifically left to other named beneficiaries.

- Nominate a personal guardian and alternate for your minor children.

- Name a property guardian (who can be the same person as the personal guardian) to manage any of your minor children's property that isn't otherwise legally controlled by an adult. It's generally preferable to leave property to your minor children in children's trusts or under the Uniform Transfers to Minors Act rather than relying on a property guardian named in a will, which you name only as a back-up for property they may acquire from some other source. (See Chapter 9.)

- Appoint your executor.

Disinheriting a child or spouse. If you want to disinherit a child or your spouse, you need to do so in your will. But before you decide to do this, re-read the materials in Chapter 8, Section H, carefully. The law may restrict your choices.

Children born or adopted after you sign your will. If you have a child after preparing your back-up will, prepare a new back-up will, naming that child and leaving him or her whatever property you choose. Re-read Chapter 8, Section H, for a reminder of why this is necessary.

You may decide that you need a more complicated will. For instance, perhaps you want to appoint different personal guardians for different minor children. Or you want to arrange for care of your pets or specifically forgive debts owed you. Some people want to use a "self-proving affidavit" (legal in most states) for their witnesses, which can make it easier to probate a will without a written statement or a court appearance by a witness. If you do want a more complicated will, consult *Nolo's Simple Will Book* or *Quicken WillMaker Plus*, software from Nolo.

C. Pour-Over Wills

A "pour-over will" takes all the property you haven't transferred to your living trust and, at your death, leaves it ("pours it over") to that trust. Some lawyers urge all people who make living trusts to make pour-over wills, arguing that it's always best to send all your property through your living trust. There seems to be something about the name pour-over will that impresses people. The term sounds, well, sophisticated, like they're doing

something really right. In fact, pour-over wills are not very desirable, in my opinion, for most people with a living trust.

1. When Not to Use a Pour-Over Will

Pour-over wills do not avoid probate. All property that is left through a will—any kind of will—must go through probate, unless the amount left is small enough to qualify for exemption from normal probate laws. Probate is most definitely not avoided simply because the beneficiary of a will is a living trust.

It's generally better to simply use a standard back-up will to take care of your leftover (nonliving trust) property rather than a pour-over will. In the back-up will, you can name the people you want to get the will property, and skip the unnecessary extra step of pouring the property through the living trust after your death.

When used as a back-up will, a pour-over will actually has a disadvantage that standard wills don't: It forces the living trust to go on for months after your death, because the property left through the pour-over will must normally go through probate before it can be transferred to the trust. Usually, the property left in a living trust can be distributed to the beneficiaries, and the trust ended, within a few weeks after the person's death.

Example

Joy transfers her valuable property to her living trust. She also makes a pour-over will, which states that any property she owns at death goes to the living trust. When Joy dies, the property left through her will goes to the trust and is distributed to the residuary beneficiary of her living trust, her son Louis. The living trust must be kept going until probate of the will is finished, when property left by the will is poured over into the living trust. Normally, keeping the living trust ongoing for several months, or however long probate takes, would not require filing a trust tax return, since there's no income to this trust. Still, it's better to wind up a living trust as quickly as feasible.

If Joy had simply named Louis as sole beneficiary of a simple back-up will, the end result would have been the same, but the process would have been simpler. The living trust would have been ended a few weeks after Joy's death. And after probate was finished, Louis would have received whatever property passed through Joy's will.

2. When You May Want a Pour-Over Will

There are, however, two situations in which you might want to use a pour-over will.

If you create an AB trust, a pour-over will can be desirable. The spouses want the maximum amount of property to eventually wind up in Trust A, the marital life estate trust. So each spouse writes a pour-over will, leaving his or her will property to their A trust. After a spouse dies, the other spouse should amend her or his will or prepare a new one, since there will no longer be a functional Trust A for the surviving spouse's property to go to.

Also, if you set up a child's subtrust for a young beneficiary in your living trust, you may want any property that child inherits through your will to go into the subtrust. Otherwise, you would create two trusts for the beneficiary: one in the will and one in your living trust.

Example

Jessica makes a living trust and leaves the bulk of her property to her 12-year-old son. She arranges, in the trust document, for any trust property her son inherits before the age of 30 to be kept in a child's trust, managed by Jessica's sister.

Jessica also makes a back-up will, in which she leaves everything to her son and again arranges for a child's trust to be set up if she should die before her son reaches age 30. So if Jessica dies before her son reaches 30, two separate child's trusts will be set up to manage property for him.

If Jessica used a pour-over will, any property her son inherited through the will would go into the trust created by her living trust. With only one trust, only half the paperwork of maintaining the trust is necessary, as compared to maintaining two separate trusts.

3. How to Create a Pour-Over Will

You can use the will forms in this book to create a pour-over will. To do so, you leave property subject to the will to your successor trustee, as trustee of your trust. A married person usually lists two people as successor trustee—first the surviving spouse (who is technically a continuing trustee), and then the person next in line.

Example

Nils, married to Mercedes, wants the property he leaves through his will to go to his living trust. In his will, he lists the beneficiary as "Mercedes Janson, trustee of the Nils and Mercedes Janson Living Trust, or, if she does not survive me, to Ingemar Janson, successor trustee of the Nils and Mercedes Janson Living Trust."

D. Avoiding Conflicts Between Your Will and Living Trust

When you make both a living trust and a will, pay attention to how the two work together. If your will and your trust document contain conflicting provisions, at the least you will create confusion among your inheritors, and at the worst, bitter disputes—maybe even a lawsuit—among friends and family. Here are some guidelines to help you avoid problems:

- **Don't leave the same property in your living trust and will, even if it's to the same beneficiary.** If you transfer the property to your living trust and name a beneficiary in the trust document, that's all you need to do. Mentioning the property in your will raises the possibility of probate.

- **Name the same person to be executor of your will and successor trustee of your living trust.** There's one important exception: If you make a basic shared trust or AB trust, you'll probably name your spouse as executor of your will, but not as successor trustee—the successor trustee takes over only after both spouses have died. The surviving spouse, however, may want to revise her will after the death of the first spouse, to name her successor trustee to be her executor.

SIMULTANEOUS DEATH CLAUSE

The will form in this book for a married person has a simultaneous death clause, which is effective if the couple dies together, or where it cannot be ascertained who died first. This clause is worded somewhat differently than the simultaneous death clause in the shared living trust or the AB trust, because each of those is a single document covering both spouses, whereas each spouse makes a separate will. But the simultaneous death clause in your will accomplishes the same task as the one in your living trust: each spouse's property is treated as if he or she survived the other.

E. Filling in the Will Form

Here are the steps necessary to prepare your own will from a will form in Appendix B or on the CD-ROM:

Step 1. Select the correct form, depending on whether you are single (Form 10) or a member of a couple (Form 11).

As with the living trust forms, the will for a member of a couple is written in terms of a married couple, using the terms "husband" and "wife." If you are a member of an unmarried couple, please make the necessary word changes ("mate," "partner," each person's name, or whatever you feel works) in the will form, so that it makes sense for your situation.

Step 2. Read through the will form carefully. There are a number of blanks to fill in. The information called for is identified below each blank. While most of this is self-explanatory, here is what you must fill in:

- Your name. This should be the form of the name you use to sign such documents as deeds, checks, and loan applications. It needn't necessarily be the way your name appears on your birth or marriage certificate.

- Your city, county, and state.

- The names of all your living children, and names of any children of a deceased child, if any.

- The names of the personal guardian, alternate personal guardian, property guardian, and alternate property guardian for your minor children. You can name only one personal guardian and one property guardian for all your children.

- Up to three specific gifts. You do not have to make any specific gifts. You can simply leave all property subject to this will to your residuary beneficiary. If you leave some property to more than one beneficiary, or alternate beneficiaries, follow the instructions in Chapter 10, Section D, for the wording of shared gifts. (Remember that in Florida, you cannot leave your house to anyone but your spouse or your children.)

- The name of your residuary beneficiary and alternate residuary beneficiary. You can name more than one residuary beneficiary if you want. For example, many people list all their children.

- The names of your executor and alternate executor.

Do not sign or date your will yet. You do this when you complete your final will, with your witnesses.

Step 3. Have the form typed, because a will with handwriting and typing combined is not valid. You may need to renumber the clauses if you omit items that don't apply to you. You do not need to initial each page; your signature at the end is all that is needed.

⚠ Don't use the form as your final will. Do not type the information required onto the form and attempt to use it as your final will. Courts are not used to wills like this. You want your will to look normal and unthreatening to a judge, which means typed, and with the fill-in-the-blank lines and instructions below these lines gone. So you can see how a final draft and a typed will should look, there are samples below of Form 10, a will for a single person.

Type or word process the final draft of your will, double-spaced, on good $8^1/2$" x 11" paper. Proofread it carefully and make sure it's letter-perfect. If you find mistakes, retype or print out the entire page. Don't ever make alterations on the face of your will by writing in words or crossing something out and initialing the change. It could make part or all of your will invalid.

4. Date and sign the will in front of witnesses. (Instructions are in Section F, below.)

F. Signing and Witnessing Your Will

To be valid, your will must be signed and dated in front of witnesses. You sign the will where the form provides. Then these witnesses must sign the will in your presence, and also in the presence of the other witnesses.

State laws vary as to how many witnesses you need, but three is enough in every state. Even if your state requires only two witnesses, three is better because it provides one more person to establish that your signature is valid, if that becomes necessary during probate. Witnesses must be:

- Adults (18 or over) and of sound mind.

- People who won't inherit under the will. That means anyone who might inherit any gift through your will, including alternate residuary beneficiaries, cannot be a witness. But someone who will receive property only from your living trust can be a valid witness.

    Sixteen states now allow a witness to inherit will property. Still, I strongly recommend against doing that in your will. Having will witnesses who do not inherit eliminates one possible reason for challenging your will.

- People who should be easy to locate in the event of your death. This usually means people who aren't likely to move around a lot and (most of all) who are younger than you are.

Here's how to go about arranging for signing and witnessing your will:

- Have the three witnesses assemble in one place.

- Tell them that the paper you hold is your will. They don't need to know what's in it.

- Sign the signature page in the witnesses' presence. Use the exact spelling of your name as you typed in the heading.

- Have each witness sign the last page in the place indicated while the other witnesses are watching. The clause immediately preceding the witnesses' signatures states ("attests") that the events outlined just above have occurred.

    The witnesses list the city, county and state of their residence (not where the will is signed). Listing the witnesses' addresses is not legally required, but can prove an aid in locating the witnesses later on, when the will becomes operational.

⚠ Get the details right. If a will doesn't comply with the technical requirements (say you had only one witness to your will), it cannot be validated by the probate court. It's not hard to do a will correctly. Double-check to be sure you've done so!

Sample Will Form, Ready to be Typed

WILL

of

_____Benjamin Werrin_____
your name

I, _____Benjamin Werrin_____, a resident of
your name

_____Fairmont_____, _____Dutchess_____ County, _____New York_____,
city   county   state

declare that this is my will.

1. I revoke all wills and codicils that I have previously made.

2. I am not married.

3. I am the _____father_____ of the _____child_____ whose _____name_____ is _____
mother/father   child/children   name(s)   is/are

Eric Werrin _____

_____

_____

There are ___ living children of my deceased child _____,
name

whose names are:

_____

_____

_____

(B) If I fail to leave, by this will or otherwise, any property to any of the children listed above, my failure to do so is intentional.

(C) If at my death any of my children are minors, and a personal guardian is needed, I nominate _____ to be appointed personal guardian
name

of my minor children. If _____ cannot serve as
name

personal guardian, I nominate _____ to be appointed
name

personal guardian.

(D) If at my death any of my children are minors, and a property guardian is needed, I appoint _____ as property guardian for my minor children.
name

If ~~_____~~ cannot serve as property ~~guardian, I appoint~~

            name

~~_____~~ ~~as property guardian.~~

            name

~~(E) I direct that no bond be required of any guardian.~~

4. (A) I leave the following specific gifts:

I leave _____ all my cameras _____

            ~~property described~~

to _Sid Tropinsky_____, or if _Sid Tropinsky_____

    ~~beneficiary's name~~   ~~beneficiary's name~~

fails to survive me, to _____ Nancy Werrin _____.

           ~~alternate beneficiary's name~~

I leave _____

            property described

to _____, or if _____

    beneficiary's name   beneficiary's name

fails to survive me, to _____.

           alternate beneficiary's name

I leave _____

            property described

to _____, or if _____

    beneficiary's name   beneficiary's name

fails to survive me, to _____.

           alternate beneficiary's name

(B) I leave all my other property subject to this will to

_Eric Werrin_____, or if _he_____ _fails_ to

     ~~residuary beneficiary's name~~   ~~he/she/they~~   ~~fails/fail~~

survive me, to _____ Gil Nason _____.

         ~~alternate residuary beneficiary's name~~

5. (A) I nominate _Gil Nason_____ to serve as executor of my will.

          ~~executor's name~~

If _____ he_____ is unable to serve or continue serving as executor, I nominate

   ~~he/she~~

_____ Nancy Werrin_____ to serve as executor.

      ~~alternate executor's name~~

(B) No bond shall be required of any executor.

I subscribe my name to this will this _____ day of _____, 20____, at

_____ Fairmont_____, ____ Dutchess County____, ___ New York_____.

       ~~city~~   ~~county~~   ~~state~~

_____

      ~~your signature~~

WITNESSES

On the date last written above, <u>Benjamin Werrin</u> declared to us, the
~~your name~~

undersigned, that this was _____his_____ will, and requested us to act as witnesses to it.
~~his/her~~

_____He_____ then signed this will in our presence, all of us being present at the same time. We now at
~~He/She~~

_____his_____ request and in _____his_____ presence, and in the presence of each other, have signed this
~~his/her~~ ~~his/her~~

Will as witnesses.

We declare under penalty of perjury that the foregoing is true and correct.

_____
witness signature

_____, _____, _____
city   county   state

_____
witness signature

_____, _____, _____
city   county   state

_____
witness signature

_____, _____, _____
city   county   state

Final, Typed Will, Ready to be Signed and Witnessed

WILL

of

Benjamin Werrin

I, Benjamin Werrin, a resident of Fairmont, Dutchess County, New York, declare that this is my will.

1. I revoke all wills and codicils that I have previously made.

2. I am not married.

3. I am the father of the child whose name is Eric Werrin.

4. (A) I make the following specific gifts:

        I leave all my cameras to Sid Tropinsky, or if Sid Tropinsky fails to survive me, to Nancy Werrin.

  (B) I leave all my other property subject to this will to Eric Werrin, or if he fails to survive me, to Gil

        Nason.

5. (A) I nominate Gil Nason to serve as executor of my will. If he is unable to serve or continue serving as

        executor, I nominate Nancy Werrin to serve as executor.

  (B) No bond shall be required of any executor.

I subscribe my name to this will this _____ day of _____, 20____, at

Fairmont, Dutchess County, New York.

_____

WITNESSES

On the date last written above, Benjamin Werrin declared to us, the undersigned, that this was his will, and requested us to act as witnesses to it. He then signed this will in our presence, all of us being present at the same time. We now at his request and in his presence, and in the presence of each other, have signed such will as witnesses.

We declare under penalty of perjury that the foregoing is true and correct.

_____
witness signature

_____, _____, _____
city   county   state

_____
witness signature

_____, _____, _____
city   county   state

_____
witness signature

_____, _____, _____
city   county   state

chapter 17

IF YOU NEED EXPERT HELP

*M*any readers, if not the majority, will find the information in this book sufficient to prepare their own living trust and back-up will. However, readers who run into a snag of some kind may sensibly decide they need a lawyer's help. Throughout this book, I've indicated "red flags" that alert you to the need for professional advice, such as the necessity to make special plans for an incapacitated or disabled beneficiary. And, of course, people with an estate over the estate tax threshold need an expert's help to review all their estate tax options and prepare the living trust best geared to their needs.

A. Hiring a Lawyer to Review Your Living Trust

Hiring a lawyer solely to review a living trust document you've prepared sounds like a good idea. It shouldn't cost much, and seems to offer a comforting security. Sadly, though, it may be difficult or even impossible to find a lawyer who will accept the job.

While this is unfortunate, I'm not willing to excoriate lawyers who won't review a do-it-yourself living trust. From their point of view, they are being asked to accept what can turn into a significant responsibility for what they regard as inadequate compensation, given their usual fees. Any prudent lawyer sees every client as a potential occasion for a malpractice claim, or at least, serious later hassles—a phone call four years down the line that begins, "We talked to you about our living trust, and now…." Many experienced lawyers want to avoid this kind of risk. Also, many lawyers feel that if they're only reviewing someone else's work, they simply don't get deeply enough into a situation to be sure of their opinions. All you can do here is to keep trying to find a sympathetic lawyer—or be prepared to pay more, enough so the lawyer can feel she has been paid adequately to review your living trust.

B. Working With an Expert

If you have decided you want legal help, the first consideration is what type of expert you should seek out. Questions about estate taxes may be better (and less expensively) answered by an experienced accountant than by a lawyer. Or if you're wondering what type of life insur-ance to buy, you may be better off talking to a financial planner. But for many sophisticated living trust issues, you'll need to see a lawyer.

1. What Type of Lawyer Do You Need?

The type of lawyer that is right for you depends on what your problem is. Before you talk to a lawyer, decide what kind of help you really need. Do you want someone to advise you on a complete estate plan or just to go over part of your trust? If you don't clearly tell the lawyer what you want, you may find yourself agreeing to turn over all your estate planning work.

If you've prepared a trust from this book, any good estate practice lawyer should be able to help you. Do make sure she's experienced with AB trusts, if you prepare that type of trust. If you want a more sophisticated document—like a QTIP trust or generation-skipping trust (see Chapter 15, Section F)—it's important that you see an estate trust specialist, who'll probably cost more than a general practice estate lawyer.

If you hire an "expert," make sure that person really has the knowledge or expertise he or she claims. Many lawyers have recently discovered the profit-making potential of trusts. Lawyers who know almost nothing about living trusts (it's easy to go through law school without ever hearing of one) have found that they can charge substantial fees—$1,500 or more is common—for a simple document. Some use computer programs to churn out trusts and may or may not take into account your specific needs.

It's also important that you feel a personal rapport with your lawyer. You want one who treats you as an equal. (Interestingly, the Latin root of the word "client" translates as "to hear, to obey.") When talking with a lawyer on the phone or at a first conference, ask specific questions that concern you. Let the lawyer know that you've read this book and that you have a good understanding of estate planning. Then, see how the lawyer responds. If he answers you clearly and concisely—explaining, but not talking down to you—fine. If he acts wise, but says little except to ask that the problem be placed in his hands (with the appropriate fee, of course), watch out. You are either talking with someone who doesn't know the answer and won't admit it (common), or someone who finds it impossible to let go of the "me expert, you peasant" way of looking at the world (even more common).

2. How to Choose a Lawyer

Finding a competent estate planning lawyer who charges a reasonable fee and respects your efforts to prepare your own living trust may not be easy. Here are some suggestions on how to go about the task.

a. Ask Friends and Business People

Personal recommendations are generally the best way to find a lawyer you'll like. If you have a close friend who's had a good experience with an estate planning lawyer, there's a good chance you'll work well with that lawyer too.

If friends can't help you, ask any business people you know for referrals. Anyone who owns a small business probably has a relationship with a lawyer. Ask around to find someone you know who is a satisfied client, and get the name of his lawyer. Even a lawyer who does not handle estate planning, will likely know someone who does. And because of the continuing relationship with your business friend, the lawyer has an incentive to recommend someone who is competent.

Also ask people in any social or other organization in which you are involved. They may well know of a good lawyer whose attitudes are similar to yours. Senior citizens' centers and other groups that advise and assist older people may have a list of local lawyers who specialize in wills and estate planning and are well-regarded.

b. Look Into a Group Legal Plan

Some unions, employers, and consumer groups offer group legal plans to their members or employees, who can obtain comprehensive legal assistance free or at low rates. If you are a member of such a plan, check with it first. Your problem may be covered free of charge. If it is, and you are satisfied that the lawyer you are referred to is knowledgeable in estate planning, this route is probably a good choice.

Some plans give you only a slight reduction in a lawyer's fee. In that case, you may be referred to a lawyer whose main virtue is the willingness to reduce fees in exchange for a high volume of referrals.

c. Try the Martindale-Hubbell Law Directory

This directory, available in most public libraries and at www.martindale.com, lists lawyers by the towns or cities they practice in, and also identifies estate planning specialists. For each lawyer or law firm listed, you'll get some information about qualifications and experience. Martindale-Hubbell tends to list established and establishment lawyers, however, so the fees they charge will not be low.

d. Call an Attorney Referral Service

A lawyer referral service will give you the name of an attorney who practices in your area. Usually, you can get a referral to an attorney who claims to specialize in estate planning and will give you an initial consultation for a low fee.

Most county bar associations have referral services. In some states, independent referral services, run by or for groups of lawyers, also operate.

Unfortunately, few referral services screen the attorneys they list, which means those who participate may not be the most experienced or competent. Often, the lawyers who sign up with referral services are just starting out and need clients. It may be possible to find a skilled estate planning specialist through a referral service, but be sure to take the time to check out the credentials and experience of the person to whom you're referred.

e. Living Trust Seminars

Newspapers, radio, and TV are full of ads for free seminars on living trusts. Usually, these events are nothing more than elaborate pitches for paying a lawyer $1,000 to $1,500 to write a living trust. Is it worth it? Probably not. For most estates, the trust forms and instructions in this book are all you need.

Often these seminars are occasions for you to be cajoled by lawyers, financial planners, and insurance agents to pay large sums of money to get your affairs in order before you die.

People are sold on the idea that much of their estate is likely to be gobbled up by estate taxes unless they set up trusts now to avoid some of the tax and buy life insurance to pay the rest. The problem is, most people don't have estates large enough to generate estate tax liability. And the seminar sponsors know it.

The sponsors try to sell:

- a lot of life insurance, to pay for supposed estate taxes, and

- their form AB trust to reduce estate taxes. (See Chapters 4 and 5.)

Be sure you need these alleged benefits before paying what will be a substantial amount to acquire them. Is your estate likely to be liable for estate taxes? What type of AB trust do you need? If your situation is more complex than what can be handled by using this book, you'll probably be better off paying the money to hire a good lawyer to draft a trust geared to your needs than paying too much for the standard form offered in these seminars.

C. Lawyer Fees

As you already know, lawyers are expensive. They charge fees usually ranging from $150 to $500 or more per hour. While fancy office trappings, dull suits, and solemn faces are no guarantee (or even a good indication) that a particular lawyer will provide top-notch service in a style you will feel comfortable with, this conventional style almost always ensures that you will be

charged at the upper end of the fee range. High fees and quality service don't necessarily go hand in hand. Indeed, the attorneys I think most highly of tend to charge moderate fees (for lawyers, that is), and seem to get along very nicely without stuffy law office trappings.

Depending on the area of the country where you live, generally, I feel that fees in the range of $200 to $250 per hour are reasonable in urban areas, given the average lawyer's overhead. In rural counties and small cities, $150 to $200 is more like it.

Be sure you've settled your fee arrangement—preferably in writing—at the start of your relationship. (In California, a written fee agreement is required by law if the bill is expected to be over $1,000.) In addition to the hourly fee, get a clear, written commitment from the lawyer stating how many hours your problem should take to handle.

D. Doing Your Own Legal Research

As an alternative to hiring a lawyer, you can explore doing your own legal research. This can work well for relatively simpler living trust questions, such as any specific state law about trust registration or a trustee's duty to manage trust property prudently.

1. Legal Research in Law Libraries

If you decide you want to do your own research in the library, how do you go about it? First, you need an introduction to how law libraries work. Since you can't hire your own law librarian, the best book explaining how nonlawyers can do their own legal work is *Legal*

Research: How to Find and Understand the Law, by Stephen Elias and Susan Levinkind (Nolo). It shows you, step-by-step, how to find answers in the law library. As far as I know, it's the only legal research book written specifically for nonprofessionals.

Next, locate a law library or a public library with a good law collection. In most counties, there's a law library in the main county courthouse, although quality varies widely. Most county law libraries are supported by tax dollars or by the fees paid to file court papers. The librarians are generally most helpful and courteous to nonlawyers who are venturing to do their own legal research. If the county library is not adequate, your best bet is a law school library. Those in state colleges and universities supported by tax dollars are almost always open to the public.

Many states have estate planning books prepared for practicing lawyers. These books contain specific clauses and forms for wills or trusts, and many other hands-on materials. The best way to locate this type of book for your state is to ask the law librarian or search the library's computerized catalog by looking for the terms "estate planning," "wills," or "trusts."

Unfortunately, I cannot recommend doing your own research for high-end living trust issues, especially regarding estate taxes. Drafting a QTIP or generation-skipping trust that complies with all federal regulations and achieves the goals you want is truly a complicated matter that requires considerable expertise. Remember, you'll consider these types of trusts only if you have substantial assets. The risk that your trust won't be legally correct and therefore won't qualify for the tax breaks you want outweighs any possible savings gained by doing your own legal work.

LIVING TRUST RESEARCH BOOKS

In most states, you can find books on trusts written for the lawyers of your state.

In California, the Continuing Education of the Bar (CEB) publishes several useful estate planning books, including *Drafting California Revocable Inter Vivos Trusts* and *Estate Planning for the General Practitioner*.

Comparable books in New York are published by the Practicing Law Institute (PLI) including *Income Taxation of Estates and Trusts*, by Michaelson & Blattmahr.

If you want to wade into the murk of estate tax issues, a standard resource is the CCH (Commerce Clearing House) *Estate and Gift Tax Reporter*, available in law libraries.

---

2. Legal Information Online

Legal research is rapidly becoming automated, and it's possible to find many answers using your computer. If you want information about a recent court decision, a new statute, a current legal issue, or more general information on some aspect of living trusts, you'll probably be able to find it somewhere on the Internet. Lots of public libraries now offer online access, if you're not connected at home or at work.

Legal Research: How to Find and Understand the Law, by Stephen Elias and Susan Levinkind (Nolo), provides extensive information on how to do legal research online.

Nolo's website offers information on living trusts and estate planning. You can find us at www .nolo.com. ■

Appendix A

HOW TO USE THE CD-ROM

$\mathcal{T}$he tear-out forms in Appendix B are included on a CD-ROM in the back of the book. This CD-ROM, which can be used with Windows computers, installs files that can be opened, printed, and edited using a word processor or other software. It is *not* a stand-alone software program. Please read this Appendix and the README.TXT file included on the CD-ROM for instructions on using the Forms CD.

Note to Mac users: This CD-ROM and its files should also work on Macintosh computers. Please note, however, that Nolo cannot provide technical support for non-Windows users.

HOW TO VIEW THE README FILE

If you do not know how to view the file README.TXT, insert the Forms CD-ROM into your computer's CD-ROM drive and follow these instructions:

- Windows 9x, 2000, Me and XP: (1) On your PC's desktop, double-click the My Computer icon; (2) double-click the icon for the CD-ROM drive into which the Forms CD-ROM was inserted; (3) double-click the file README.TXT.
- Macintosh: (1) On your Mac desktop, double-click the icon for the CD-ROM that you inserted; (2) double-click on the file README.TXT.

While the README file is open, print it out by using the Print command in the File menu.

A. Installing the Form Files Onto Your Computer

Word processing forms that you can open, complete, print, and save with your word processing program (see Section B, below) are contained on the CD-ROM. Before you can do anything with the files on the CD-ROM, you need to install them onto your hard disk. In accordance with U.S. copyright laws, remember that copies of the CD-ROM and its files are for your personal use only.

Insert the Forms CD and do the following:

1. Windows 9x, 2000, Me, and XP Users

Follow the instructions that appear on the screen. (If nothing happens when you insert the Forms CD-ROM, then (1) double-click the My Computer icon; (2) double-click the icon for the CD-ROM drive into which the Forms CD-ROM was inserted; and (3) double-click the file WELCOME.EXE.)

By default, all the files are installed to the \Living Trust Forms folder in the \Program Files folder of your computer. A folder called "Living Trust Forms" is added to the "Programs" folder of the Start menu.

2. Macintosh Users

Step 1: If the "Living Trust Forms CD" window is not open, open it by double-clicking the "Living Trust Forms CD" icon.

Step 2: Select the "Living Trust Forms" folder icon.

Step 3: Drag and drop the folder icon onto the icon of your hard disk.

B. Using the Word Processing Files to Create Documents

This section concerns the files for forms that can be opened and edited with your word processing program.

All word processing forms come in rich text format. These files have the extension ".RTF." For example, the form for the AB Living Trust discussed in Chapter 4 is on the file FORM03.RTF. All forms and their filenames are listed at the beginning of Appendix B.

RTF files can be read by most recent word processing programs including all versions of MS Word for Windows and Macintosh, WordPad for Windows, and recent versions of WordPerfect for Windows and Macintosh.

To use a form from the CD to create your documents you must: (1) open a file in your word processor or text editor; (2) edit the form by filling in the required information; (3) print it out; (4) rename and save your revised file.

The following are general instructions on how to do this. However, each word processor uses different commands to open, format, save and print documents. Please read your word processor's manual for specific instructions on performing these tasks.

Do not call Nolo's technical support if you have questions on how to use your word processor.

Step 1: Opening a File

There are three ways to open the word processing files included on the CD-ROM after you have installed them onto your computer.

- Windows users can open a file by selecting its "shortcut" as follows: (1) Click the Windows "Start" button; (2) open the "Programs" folder; (3) open the "Living Trust Forms" subfolder; and (4) click on the shortcut to the form you want to work with.

- Both Windows and Macintosh users can open a file directly by double-clicking on it. Use My Computer or Windows Explorer (Windows 9x, 2000, Me, or XP) or the Finder (Macintosh) to go to the folder you installed or copied the CD-ROM's files to. Then, double-click on the specific file you want to open.

- You can also open a file from within your word processor. To do this, you must first start your word processor. Then, go to the File menu and choose the Open command. This opens a dialog box where you will tell the program (1) the type of file you want to open (*.RTF); and (2) the location and name of the file (you will need to navigate through the directory tree to get to the folder on your hard disk where the CD's files have been installed). If these directions are unclear, you will need to look through the manual for your word processing program—Nolo's technical support department will *not* be able to help you with the use of your word processing program.

WHERE ARE THE FILES INSTALLED?

Windows Users
- RTF files are installed by default to a folder named \Living Trust Forms in the \Program Files folder of your computer.

Macintosh Users
- RTF files are located in the "Living Trust Forms" folder.

Step 2: Editing Your Document

Fill in the appropriate information according to the instructions and sample agreements in the book. Underlines are used to indicate where you need to enter your information, frequently followed by instructions in brackets. *Be sure to delete the underlines and instructions from your edited document.* If you do not know how to use your word processor to edit a document, you will need to look through the manual for your word processing program—Nolo's technical support department will *not* be able to help you with the use of your word processing program.

EDITING FORMS THAT HAVE OPTIONAL OR ALTERNATIVE TEXT

Some of the forms have optional or alternate text:
- With optional text, you choose whether to include or exclude the given text.
- With alternative text, you select one alternative to include and exclude the other alternatives.

When editing these forms, we suggest you do the following:

Optional text

If you **don't want** to include optional text, just delete it from your document.

If you **do want** to include optional text, just leave it in your document.

In either case, delete the italicized instructions.

NOTE: if you choose not to include an optional numbered clause, be sure to renumber all the subsequent clauses after you delete it.

Alternative text

First delete all the alternatives that you do not want to include, then delete the italicized instructions.

Step 3: Printing Out the Document

Use your word processor's or text editor's "Print" command to print out your document. If you do not know how to use your word processor to print a document, you will need to look through the manual for your word processing program—Nolo's technical support department will *not* be able to help you with the use of your word processing program.

Step 4: Saving Your Document

After filling in the form, use the "Save As" command to save and rename the file. Because all the files are "read-only," you will not be able to use the "Save" command. This is for your protection. *If you save the file without renaming it, the underlines that indicate where you need to enter your information will be lost, and you will not be able to create a new document with this file without recopying the original file from the CD-ROM.*

If you do not know how to use your word processor to save a document, you will need to look through the manual for your word processing program—Nolo's technical support department will *not* be able to help you with the use of your word processing program. ■

Appendix B

FORMS

REMINDER

The circled numbers on the trust forms (①, ④, ⑦, etc.) refer to the specific steps, or instructions, described in Chapter 10, "Preparing Your Living Trust Document," Section D, which explain what information you need to write on the blank lines. Thus the circled ② refers you to Step 2 of Chapter 10, Section D, "Decide How Many Property Schedules Your Trust Needs." Each step also explains how you can make any appropriate revision for that trust section. If you have any trouble completing a trust form or are puzzled by these numbers, please re-read Section D of Chapter 10.

Form 1: Basic Living Trust for One Person

The ①_____ Living Trust

your name (or name of trust, if different)

DECLARATION OF TRUST

I. TRUST NAME

This trust shall be known as The ①_____ Living Trust.

your name

II. TRUST PROPERTY

(A) Property Placed in Trust

①_____ , called the grantor or trustee, declares

your name

that _____ has set aside and holds in The ①_____

he/she your name

Living Trust all _____ interest in that property described in the attached Schedule A.②

his/her

The trust property shall be used for the benefit of the trust beneficiaries and shall be administered and distributed by the trustee in accordance with this Declaration of Trust.

(B) Additional or After-Acquired Property

The grantor may add property to the trust at any time.

III. RESERVED POWERS OF GRANTOR

(A) Amendment or Revocation

The grantor reserves the power to amend or revoke this trust at any time during _____ lifetime,

his/her

without notifying any beneficiary.

(B) Rights to Trust Property

Until the death of the grantor, all rights to all income, profits and control of the trust property shall be retained by the grantor.

(C) Homestead Rights

If the grantor's principal residence is transferred to the trust, grantor has the right to possess and occupy it for life, rent-free and without charge, except for taxes, insurance, maintenance and related costs and expenses. This right is intended to give grantor a beneficial interest in the property and to ensure that grantor does not lose eligibility for a state homestead tax exemption for which grantor otherwise qualifies.

⑤Ⓐ **(D) Incapacity of Grantor**

If the grantor has become physically or mentally incapacitated, as certified in writing by a licensed physician, the successor trustee shall manage this trust. The successor trustee shall pay trust income at least annually to, or for the benefit of, the grantor and may also spend any amount of trust principal necessary in the trustee's discretion for the needs of the grantor, until a licensed physician certifies that the grantor is no longer incapacitated or until the grantor's death.

(E) Grantor's Death

After the death of the grantor, this trust becomes irrevocable. It may not be altered or amended in any respect, and may not be terminated except through distributions permitted by this Declaration of Trust.

IV. TRUSTEES

(A) Original Trustee

The trustee of The ①_____ Living Trust and all
                                                          your name

children's trusts created under this Declaration of Trust shall be ①_____ _____.

(B) Successor Trustee

Upon the death of the trustee, or _____ incapacity as certified in writing by a licensed physician, the
                                                        his/her

successor trustee shall be ⑥_____. If _____ is/are
                                                          name(s)   he/she/all of them

unable to serve or continue serving as successor trustee, the successor trustee shall be

⑥_____.
                                            name

[If you named more than one successor trustee, include ONE of the following two paragraphs here:]

Any of the successor trustees has full and independent authority to act for and represent the trust.

[or]

All of the successor trustees must consent, in writing, to any transaction involving the trust or trust property.

(C) Resignation of Trustee

Any trustee in office may resign at any time by signing a notice of resignation. The resignation must be delivered to the person or institution who is either named in this Declaration of Trust, or appointed by the trustee under Section IV, Paragraph (D), to next serve as trustee.

(D) Power to Appoint Successor Trustee

If all the successor trustees named in this Declaration of Trust cease to, or are unable to, serve as trustee, any trustee may appoint an additional successor trustee or trustees to serve in the order nominated. The appointment must be made in writing, signed by the trustee and notarized.

(E) Terminology

In this Declaration of Trust, the term "trustee" includes any successor trustee or successor trustees.

(F) Bond Waived

No bond shall be required of any trustee.

(G) Compensation

No trustee shall receive any compensation for serving as trustee, except that a trustee shall be entitled to reasonable compensation, as determined by the trustee, for serving as a trustee of a child's trust created by this Declaration of Trust, or for serving as trustee because the grantor has become incapacitated.

(H) Liability of Trustee

With respect to the exercise or non-exercise of discretionary powers granted by this Declaration of Trust, the trustee shall not be liable for actions taken in good faith.

V. BENEFICIARIES

Upon the death of the grantor, the property listed on Schedule A shall be distributed to the beneficiaries named in this section.

(A) Primary and Alternate Beneficiaries

1. ⑦_____ shall be given
beneficiary

_____.
property identified

If _____ does not survive the grantor, that property shall be
beneficiary

given to _____.
alternate beneficiary

2. ⑦ _____ shall be given
beneficiary

_____.
property identified

If _____ does not survive the grantor, that property shall be
beneficiary

given to _____.
alternate beneficiary

3. ⑦ _____ shall be given
beneficiary

_____.
property identified

If _____ does not survive the grantor, that property shall be
beneficiary

given to _____.
alternate beneficiary

4. ⑦ _____ shall be given
beneficiary

_____.
property identified

If _____ does not survive the grantor, that property shall be
beneficiary

given to _____.
alternate beneficiary

5. ⑦ _____ shall be given
beneficiary

_____.
property identified

If _____ does not survive the grantor, that property shall be
beneficiary

given to _____.
alternate beneficiary

(B) Residuary Beneficiary

The residuary beneficiary of the trust shall be ⑧Ⓐ _____,
residuary beneficiary

who shall be given all trust property not specifically and validly disposed of by Section V, Paragraph (A). If

_____ does not survive the grantor, that property shall be given to
residuary beneficiary

⑧Ⓐ _____.
alternate residuary beneficiary

VI. DISTRIBUTION OF TRUST PROPERTY UPON DEATH OF GRANTOR

Upon the death of the grantor, the trustee shall distribute the trust property outright to the beneficiaries

named in Section V, Paragraphs (A) and (B), subject to any provision in this Declaration of Trust that creates

children's trusts or creates custodianships under the Uniform Transfers to Minors Act.

VII. TRUSTEE'S POWERS AND DUTIES

(A) Powers Under State Law

To carry out the provisions of The ① _____
your name

Living Trust , and any children's trusts created under this Declaration of Trust, the trustee shall have all

authority and powers allowed or conferred on a trustee under _____ law,
your state

subject to the trustee's fiduciary duty to the grantor and the beneficiaries.

(B) Specified Powers

The trustee's powers include, but are not limited to:

1. The power to sell trust property, and to borrow money and to encumber that property, specifically including trust real estate, by mortgage, deed of trust or other method.

2. The power to manage trust real estate as if the trustee were the absolute owner of it, including the power to lease (even if the lease term may extend beyond the period of any trust) or grant options to lease the property, to make repairs or alterations and to insure against loss.

3. The power to sell or grant options for the sale or exchange of any trust property, including stocks, bonds, debentures and any other form of security or security account, at public or private sale for cash or on credit.

4. The power to invest trust property in property of any kind, including but not limited to bonds, debentures, notes, mortgages and stocks.

5. The power to receive additional property from any source and add to any trust created by this Declaration of Trust.

6. The power to employ and pay reasonable fees to accountants, lawyers or investment experts for information or advice relating to the trust.

7. The power to deposit and hold trust funds in both interest-bearing and non-interest-bearing accounts.

8. The power to deposit funds in bank or other accounts uninsured by FDIC coverage.

9. The power to enter into electronic fund transfer or safe deposit arrangements with financial institutions.

10. The power to continue any business of the grantor.

11. The power to institute or defend legal actions concerning the trust or grantor's affairs.

12. The power to execute any document necessary to administer any child's trust created in this Declaration of Trust.

13. The power to diversify investments, including authority to decide that some or all of the trust property need not produce income.

(C) Payment by Trustee of the Grantor's Debts and Taxes

The grantor's debts and death taxes shall be paid by the trustee. The trustee shall pay these from the following trust property:

⑨ _____

_____

_____.

If the property specified above is insufficient to pay all the grantor's debts and death taxes, the trustee shall determine how such debts and death taxes shall be paid from trust property.

VIII. GENERAL ADMINISTRATIVE PROVISIONS

(A) Controlling Law

The validity of The ① _____ Living Trust shall
your name

be governed by the laws of _____.
your state

(B) Severability

If any provision of this Declaration of Trust is ruled unenforceable, the remaining provisions shall nevertheless remain in effect.

(C) Amendments

The term "Declaration of Trust" includes any provisions added by amendments.

(D) Accountings

No accountings or reports shall be required of the trustee.

IX. CHILDREN'S TRUSTS

All trust property left to any of the minor or young adult beneficiaries listed below in Section IX, Paragraph (A), shall be retained in trust for each such beneficiary in a separate trust of this

① _____ Living Trust. Each trust may be identified
your name

and referred to by adding the name of that trust's beneficiary to the name of this trust. The following terms apply to each children's trust:

(A) Trust Beneficiaries and Age Limits

A trust shall end when the beneficiary of that trust, listed below, becomes 35, except as otherwise specified in this section:

⑩ Trust for   Shall end at age

_____   _____

_____   _____

_____   _____

_____   _____

_____   _____

(B) Powers and Duties of Children's Trust Trustee

1. Until a child's trust ends, the trustee may distribute to or use for the benefit of the beneficiary as much of the net income or principal of the child's trust as the trustee deems necessary for the beneficiary's health, support, maintenance or education. Education includes, but is not limited to, college, graduate, postgraduate and vocational studies, and reasonably related living expenses.

2. In deciding whether to make a distribution to the beneficiary, the trustee may take into account the beneficiary's other income, resources and sources of support.

3. Any children's trust income that is not distributed to a beneficiary by the trustee shall be accumulated and added to the principal of the trust for that beneficiary.

4. The trustee of a child's trust is not required to make any accounting or report to the trust beneficiary.

(C) Assignment of Interest of Beneficiary Prohibited

The interests of the beneficiary of a child's trust shall not be transferable by voluntary or involuntary assignment or by operation of law before actual receipt by the beneficiary. These interests shall be free from the claims of creditors and from attachments, execution, bankruptcy or other legal process to the fullest extent permitted by law.

(D) Compensation of Trustee

Any trustee of a child's trust created under this Declaration of Trust shall be entitled to reasonable compensation out of the trust assets for ordinary and extraordinary services, and for all services in connection with the termination of any trust.

(E) Termination of Children's Trusts

A child's trust shall end when any of the following events occur:

1. The beneficiary reaches the age specified in Section IX, Paragraph (A). If the trust ends for this reason, the remaining principal and accumulated income of the trust shall be given outright to the beneficiary.

2. The beneficiary dies. If the trust ends for this reason, the trust property shall pass to the beneficiary's heirs.

3. The trustee distributes all trust property under the provisions of this Declaration of Trust.

X. CUSTODIANSHIPS UNDER THE UNIFORM TRANSFERS TO MINORS ACT

1. All property ⑪_____ becomes entitled to
beneficiary

under this trust document shall be given to _____ as
custodian's name

custodian for _____ under the _____
beneficiary   state

Uniform Transfers to Minors Act, until _____ reaches age _____.
beneficiary

2. All property ⑪_____ becomes entitled to
beneficiary

under this trust document shall be given to _____ as
custodian's name

custodian for _____ under the _____
beneficiary   state

Uniform Transfers to Minors Act, until _____ reaches age _____.
beneficiary

3. All property ⑪_____ becomes entitled to
beneficiary

under this trust document shall be given to _____ as
custodian's name

custodian for _____ under the _____
beneficiary   state

Uniform Transfers to Minors Act, until _____ reaches age _____.
beneficiary

Certification by Grantor

I certify that I have read this Declaration of Trust and that it correctly states the terms and conditions under which the trust property is to be held, managed and disposed of by the trustee and I approve the Declaration of Trust.

Dated: _____

_____
Grantor and Trustee

NOTARY'S ACKNOWLEDGMENT

State of _____

County of _____

On _____ _____, 20_____, before me, _____,

a notary public in and for said state, personally appeared _____,

personally known to me (or proved to me on the basis of satisfactory evidence) to be the person whose name is

subscribed to the within Declaration of Trust, and acknowledged to me that he/she executed the same in his/her

authorized capacity and that by his/her signature on the instrument he/she executed the Declaration of Trust.

_____
Signature of Notary   [SEAL]

SCHEDULE A②

All the grantor's interest in the following property:

Form 2: Basic Shared Living Trust

The ① _____ Living Trust

your name (or name of trust, if different)

DECLARATION OF TRUST

I. TRUST NAME

This trust shall be known as The ① _____ _____

your names

Living Trust.

II. TRUST PROPERTY

(A) Property Placed in Trust

① _____ , called the grantors

your names

or trustees, declare that they have set aside and hold in The ① _____

your names

Living Trust all their interest in the property described in the attached Schedules A, B and C. ②

The trust property shall be used for the benefit of the trust beneficiaries, and shall be administered and

distributed by the trustees in accordance with this Declaration of Trust.

(B) Rights Retained by Grantors

As long as both grantors are alive, both grantors retain all rights to all income, profits and control of the

trust property listed on Schedule A of The ① _____ _____

your names

Living Trust.

(1) As long as _____ is alive, she shall retain all

wife's name

rights to all income, profits and control of her separate property listed on Schedule B of The

① _____ Living Trust.

your names

(2) As long as _____ is alive, he shall retain all

husband's name

rights to all income, profits and control of his separate property listed on Schedule C of The

① _____ Living Trust.

your names

(C) Additional or After-Acquired Property

Either grantor, or both, may add property to the trust at any time.

(D) Character of Property Placed in Trust

While both grantors are alive, property transferred to this trust shall retain its original character. If the trust is revoked, the trustee shall distribute the trust property to the grantors based on the same ownership rights they had before the property was transferred to the trust, as specified below.

1. Shared Property

All trust property listed on Schedule A was shared property:

④ _____

identify the character of shared property listed in Schedule A

_____

_____

_____

_____.

2. Separate Property

The trust property listed on Schedule B shall retain its character as the separate property of

_____. The trust property listed on Schedule C

wife's name

shall retain its character as the separate property of _____.

husband's name

[Make appropriate deletions if wife and/or husband has no separate property.]

(E) Revocation

As long as both grantors live, either grantor may revoke The ① _____

your names

Living Trust at any time by writing given to the other grantor. No beneficiary need be given any notice of revocation. After the death of a spouse, the surviving spouse can amend his or her continuing revocable living trust, Trust 2, as defined in Section V, Paragraph (B).

(F) Amendment

As long as both grantors live, The ① _____

your names

Living Trust may be altered, amended or modified only by a writing signed by both grantors.

(G) Homestead Rights

If the grantors' principal residence is transferred to the trust, grantors have the right to possess and occupy it for life, rent-free and without charge, except for taxes, insurance, maintenance and related costs and expenses. This right is intended to give grantors a beneficial interest in the property and to ensure that the grantors, or either of them, do not lose eligibility for a state homestead tax exemption for which either grantor otherwise qualifies.

III. TRUSTEES

(A) Original Trustees

The trustees of The ① _____ _____ Living Trust and
<small>your names</small>

any other trusts or children's trusts created under this Declaration of Trust shall be

① _____ . Either trustee may act for, and represent, the
<small>your names</small>

trust in any transaction.

(B) Trustee on Death or Incapacity of Original Trustee

Upon the death or incapacity, as certified in writing by a licensed physician, of

_____ _____ or
<small>wife's name</small>

_____ , the other spouse shall serve as sole trustee
<small>husband's name</small>

of this trust and any children's trusts created under this Declaration of Trust.

(C) Trustee's Responsibility

The trustee in office shall serve as trustee of all trusts created under this Declaration of Trust, including all children's trusts.

(D) Terminology

In this Declaration of Trust, the term "trustee" includes any successor trustee or trustees. The singular "trustee" also includes the plural.

(E) Successor Trustee

Upon the death or incapacity of the surviving spouse, or the incapacity of both spouses, the successor

trustee shall be ⑥ _____ . If _____ is/are unable to
<small>name(s)　　　　　　　　　　　　　he/she/all of them</small>

serve or to continue serving as successor trustee, the next successor trustee shall be

⑥ _____ .
<small>name</small>

[If you named more than one successor trustee, include ONE of the following two paragraphs here:]

Any of the successor trustees has full and independent authority to act for and represent the trust.

[or]

All of the successor trustees must consent, in writing, to any transaction involving the trust or trust property.

(F) Resignation of Trustee

Any trustee in office may resign at any time by signing a notice of resignation. The resignation must be delivered to the person or institution who is either named in this Declaration of Trust, or appointed by the trustee under Section III, Paragraph (G), to next serve as trustee.

(G) Power to Appoint Successor Trustee

If all the successor trustees named in this Declaration of Trust cease to, or are unable to, serve as trustee, any trustee may appoint an additional successor trustee or trustees to serve in the order nominated. The appointment must be made in writing, signed by the trustee and notarized.

(H) Bond Waived

No bond shall be required of any trustee.

(I) Compensation

No trustee shall receive any compensation for serving as trustee, except that a trustee shall be entitled to reasonable compensation, as determined by the trustee, for serving as a trustee of a child's trust created by this Declaration of Trust, or for serving as trustee because the grantors or a grantor becomes incapacitated.

(J) Liability of Trustee

With respect to the exercise or non-exercise of discretionary powers granted by this Declaration of Trust, the trustee shall not be liable for actions taken in good faith.

IV. BENEFICIARIES

(A) Husband's Primary and Alternate Beneficiaries

Upon the death of _____, trust property
husband's name

owned by _____, as his share of the trust property
husband's name

listed on Schedule A and any separate property listed on Schedule C, shall be distributed as specified to the beneficiaries named in this section.

1. Husband's Specific Beneficiaries

a. ⑦ _____ shall be given
   beneficiary's name(s)

_____ .
property identified

If _____ does not survive _____ ,
     beneficiary   husband's name

that property shall be given to _____ .
alternate beneficiary

b. ⑦ _____ shall be given
   beneficiary's name(s)

_____ .
property identified

If _____ does not survive _____ ,
     beneficiary   husband's name

that property shall be given to _____ .
alternate beneficiary

c. ⑦ _____ shall be given
   beneficiary's name(s)

_____ .
property identified

If _____ does not survive _____ ,
     beneficiary   husband's name

that property shall be given to _____ .
alternate beneficiary

d. ⑦ _____ shall be given
   beneficiary's name(s)

_____ .
property identified

If _____ does not survive _____ ,
     beneficiary   husband's name

that property shall be given to _____ .
alternate beneficiary

e. ⑦ _____ shall be given
   beneficiary's name(s)

_____ .
property identified

If _____ does not survive _____ ,
     beneficiary   husband's name

that property shall be given to _____ .
alternate beneficiary

2. Husband's Residuary Beneficiary

The residuary beneficiary of any trust property owned by _____
husband's name

as his share of the trust property listed on Schedule A or any separate property listed on Schedule C, and not

specifically and validly disposed of by Section IV, Paragraph (A)1, shall be

(8A) _____. If _____
residuary beneficiary   residuary beneficiary

does not survive _____, that property shall be given to
husband's name

(8A)_____.
alternate residuary beneficiary

(B) Wife's Primary and Alternate Beneficiaries

Upon the death of _____, trust property
wife's name

owned by _____, as her share of the trust property
wife's name

listed on Schedule A and any separate property listed on Schedule B shall be distributed as specified to the

beneficiaries named in this section.

1. Wife's Specific Beneficiaries

a. (7)_____ shall be given
beneficiary's name(s)

_____.
property identified

If _____ does not survive _____ ,
beneficiary   wife's name

that property shall be given to _____ .
alternate beneficiary

b. (7)_____ shall be given
beneficiary's name(s)

_____.
property identified

If _____ does not survive _____ ,
beneficiary   wife's name

that property shall be given to _____ .
alternate beneficiary

c. (7)_____ shall be given
beneficiary's name(s)

_____.
property identified

If _____ does not survive _____ ,
beneficiary   wife's name

that property shall be given to _____ .
alternate beneficiary

d. ⑦_____ shall be given
beneficiary's name(s)

_____.
property identified

If _____ does not survive _____ ,
               beneficiary   wife's name

that property shall be given to _____ .
                                              alternate beneficiary

e. ⑦_____ shall be given
beneficiary's name(s)

_____.
property identified

If _____ does not survive _____ ,
               beneficiary   wife's name

that property shall be given to _____ .
                                              alternate beneficiary

2. Wife's Residuary Beneficiary

The residuary beneficiary of any trust property owned by _____
wife's name

as her share of the trust property listed on Schedule A or any separate property listed on Schedule B, and not

specifically and validly disposed of by Section IV, Paragraph (B)1, shall be

⑧Ⓐ _____ . If _____
                 residuary beneficiary   residuary beneficiary

does not survive _____ , that property shall be given to
                                                wife's name

⑧Ⓐ_____ .
                 alternate residuary beneficiary

V. ADMINISTRATION OF TRUST PROPERTY

(A) Terminology

The first grantor to die shall be called the "deceased spouse." The living grantor shall be called the

"surviving spouse."

(B) Division and Distribution of Trust Property on Death of Grantor

1. Upon the death of the deceased spouse, the trustee shall divide the property of The

①_____ Living Trust listed on Schedules A, B and C
                 your names

into two separate trusts, Trust 1 and Trust 2. The trustee shall serve as trustee of Trust 1 and Trust 2.

2. Trust 1 shall contain all the property of The ①_____
your names

Living Trust owned by the deceased spouse at the time it was transferred to the trust, plus accumulated income,

appreciation in value and the like attributable to the ownership interest of the deceased spouse and his or her share

of any property acquired in the trust's name, except trust property left by the terms of this trust to the surviving

spouse. Trust 1 becomes irrevocable at the death of the deceased spouse. The trustee shall distribute the property in

Trust 1 to the beneficiaries named by the deceased spouse in Section IV of this Declaration of Trust, subject to any

provision of this Declaration of Trust that creates children's trusts or creates custodianships under the Uniform

Transfers to Minors Act.

3. Trust 2 shall contain all the property of The ①_____
your names

Living Trust owned by the surviving spouse at the time it was transferred to the trust, plus accumulated income,

appreciation in value and the like attributable to the ownership interest of the surviving spouse and any trust

property left by the deceased spouse to the surviving spouse.

4. The trustee shall have exclusive authority to determine the paperwork and recordkeeping necessary to

establish Trust 1 and Trust 2.

(C) Property Left to the Surviving Spouse

Any trust property left by the deceased spouse to the surviving spouse shall remain in the surviving

spouse's revocable trust, Trust 2, without necessity of a formal transfer to that trust.

(D) Administration of Trust 2

1. Rights Retained by Surviving Spouse

Until the death of the surviving spouse, all rights to all income, profits and control of property in Trust 2

shall be retained by or distributed to the surviving spouse.

2. Revocation

The surviving spouse may amend or revoke Trust 2 at any time during his or her lifetime, without

notifying any beneficiary.

3. Distribution of Property in Trust 2

Upon the death of the surviving spouse, Trust 2 becomes irrevocable, and the property in Trust 2 shall be

distributed to the beneficiaries listed in Section IV, subject to any provision of this Declaration of Trust that creates

children's trusts or creates custodianships under the Uniform Transfers to Minors Act.

VI. INCAPACITY

(A) Incapacity of Both Grantors

⑤Ⓐ If both grantors of The ① _____ Living

your names

Trust become physically or mentally incapacitated, as certified in writing by a licensed physician, the successor

trustee shall serve as trustee and manage The ① _____ Living Trust,

your names

and pay trust income at least annually to, or for the benefit of, the grantors and may also spend any amount of trust

principal necessary, in the successor trustee's discretion, for the needs of the grantors, until a licensed physician

certifies that the grantors, or either of them, are no longer incapacitated, or until their deaths.

⑥Ⓐ (B) Incapacity of Surviving Spouse

If, after the death of the deceased spouse, the surviving spouse becomes physically or mentally

incapacitated, as certified in writing by a licensed physician, the successor trustee shall manage Trust 2, and pay

trust income at least annually to, or for the benefit of, the surviving spouse and may also spend any amount of the

trust principal necessary in the successor trustee's discretion, for the needs of the surviving spouse, until a licensed

physician certifies that the surviving spouse is again able to manage his or her own affairs, or until his or her death.

VII. SIMULTANEOUS DEATH

If both grantors should die simultaneously, or under such circumstances as to render it difficult or

impossible to determine who predeceased the other, for purposes of this living trust, it shall be conclusively

presumed that both died at the same moment, and neither shall be presumed to have survived the other for

purposes of this living trust. The trustee shall distribute the trust property to the named beneficiaries.

VIII. TRUSTEE'S POWERS AND DUTIES

(A) Powers Under State Law

To carry out the provisions of this Declaration of Trust, and to manage the trust property of The

① _____ Living Trust, Trust 1, Trust 2 and any child's

your names

trust created under this Declaration of Trust, the trustee shall have all authority and power allowed or conferred

under _____ law, subject to the rights retained by each grantor in Section II (B)

your state

and to the trustee's fiduciary duty to the grantors and the beneficiaries.

(B) Specified Powers

The trustee's powers include, but are not limited to:

1. The power to sell trust property, and to borrow money and to encumber property, specifically including trust real estate, by mortgage, deed of trust or other method.

2. The power to manage trust real estate as if the trustee were the absolute owner of it, including the power to lease (even if the lease term may extend beyond the period of any trust) or grant options to lease the property, to make repairs or alterations and to insure against loss.

3. The power to sell or grant options for the sale or exchange of any trust property, including stocks, bonds, debentures and any other form of security or security account, at public or private sale for cash or on credit.

4. The power to invest trust property in property of any kind, including but not limited to bonds, debentures, notes, mortgages and stocks.

5. The power to receive additional property from any source and add to any trust created by this Declaration of Trust.

6. The power to employ and pay reasonable fees to accountants, lawyers or investment experts for information or advice relating to the trust.

7. The power to deposit and hold trust funds in both interest-bearing and non-interest-bearing accounts.

8. The power to deposit funds in bank or other accounts uninsured by FDIC coverage.

9. The power to enter into electronic fund transfer or safe deposit arrangements with financial institutions.

10. The power to continue any business of either grantor.

11. The power to institute or defend legal actions concerning the trust or grantor's affairs.

12. The power to execute any document necessary to administer any trust created in this Declaration of Trust.

13. The power to diversify investments, including authority to decide that some or all of the trust property need not produce income.

(C) Payment by the Trustee of the Grantors' Debts and Taxes

1. Wife's Debts and Taxes

_____'s debts and death taxes shall be paid
wife's name

by the trustee. The trustee shall pay these from the following trust property:

⑨_____

_____

_____.

2. Husband's Debts and Taxes

_____ _____'s debts and death taxes shall be paid

husband's name

by the trustee. The trustee shall pay these from the following trust property:

⑨_____

_____

_____.

3. If Specified Property Insufficient

If the property specified above is insufficient to pay all a grantor's debts and death taxes, the trustee shall

determine how such debts and death taxes shall be paid from that grantor's trust property.

IX. GENERAL ADMINISTRATIVE PROVISIONS

(A) Controlling Law

The validity of The ①_____ _____ Living Trust and

your names

construction of its provisions shall be governed by the laws of _____.

your state

(B) Severability

If any provision of this Declaration of Trust is ruled unenforceable, the remaining provisions shall

nevertheless remain in effect.

(C) Amendments

The term "Declaration of Trust" includes any provisions added by valid amendment.

(D) Accountings

No accountings or reports shall be required of the trustee.

X. CHILDREN'S TRUSTS

All trust property left to any of the minor or young adult beneficiaries listed below in Section X, Paragraph (A), shall be retained in trust for each such beneficiary in a separate trust of this

① _____ Living Trust. Each trust may be identified
                          your names

and referred to by adding the name of that trust's beneficiary to the name of this trust. The following terms apply to each children's trust:

(A) Trust Beneficiaries and Age Limits

A trust shall end when the beneficiary of that trust, listed below, becomes 35, except as otherwise specified in this section:

⑩ Trust for	Shall end at age
_____	_____
_____	_____
_____	_____
_____	_____
_____	_____

(B) Powers and Duties of Children's Trust Trustee

1. Until a child's trust ends, the trustee may distribute to or use for the benefit of the beneficiary as much of the net income or principal of the child's trust as the trustee deems necessary for the beneficiary's health, support, maintenance or education. Education includes, but is not limited to, college, graduate, postgraduate and vocational studies, and reasonably related living expenses.

2. In deciding whether to make a distribution to the beneficiary, the trustee may take into account the beneficiary's other income, resources and sources of support.

3. Any children's trust income that is not distributed to a beneficiary by the trustee shall be accumulated and added to the principal of the trust for that beneficiary.

4. The trustee of a child's trust is not required to make any accounting or report to the trust beneficiary.

(C) Assignment of Interest of Beneficiary Prohibited

The interests of the beneficiary of a child's trust shall not be transferable by voluntary or involuntary assignment or by operation of law before actual receipt by the beneficiary. These interests shall be free from the claims of creditors and from attachments, execution, bankruptcy or other legal process to the fullest extent permitted by law.

(D) Compensation of Trustee

Any trustee of a child's trust created under this Declaration of Trust shall be entitled to reasonable compensation without court approval out of the trust assets for ordinary and extraordinary services, and for all services in connection with the termination of any trust.

(E) Termination of Children's Trusts

A child's trust shall end when any of the following events occurs:

1. The beneficiary reaches the age specified in Section X, Paragraph (A). If the trust ends for this reason, the remaining principal and accumulated income of the trust shall be given outright to the beneficiary.

2. The beneficiary dies. If the trust ends for this reason, the trust property shall pass to the beneficiary's heirs.

3. The trustee distributes all trust property under the provisions of this Declaration of Trust.

XI. CUSTODIANSHIPS UNDER THE UNIFORM TRANSFERS TO MINORS ACT

1. All property ⑪_____ becomes entitled to
beneficiary

under this trust document shall be given to _____ as
custodian's name

custodian for _____ under the _____
beneficiary   state

Uniform Transfers to Minors Act, until _____ reaches age _____.
beneficiary

2. All property ⑪_____ becomes entitled to
beneficiary

under this trust document shall be given to _____ as
custodian's name

custodian for _____ under the _____
beneficiary   state

Uniform Transfers to Minors Act, until _____ reaches age _____.
beneficiary

3. All property ⑪_____ becomes entitled to
beneficiary

under this trust document shall be given to _____ as
custodian's name

custodian for _____ under the _____
beneficiary   state

Uniform Transfers to Minors Act, until _____ reaches age _____.
beneficiary

Certification by Grantors

We certify that we have read this Declaration of Trust and that it correctly states the terms and conditions

under which the trust property is to be held, managed and disposed of by the trustees and we approve the

Declaration of Trust.

Dated: _____

_____

Grantor and Trustee

_____

Grantor and Trustee

NOTARY'S ACKNOWLEDGMENT

State of _____

County of _____

On _____, 20_____, before me, _____,

a notary public in and for said state, personally appeared _____

_____, personally known to me (or proved to me on the basis of

satisfactory evidence) to be the persons whose names are subscribed to the within Declaration of Trust, and

acknowledged to me that they executed the same in their authorized capacities and that by their signatures on the

instrument they executed the Declaration of Trust.

_____
Signature of Notary   [SEAL]

SCHEDULE A ③

SHARED PROPERTY PLACED IN TRUST

SCHEDULE B

WIFE'S SEPARATE PROPERTY PLACED IN TRUST

All Wife's interest in the following property:

SCHEDULE C

HUSBAND'S SEPARATE PROPERTY PLACED IN TRUST

All Husband's interest in the following property:

Form 3: AB Living Trust

The ①_____ AB Living Trust.
your names (or name of trust, if different)

DECLARATION OF TRUST

I. TRUST NAME

This trust shall be known as The ①_____ _____
your names

Living Trust.

II. TRUST PROPERTY

(A) Property Placed in Trust

①_____ _____ _____, called the grantors or
your names

trustees, declare that they have set aside and hold in The ①_____
your names

Living Trust all their interest in the property described in the attached Schedules A, B and C.②

The trust property shall be used for the benefit of the trust beneficiaries and shall be administered and

distributed by the trustees in accordance with this Declaration of Trust.

(B) Rights Retained by Grantors

As long as both grantors are alive, both grantors retain all rights to all income, profits and control of the

trust property listed on Schedule A of The ①_____ Living Trust.
your names

(1) As long as _____ is alive, she shall retain all rights to all income,
wife's name

profits and control of her separate property listed on Schedule B of The

①_____ Living Trust.
your names

(2) As long as _____ is alive, he shall retain all rights to all income,
husband's name

profits and control of his separate property listed on Schedule C of The

①_____ Living Trust.
your names

(C) Additional or After-Acquired Property

Either grantor, or both, may add property to the trust at any time.

(D) Character of Property Placed in Trust

While both grantors are alive, property transferred to this trust shall retain its original character. If the trust is revoked, the trustee shall distribute the trust property to the grantors based on the same ownership rights they had before the property was transferred to the trust.

Specifically:

1. Shared Property

All trust property listed on Schedule A was shared property:

④ _____

identify the character of shared property listed in Schedule A

_____

_____

_____

_____.

2. Separate Property

The trust property listed on Schedule B shall retain its character as the separate property of

_____. The trust property listed on

wife's name

Schedule C shall retain its character as the separate property of _____.

husband's name

[Make appropriate deletions if wife and/or husband has no separate property.]

(E) Revocation

Except as provided in Section VII(A), for as long as both grantors live, either grantor may revoke The

① _____ Living Trust at any time

your names

by writing given to the other grantor. No beneficiary need be given any notice of revocation.

(F) Amendment

Except as provided in Section VII, Paragraph (A), for as long as both grantors live, The

① _____ Living Trust may be altered, amended or

your names

modified only by a writing signed by both grantors.

After the death of a spouse, the surviving spouse can amend his or her revocable living trust, Trust B, The Surviving Spouse's Trust, as defined in Section V Paragraph (A)3 and (B)3, and in Section VI.

(G) Homestead Rights

If the grantors' principal residence is transferred to the trust, grantors have the right to possess and occupy it for life, rent-free and without charge, except for taxes, insurance, maintenance and related costs and expenses. This right is intended to give grantors a beneficial interest in the property and to ensure that the grantors, or either of them, do not lose eligibility for a state homestead tax exemption for which either grantor otherwise qualifies.

III. TRUSTEES

(A) Original Trustees

The trustees of The ① _____
your names

Living Trust and any AB trust or other trust, including any children's trusts created under this Declaration of Trust shall be ① _____.
your names

Either trustee may act for, and represent, the trust, in any transaction.

(B) Trustee on Death or Incapacity of Original Trustee

Upon the death or incapacity, as certified in writing by a licensed physician, of

_____ or _____ ,
wife's name   husband's name

the other spouse shall serve as sole trustee of this trust and all trusts and any child's trusts created under this Declaration of Trust.

(C) Trustee's Responsibility

The trustee in office shall serve as trustee of this trust and all trusts and any child's trusts created under this Declaration of Trust.

(D) Terminology

In this Declaration of Trust, the term "trustee" includes any successor trustee or trustees. The singular "trustee" also includes the plural.

(E) Successor Trustee

⑤Ⓐ Upon the death or incapacity of the surviving spouse, or the incapacity of both spouses, the successor trustee shall be ⑥ _____ . If _____

name(s)   he/she/all of them

is/are unable to serve or to continue serving as successor trustee, the next successor trustee shall be
⑥ _____ .

name

[If you named more than one successor trustee, include ONE of the following two paragraphs here:]

Any of the successor trustees has full and independent authority to act for and represent the trust.

[or]

All of the successor trustees must consent, in writing, to any transaction involving the trust or trust property.

(F) Resignation of Trustee

Any trustee in office may resign at any time by signing a notice of resignation. The resignation must be delivered to the person or institution who is either named in this Declaration of Trust, or appointed by the trustee under Section III, Paragraph (G), to next serve as the trustee.

(G) Power to Appoint Successor Trustee

If all the successor trustees named in this Declaration of Trust cease to, or are unable to, serve as trustee, the last acting trustee may appoint an additional successor trustee or trustees to serve in the order nominated. The appointment must be made in writing, signed by the trustee, and notarized.

(H) Bond Waived

No bond shall be required of any trustee.

(I) Compensation

No trustee shall receive any compensation for serving as trustee, except that a trustee shall be entitled to reasonable compensation, as determined by the trustee, for serving as a trustee of Trust A, or a child's trust created by this Declaration of Trust, for serving as trustee because the grantors or a grantor has become incapacitated.

(J) Liability of Trustee

With respect to the exercise or non-exercise of discretionary powers granted by this Declaration of Trust, the trustee shall not be liable for actions taken in good faith.

IV. BENEFICIARIES

(A) Wife's Specific and Alternate Beneficiaries

Upon the death of _____, trust property
wife's name

owned by _____, as her share of the trust property
wife's name

listed on Schedule A and any separate property listed on Schedule B shall be distributed as specified to the

beneficiaries named in this section.

⑦1. _____ shall be given
beneficiary's name(s)

_____.
property identified

If _____ does not survive _____,
beneficiary   wife's name

that property shall be given to _____ .
alternate beneficiary

⑦2. _____ shall be given
beneficiary's name(s)

_____.
property identified

If _____ does not survive _____,
beneficiary   wife's name

that property shall be given to _____ .
alternate beneficiary

⑦3. _____ shall be given
beneficiary's name(s)

_____.
property identified

If _____ does not survive _____,
beneficiary   wife's name

that property shall be given to _____ .
alternate beneficiary

(B) Husband's Specific and Alternate Beneficiaries

Upon the death of _____, trust property owned by
husband's name

_____, as his share of the trust property listed on Schedule A and
husband's name

any separate property listed on Schedule C shall be distributed as specified to the beneficiaries named in this

section.

⑦1. _____ shall be given
                    beneficiary's name(s)

_____ .
                                property identified

If _____ does not survive _____ ,
              beneficiary   husband's name

that property shall be given to _____ .
                                        alternate beneficiary

⑦2. _____ shall be given
                    beneficiary's name(s)

_____ .
                                property identified

If _____ does not survive _____ ,
              beneficiary   husband's name

that property shall be given to _____ .
                                        alternate beneficiary

⑦3. _____ shall be given
                    beneficiary's name(s)

_____ .
                                property identified

If _____ does not survive _____ ,
              beneficiary   husband's name

that property shall be given to _____ .
                                        alternate beneficiary

(C) Remaining Trust Property

Except as provided by Section IV, Paragraph (A) or (B), all other trust property of the deceased spouse

shall be transferred to, and administered as part of, Trust A, defined in Section V.

V. CREATION OF TRUST A ON DEATH OF DECEASED SPOUSE

(A) Terminology

1. The first grantor to die shall be called the "deceased spouse." The living grantor shall then be called the

"surviving spouse."

2. The "trust property of the deceased spouse" shall consist of all property of The

① _____ Living Trust individually owned by the
                              your names

deceased spouse at the time it was transferred to the trustee, plus shared ownership porperty with a total value equal

to one-half of the total value at the time of the deceased spouse's death of the shared ownership trust property, plus

accumulated income, appreciation in value and the like, attributable to the ownership interest of the deceased

spouse, and his or her share of all property acquired in the trust's name or the trustees' names.

3. The "trust property of the surviving spouse" shall consist of all property of The

① _____ Living Trust individually owned by the surviving
your names

spouse at the time it was transferred to the trustee, plus shared ownership property with a total value equal to one-

half of the total value at the time of the deceased spouse's death of the shared ownership trust property, plus

accumulated income, appreciation in value and the like, attributable to the ownership interest of the surviving

spouse, and his or her share of all property acquired in the trust's name or the trustees' names.

(B) Division of Trust Property on Death of Deceased Spouse

1. Upon the death of the deceased spouse, the trustee shall divide the property of The

① _____ Living Trust listed on Schedules A, B and C
your names

into two separate trusts, Trust A and Trust B.

2. All trust assets of the deceased spouse, as defined in Section V, Paragraph (A)2, shall be placed in a

trust known as Trust A, after making any specific gifts provided for in Section IV, Paragraph (A) or (B), subject to

any provision in this Declaration of Trust that creates childrens' trusts or creates custodianship under the Uniform

Transfers to Minors Act.

3. The trustee shall place all trust assets of the surviving spouse, as defined in Section V, Paragraph (A)3,

in a trust known as Trust B (The Surviving Spouse's Trust).

4. Physical segregation of the assets of The ① _____
your names

Living Trust is not required to divide that trust's property into Trust A and Trust B. The trustee shall exclusively

determine what records, documents and actions are required to establish and maintain Trust A and Trust B.

(C) Administration of Trust A

All property held in Trust A shall be administered as follows:

1. Upon the death of the deceased spouse, Trust A shall be irrevocable.

2. The life beneficiary of Trust A shall be the surviving spouse.

3. If _____ is the deceased spouse, the final
wife's name

beneficiaries of Trust A shall be:

⑧B _____

_____

_____

If _____ is the deceased spouse, the alternate final beneficiaries of
                wife's name

Trust A shall be:

(8B) _____

_____

_____

_____ : _____

4. If _____ is the deceased spouse, the final beneficiaries
                husband's name

of Trust A shall be:

(8B) _____

_____

_____

_____

If _____ is the deceased spouse, the alternate final beneficiaries of
                husband's name

Trust A shall be:

(8B) _____

_____

_____

_____

5. After the deceased spouse's death, the trustee shall pay to or spend for the benefit of the surviving

spouse the net income of Trust A at least quarterly. The trustee shall also pay to or spend for the benefit of the

surviving spouse any sums from the principal of Trust A necessary for the surviving spouse's health, education,

support and maintenance, in accord with his or her accustomed manner of living.

6. (12) No accounting of Trust A shall be required of the trustee, except that the final beneficiaries shall be

provided with copies of the annual federal income tax return.

7. The trustee shall be entitled to reasonable compensation from assets of Trust A for services rendered

managing Trust A, without court approval.

8. Upon the death of the life beneficiary, the trustee shall distribute the property of Trust A to the final or

alternate final beneficiary or beneficiaries, as named in Section V, Paragraph C(3) or C(4).

VI. TRUST B: THE SURVIVING SPOUSE'S TRUST

(A) Creation of Trust B, The Surviving Spouse's Trust

Upon the death of the deceased spouse, all trust property owned by the surviving spouse, as defined in Section V, Paragraph (A)3, shall be held in Trust B, The Surviving Spouse's Trust.

(B) Administration of Trust B

Until the death of the surviving spouse, the surviving spouse retains all rights to all income, profits and control of the property in Trust B. The surviving spouse may amend or revoke Trust B at any time during his or her lifetime, without notifying any beneficiary.

(C) Distribution of Property in Trust B

1. Upon the death of the surviving spouse, Trust B becomes irrevocable.

2. The trustee shall first distribute any specific gifts of the surviving spouse to the beneficiaries named in Section IV, Paragraph (A) or (B). The trustee shall then distribute all remaining property of Trust B to his or her final, or alternate final, beneficiaries, as named in Section V, Paragraph (C)3 or (C)4.

3. All distributions under Section VI, Paragraph (C), are subject to any provision in this Declaration of Trust that creates children's trusts or creates custodianships under the Uniform Transfers to Minors Act.

VII. INCAPACITY

(A) Incapacity of Grantors

5A If both grantors of The ① _____

your names

Living Trust become physically or mentally incapacitated, as certified in writing by a licensed physician, the successor trustee shall serve as trustee and shall manage The ① _____

your names

Living Trust, and pay trust income at least annually to, or for the benefit of, the grantors and may also spend any amount of trust principal necessary, in the successor trustee's discretion, for the needs of the grantors, until a licensed physician certifies that the grantors or either of them are no longer incapacitated or until their deaths.

5B (B) Amending AB Trust If Estate Tax Law Changes

Not withstanding any other provision of this trust, if both grantors are alive and one is incapacitated, and Congress changes the estate tax law, the competent spouse shall have authority to amend this AB trust in order to take best advantage of the new tax law. If both grantors are alive and both are incapacitated, and Congress changes the estate tax law, the successor trustee shall have authority to amend this AB trust in order to take best advantage of the new tax law.

(5A) **(C) Incapacity of Surviving Spouse**

If, after the death of the deceased spouse, the surviving spouse becomes physically or mentally incapacitated, as certified in writing by a licensed physician, the successor trustee shall:

1. Manage Trust B and pay trust income at least annually to, or for the benefit of, the surviving spouse, and spend any amount of that trust's principal necessary in the successor trustee's discretion, for the needs of the surviving spouse, until a licensed physician certifies that the surviving spouse is no longer incapacitated, or until his or her death.

Any income not spent for the benefit of the surviving spouse shall be accumulated and added to the property of Trust B.

2. Manage Trust A, under the terms of this Declaration of Trust, until a licensed physician certifies that the surviving spouse is again able to manage his or her own affairs and is able to serve as trustee of that trust, or until the death of the surviving spouse.

3. Manage any operational child's trust created by their Declaration of Trust.

The successor trustee shall continue to serve as trustee unless the surviving spouse is no longer incapacitated.

VIII. SIMULTANEOUS DEATH

If both grantors should die simultaneously, or under such circumstances as to render it difficult or impossible to determine who predeceased the other, for the purposes of this living trust it shall be conclusively presumed that both died at the same moment, and neither shall be presumed to have survived the other. The trustee shall make any specific gifts left by either spouse, and then distribute all remaining property to each spouse's final beneficiaries.

IX. TRUSTEE'S POWERS AND DUTIES

(A) Powers Under State Law

To carry out the provisions of this Declaration of Trust and to manage the trust property of The

① _____ Living Trust, Trust A and Trust B,
　　　　　　　　　　　　your names

and any child's trust created under this Declaration of Trust, the trustee shall have all authority and power allowed or conferred under _____ law, subject to the rights retained by each grantor in
　　　　　　　　　　　　　your state

Section II (B) and to the trustee's fiduciary duty to the grantors and the beneficiaries.

(B) Specified Powers

The trustee's powers include, but are not limited to:

1. The power to sell trust property, and to borrow money and to encumber property, specifically including trust real estate, by mortgage, deed of trust or other method.

2. The power to manage trust real estate as if the trustee were the absolute owner of it, including the power to lease (even if the lease term may extend beyond the period of any trust) or grant options to lease the property, to make repairs or alterations and to insure against loss.

3. The power to sell or grant options for the sale or exchange of any trust property, including stocks, bonds, debentures and any other form of security or security account, at public or private sale for cash or on credit.

4. The power to invest trust property in property of any kind, including but not limited to bonds, debentures, notes, mortgages and stocks.

5. The power to receive additional property from any source and add to any trust created by this Declaration of Trust.

6. The power to employ and pay reasonable fees to accountants, lawyers or investment experts for information or advice relating to the trust.

7. The power to deposit and hold trust funds in both interest-bearing and non-interest-bearing accounts.

8. The power to deposit funds in bank or other accounts uninsured by FDIC coverage.

9. The power to enter into electronic fund transfer or safe deposit arrangements with financial institutions.

10. The power to continue any business of either grantor.

11. The power to institute or defend legal actions concerning the trust or the grantors' affairs.

12. The power to execute any documents necessary to administer any trust created in this Declaration of Trust.

13. The power to diversify investments, including authority to decide that some or all of the trust property need not produce income.

(C) Payment by the Trustee of the Grantors' Debts and Taxes

1. Wife's Debts and Taxes

_____'s debts and death taxes shall be paid
wife's name
by the trustee. The trustee shall pay these from the following trust property: ⑨_____

_____

_____.

2. Husband's Debts and Taxes

_____'s debts and death taxes shall be paid

husband's name

by the trustee. The trustee shall pay these from the following trust property: ⑨_____

_____

_____.

3. If Specified Property Insufficient

If the property specified above is insufficient to pay all a grantor's debts and death taxes, the trustee shall

determine how such debts and death taxes shall be paid from that grantor's trust property, except as limited by any

law or IRS regulation controlling the property in Trust A.

X. GENERAL ADMINISTRATIVE PROVISIONS

(A) Controlling Law

The validity of The ①_____ Living Trust and

your names

construction of its provisions shall be governed by the laws of _____.

your state

(B) Severability

If any provision of this Declaration of Trust is ruled unenforceable, the remaining provisions shall

nevertheless remain in effect.

(C) Amendments

The term "Declaration of Trust" includes any provisions added by valid amendment.

XI. CHILDREN'S TRUSTS

All trust property left to any of the minor or young adult beneficiaries listed below in Section XI,

Paragraph (A), shall be retained in trust for each such beneficiary in a separate trust of this

①_____ Living Trust.

your names

Each trust may be identified and referred to by adding the name of that trust's beneficiary to the name of this

trust. The following terms apply to each children's trust:

(A) Trust Beneficiaries and Age Limits

A trust shall end when the beneficiary of that trust, listed below, becomes 35, except as otherwise specified in this section:

⑩ Trust for   Shall end at age

_____   _____

_____   _____

_____   _____

_____   _____

_____   _____

(B) Powers and Duties of Children's Trust Trustee

1. Until a child's trust ends, the trustee may distribute to or use for the benefit of the beneficiary as much of the net income or principal of the child's trust as the trustee deems necessary for the beneficiary's health, support, maintenance or education. Education includes, but is not limited to, college, graduate, postgraduate and vocational studies, and reasonably related living expenses.

2. In deciding whether to make a distribution to the beneficiary, the trustee may take into account the beneficiary's other income, resources and sources of support.

3. Any child's trust income that is not distributed to a beneficiary by the trustee shall be accumulated and added to the principal of the trust for that beneficiary.

4. The trustee of a child's trust is not required to make any accounting or report to the trust beneficiary.

(C) Assignment of Interest of Beneficiary Prohibited

The interests of the beneficiary of a child's trust shall not be transferable by voluntary or involuntary assignment or by operation of law before actual receipt by the beneficiary. These interests shall be free from the claims of creditors and from attachments, execution, bankruptcy or other legal process to the fullest extent permitted by law.

(D) Compensation of Trustee

Any trustee of a child's trust created under this Declaration of Trust shall be entitled to reasonable compensation without court approval out of the trust assets for ordinary and extraordinary services, and for all services in connection with the termination of any trust.

(E) Termination of Children's Trusts

A child's trust shall end when any of the following events occurs:

1. The beneficiary reaches the age specified in Section XI, Paragraph (A). If the trust ends for this reason, the remaining principal and accumulated income of the trust shall be given outright to the beneficiary.

2. The beneficiary dies. If the trust ends for this reason, the trust property shall pass to the beneficiary's heirs.

3. The trustee distributes all trust property under the provisions of this Declaration of Trust.

XII. CUSTODIANSHIPS UNDER THE UNIFORM TRANSFERS TO MINORS ACT

1. All property ⑪_____ becomes entitled to
beneficiary

under this trust document shall be given to _____ as
custodian's name

custodian for _____ under the _____
beneficiary   state

Uniform Transfers to Minors Act, until _____ reaches age _____.
beneficiary

2. All property ⑪_____ becomes entitled to
beneficiary

under this trust document shall be given to _____ as
custodian's name

custodian for _____ under the _____
beneficiary   state

Uniform Transfers to Minors Act, until _____ reaches age _____.
beneficiary

3. All property ⑪_____ becomes entitled to
beneficiary

under this trust document shall be given to _____ as
custodian's name

custodian for _____ under the _____
beneficiary   state

Uniform Transfers to Minors Act, until _____ reaches age _____.
beneficiary

Certification by Grantors

We certify that we have read this Declaration of Trust and that it correctly states the terms and conditions under which the trust property is to be held, managed and disposed of by the trustees and we approve the Declaration of Trust.

Dated: _____

_____
Grantor and Trustee

_____
Grantor and Trustee

NOTARY'S ACKNOWLEDGMENT

State of _____

County of _____

On _____, 20_____, before me, _____,

a notary public in and for said state, personally appeared _____

_____, personally known to me (or proved to me on the basis of

satisfactory evidence) to be the persons whose names are subscribed to the within Declaration of Trust, and

acknowledged to me that they executed the same in their authorized capacities and that by their signatures on the

instrument they executed the Declaration of Trust.

_____

Signature of Notary   [SEAL]

SCHEDULE A ③

SHARED PROPERTY PLACED IN TRUST

SCHEDULE B

WIFE'S SEPARATE PROPERTY PLACED IN TRUST

All Wife's interest in the following property:

SCHEDULE C

HUSBAND'S SEPARATE PROPERTY PLACED IN TRUST

All Husband's interest in the following property:

Form 4: Witness Statement for a Florida Living Trust

STATEMENT OF WITNESS

On this _____ day of _____, 20___ ,

_____ declared to me, the undersigned, that this

your name(s)

Declaration of Trust was _____ living trust and requested me to act as witness to it.

his/her/their

_____ then signed this living trust in my presence. I now

your name(s)

at _____ request, in _____ presence, subscribe my name as witness and declare I understand this

his/her/their _his/her/their_

to be _____ living trust.

his/her/their

I declare under penalty of perjury that the foregoing is true and correct, this _____ day of

_____, 20_____.

_____
witness's signature

_____
witness's typed name

_____, _____, _____
city   county   state

Form 5: Assignment of Property to a Trust for One Person

ASSIGNMENT OF PROPERTY

I, _____ _____, as grantor, hereby assign and transfer all my
                            your name

rights, title and interest in the following property   _____

_____

_____ to

_____, as trustee of the _____
            your name   your name

Living Trust, dated _____, 20____.

Executed at _____, _____, on
                   city   state

_____, 20 ____.
       date

_____

Grantor and Trustee

Form 6: Assignment of Shared Property to a Trust for a Couple

ASSIGNMENT OF PROPERTY

We, _____,
your names

as grantors, hereby assign and transfer all our rights, title and interest in the following property

_____

_____

_____ to

_____, as trustees of
your names

The _____ Living Trust,
your names

dated _____, 20_____.

Executed at _____, _____, on
city   state

_____, 20_____.
date

_____
Grantor and Trustee

_____
Grantor and Trustee

AMENDMENT TO LIVING TRUST

This Amendment to The ① _____ Living Trust

your name

dated _____, 20_____, is made this _____ day of _____, 20_____,

date Declaration of Trust signed

by _____, the grantor and trustee of the trust. Under the

your name

power of amendment reserved to the grantor by Section III, Paragraph (A), of the trust, the grantor amends the

trust as follows:

1. The following is added to the Declaration of Trust:

_____

_____

2. The following is deleted from the Declaration of Trust:

_____

_____

[Repeat as needed]

In all other respects, the Declaration of Trust as executed on _____, 20_____,

by the grantor is hereby affirmed.

Executed at _____, _____, on

city   state

_____, 20_____.

date

_____

Grantor and Trustee

NOLO
www.nolo.com
Amendment to Living Trust for One Person
Page 1 of 2

NOTARY'S ACKNOWLEDGMENT

State of _____

County of _____

      On _____, 20_____, before me, _____,

a notary public in and for said state, personally appeared _____,

personally known to me (or proved to me on the basis of satisfactory evidence) to be the person whose name is

subscribed to the within Amendment to Living Trust, and acknowledged to me that he/she executed the same in

his/her authorized capacity and that by his/her signature on the instrument he/she executed the Amendment to

Living Trust.

_____
Signature of Notary   [SEAL]

Form 8: Amendment to Basic Shared Living Trust or AB Trust

AMENDMENT TO LIVING TRUST

This Amendment to The ① _____ Living Trust

                                                          your names

dated _____, 20____, is made this _____ day of _____, 20_____,

        date Declaration of Trust signed

by _____,

                                      your names

the grantors and trustees of the trust. Under the power of amendment reserved to the grantors by Section II,

Paragraph (F), of the Declaration of Trust, the grantors amend the trust as follows:

    1. The following is added to the Declaration of Trust:

_____

_____

    2. The following is deleted from the Declaration of Trust:

_____

_____

    [Repeat as needed]

    In all other respects, the Declaration of Trust as executed on _____, 20_____,

by the grantors is hereby affirmed.

    Executed at _____, _____, on

                    city   state

_____, 20_____.

        date

_____

Grantor and Trustee

_____

Grantor and Trustee

NOTARY'S ACKNOWLEDGMENT

State of _____

County of _____

On _____, 20_____, before me, _____,

a notary public in and for said state, personally appeared _____

_____, personally known to me (or proved to me on the basis of

satisfactory evidence) to be the persons whose names are subscribed to the within Amendment to Living Trust, and

acknowledged to me that they executed the same in their authorized capacities and that by their signatures on the

instrument they executed the Amendment to Living Trust.

_____
Signature of Notary   [SEAL]

Form 9: Revocation

REVOCATION OF LIVING TRUST

On _____ , 20 ____ , _____ created

your name(s)

a revocable living trust, called "The _____

your name(s)

Living Trust," with _____ as the grantor(s) and

your name(s)

trustee(s). Under the terms of the trust, the grantor(s) reserved to _____ the full

himself/herself/themselves

power to revoke the trust.

    According to the terms of the Declaration of Trust, and the laws of the State of _____ ,

your state

the grantor(s) hereby revoke the Declaration of Trust and state that the trust is completely revoked. All property of

The _____ Living Trust shall be returned to the grantor(s)

your name(s)

and legally owned by _____ as defined in the Declaration of Trust.

him/her/them

Dated: _____

_____
Grantor & Trustee

_____
Grantor & Trustee

Notary's Acknowledgment

State of _____

County of _____

    On _____ , 20 _____ , before me, _____ ,

a notary public in and for said state, personally appeared _____

_____ , personally known to me (or proved to me on the basis of

satisfactory evidence) to be the person(s) whose name(s) is/are subscribed to the within Revocation of Living Trust,

and acknowledged to me that he/she/they executed the same in his/her/their authorized capacity(ies) and that by

his/her/their signature(s) on the instrument the person(s), or the entity upon behalf of which the person(s) acted,

executed this Revocation of Living Trust.

_____
Signature of Notary   [SEAL]

WILL

of

_____

your name

I, _____, a resident of

your name

_____, _____ County, _____,

city   county   state

declare that this is my will.

    1. I revoke all wills and codicils that I have previously made.

    2. I am not married.

    3. (A) I am the _____ of the _____ whose _____ _____

mother/father   child/children   name(s)   is/are

_____

_____

_____

_____

_____.

    There are ___ living children of my deceased child _____,

name

whose names are:

_____

_____

_____.

    (B) If I fail to leave, by this will or otherwise, any property to any of the children listed above, my failure to do so is intentional.

    (C) If at my death any of my children are minors, and a personal guardian is needed, I nominate

_____ to be appointed personal guardian

name

of my minor children. If _____ cannot serve as

name

personal guardian, I nominate _____ to be appointed

name

personal guardian.

(D) If at my death any of my children are minors, and a property guardian is needed,

I appoint _____ as property guardian for my minor children.
name

If _____ cannot serve as property guardian, I appoint
name

_____ as property guardian.
name

(E) I direct that no bond be required of any guardian.

4. (A) I make the following specific gifts:

I leave _____
property described

to _____, or if _____
beneficiary's name beneficiary's name

fails to survive me, to _____.
alternate beneficiary's name

I leave _____
property described

to _____, or if _____
beneficiary's name beneficiary's name

fails to survive me, to _____.
alternate beneficiary's name

I leave _____
property described

to _____, or if _____
beneficiary's name beneficiary's name

fails to survive me, to _____.
alternate beneficiary's name

(B) I leave all my other property subject to this will to

_____, or if _____ fails to
residuary beneficiary's name he/she

survive me, to _____.
alternate residuary beneficiary's name

5. (A) I nominate _____ to serve as executor of my will.
executor's name

If _____ is unable to serve or continue serving as executor, I nominate
he/she

_____ to serve as executor.
alternate executor's name

(B) No bond shall be required of any executor.

I subscribe my name to this will this _____ day of _____, 20____, at

_____, _____, _____.
city county state

_____
your signature

WITNESSES

On the date last written above, _____ _____ declared to us, the
your name

undersigned, that this was _____ will, and requested us to act as witnesses to it. _____ then
his/her He/She

signed this will in our presence, all of us being present at the same time. We now at _____ request
his/her

and in _____ presence, and in the presence of each other, have signed this will as witnesses.
his/her

We declare under penalty of perjury that the foregoing is true and correct.

_____
witness signature

_____
witness printed name

_____, _____, _____
city   county   state

_____
witness signature

_____
witness printed name

_____, _____, _____
city   county   state

_____
witness signature

_____
witness printed name

_____, _____, _____
city   county   state

Form 11: Basic Will for a Member of a Couple

WILL

of

_____
your name

I, _____, a resident of
your name

_____, _____ County, _____,
city   county   state

declare that this is my will.

1. I revoke all wills and codicils that I have previously made.

2. I am married to _____.
name

3. (A) I am the _____ of the _____ whose _____ _____
mother/father   child/children   name(s)   is/are

_____

_____

_____

_____
                                                                                          .

There are ___ living children of my deceased child _____,
name

whose names are:

_____

_____

_____
                                                                                          .

(B) If I fail to leave, by this will or otherwise, any property to any of the children listed above, my failure to do so is intentional.

(C) If at my death any of my children are minors, and a personal guardian is needed, I nominate

_____ to be appointed personal guardian
name

of my minor children. If _____ cannot serve as
name

personal guardian, I nominate _____ to be appointed

name

personal guardian.

      (D) If at my death any of my children are minors, and a property guardian is needed,

I appoint _____ as property guardian for my minor children.

name

If _____ cannot serve as property guardian, I appoint

name

_____ as property guardian.

name

      (E) I direct that no bond be required of any guardian.

    4. (A) I make the following specific gifts:

      I leave _____

property described

to _____, or if _____

beneficiary's name   beneficiary's name

fails to survive me, to _____.

alternate beneficiary's name

      I leave _____

property described

to _____, or if _____

beneficiary's name   beneficiary's name

fails to survive me, to _____.

alternate beneficiary's name

      I leave _____

property described

to _____, or if _____

beneficiary's name   beneficiary's name

fails to survive me, to _____.

alternate beneficiary's name

      (B) I leave all my other property subject to this will to

_____, or if _____ fails to

residuary beneficiary's name   he/she

survive me, to _____.

alternate residuary beneficiary's name

    5. (A) I nominate _____ to serve as executor of my will.

executor's name

If _____ is unable to serve or continue serving as executor, I nominate

he/she

_____ to serve as executor.

alternate executor's name

      (B) No bond shall be required of any executor.

6. If my spouse and I should die simultaneously, or under such circumstances as to render it difficult or impossible to determine who predeceased the other, I shall be conclusively presumed to have survived my spouse for purposes of this will.

I subscribe my name to this will this _____ _____ day of _____, 20____, at

_____, _____, _____.
     city   county   state

       _____
       your signature

WITNESSES

On the date last written above, _____ declared to us, the
                your name

undersigned, that this was _____ will, and requested us to act as witnesses to it. _____ then
        his/her   He/She

signed this will in our presence, all of us being present at the same time. We now at _____ request and
                          his/her

presence, and in the presence of each other, have signed this will as witnesses.

We declare under penalty of perjury that the foregoing is true and correct.

_____
witness signature

_____
witness printed name

_____, _____, _____
city   county   state

_____
witness signature

_____
witness printed name

_____, _____, _____
city   county   state

_____
witness signature

_____
witness printed name

_____, _____, _____
city   county   state

Form 12: Affidavit of Successor Trustee

AFFIDAVIT OF ASSUMPTION OF DUTIES BY SUCCESSOR TRUSTEE

State of _____, County of _____.
                               state   county of successor trustee

_____, of legal age, first being duly sworn, declares:
             successor trustee's name

On _____, 20_____, _____ created
            date   name(s) of grantor(s)

The _____ Living Trust.
                name(s) of grantor(s)

On _____, 20_____, _____ died, as
            date   grantor's name

established in the attached certified copy of the Certificate of Death.

[for a shared or AB trust, add:]

On _____, 20_____, _____ died, as
            date   second grantor's name

established in the attached certified copy of the Certificate of Death.

The Declaration of Trust creating The _____ Living Trust
                                       name(s) of grantor(s)

provides that upon the death of the grantors, I, _____,
                                     successor trustee's name

become the trustee of the trust.

I hereby accept the office of trustee of the trust, and am now acting as trustee of the trust.

Dated: _____

_____
Successor Trustee

ances by one spouse, and, in some community property states, income from property owned by one spouse prior to marriage. Spouses can, however, enter into an agreement to the contrary.

A surviving spouse automatically owns one-half of all community property. The other spouse has no legal power to affect this.

Conservator. Someone appointed by a court to manage the affairs of a mentally incompetent person. In some states, this person is called a guardian.

Creditor. A person or institution to whom money is owed. A creditor may be the person who actually lent the money, or a lawyer or bill collector who is trying to collect the money for the original creditor.

Curtesy. *See* **dower and curtesy.**

Custodian. A person named to care for property left to a minor under the Uniform Transfers to Minors Act. The custodian manages the property until the minor reaches the age at which state law says she must receive it. (In some states, the giver can specify, within limits, at what age the custodianship will end.)

The custodian has essentially the same powers as a child's trust trustee and may use the property for the minor's health, education, and support. The custodian's authority and duties are clearly set out by state law (the Uniform Transfers to Minors Act). No court supervises the custodian.

Death taxes. Taxes levied on the property of a person who died. Federal death taxes are called estate taxes. State death taxes (if any) go by various names, including inheritance tax.

Debtor. A person who owes money.

Deceased spouse. With a shared living trust created by both spouses, the first spouse to die.

Decedent. A person who has died.

Deed. The legal document by which one person (or persons) transfers title (recorded ownership) to real estate.

Disclaimer trust. A trust where a beneficiary has the specific right to disclaim all or any portion of a gift left to him or her, so the gift goes to whomever is next entitled to receive it.

Domicile. The state, or country, where one has his or her primary home.

Donee. Someone who receives a gift.

Donor. Someone who gives a gift.

Dower and curtesy. The right of a widow or widower to receive or enjoy the use of a set portion of the deceased spouse's property (usually one-third to one-half) if the surviving spouse is not left at least that share. Dower refers to the title that a surviving wife gets, while curtesy refers to what a man receives. Until recently, these amounts differed in a number of states. However, states generally provide the same benefits regardless of sex.

Durable power of attorney. A power of attorney that remains effective even if the person who created it (called the "principal") becomes incapacitated. The person authorized to act (called the "attorney-in-fact" or "agent") can make health care decisions or handle financial affairs of the principal, depending on the authority granted by the document.

Estate. Generally, all the property you own when you die. There are different kinds of estates: the taxable estate (property subject to estate taxation), the probate estate (property that must go through probate), or the net estate (the net value of the property).

Estate planning. Figuring out how to prosper when you're alive, die with the smallest taxable estate and probate estate possible and pass property to loved ones with a minimum of fuss and expense.

Estate taxes. Taxes imposed on property as it passes from the dead to the living. The federal government exempts a set amount of property, depending on the year of death. Also exempt is all property left to a surviving spouse who is a U.S. citizen. Taxes are imposed only on property actually owned at the time of death. So techniques designed to reduce taxes usually concentrate on the legal transfer of ownership of property while you are living, to minimize the amount of property owned at death.

Executor. The person named in a will to manage the deceased person's estate, deal with the probate court, collect assets, and distribute them as the will specifies. In some states this person is called the "personal representative." If someone dies without a will, the probate court will appoint such a person, who is called the administrator of the estate.

Exemption trust. *See* **AB trust.**

Final beneficiary. The person(s) or institution(s) who receive the property in a marital life estate trust, after the life beneficiary of that trust dies.

Financial guardian. *See* **property guardian.**

Funding a trust. Transferring ownership of property to a trust, in the name of the trustee.

Generation-skipping trust. An estate tax-saving trust, where the principal is left in trust for one's grandchildren, with one's children receiving only the trust income.

Gift. Any property given to another person or organization, either during the giver's lifetime, or by will or living trust after his or her death.

Gift tax. Tax on gifts made during a person's lifetime. Many gifts are exempt from tax: gifts to tax-exempt charities or the giver's spouse (if the recipient spouse is a U.S. citizen) and, currently, gifts of $11,000 or less to any one recipient in a calendar year.

Grantor. The person or persons who create a trust. Also called the "trustor," "settlor," or "creator."

Heirs. Persons who are entitled by state intestate law to inherit a deceased person's property if that person didn't make arrangements for what should happen to the property at his or her death.

Inherit. To receive property from one who dies.

Inheritance taxes. Taxes some states impose on property received by inheritors from a deceased's estate.

Inheritors. Persons or organizations who inherit property.

Instrument. Legalese for document; sometimes used to refer to the document that creates a living trust.

Inter vivos trust. Same as **living trust.** ("Inter vivos" is Latin for "between the living.")

Intestate. Someone who dies without a will or other valid estate transfer device dies "intestate."

Intestate succession. The method by which property is distributed when a person fails to distribute it in a will or other estate transfer device. In such cases, the law of each state provides that the property be distributed in certain shares to the closest surviving relatives. In most states, these are a surviving spouse, children, parents, siblings, nieces and nephews, and next of kin, in that order. The intestate succession laws are also used in the event an heir is found to be pretermitted (not mentioned or otherwise provided for in the will).

Irrevocable trust. Means what it says. Once you create it, that's it. A trust that cannot be revoked by the person who created it once it's created. Unlike a revocable, probate-avoidance trust, it can't be amended or changed in any way.

Joint tenancy. A way to own jointly owned real or personal property. When two or more people own property as joint tenants, and one of the owners dies, the other owners automatically become owners of the deceased owner's share. Thus, if a parent and child own a house as joint tenants, and the parent dies, the child automatically becomes full owner. Because of this "right of survivorship," a joint tenancy interest in property does not go through probate, or, put another way, is not part of the probate estate. Instead it goes directly to the surviving joint tenant(s).

Liquid assets. Cash or assets that can readily be turned into cash.

Living trust. A trust set up while a person is alive and which remains under the control of that person until death. Also referred to as "inter vivos trust." Living trusts are an excellent way to minimize the value of property passing through probate. This is because they enable people (called "grantors") to specify that money or other property will pass directly to their beneficiaries after their death, free of probate, and yet allow the grantors to continue to control the property during their lifetime and even end the trust or change the beneficiaries if they wish.

Living trust with marital life estate. *See* **AB trust.**

Living will. A document, directed to physicians, in which you state that you do not want to have your life artificially prolonged by technological means.

Marital deduction. A deduction allowed by the federal estate tax law for all property passed to a surviving spouse who is a U.S. citizen. This deduction (which really acts like an exemption) allows anyone, even a billionaire, to pass his or her entire estate to a surviving spouse without any tax at all. Tax problems, however, are usually made worse by relying exclusively on the marital deduction.

Marriage. A specific status conferred on a couple by the state. In most states, it is necessary to file papers with a county clerk and have a marriage ceremony conducted by an authorized individual to be married.

In some states, however, couples may be considered married without a ceremony in certain circumstances. *See* **common law marriage.**

Minor. In most states, persons under 18 years of age. All minors must be under the care of a competent adult (parent or guardian) unless they are "emancipated"—in the military, married or living independently with court permission. Property left to a minor must be handled by an adult until the minor becomes an adult under the laws of the state.

Mortgage. A document that makes a piece of real estate the security (collateral) for the payment of a debt. Most house buyers sign a mortgage when they buy; the bank lends money to buy the house, and the house serves as security for the debt. If the owners don't pay back the loan on time, the bank can seize the house and have it sold to pay off the loan.

Pay-on-death account. An account, usually a bank account, where you name a beneficiary to receive the account assets outside of probate when you die.

Personal guardian. An adult appointed or selected to care for a minor child in the event no biological or adoptive parent (legal parent) of the child is able to do so. If one legal parent is alive when the other dies, the child will automatically go to that parent, unless the best interests of the child require something else.

Personal property. All property other than land and buildings attached to land. Cars, bank accounts, wages, securities, a small business, furniture, insurance policies, jewelry, pets, and season baseball tickets are all personal property.

Personal representative. *See* **executor.**

Pour-over will. A will that "pours over" property into a trust. Property left through the will must go through probate before it goes into the trust.

Power of attorney. A legal document in which you authorize someone else to act for you. *See* **durable power of attorney.**

Pretermitted heir. A child (or the child of a deceased child) who is either not named or (in some states) not provided for in a will. Most states presume that persons want their children to inherit. Accordingly, children, or the children of a child who has died, who are not mentioned or provided for in the will are entitled to a share of the estate.

Principal. Property owned by a trust, as distinguished from the income generated by that property.

Probate. The court proceeding in which: (1) the authenticity of your will (if any) is established, (2) your executor or administrator is appointed, (3) your debts and taxes are paid, (4) your heirs are identified, and (5) your property in your probate estate is distributed according to your will (if there is a will).

Probate estate. All a decedent's property that passes through probate. Generally, this means all property owned at death less any property that has been placed in joint tenancy, a living trust, a bank account trust, or in life insurance.

Probate fees. Fees paid from a decedent's property to an attorney or court during probate. Typically, fees take about 5% of the decedent's estate.

Property guardian. The person named in a will to care for property of a minor child not supervised by some other legal method, such as a minor's trust. Also called "the guardian of the minor's estate" or "financial guardian."

QTIP trust. A type of trust that allows a surviving spouse to postpone, until her death, paying estate taxes that were assessed on the death of the other spouse.

Quasi-community property. A rule that applies to married couples who have moved to Washington, Idaho, or California. Laws in those states require all property acquired by people during their marriage in other states to be treated as community property at their death.

Real estate. Same as **real property.**

Real property. All land and items attached to the land, such as buildings, houses, stationary mobile homes, fences, and trees are real property or "real estate." All property that is not real property is personal property.

Recording. The process of filing a copy of a deed with the county land records office. Recording creates a public record of all changes in ownership of property in the state.

Residuary beneficiary. The residuary beneficiary of a trust for one person, or a basic shared trust created from this book, is that beneficiary who receives any trust property not otherwise given away by the trust document. The residuary beneficiary of a will is the beneficiary who receives any property the will writer owned that was not left to beneficiaries by the will or other method.

Residuary estate. Property that goes to the residuary beneficiary of a will or trust, after all specific gifts of property have been made.

Right of survivorship. The right of a surviving joint tenant to take ownership of a deceased joint tenant's share of the property.

Separate property. In states which have community property, all property that is not community property. *See* **community property.**

Sprinkling trust. A trust that authorizes the trustee to decide how to distribute trust income or principal among different beneficiaries.

Stepped-up basis. Under current federal law, the tax basis of inherited property is "stepped up" to the market value of the property at the date of the decedent's death.

Successor trustee. The person (or institution) who takes over as trustee of a trust when the original trustee(s) have died or become incapacitated.

Surviving spouse. With a shared living trust created by both spouses, the living spouse after the other spouse dies.

Surviving spouse's trust. Where a couple has created an AB trust, the revocable living trust of the surviving spouse, after the other spouse has died.

Taking against the will. State law gives a surviving spouse the right to demand a certain share (in most states, one-third to one-half) of the deceased spouse's property. The surviving spouse can take that share instead of accepting whatever he or she inherited through the deceased spouse's will. If the surviving spouse decides to take the statutory share, it's called "taking against the will." *See* **dower and curtesy.**

Tax basis. *See* **basis.**

Taxable estate. The portion of an estate that is subject to federal or state estate taxes.

Tenancy by the entirety. A form of property ownership available in many states. It is similar to joint tenancy, but is allowed only for property owned by a husband and wife.

Tenancy in common. A way for co-owners to hold title to property that allows them maximum freedom to dispose of their interests by sale, gift, or will. At a co-owner's death, his or her share goes to beneficiaries named in a will or trust or to the legal heirs, not to the other co-owners. Compare **joint tenancy.**

Testamentary trust. A trust created by a will.

Testate. Someone who dies leaving a valid will or other valid property transfer devices dies "testate."

Testator. A person who makes a will, also called the will writer.

Title. A document that proves ownership of property.

Totten trust. *See* **pay-on-death account.**

Trust. A legal arrangement under which one person or institution (called a "trustee") controls property given by another person (called a "grantor," "settlor" or "trustor") for the benefit of a third person (called a "beneficiary").

Trust corpus or **res.** Latin for the property transferred to a trust.

Trustee. The people or institutions who manage trust property under the terms of the trust document. With a revocable living trust created from the forms in this book, the creators of the trust (grantors) are the original trustees.

Trustee powers. The provisions in a trust document defining what the trustee may and may not do.

Uniform Transfers to Minors Act. A statute, adopted by most states, that provides a method for transferring property to minors and arranging for an adult to manage it until the child is older. *See* **custodian.**

Will. A legal document in which a person directs what is to be done with his or her property after death. ■

Index

Remember:

Little publishers have big ears.
We really listen to you.

Take 2 Minutes
& Give Us
Your 2 cents

Your comments make a big difference in the development
and revision of Nolo books and software. Please take a few
minutes and register your Nolo product—and your comments—with us.
Not only will your input make a difference, you'll receive special offers available
only to registered owners of Nolo products on our newest books and software.
Register now by:

PHONE
1-800-728-3555

FAX
1-800-645-0895

EMAIL
cs@nolo.com

or **MAIL** us
this registration card

fold here

Registration Card

NAME _____ DATE _____

ADDRESS _____

_____

CITY _____ STATE _____ ZIP _____

PHONE _____ E-MAIL _____

WHERE DID YOU HEAR ABOUT THIS PRODUCT? _____

WHERE DID YOU PURCHASE THIS PRODUCT? _____

DID YOU CONSULT A LAWYER? (PLEASE CIRCLE ONE)   YES   NO   NOT APPLICABLE

DID YOU FIND THIS BOOK HELPFUL?   (VERY)   5   4   3   2   1   (NOT AT ALL)

COMMENTS _____

_____

_____

WAS IT EASY TO USE?   (VERY EASY)   5   4   3   2   1   (VERY DIFFICULT)

We occasionally make our mailing list available to carefully selected companies whose products may be of interest to you.

❑   If you do not wish to receive mailings from these companies, please check this box.

❑   You can quote me in future Nolo promotional materials.
    Daytime phone number _____.

LITR 6.0

Nolo in the NEWS

"Nolo helps lay people perform legal tasks without the aid—or fees—of lawyers."

—USA TODAY

Nolo books are ..."written in plain language, free of legal mumbo jumbo, and spiced with witty personal observations."

—ASSOCIATED PRESS

"...Nolo publications...guide people simply through the how, when, where and why of law."

—WASHINGTON POST

"Increasingly, people who are not lawyers are performing tasks usually regarded as legal work... And consumers, using books like Nolo's, do routine legal work themselves."

—NEW YORK TIMES

"...All of [Nolo's] books are easy-to-understand, are updated regularly, provide pull-out forms...and are often quite moving in their sense of compassion for the struggles of the lay reader."

—SAN FRANCISCO CHRONICLE

- - - - - - - - - - - - - - - - fold here - - - - - - - - - - - - - - - -

Nolo
950 Parker Street
Berkeley, CA 94710-9867

Attn: LITR 6.0